The Collected Courses of the Academy of European Law

Series Editors: Professor Nehal Bhuta
Professor Claire Kilpatrick
Professor Joanne Scott
European University Institute, Florence
Assistant Editors: Anny Bremner and Joyce Davies
European University Institute, Florence

VOLUME XXVII/1

EU Law Beyond EU Borders

The Extraterritorial Reach of EU Law

The Collected Courses of the Academy of European Law
Edited by Professor Nehal Bhuta, Professor Claire Kilpatrick, and Professor Joanne Scott
Assistant Editors: Anny Bremner and Joyce Davies

Each year the Academy of European Law in Florence, Italy, invites a group of outstanding lecturers to teach at its summer courses on Human Rights Law and the Law of the European Union. A 'general course' is given in each of the two fields by a distinguished scholar or practitioner, who examines the field as a whole through a particular thematic, conceptual, or philosophical lens, or looks at a theme in the context of the overall body of law. In addition, a series of 'specialized courses' brings together a group of highly qualified scholars to explore and analyse a specific theme in relation to human rights law and EU law. The Academy's mission, to produce scholarly analyses which are at the cutting edge of the two fields, is achieved through publication of this series, the Collected Courses of the Academy of European Law.

EU Law Beyond EU Borders

The Extraterritorial Reach of EU Law

Edited by
MARISE CREMONA
and
JOANNE SCOTT

OXFORD
UNIVERSITY PRESS

OXFORD
UNIVERSITY PRESS

Great Clarendon Street, Oxford, OX2 6DP,
United Kingdom

Oxford University Press is a department of the University of Oxford.
It furthers the University's objective of excellence in research, scholarship,
and education by publishing worldwide. Oxford is a registered trade mark of
Oxford University Press in the UK and in certain other countries

First Edition published in 2019

Published in the United States of America by Oxford University Press
198 Madison Avenue, New York, NY 10016, United States of America

British Library Cataloguing in Publication Data
Data available

Library of Congress Control Number: 2019934139

ISBN 978–0–19–884217–0

Contents

Table of Cases

n = footnote.

CJEU CASES (in number order)

GENERAL COURT CASES (in number order)

NATIONAL AND INTERNATIONAL CASES

European Court of Human Rights

International Court of Justice

Ireland

Republic of South Africa

USA

Table of Legislation

n = footnote

EUROPEAN LEGISLATION

Treaties and Conventions (in alphabetical order)

Directives (in chronological order)

Regulations (in chronological order)

Resolutions (in chronological order)

Decisions (in chronological order)

Declarations, Guidelines and other Non-Binding Instruments

Draft Legislation and legal acts not yet in force

INTERNATIONAL CONVENTIONS

BILATERAL/TRILATERAL AGREEMENTS

Notes on Contributors

Marise Cremona is Professor Emeritus at the European University Institute, Florence. She was Professor of European Law, and a Co-Director of the Academy of European Law, at the European University Institute from 2006 to 2017. She is a member of the Editorial Board of the *Common Market Law Review*. Her research interests are in the external relations law of the European Union, in particular the constitutional basis for EU external relations law and the legal and institutional dimensions of EU foreign policy.

Paul Davies is a Senior Research Fellow at Harris Manchester College, Oxford, UK. He was the Allen & Overy Professor of Corporate Law, University of Oxford, from 2009 to 2014; prior to that he was the Cassel Professor of Commercial Law at the London School of Economics and Political Science, 1998–2009; and, before that, Professor of the Law of the Enterprise, University of Oxford. He is an honorary Queen's Counsel and an honorary Bencher of Gray's Inn. Professor Davies' main interests are in labour law, corporate law and banking law. He is the editor (with Sarah Worthington) of *Gower's Principles of Modern Company Law*; author (with numerous others) of *The Anatomy of Corporate Law*; and (on his own) of *Introduction to Company Law*. His most recent book (with others) is *Principles of Financial Regulation*. He has also written widely in the labour law field. Professor Davies was a member of the Steering Group whose reports led to the Companies Act 2006 (UK).

Christopher Kuner is Professor of Law at the Vrije Universiteit Brussel (VUB) and Co-Director of the Brussels Privacy Hub, as well as being Visiting Professor of Law at Maastricht University. The author of numerous books and articles, he is Editor-in-Chief of the journal *International Data Privacy Law*. He has taught at the Hague Academy of International Law, as well as at numerous universities, including the University of Cambridge.

Giorgio Monti is Professor of Competition Law at the Law Department and the Robert Schuman Centre of the European University Institute. He works in all fields of competition law and economic regulation more generally. He is scientific director of the Florence Competition Programme at the EUI and is one of the editors of the *Common Market Law Review*. He is co-author of *European Union Law: Text and Materials*, with a fourth edition forthcoming in 2019.

Bernard Ryan is Professor of Migration Law at the University of Leicester. He has published on many aspects of migration law and policy, including the British-Irish common travel area, migration control at sea, integration tests and employer checks of immigration status. His current research is concerned with the intersection between migration policy and employment law, and with the implications of Brexit for migration law.

Joanne Scott is Professor of European Law and Co-Director of the Academy of European Law at the European University Institute. She is currently on leave from University College London, Faculty of Laws, where she taught from 2005 to 2017. Her research interests lie in the areas of environmental law and climate change law, EU extraterritoriality, new modes of EU governance and the relationships between different legal orders. Professor Scott was elected as a Fellow of the British Academy in 2013 and as a Fellow of the Royal Society of Edinburgh in 2012.

List of Abbreviations

ACTA	Anti-Counterfeiting Trade Agreement
AFSJ	Area of Freedom, Security and Justice
AG	Advocate General
AIFM	alternative investment fund manager
BCBS	Basel Committee on Banking Supervision
BCRs	binding corporate rules
CCP	central counterparty
CDS	credit default swap
CFSP	Common Foreign and Security Policy
CFTC	Commodity Futures Trading Commission (US)
CJEU	Court of Justice of the European Union
DCFTA	deep and comprehensive free trade agreement
DCOs	Derivatives Clearing Organizations
DNS	domain name system
DOJ	Department of Justice (US)
DPAs	data protection authorities
EaP	Eastern Partnership
EASO	European Asylum Support Office
ECB	European Central Bank
ECHR	European Convention on Human Rights
ECtHR	European Court of Human Rights
EDPS	EU Data Protection Supervisor
EEA	European Economic Area
EFTA	European Free Trade Area
EMIR	European Market Infrastructure Regulation
EMSA	European Maritime Safety Authority
ENP	European Neighbourhood Policy
ESMA	European Securities and Markets Authority
FIDH	International Federation for Human Rights
FNC	Federal Networking Council (US)
FSB	Financial Stability Board
FTC	Federal Trade Commission (US)
FATF	Financial Action Task Force
G20	Group of Twenty
GAMM	Global Approach to Migration and Mobility
GDPR	General Data Protection Regulation
GHG	extraterritorial greenhouse gas
GMRIO	global multi-region input-output
ICANN	Internet Corporation for Assigned Names and Numbers
ICN	International Competition Network
ICRC	International Committee of the Red Cross
IETF	Internet Engineering Task Force
IGF	Internet Governance Forum

IOM	International Organization for Migration
IOSCO	International Organization of Securities Commissions
IP	Internet Protocol
IPA II	Regulation establishing an Instrument for Pre-accession Assistance
ISS	Internal Security Strategy
IUU	illegal, unreported or unregulated (fishing)
LCD	liquid crystal display
NGO	non-governmental organization
OECD	Organisation for Economic Co-operation and Development
OEM	Original Equipment Manufacturer
OTC	over the counter
PCA	Partnership and Cooperation Agreement
PNR	passenger name records
RAA	Registrar Accreditation Agreement
RFMO	regional fisheries management organisation
SAA	Stabilisation and Association Agreement
SDG12	Sustainable Development Goal 12 (relating to sustainable production and consumption)
SEC	Securities Exchange Commission (US)
SIV	structured investment vehicle
SSM	Single Supervisory Mechanism (of the BCBS)
SPS	sanitary and phytosanitary (standards, WTO)
TCP	Transmission Control Protocol
TEU	Treaty on European Union
TFEU	Treaty on the Functioning of the European Union
UAA	Ukraine Association Agreement
UCITS	Undertakings for Collective Investment in Transferable Securities
UNCITRAL	United Nations Commission for International Trade Law
UNEP	United Nations Environment Programme
UNHCR	United Nations High Commissioner for Refugees
UNTS	United Nations Treaty Series
VCHR	Vietnam Committee on Human Rights
W3C	World Wide Web Consortium
WIPO	World Intellectual Property Organization
WTO	World Trade Organization

Introduction

EU Law Beyond EU Borders

Marise Cremona and Joanne Scott

1. The Aim of this Book

The former Advocate General Francis Jacobs recently expressed a view, certainly shared by many, that 'the EU is based exclusively on law, not on power . . . [and] that over the past sixty years or so law has made a unique contribution to the European story'.[1] While it may be true that the EU is based on law not on power, this book explores the possibility that in its international relations we can also see law *as* power. As an international legal actor, law is at the foundation of the EU's external power; it may have profound effects on the laws and governance arrangements of other countries, upon global governance arrangements and international and transnational norms. This book will address the impact of EU law beyond its own borders, which may be termed the 'global reach' of EU law;[2] it examines the ways that law is used as a powerful instrument of EU external action, the impact this has on the nature of the EU's external relationships and some of the normative challenges this poses.

What do we mean by the global reach of EU law? It includes the extraterritorial application of EU law, the presence of territorial extension,[3] and the so-called 'Brussels Effect',[4] all phenomena concerned with the effects of unilateral legislative instruments and regulatory action beyond the EU's borders.[5] But 'global reach' also refers to the impact of the EU's bilateral relationships in the form of agreements with third countries or third country agencies, and of the EU's engagement with multilateral fora and the negotiation of international legal instruments.[6] Although this book is concerned with the impact of (EU) *law*, the instruments used by the EU to

[1] Jacobs, Foreword to R. Schütze and T. Tridimas (eds), *Oxford Principles of European Union Law, Volume 1: The European Union Legal Order* (2018).

[2] Scott, 'Extraterritoriality and Territorial Extension in EU Law', 62 *American Journal of Comparative Law* (2014) 87. See also E. Fahey, *The Global Reach of EU Law* (2016) which focuses on the EU's Area of Freedom, Security and Justice.

[3] Scott, 'The New EU "Extraterritoriality"', 51 *Common Market Law Review* (2014) 1343.

[4] Bradford, 'The Brussels Effect', 107 *Northwestern University Law Review* (2013) 1.

[5] See further Joanne Scott, Chapter 1 in this volume.

[6] See further Marise Cremona, Chapter 2 in this volume.

facilitate its global reach include, alongside 'hard' law such as legislation and international agreements, non-binding—though sometimes highly institutionalized—instruments, such as dialogues, agendas for action and guidelines.

Three points flow from this conception of 'global reach'. First is the need to appreciate the relationship between these different modes of EU action—unilateral, bilateral and multilateral—and the ways in which they interact. As we will see in the following chapters, the movement is not all one way and cannot simply be characterized as the export or import of norms. Second, this interplay indicates that the global reach of EU law is not limited to the export of the EU's own internal *acquis*; it may involve the use of EU instruments (both unilateral and bilateral) to support the adoption and application of international law. And, third, the instruments of the global reach of EU law are often presented (not least by the EU itself) as mechanisms for the promotion of its values, as part of the EU's external mandate under Articles 3(5) and 21 of the Treaty on European Union (TEU).

This external mandate also explicitly requires the EU to promote and safeguard its interests; claims that the EU's interests and values coincide—that, in fact, it is in the EU's interest to see its values more widely accepted[7]—reveal the tensions implicit in this relation between values and interests. This tension permeates discussion of the global reach of EU law. Instances can be identified where the EU's value-promotion represents an attempt to extend to third countries international law norms by which it is itself constrained. But the EU also faces the charge that it seeks to export to third countries values and standards which it is less rigorous about applying to itself, and that the external application of EU law may in some instances put into question the EU's own responsibility to comply with international law. In any event, the EU's desire to promote its own values as global is clearly linked to EU interests in promoting the EU law norms based on those values; however, as Christopher Kuner points out in Chapter 3, 'it would be unreasonable to expect third countries to accept the EU's political interests as universal values'.

2. The Structure and Scope of this Book

The book starts with two introductory chapters by Joanne Scott and Marise Cremona that descriptively map this phenomenon and offer some analytical tools for understanding it. These are followed by four chapters, all looking at very different legal fields, which seek to assess to what extent we can indeed identify an extraterritorial impact of EU law; explore the interaction between EU law, the domestic laws of third countries and international or transnational governance regimes; and identify some of the normative issues raised by these interactions. The legal fields chosen—the environment, the Internet and data protection, banking and financial markets, competition policy and migration—each possess natural cross-border characteristics, as well as being fields in which the EU has been notably active, both internally

[7] European Union, 'Shared Vision, Common Action: A Stronger Europe. A Global Strategy for the European Union's Foreign and Security Policy' (June 2016), at 13. See further Marise Cremona, Chapter 2 in this volume.

and externally. The EU may seek to influence conduct and governance regimes beyond its borders for a multiplicity of reasons, whether through the extraterritorial impact of its own legislation, participation in international governance structures, or entering into bi- or multilateral agreements. It may be concerned with ensuring the integrity and efficacy of its own internal regulatory regime and preventing evasion; it may wish to influence the development of regulation in line with its own values and interests, and then seek to promote a specific regulatory approach more widely; or it may claim wider jurisdictional responsibility or seek to divert responsibility to other actors. The five diverse policy fields examined here by Joanne Scott, Marise Cremona, Christopher Kuner, Paul Davies, Giorgio Monti and Bernard Ryan each offer a different balance between these motivations and techniques, and the conclusions reached by these authors indicate that the EU's willingness and ability to exercise global influence is by no means uniform.

The complexity of the concept of the global reach of EU law and the diversity of its operation in (and within) different policy fields suggests the difficulty of drawing firm conclusions. Some initial interpretations and assessment of the material presented in this book are offered below, with the hope that this may encourage both further empirical research and further work on developing an understanding of the normative justifications for EU law's global reach, and of the conditions that would help to ensure that it operates in compliance with its own self-proclaimed values.

Joanne Scott's chapter (Chapter 1) performs two functions. The first part of the chapter provides an overview of some of the key techniques which the EU uses to extend the global reach of its laws. It highlights the variety of jurisdictional triggers upon which the EU relies and draws a distinction between extraterritoriality and territorial extension. It also considers the relationship between territorial extension and the influential concept of the Brussels Effect. Although the EU's effort to extend the global reach of its laws has sometimes proven to be controversial, Scott explores the permissive approach of the Court of Justice of the European Union (CJEU). Many of the concepts introduced by Scott in this chapter are illustrated by examples in the chapters that follow. The first part of Scott's chapter is intended to be descriptive and analytical rather than normative.

The second part of Scott's chapter is, however, to some degree normative. She uses environmental protection as a case study to evaluate territorial extension in EU law. To this end, she provides an overview of the EU's global environmental footprint, arguing that the EU is a major importer of raw materials and ecological assets and that it uses more than its fair share of these. She argues further that the processes of extracting, harvesting or making products destined for the EU market, or managing the associated waste products, frequently cause severely negative impacts globally and in third countries. With this in mind, Scott explores the question of whether an understanding of the EU as being complicit in environmental wrongdoing in third countries can help to justify the presence of territorial extension in EU environmental law. Drawing upon the understanding of complicity developed by Lepora and Goodin,[8] she argues that complicity can serve both as a justification for territorial

[8] C. Lepora and R. E. Goodin, *On Complicity and Compromise* (2013).

extension and as a launching pad for critique. Thus, in contrast with much recent literature on this theme, Scott argues that territorial extension can sometimes be justified even where activities in third countries do not cause direct, substantial and foreseeable effects within the EU.

The aim of Marise Cremona in Chapter 2 is to explore the ways in which, and for what purposes, the EU uses its external relations powers and its wide range of external instruments to extend the reach of EU law beyond its borders. Within the framework of its external policies and governed by EU constitutional law, the EU maintains a complex web of international legal relations, taking part in a multi-layered process of unilateral, bilateral and multilateral normative interactions which cannot be categorized simply as either norm export or import. In exploring this process the chapter clarifies the way in which the law shapes the EU's external action, and the centrality of law to the EU's international actorness. Cremona examines three dimensions of the EU's 'actorness' which illustrate different meanings that might be attributed to the notion of 'the global reach of EU law' in the context of external relations and show three distinct—though overlapping—dynamics to the relationship between law and external action.

First, the role law plays in the construction of the EU's international legal presence as a Union of values, as it navigates between its own constitution and international legal principles. To what extent is law used to promote EU values externally, and to what extent does law act as a constraint, ensuring that the EU upholds its values (including human rights norms) in its external relations?

Second, law mediates between the EU and its external partners. The EU uses law as a way of conducting its foreign policy, and of promoting its interests. Cremona argues that the building of the EU as an integration project—'integration through law'—has an external as well as an internal quality. It is as a legal order that the EU relates to the outside world, and the boundary between what is internal and what is external to that order is a legal one; establishing that boundary is a necessary part of defining the EU's autonomous identity in relation to other actors. Law thus constrains the degree to which it is possible to integrate third countries into EU structures as well as the ways in which the EU can integrate itself into external, international, legal regimes.

The third dimension presented by Cremona shows the EU as a regulatory actor with a Treaty-based commitment to 'multilateral solutions to common problems' and 'good global governance'; an actor engaged in shaping, importing and promoting international legal norms. Its participation in these processes involves an interaction between unilateral, bilateral and multilateral relations. If we look at the ways in which the EU engages with the creation of norms at the international level, what challenges does this pose for its claim to be a Union of values?

The governance of the Internet, and especially the application of the EU data protection rules which are examined by Christopher Kuner in Chapter 3, might be said to be a paradigmatic illustration of the phenomena introduced in these first two chapters. The interaction between EU law and the Internet is multi-directional: while EU law has impacts beyond its borders, the Internet poses both jurisdictional and normative challenges for EU law. As Kuner shows, the global reach of EU law is manifested in a variety of ways, ranging from requiring compliance with EU legal standards beyond its borders to influencing the scope and content of third country legislation and undertaking regulatory investigations in third countries. After introducing the complex multi-level structure and highly fragmented character of Internet governance, including the interplay between EU and Member State competence and action, Kuner's chapter addresses four sets of issues. First, it explains the role played in this field by key principles (or values) of EU law introduced in Chapter 2: the principle of autonomy ensures that the EU's constitutional principles, including the rule of law and fundamental rights, are given priority even over international obligations, and indeed constrain the type of international obligation that the EU may contract. Given the fragmentation of Internet governance and the resulting overlap of jurisdictions, this principle has become a powerful tool in the hands of the CJEU, as *Opinion 1/15* and the *Schrems* case illustrate.[9]

Second, the chapter outlines the areas of law where the Internet and EU law interact, directly or indirectly, notably Internet governance, data protection and rules on jurisdiction and applicable law such as those contained in the General Data Protection Regulation (GDPR). The GDPR in particular is an example of the application of EU law beyond its territory, with its reach capable of extending to Internet activity in third countries. The chapter then considers the mechanisms of global reach, many but not all of which are the result of deliberate policy choices by the EU: emulation and learning (from judgments such as *Google Spain* as well as legislation such as the GDPR); participation in international fora and negotiations (where the EU may compete for influence with others, such as the US); coercion and conditionality, including adequacy decisions; and the (non-)recognition of third country regulation or other legal measures such as court judgments.

Finally, Kuner addresses some of the normative issues raised by these mechanisms and the EU's approach to Internet governance beyond its borders. These include the tension, referred to in Chapters 2 and 3 (Cremona and Kuner), between the EU's legal values and its political interests; Kuner advocates greater honesty in differentiating political agenda from law and warns of the 'risk that legal values will be diluted to fit a particular political agenda'. Closely connected is the risk that the EU's stated commitment to promoting rules-based 'multilateral solutions to common problems' will turn into an attempt to promote its own legal solutions by equating the latter with universal values. And, Kuner argues, if the EU is seeking to gain widespread acceptance for its own regulatory model of data protection, including in developing countries, then this carries responsibilities; the EU needs to recognize the commitment that this will entail, as well as being alert to the risk of double standards.

In Chapter 4, Paul Davies explores the global influence of EU law in relation to the pursuit of financial stability. He starts by explaining why the EU has a strong incentive to exert global influence in this domain, having regard to the fragility of the business model in global finance and to the high probability that a financial crisis starting in one

[9] *Opinion 1/15*, Draft agreement between Canada and the European Union—Transfer of Passenger Name Record data from the European Union to Canada (ECLI:EU:C:2017:592); Case C-362/14, *Schrems v. Data Protection Commissioner* (ECLI:EU:C:2015:650), paras 84–87.

country will spread contagion across borders. Davies then turns to consider the implications of this for regulation, pointing out that there are three distinct ways in which a country can respond to these challenges: reversing globalization; imposing its rules extraterritorially; or coordinating laws at an international level.

Having identified these three possible routes, Davies then assesses the influence of EU financial regulation. He starts by considering the EU's influence at the international level in bodies such as the G20/Financial Stability Board or the Basel Committee on Banking Supervision. He then considers the extent of the EU's influence via 'mutual recognition' by analysing the EU's influence on the regulation of central counterparties (CCPs) which are responsible for clearing over-the-counter derivatives. He sees mutual recognition as a modified form of extraterritoriality, whereby one country's legislation includes an exception which allows for the recognition of another jurisdiction's rules where these are regarded as equivalent to its own. Davies points out that the extent of the EU's global influence may be expected to depend not only upon the pull factor of the EU's market for third country institutions, but also upon the desire of EU institutions to be able to sell their products on third country markets while being subject to EU rather than third country law.

In discussing the EU's influence via mutual recognition, Davies provides a careful exploration of the progress of mutual recognition between the EU and the US. He alerts us to the important difference between the 'equivalence' mechanism in EU law and 'substituted compliance' in US law. Whereas the former permits mutual recognition of a third country's substantive rules and its system for supervision and enforcement, the latter only permits the mutual recognition of a third country's substantive rules. Focusing on the example of CCPs, Davies illustrates the lengthy and acrimonious nature of the EU-US dialogue on mutual recognition of CCPs.

Davies is alert to the implications of his analysis for the UK on the occasion of its departure from the EU. He points out that at present three-quarters of all euro-denominated interest rate derivatives are cleared by clearing houses established in the UK. The Commission has formulated proposals that could require some systemically important third country CCPs to become established within the EU. Even where third country CCPs can continue to benefit from mutual recognition, this would operate in a manner that is more akin to 'substituted compliance' in the US than to equivalence, which has been the norm within the EU. An equivalence determination would therefore imply recognition of the adequacy of a third country's substantive rules but not of its arrangements for supervision and enforcement.

In his chapter on the extraterritorial effect and global reach of EU competition law (Chapter 5), Giorgio Monti assesses the degree to which it is possible to identify a 'Brussels Effect'. He argues that although the Commission's application of EU competition law has a global reach, claims of a Brussels Effect or hegemony are overstated. The global reach of EU competition law is, rather, based on cooperation between agencies and an incremental convergence which emerges as the result of sharing ideas and information. Identifying the risk of over- and under-enforcement as being of more concern than the risk of EU hegemony, and considering the prospect of the establishment of a global antitrust authority to be unrealistic, Monti asks to what extent the two main external relations techniques used by the EU in this field—cooperation agreements and the inclusion of antitrust clauses in bilateral agreements—may help with these concerns.

The chapter takes the three core elements of EU competition law in turn: merger control; unilateral conduct by dominant companies; and cartels. In the case of merger control, Monti argues that the Brussels Effect (the wielding of unilateral regulatory power) does not explain the global reach of EU antitrust law, and there is little evidence of EU hegemony. Companies in merger cases are more concerned by the problems caused by overlapping jurisdictions and the need for multiple notifications. Cooperation between antitrust agencies has become the norm; it is designed to ensure coordination and where possible avoid divergent outcomes and the consequent enforcement difficulties. In contrast, in the case of unilateral conduct by dominant companies, the basis on which the EU exercises jurisdiction has been controversial. The tests used (the economic entity and implementation doctrines) mean in practice that EU law will apply if conduct which takes place abroad has an effect on the EU market. There is, as Monti shows, more divergence between antitrust agencies and laws than in the case of either mergers or cartels, and coordination between agencies has proved difficult. In the case of cartels, where the jurisdiction rules are essentially the same as for unilateral conduct, the main controversy over the reach of EU law has been over the level of fines imposed, although, as Monti points out, it can be argued that in this way the EU contributes to global deterrence. Agencies cooperate in handling investigations (e.g. in coordinating the inspection of premises), with the most significant barrier to cooperation being the absence of agreements on the sharing of confidential information.

Unilateral antitrust enforcement may be tempered by comity, but in Monti's opinion comity is more a matter of rhetorical goodwill than of practical value. More important are inter-agency cooperation and exchanges of information, facilitated by agreements. For the EU, especially in relation to the more significant economies, it appears that cooperation is more important than seeking to export norms. As Monti shows, the latest generation of antitrust cooperation agreements, such as the agreement with Switzerland, establishes a level of cooperation close to that between the European Commission and Member State national authorities. Where clauses on antitrust are included within broader agreements, they may—depending on the nature of the relationship—seek to align the partner country to the EU's model of competition law, but in other cases such as agreements with emerging economies, 'the emphasis is placed more on conversation than on exporting rules'. Contact between authorities, cooperation and conversation may lead to convergence of rules, but Monti counsels caution here: in his view it is important to maintain sufficient divergence to allow for different positions (particularly between countries at different levels of development) on the role played by antitrust law.

In Chapter 6, Bernard Ryan begins by charting the history and development of the EU's border regime before 2011. He sees this as 'the joint product of the functional and intergovernmental forces which shape EU integration' and explores the relationship between functional and intergovernmental elements. Already in this pre-2011 phase, third countries were encouraged to play a role in EU border control by preventing irregular migration and by readmitting persons who were present in the EU on an irregular basis. Ryan's chapter includes a detailed overview of EU cooperation on migration, which was conducted on a largely regional basis.

In the second part of his chapter, Ryan charts the shifting nature of the EU's border control regime, arguing that migration developments in the Central Mediterranean (e.g. Albania, Tunisia and Libya) and Eastern Mediterranean (e.g. Syria, Afghanistan and Iraq) served as a catalyst for these changes. Among the most important of the changes tracked by Ryan is an expansion in the substantive and geographical reach of EU law through cooperation with third countries. The conclusion of a revised agreement with Tunisia in 2011 is exemplary in this respect. It provided for a simplified procedure for the readmission of irregular migrants, an enhancement of Tunisia's efforts to prevent departures, and the supply of boats and vehicles to the Tunisian authorities.

The migration crisis transformed the EU's border control regime in both its internal and external dimensions. As far as the internal dimension is concerned, it led to a strengthening of the powers of the EU's border control agency, Frontex. Ryan demonstrates how the evolution of Frontex's powers has led to 'an enhancement of the territorial reach of Frontex, by enabling far closer cooperation with third states'. This includes the deployment of Frontex officials and teams to the territory of third countries. This period also witnessed a series of Schengen governance reforms which both sanctioned the reintroduction of internal controls by Member States and enhanced EU supervision of Schengen states struggling to police their external borders. This latter element served to enhance the substantive reach of EU law.

As far as the external dimension is concerned, the EU has engaged in enhanced cooperation with third countries both to prevent irregular migration to the EU and to facilitate the return of irregular migrants to these third states. The EU relaunched its Global Approach to Migration and Mobility (GAMM) in 2011 and pursued dialogue and cooperation with a wide range of third countries. The EU has both broadened the range of countries with which it engages and altered the forms of cooperation that it has pursued. For example, the EU has started to work more closely with countries of transit such as Libya and Niger in order to prevent the departure of irregular migrants from those countries. This includes cooperation with African states and the launch of the EU Trust Fund for Africa in 2015. This fund has committed funding of nearly €2bn and has financed initiatives aimed at migration control and at improving employment opportunities and social services within the countries from which the greatest number of irregular migrants originate. Substantial financial support has also been provided to state authorities in Turkey and to humanitarian organizations assisting Syrian refugees in Turkey (€3bn made up of EU and Member State contributions).

Significantly, Ryan argues that the EU's strategy of preventing irregular migration is not intended to export EU norms but rather to reduce the level of protection accruing to migrants, while simultaneously enabling the EU and its Member States to avoid acquiring legal responsibility for them. The EU's desire to side-step this responsibility is apparent even in situations where third countries are unable to provide an adequate level of protection. Ryan points out that this is particularly an issue in relation to Libya, which is not a party to the Refugee Convention. Ryan raises the question of whether EU support to third countries for the purpose of controlling irregular migration may in itself be sufficient to trigger international responsibility under the European Convention on Human Rights (ECHR) or international law. Ryan also raises concerns in relation to EU-Turkey cooperation which similarly weakens guarantees of legal protection, even providing for the possibility of the return of applicants who are currently seeking legal protection to third countries. This includes Turkey, even though Turkey does not include non-Europeans within the scope of the protection conferred by the Refugee Convention.

3. What Kinds of Global Reach?

All of the chapters included in this volume include examples of the global reach of EU law. Cremona offers examples across the spectrum, ranging from unilateral EU measures to bilateral and multilateral agreements which the EU has entered into. The EU has endeavoured to export its *acquis* to its close neighbours, particularly in the economic domain, and has developed sophisticated institutional mechanisms for tracking developments in EU law.

Cremona also offers an example of the EU seeking to promote its own fundamental rights values globally by taking steps to avoid being complicit in the administration of the death penalty in third countries. It does so with the aim of building acceptance and working towards a universalization of an anti-death-penalty norm, seeking to further reinforce its status in third country and international law. In relation to this and other examples, the EU can be seen 'taking' norms from international law, including soft law such as recommendations, and seeking to influence their content. The EU then promotes these international norms via bilateral instruments within and beyond its immediate neighbourhood. The area of money-laundering offers a good example of this elaborate interplay between the unilateral, bilateral and multilateral techniques that the EU uses to influence third country and international law.

Scott introduces the concept of 'territorial extension' and exemplifies the different levels at which this operates in EU law. She offers multiple examples of territorial extension, including country-level territorial extension, to explore the different modalities used by the EU to extend the global reach of its data protection laws. Kuner uses this concept of territorial extension to explain the global reach of EU data protection law. In this example, the effects of extending the EU *acquis* are felt at different levels: internationally as the EU acts in international fora to shape international norms; and in third countries as the EU *acquis* is used as a model to incentivize the adoption by third countries of 'adequate' data protection laws. EU data protection law is also shown to influence private actors in third countries. Private actors exhibit a willingness to abide by EU norms in order to ensure the free flow of data across EU borders through the inclusion of EU-recognized standard contractual clauses.

Monti offers the clear example in competition policy of the EU targeting actions that take place outside the EU if their effects will be felt within the EU. Though the

EU has exhibited a willingness to act unilaterally in this respect, it has also cooperated bilaterally with third countries to facilitate the enforcement of EU and third country competition law. In the merger field, firms are keen to avoid being faced with multiple, overlapping, regulations, and so they generally do not object to bilateral cooperation when it is designed to prevent this. Nonetheless, by contrast to other examples discussed in this book, including data protection, there is little evidence of the EU seeking to influence the substantive content of third country competition law through binding means. There is likewise limited evidence of a 'Brussels Effect'.

While Davies understands why the EU may wish to exert global influence on financial regulation, he paints a picture of the EU which suggests that it has not been very successful in this respect. He appraises the extent of the EU's global influence at the international level and as a result of its equivalence dialogue with the US in relation to CCPs. As far as the EU's influence in international standard-setting is concerned, Davies reaches a quite stark conclusion. The EU's influence on the development of international standards since the financial crisis has been low, and Davies explores some of the reasons for this. The EU has largely been a rule-taker rather than a rule-maker in this respect, and even where the EU has 'struck out on its own', Davies suggests that it has struggled to find followers.

As far as the EU's influence through mutual recognition/equivalence is concerned, Davies argues that the EU has made only limited gains as a result of its efforts to 'export' its norms regarding CCPs to the US. While it may appear as if the EU has made better 'defensive' use of equivalence in order to resist the importation of US norms, the EU's victory regarding the preservation of its net margining model for CCPs was no more than a pyrrhic one. Retention of this model resulted in EU financial institutions being placed at a competitive disadvantage. Ultimately, therefore, the EU decided to revise its previously hard-fought-for norms. 'One might say that the impact of mutual recognition dialogue was in fact to undermine, not to preserve, the EU net margining rule'. Interestingly though, Davies points out that third country law can only be recognized as equivalent under EU law if the third country in question has a comparable system of mutual recognition in place. The EU does therefore seek to project the concept of equivalence as a norm externally.

Ryan traces EU cooperation with third countries aimed at reducing irregular migration and readmitting irregular migrants who do reach the EU. Overall, he argues, there has been an unprecedented level of EU involvement in the migration policies of third countries since 2011. As was noted previously, the EU has broadened the range of countries that it engages with and has engaged in novel forms of cooperation, including on operational matters. Ryan observes that cooperation has been more successful in relation to some countries (e.g. Libya) than others (e.g. Morocco, Algeria, Tunisia and Egypt).

In the Central Mediterranean, the cumulative effect of EU initiatives (together with Italy's cooperation with the Libyan authorities) has been a reduction in the level of irregular migration to the EU. For example, in the first four months of 2018, arrivals from Libya were down by 82 per cent compared with the previous year. In the Eastern Mediterranean, EU cooperation with Turkey and border controls in the Western Balkans has led to a dramatic decline in the number of migrants arriving on the Greek islands in 2016 and 2017. Ryan notes that this latter decline can help us to understand why EU-Turkey cooperation in relation to migration is ongoing, notwithstanding the Turkish Government's suppression of dissent and opposition internally since the failed coup in 2016.

However, it bears repeating that Ryan makes a convincing case that EU-third country cooperation on migration results in a reduction of the level of international protection accruing to migrants, including current applicants for protection, rather than in exporting higher standards of protection enshrined in EU law.

4. The Role of Law: Enabling and Constraining the Extraterritorial Reach of EU Law

This book seeks to understand more fully the role of law as a foundation of EU external power. Our contention is that there is a need to look beyond the instrumental function of law and the use by the EU of the legal tools in its toolbox—although this function is undoubtedly important—and to identify the ways in which law shapes the EU's external identity and its relations with other legal regimes. In this, the law may both enable and constrain the EU's external action. Each of the chapters in this volume exemplifies the important role that law plays in enabling and constraining the extraterritorial reach of EU law, and some elements of this are highlighted below. Although the enabling and constraining functions of law have been separated out, there is often an iterative dimension present whereby constraints serve as a catalyst for the emergence of enabling devices and the emergence of new enabling devices will occasionally provoke the emergence of additional constraints.

5. Law as an Enabler

A. The Permissive Stance of the CJEU

The CJEU has accepted that EU law may operate outside the borders of the EU, and multiple examples can be found in the CJEU's case law to support this claim. In her chapter, Scott points to many of the relevant cases, particularly as they relate to the lawfulness of territorial extension in EU law. She points out that the CJEU has upheld the validity of measures giving rise to territorial extension and exhibited a willingness to construe EU legislation broadly to permit its application to foreign conduct.[10] Following the *Zuchtvieh* case, Scott concludes that there appears to be no presumption against extraterritoriality in EU law.[11] Monti also explores the case law of the CJEU, including a discussion of the recent *Intel* case in which it endorsed the

[10] For one example of the former, see Case C-366/10, *Air Transportation of America ex parte Secretary of State for Energy and Climate Change* (*ATAA*) (ECLI:EU:C:2011:864) and of the latter see Case C-424/13, *Zuchtvieh-Export GmbH* (ECLI:EU:C:2015:259).

[11] *Zuchtvieh*, note 10.

presence of a 'qualified effects' doctrine in EU law.[12] Monti also points to the fact that the CJEU has upheld the Commission's practice of setting fines for breach of competition law without taking account of fines that have been imposed by third country agencies. Kuner also offers examples of the CJEU's permissive stance, including the well-known cases of *Google Spain*[13] and *Schrems*.[14] In the latter, the CJEU adopted a strict approach to enforcing country-level territorial extension in EU law.

B. Equivalence as an Emerging Principle of EU Law

As is explained by Davies in his chapter, the concept of equivalence operates to soften the impact of a full-blown extraterritorial application of norms. It does so by preventing direct conflicts of norms and/or by preventing the emergence of overlapping norms from different jurisdictions even where these norms are not in direct conflict. The concept of equivalence also serves to accommodate differences in regulatory approach, at least up to the point where these differences are deemed to impede unduly the attainment of the EU's regulatory objectives.

Equivalence is found in different forms throughout EU law giving rise to territorial extension. In its narrow form, it permits the disapplication of EU law when it is in direct conflict with EU-equivalent third country laws. In its broader form, it permits the disapplication of EU law in favour of third country law, even in the absence of a direct conflict. An example of a broader conception of equivalence can be seen in Kuner's discussion of the *Schrems* case.[15] Here, the CJEU has interpreted the concept of adequacy in the data protection directive as necessitating an evaluation of whether a third country has EU-equivalent standards of protection in place. In its narrow form, the concept of equivalence has recently found favour with the CJEU when construing legislation that did not contain an explicit reference to this concept. In *Zuchtvieh*, the CJEU emphasized that where the law or administrative practice of a third country verifiably and demonstrably precludes full compliance with EU law, EU competent authorities are entitled to accept compliance with third country measures which ensure an EU-equivalent level of protection.[16] This indicates that at least in its narrow form, which aims at the avoidance of direct conflict, equivalence may be emerging as a principle of EU law.

C. Law Enabling New Forms of Integration

Cremona's chapter notes the central importance in the EU's external relations (as in the EU's internal evolution) of the development of relationships based on economic, political and legal integration. These relationships are driven by and based on law; complex institutional frameworks have enabled new highly dynamic forms and structures of close integration, which, as illustrated by the European Economic

[12] Case C-413/14 P, *Intel Corporation* (ECLI:EU:C:2017:632), judgment of 6 September 2017.

[13] Case C-131/12, *Google Spain SL, Google Inc. v. Agencia Española de Protección de Datos (AEPD), Mario Costeja González* (ECLI:EU:C:2014:317).

[14] *Schrems*, note 9. [15] See note 9. [16] *Zuchtvieh*, note 10, para. 54.

Area Agreement and the Association Agreement with Ukraine, have been especially effective in the EU's neighbourhood. This external law of integration, as well as promoting the EU's regulatory approaches across a wide range of economic fields, enables the EU's efforts to achieve further objectives, such as the modernization of the economies of neighbouring countries, and an increase in their legal and political stability. The innovative solutions found, such as the EFTA Court and the EFTA Surveillance Authority, have at least in part been prompted by the legal constraints imposed by the principle of autonomy, as examined later, at section 6.A.

Law also acts as a catalyst for cooperation. The extraterritorial application of EU law may trigger agreements with third countries which mitigate these effects, either through mechanisms of equivalence, as mentioned earlier, or by facilitating cooperation in enforcement. In the field of data protection, for example, an impetus can be seen towards bilateral agreements with third countries, which are designed to ensure the adequacy (equivalence) required by the EU's own legislation, such as the 'Privacy Shield' agreed with the US. Agreements may also be designed to meet the requirements of the EU's Charter of Fundamental Rights, such as the agreements on the transfer of airline passenger name records (PNR) to third countries. Cooperation agreements in the domain of competition law are more concerned with enforcement than the equivalence of substantive norms.

D. Law Enabling New Forms of Extraterritorial Enforcement of EU Law

As will be discussed later, public international law precludes states from enforcing their laws extraterritorially. However, the chapters included in this volume illustrate that the EU has developed mechanisms and strategies that aim to ensure that its laws are enforced in third countries while not breaching the norm prohibiting extraterritorial enforcement. Four such mechanisms will be highlighted here.

First, as was noted in the discussion of Davies' contribution, mutual recognition in EU law extends not only to a third country's substantive rules but also to its system for ensuring compliance with EU law. Thus, when the EU makes market access conditional upon a third country achieving an EU-equivalent level of protection, it performs a meta-regulatory function by, on the one hand, outsourcing responsibility for securing compliance to third countries and, on the other hand, by overseeing the adequacy of their arrangements for supervision and enforcement.

Second, and closely related, the EU frequently makes access to the EU's market conditional upon a third country and/or private actors within that country making it permissible for EU or EU-approved personnel to conduct inspections within the territory of that third country. EU law is replete with examples of this kind. For example, EU aviation security validators act on behalf of EU Member States when they assess the appropriateness of security measures applied by air-cargo handling entities in third country airports.[17] EU aviation security validators must be approved

[17] Commission Implementing Regulation 2015/1998 of 5 November 2015 laying down detailed measures for the implementation of common basic standards on aviation security, OJ 2009 L 299/1.

by an EU Member State. EU regulation of recognized organizations in the maritime sector offers another good example.[18] The European Maritime Safety Authority regularly inspects third country recognized organizations in third country ports; and in entering into contracts with shipowners, such organizations must include a contractual clause to ensure that the EU Commission may gain access to ships, even when they are situated in third country ports.

Third, the EU enters into cooperation agreements with third countries to facilitate enforcement of its laws extraterritorially. Monti offers an excellent example of this in his chapter on competition law. In this arena, cooperation agreements serve not only formalize comity (e.g. by ensuring that a merger will be acceptable to both authorities), but also lay down rules enabling joint investigations and the transfer of confidential information.

Finally, in at least one recent example, the EU has sought input from individuals within third countries to assist in monitoring compliance with EU law. Thus, natural and legal persons affected or likely to be affected by a breach of relevant provisions in the EU's ship recycling regulation, or having a sufficient interest in environmental decision-making in relation to such matters, are entitled to request the Commission to take action with respect to such a breach or imminent threat of such a breach.[19] Where such a request shows in a plausible manner that a breach is imminent or has already occurred, the Commission shall give the ship recycling company in question a right to be heard, and shall inform the party making the request of its decision to accede to or refuse the request for action, and provide reasons for this decision. In this scenario, individuals or organizations within third countries are empowered to alert the Commission to the existence of a breach of EU law.

6. Law as a Constraint

In identifying some of the ways in which law may act as a constraint to the extraterritorial reach of EU law, it becomes clear that although these responses form part of the broader structure of EU constitutional and administrative law, they are not as such parts of a considered legal response to extraterritorial reach. In that sense, they are ad hoc. Some (such as autonomy) are rather fully developed through case law; others are in a process of evolution (such as the extraterritorial impact of fundamental rights); others are rather under-developed (such as the principles governing third country interests, and procedural constraints).

[18] Regulation 391/2009 of 23 April 2009 on common rules and standards for ship inspection and survey organisations, OJ 2009 L 131/11. For details of inspections in the EU and in third countries see http://www.emsa.europa.eu/visits-a-inspections/assessment-of-classification-societies.html. (Both website references in this chapter were last visited on XX XXXX.)

[19] Regulation 1257/2013 of 20 November 2013 on ship recycling, OJ 2013 L 330/1, Article 23 on 'request for action'.

A. The Principle of Autonomy

The principle of the autonomy of EU law imposes constraints on institutional arrangements negotiated with third countries. It requires that these ensure the independence of EU institutions in matters of decision-making, and the primacy of the CJEU in its interpretation of EU law, including in particular the division of competence between the EU and its Member States. As the EEA case law demonstrates, this poses a challenge for the EU in developing close relationships of integration with third countries under conditions of equality. Since it precludes full third country participation in EU decision-making, agreements which envisage a high degree of integration or even homogeneity between the EU *acquis* and the integration regime, will essentially require the third country partner to become a norm-taker. In other contexts where equivalence rather than legal integration is the basis of an external relationship—such as in the EU's bilateral agreements on data protection—the principle of autonomy is less constraining, although it may impact institutional choices, for example on the role of the CJEU.

The principle of autonomy also makes it difficult for the EU to participate in external regulatory regimes, especially if these include decision-making or adjudication.[20] Where the EU has sufficient negotiating strength it may be able both to influence the content of an external regime and to ensure—through the insertion of a 'disconnection clause'—that as far as the EU Member States are concerned the external regime does not displace the operation of EU law.[21] The EU *acquis* is protected but at a cost in terms of fragmentation of the international regime.

B. Public International Law

The CJEU has stated repeatedly that when the EU adopts an act, it is 'bound to observe international law in its entirety', including customary international law.[22] The CJEU has been willing to review the validity or legality of an EU act in light of customary international law, albeit that it limits judicial review to appraising whether the EU has committed a manifest error of assessment as far as the principles of customary international law are concerned.[23] In the *Air Transportation of America* case, the CJEU endorsed the validity of an EU measure giving rise to territorial extension on the basis that aircraft that are physically present within the EU are subject to the unlimited jurisdiction of the EU and its Member States.[24] Regardless of whether one

[20] See, e.g., *Opinion 1/09* on the European and Community Patents Court (ECLI:EU:C:2011:123).

[21] See, e.g., the United Nations Convention on the Use of Electronic Communications in International Contracts 2005, 2898 UNTS, Registration No. 50525, Art. 17, cited by Kuner. See also the priority given by the CJEU to the EU's internal integration objectives over wider international co-operation in private international law in Case C-533/08, *TNT Express Nederland BV v. AXA Versicherung AG* [2010] ECR I-4107 (ECLI:EU:C:2010:243). See further Cremona, 'A Triple Braid—Interactions between International Law, EU law and Private Law', in M. Cremona and H.-W. Micklitz (eds), *Private Law in the External Relations of the EU* (2016).

[22] *ATAA*, note 10, para. 122; citing Case C-286/90, *Anklagemyndigheden v. Peter Michael Poulsen and Diva Navigation Corp.*, [1992] ECR I-6019 (ECLI:EU:C:1992:453).

[23] *ATAA*, note 10, para. 110.

[24] *Ibid.*, para. 124.

reads this case as being concerned with the exercise of prescriptive or enforcement jurisdiction by the EU, it remains true that customary international law prohibits states from enforcing (as opposed to prescribing) their laws extraterritorially.[25] However, as was noted earlier, the EU has developed a number of novel mechanisms to facilitate the extraterritorial enforcement of EU law.

The CJEU has also been willing to assess the validity or legality of an EU act by reference to the standards laid down in an international agreement where a number of conditions are met. The agreement in question must be binding on the EU, its nature and broad logic must not be such as to preclude it being relied upon by individuals, and the content of the agreement must be unconditional and sufficiently precise.[26] In practice, these conditions can be difficult to fulfil and the CJEU has often concluded that international agreements that are binding on the EU are not suitable to confer rights on individuals which they can rely on in court.[27] For example, subject to exceptions which have been narrowly construed, the CJEU has not proven to be willing to review the validity or legality of an EU act on the basis that it is alleged to infringe World Trade Organization (WTO) law.[28]

C. Fundamental Human Rights in EU Law and International Law

Fundamental human rights are among the EU's values as set out in Article 2 TEU and the CJEU has taken a clear position that human rights compliance 'is required of all actions of the European Union', including external action.[29] Likewise, international agreements concluded by the EU are required to comply with EU primary law, including fundamental human rights as protected by the Charter.[30] The priority of EU constitutional law (including the Charter) imposes constraints on what the EU can agree to, and the Charter thus provides a baseline or set of minimum standards which third countries wanting to conclude agreements with the EU have to accept, given the risk of an *ex ante* or *ex post* finding of illegality.[31] This legal constraint on the EU may thus appear as a strength: as Kuner points out, the priority that the CJEU insists should be given to fundamental principles of EU law in cases such as *Schrems* gives the EU some leverage in a 'pluralistic and fragmented' scenario where several jurisdictions may cover the same actors or conduct without clear priority rules.

The precise degree to which the EU Charter of Fundamental Rights applies in extraterritorial contexts may still be debated, although it seems clear that the references to human rights in Article 3(5) and 21 TEU provide a firm basis for arguing

[25] See C. Ryngaert, *Jurisdiction in International Law* (2nd edn, 2015), at 31.

[26] *ATAA*, note 10, paras 52–54.

[27] *Ibid.*, para. 77 as far as the Kyoto Protocol is concerned and Case C-308/06, *Intertanko v. Secretary of State for Transport*, [2008] ECR I-4057 (ECLI:EU:C:2008:312).

[28] Case C-149/96, *Portugal v. Council*, [1999] ECR I-8395 (ECLI:EU:C:1999:574).

[29] Case C-263/14, *European Parliament v. Council* (ECLI:EU:C:2016:435), para. 47.

[30] *Opinion 1/15*, note 9, para. 70.

[31] The *ex ante* declaration of incompatibility of the proposed agreement on PNR data with Canada in *Opinion 1/15* means that the agreement will have to be revised before it can come into force: Art. 218(11) TFEU. The *ex post* declaration of illegality in *Schrems*, note 9 made it necessary to renegotiate the EU-USA Safe Harbour (adequacy) arrangement.

that it carries a legal effect beyond the EU's territorial borders.[32] Although Advocate General Wathelet in the *Polisario* case rejected the applicability of the Charter outside the EU on the grounds that none of the conditions established by the European Court of Human Rights (ECtHR) for the extraterritorial application of the ECHR were met,[33] he accepted the argument that the EU was bound to consider the impact of its external actions as regards *erga omnes* and peremptory international law obligations, including the right of self-determination.

In principle, the constitutional conditions for the legality of an EU act concluding an international agreement include compliance with peremptory norms of international law.[34] The CJEU in both the *Polisario* and *Western Sahara* cases refused to interpret an EU agreement in contravention of peremptory norms of international law, despite institutional practice.[35] However, the EU's (and the Member States') potential responsibility for breaches of international human rights law beyond its borders may influence policy in a less benign manner. The ruling of the ECtHR in *Hirsi Jamaa* to the effect that Italy has jurisdiction over migrants intercepted by its vessels at sea, and that it would be unlawful to return them to Libya where this would expose them to the risk of inhuman and degrading treatment, has, Ryan argues, shaped EU policy on irregular migration, putting an emphasis on preventing departure from third countries, and encouraging return to third countries which—like Turkey—are deemed safe despite concerns over compliance with the Refugee Convention.[36] This strategy is aimed not at exporting EU human rights norms, nor on promoting international human rights law, but rather at avoiding legal responsibility being placed on the EU and its Member States. Ryan questions the extent of the EU's responsibility for human rights abuses that are not attributable to EU Member States directly, but in relation to which the EU may be considered to be a secondary agent from a complicity perspective.

D. The Duty to Take into Account Third Country Interests

In some of the chapters that follow, the EU is criticized for failing to take third country interests sufficiently into account when it extends (or indeed fails to extend)

[32] Case T-512/12, *Front populaire pour la liberation de la saguia-elhamra et du rio de oro (Front Polisario) v. Council*, ECLI:EU:T:2015:953; V. Kube, 'The EU's human rights obligations towards the wider world and the international investment regime: Making the promise enforceable' (2018) (PhD thesis on file at the EUI, Florence), chapter 1.III.

[33] Case C-104/16 P, *Council v. Front Polisario*, Opinion of AG Wathelet, (ECLI:EU:C:2016:677). For an argument that the EU Charter is not limited by the territorial principle applicable to the ECHR, see further Moreno-Lax and Costello, 'The Extraterritorial Application of the EU Charter of Fundamental Rights: From Territoriality to Facticity, the Effectiveness Model', in S. Peers *et al.* (eds), *The EU Charter of Fundamental Rights: A Commentary* (2014).

[34] Case C-266/16, *Western Sahara* (ECLI:EU:C:2018:118), paras 47–50. As the Court points out at para. 50: 'where . . . the Court has received a request for a preliminary ruling concerning the validity of an international agreement concluded by the European Union, that request must be understood as relating to the EU act approving the conclusion of that international agreement'.

[35] *Front Polisario*, note 33; *Western Sahara*, note 34. See further Marise Cremona, Chapter 2 in this volume.

[36] ECtHR, *Hirsi Jamaa v. Italy*, Appl. no. 27765/09, Judgment of 23 February 2012. Decision available online at http://hudoc.echr.coe.int/.

the geographical reach of its laws. For example, Scott argues that the EU is not sufficiently attentive to potential negative third country consequences during the process leading to the adoption of the sustainable fishing and ship recycling regulations. Monti points to the fact that the EU does not take action against export cartels in the EU if their effects are not felt within the Union, even though these cartels may be very damaging to the developing countries in which the effects are felt. Needless to say, contrary examples can be found. In its seals regulation,[37] for example, the EU included an indigenous peoples exception which was intended to protect the fundamental economic and social interests of Inuit communities engaged in the hunting of seals as a means of ensuring their subsistence.[38]

This raises the question of whether the EU is under a legal obligation to take third country interests into account when it adopts measures that render EU law applicable in relation to foreign conduct. As a preliminary point, it is clear that WTO law permits members to design their regulations in a manner that achieves a balance between different objectives. For example, it would, in principle, be permissible for the EU to include an indigenous peoples exception in its seals regulation even where this undermines to some degree the contribution made by the measure to the attainment of its principal objective. However, it would be incumbent on the EU to explain why 'the need to protect the economic and social interests of the Inuit and other indigenous peoples necessarily implies that the European Union cannot do anything further to ensure that the welfare of seals is addressed in the context of [indigenous communities'] hunts'.[39]

It is also arguable that the WTO goes one step further, by requiring members to take into account 'different conditions which may occur in the territories of... other Members'.[40] The Appellate Body suggested that discrimination may occur not only when countries in which the same conditions prevail are treated differently, but also when the application of a regulatory measure 'does not allow for any inquiry into the appropriateness of the regulatory program for the conditions prevailing in those exporting countries'.[41] Nonetheless, the implications of this statement have not been spelt out.

Within the EU, Commission initiatives and EU legislation should be prepared on the basis of transparent, comprehensive and balanced evidence, making use of the tool of impact assessments.[42] Those preparing such assessments are assisted by guidelines that have been drawn up by the EU Commission which list the different categories of impacts that are to be identified.

Impacts that may occur within third countries feature quite prominently in the tables specifying the kinds of impacts that are to be taken into account. This includes economic impacts, such as impacts on foreign businesses and consumers and

[37] Regulation 1007/2009 of 16 September 2009 on trade in seal products, OJ 2015 L 262/1.

[38] *Ibid.*, Art. 3.

[39] WT/DS401/AB/R, *European Communities—Measures Prohibiting the Importation and Marketing of Seals*, para. 5.320.

[40] WT/DS58/AB/R, *United States—Import Prohibition of Certain Shrimp and Shrimp Products*, para. 164.

[41] *Ibid.*, para. 165.

[42] European Commission, *Impact Assessment Guidelines* (15 January 2009).

impacts on developing countries;[43] together with social and environmental impacts in third countries.[44] Among the questions to be addressed in terms of social impacts is whether the initiative will increase poverty in developing countries or have an impact on the income of the poorest populations.[45]

Even when it comes to providing guidance on 'in-depth analysis of the most significant impacts', international impacts are to be considered, including impacts on developing countries, with a view to ensuring the coherence of the initiative with the EU's development policy.[46] Moreover, the guidelines make clear that efforts are to be made to ensure that third country 'stakeholders' can participate in the consultation process.[47] However, no specific guidance is given on how to strike a balance between the EU and third country impacts.[48]

While the EU has an elaborate framework for impact assessment which has been developed and implemented over many years, some of the examples included in this volume raise questions about the extent to which negative third country impacts are even identified, let alone taken into account. Assessing the adequacy of EU impact assessments from this point of view, with a particular view to strengthening the assessment and weighting of negative impacts on developing countries and on vulnerable groups within them, emerges from this volume as an important topic for future research.

E. Proceduralization

This then brings us back to Article 21 TEU which was highlighted earlier in the discussion of the role of fundamental human rights as a legal constraint. This lays down a series of principles which are to guide EU action on the international scene, including the principles of equality and solidarity. It establishes objectives for the EU which relate to the conditions prevailing in third countries. For example, the EU is required to define and pursue common policies and actions, and work for a high degree of cooperation in all fields of international relations in order, *inter alia*, to foster the sustainable economic, social and environmental development of developing countries, with the primary aim of reducing poverty.[49]

Such is the open-ended nature of the EU's constitutional commitments contained in Article 21 TEU, and the complexity of achieving a balance between the different elements contained within them, that they are unlikely to serve as a basis for substantive judicial review of EU measures. However, they can and should serve as a basis for courts and other actors to scrutinize the adequacy of the procedures followed by the EU institutions, particularly in relation to measures that seek to govern conduct or circumstances in third countries.

43 *Ibid.*, under 'third countries and international relations', at 34.

44 *Ibid.*, under 'social inclusion and protection of particular groups', at 35, 'social impacts in third countries', at 36 and 'international environmental impacts', at 38.

45 *Ibid.*, under 'social impacts in third countries', at 26.

46 *Ibid.*, at 42.

47 *Ibid.*, at 42.

48 See the section on 'cost-benefit thinking through multi-criteria analysis', *ibid.*, at 47–49.

49 Art. 21(2)(d) TEU.

As highlighted previously, both the General Court and the European Ombudsman have taken steps in this direction in so far as the EU's commitment to the protection of human rights is concerned. In *Front Polisario*,[50] the General Court found that the Council was obliged to address the question of the protection of the fundamental human rights of the population of Western Sahara before entering into an agreement with Morocco.[51] While it accepted that the EU would not be directly liable for breaches of human rights within the Western Sahara, it did consider that the EU could be complicit in such breaches were it to permit the importation of products produced in conditions that did not respect human rights into the EU.[52] The Ombudsman accepted that there was no legally binding requirement to carry out a human rights impact assessment in relation to the EU-Vietnam Free Trade Agreement; however, she considered that it would be in accordance with 'the spirit' of Article 21 TEU for the Commission to carry out an assessment of this kind and considered that the Commission's failure to provide valid reasons for refusing to carry out a human rights impact assessment constituted maladministration.[53]

In keeping with these recent developments, it is the present authors' contention that the Commission ought to be required to pay close attention to the possible impacts of EU measures on third countries, and to develop a transparent framework for assessing trade-offs between competing interests in third countries, and between interests inside and outside the EU.[54] The EU Treaties, including Article 21 TEU, can assist in identifying which types of impacts should be taken into account. The case studies included in this volume demonstrate that significant impacts can occur within third countries not only when the EU adopts measures that form part of its outwards-focused, external relations law; but also when it adopts 'domestic' measures that nonetheless necessitate a judgement about the adequacy of third country conduct or third country law.

[50] *Front* Polisario, note 32. [51] *Ibid.*, paras 223–247.

[52] *Ibid.*, paras 227 and 228. For a discussion of the concept of complicity which is relevant to many of the examples discussed in this volume, see Joanne Scott, Chapter 1 in this volume.

[53] Decision in Case 1409/2014/MHZ on the European Commission's failure to carry out a prior human rights impact assessment of the EU-Vietnam free trade agreement.

[54] For an exploration of the application of administrative rules and principles to EU external administrative action, see I. Vianello, 'EU External Action and the Administrative Rule of Law: A Long-Overdue Encounter' (2016) (PhD thesis on file at the EUI, Florence) and, in the context of environmental protection, I. Hadjiyianni, *The EU as a Global Regulator for Environmental Protection: A Legitimacy Perspective* (2019).

1

The Global Reach of EU Law

*Joanne Scott**

1. Introduction

Over recent years, I have explored the concept of 'territorial extension' in EU law and shown how this phenomenon has enabled the EU to exploit the existence of a territorial connection to gain influence over foreign conduct and foreign law.[1] Some examples of territorial extension are well known and highly controversial. Among these, I would include the EU's ill-fated decision to include extraterritorial greenhouse gas (GHG) emissions within the scope of its emissions trading scheme;[2] and its well-known practice of rendering the transfer of personal data to third countries contingent upon the country in question having adequate data protection policies in place.[3] However, many examples of territorial extension in EU law operate under the radar and, while important, are much more mundane. We take for granted the application of process-based food-safety standards to imported food;[4] and the fact that the aviation safety assessments undertaken by EU aviation authorities take into consideration aviation incidents outside the EU.[5]

* Many thanks to the participants in the Academy of European Law summer school in Florence on 'The Global Reach of EU Law' for their contribution to this project. The chapter has been improved thanks to the many comments and questions received following presentations at the EUI and the Universities of Siena and Strathclyde. I would offer particular thanks to Claire Kilpatrick, Fergus Murray, Ioanna Hadjiyianni, Jaap Waverijn, Bruno de Witte and Eva van der Marel.

1 Scott, 'Extraterritoriality and Territorial Extension in EU Law', 62 *American Journal of Comparative Law* (2014) 87.

2 Directive 2008/101 of 19 November 2008 amending Directive 2003/87 so as to include aviation activities in the scheme for greenhouse gas emissions allowance trading within the Community, OJ 2009 L 8/3.

3 Directive 95/46 of 24 October 1995 on the protection of individuals with regard to the processing of personal data and on the free movement of such data, OJ 1995 L 281/31, Art. 25, which was recently repealed by Regulation 2016/679 of 27 April 2016 on the protection of individuals with regard to the processing of personal data and on the free movement of such data (General Data Protection Regulation—GDPR), OJ 2016 L 119/1, Art. 45. On territorial extension in relation to data protection, see Christopher Kuner, Chapter 3 in this volume.

4 Regulation 854/2004 of 29 April 2004 on the hygiene of foodstuffs, OJ 2004 L 226/83, Art. 5.

5 Regulation 2111/2005 of 8 December 2005 on the establishment of a Community list of air carriers subject to an operating ban within the Community and on informing air transport passengers of the identity of the operating air carrier, OJ 2005 L 322/17.

To date, my research on territorial extension in EU law has been largely descriptive and analytical, seeking to map and categorize the multiple manifestations of territorial extension in EU law. In this chapter, however, I aim not only to provide an overview of this and related concepts, but also to take a first step down the road of appraising territorial extension. To this end, the chapter includes a case study on environmental protection. Against the backdrop of the EU's large and damaging global environmental footprint, the second part of the chapter considers whether the concept of complicity can help to provide a justification for territorial extension, even in relation to foreign conduct that does not cause significant effects within the EU. While it is argued that complicity can sometimes provide a justification for territorial extension, the chapter also suggests that it can offer a launching pad for critique.

2. Extraterritoriality and Territorial Extension

A. Introduction

In my earlier work, I drew a distinction between the concept of extraterritoriality and the concept that was labelled 'territorial extension'.[6] I argued that a measure may be considered to be extraterritorial when its application does not depend on the existence of a territorial connection between a regulated activity and an EU Member State. A measure that regulates the foreign conduct of EU citizens would be extraterritorial in this sense because its application posits nationality rather than territory as the relevant connection.[7] By contrast, a measure is considered to give rise to territorial extension where its application is triggered by the existence of a territorial connection with the EU, but where an assessment of compliance with the law requires an evaluation of foreign conduct and/or third country law. A territorial connection may take the form of conduct within the territory of an EU Member State or physical

Table 1.1 Extraterritoriality and territorial extension

Concept	Definition
Extraterritoriality	The application of a measure does not depend upon the existence of a territorial connection.
Territorial extension	Although the application of a measure is triggered by a territorial connection, evaluation of compliance with the measure requires an assessment of foreign conduct and/or third country law.

[6] Scott, note 1.

[7] For an example concerning natural persons, see Directive 2011/36 of 5 April 2011 on combating and preventing trafficking in human beings and protecting its victims, OJ 2011 L 101/1, Art. 10(1) of which requires a Member State to establish jurisdiction over offenders where the offence is committed in whole or in part within its territory or when the offender is a national of that Member State. For an example concerning legal persons, see Directive 2011/61 of 8 June 2011 on alternative investment fund managers, OJ 2011 L 174/1. This considers an alternative investment fund manager (AIFM) to be an EU-AIFM where it has its registered office in an EU Member State (recital 4).

or legal presence within the EU.[8] The concepts of extraterritoriality and territorial extension understood in this way are summarized in Table 1.1.

There is sometimes reasonable disagreement about how a particular jurisdictional trigger should be characterized. For example, where EU law applies to legal persons that are established within the territory of an EU Member State, there may be uncertainty about whether the application of this law is triggered by a non-territorial connection (nationality) or a territorial connection (presence). Ultimately, this will depend both on how the concept of establishment is defined (e.g. does it include branches as well as subsidiaries?) and upon how broadly the concept of nationality is drawn.[9] Equally, there is still some disagreement about whether effects-based jurisdiction should best be conceived of as a form of territorial or extraterritorial jurisdiction.[10]

B. Extraterritoriality

Notwithstanding this ambiguity, it is clear that in recent years, and especially in the wake of the 2007–2008 financial crisis, the EU legislature has made more frequent recourse to non-territorial connecting factors to trigger the application of EU law.[11]

On the one hand, it has relied upon an expansive understanding of nationality jurisdiction in order to bring the foreign subsidiaries of EU-established companies within the scope of its laws. For example, EU provisions concerning the remuneration of bankers operate at 'group, parent company and subsidiary levels', and include institutions that are established in offshore financial centres.[12] These provisions therefore apply to staff employed in the third country branches and subsidiaries of EU-headquartered banks and investment firms.[13]

On the other hand, the EU has also relied upon more novel non-territorial triggers to bring 'foreign' transactions within the scope of its laws. For example, the EU has not only relied upon the territorially ambiguous effects doctrine, but also relied

[8] The line separating nationality and presence within Member State territory can be hard to identify as far an 'establishment' is concerned. This depends upon how establishment is defined and whether, e.g., it includes branches as well as subsidiaries.

[9] Art. 54 TFEU implicitly provides a definition of nationality for legal persons for the purposes of internal market law. This includes '[c]ompanies or firms formed in accordance with the law of a Member State and having their registered office, central administration or principal place of business within the [EU]'.

[10] For a discussion of effects-based jurisdiction in the competition law domain, see Giorgio Monti, Chapter 5 in this volume. See, e.g., 'Amicus Curiae Brief by the European Commission on Behalf of the European Union in Support of Neither Part in *Kiobel et al. v. Royal Dutch Petroleum et al.*', at footnote 28.

[11] For a fuller discussion, see Scott, 'The New EU "Extraterritoriality"' (2014) 51 *Common Market Law Review* 1343.

[12] Directive 2013/36 of 26 June 2013 on access to the activity of credit institutions and the prudential supervision of credit institutions and investment firms (CRD IV), OJ 2013 L 176/338, Arts 92 and 94. Here, the EU famously introduced a bankers' 'bonus cap' that fixes the variable element of remuneration at a maximum of 100% of salary or twice this level with explicit shareholder approval.

[13] Marise Cremona points to a further example of an expansive interpretation of the nationality principle in Chapter 2 in this volume. She observes that the EU's fourth money-laundering directive requires the foreign subsidiaries of EU companies to apply EU standards where possible. See Directive 2015/849 of 20 May 2015 on the prevention of the use of the financial system for the purposes of money laundering or terrorist financing, OJ 2015 L 141/73. This includes third country branches too but this is less controversial because these do not enjoy separate legal personality from the parent firm.

upon triggers which are more emphatically extraterritorial, to bring foreign conduct within the scope of its laws. For example, according to the counterparty principle, third country actors incur obligations under EU law when they enter into a contract with an EU counterparty, even where the contract in question is concluded abroad.[14] Likewise, the inclusion of an anti-evasion clause in EU legislation can serve to extend the geographical scope of EU law to include foreign transactions to the extent that this is necessary or appropriate to prevent the evasion of EU law.[15]

Despite these examples, instances of genuine extraterritoriality remain rare in EU law and are very largely confined to the domain of financial regulation. It is no doubt due to this that there is often a perception that, by contrast with the United States, the EU is reluctant to extend the extraterritorial reach of its laws. Indeed, when the European Parliament commissioned a study on the extraterritorial effects of EU and US legislation, of the 12 featured case studies, only one involved the EU.[16] And this one EU case study actually served to exemplify territorial extension rather than extraterritoriality in EU law.[17]

C. Territorial Extension

While it remains relatively rare to find examples of extraterritoriality in EU law (other than those relying upon the normally uncontroversial category of nationality jurisdiction), the phenomenon of territorial extension is very widespread in EU law. As a starting point, the concept of territorial extension can be illustrated by reference to a single example.

The EU has adopted a regulation for the protection of animals at the time of killing. This regulates the killing of animals bred or kept for the production of food, wood, skin, fur or other products.[18] It requires that animals be spared any avoidable pain, distress or suffering during their killing and related operations. Article 12 of this regulation applies to imported animal products and demands that they be accompanied by a certificate attesting that requirements at least equivalent to those laid down in this EU law have been met. As such, animal products imported into the EU must be derived from animals that have been slaughtered in a manner that meets EU-equivalent standards. This measure gives rise to territorial extension. This is because, on the one hand, its application is triggered by the existence of a territorial connection (the import into the EU of animal products) and, on the other, an evaluation of compliance with the regulation necessitates an assessment of foreign

[14] See, for one example, Regulation 648/2012 of 4 July 2012 on OTC derivatives, central counterparties and trade repositories (EMIR), OJ 2012 L 201/1, Art. 4(1)(a)(iv) as well as the discussion of this instrument by Paul Davies in Chapter 4 in this volume.

[15] Regulation 648/2012, note 14, Arts 4(1)(a)(v) and 11(2).

[16] R. Dover and J. Fronsini, 'Extraterritorial Effects of Legislation and Policies in the EU and the US' (European Parliament, 2012). The authors explain this imbalance by reference to the 'far stronger preference' exhibited by US legislators in favour of extraterritoriality, and because as EU researchers they were most interested in the impacts of extraterritoriality upon actors situated in the EU (at 14).

[17] This concerned the EU's infamous decision to include extraterritorial GHG emissions within the scope of its law (note 2).

[18] Council Regulation 1099/2009 of 24 September 2009 on the protection of animals at the time of killing, OJ 2009 L 303/1.

Table 1.2 A simple example of territorial extension

Instrument	Territorial trigger	Territorial extension
Regulation 1099/2009 on the protection of animals at the time of killing	The importation of animal products into the EU	Compliance in third countries with EU-equivalent standards

conduct (the question of whether EU-equivalent standards have been met). The presence of territorial extension in this instrument is summarized in Table 1.2.

Territorial extension operates at different levels and in pursuit of different kinds of objectives.

D. Levels of Territorial Extension

At its narrowest, territorial extension operates at the level of an individual transaction, journey or shipment of goods that is itself centred on the territory of the EU. This can be labelled as transaction-level territorial extension. The EU regulation on the protection of animals at the time of killing, discussed earlier, offers an example of this.[19] This regulation only applies to third country animals that are killed to produce animal products that are imported into the EU. It does not govern the killing of animals that are destined for consumption outside the EU. While this may appear to be self-evident, there are in fact many examples of territorial extension that seek to carve out a broader sphere of regulatory intervention. Territorial extension may operate at 'firm-level' or 'country-level' and examples of each are identified in the following paragraphs.

In the case of firm-level territorial extension, an evaluation of compliance with EU law will assess the overall conduct, organization or governance of a firm and not just its conduct when it is servicing the EU market. For example, if the protection of animals at the time of killing regulation had embodied firm-level as opposed to transaction-level territorial extension, it would have required an appraisal of the overall governance structures of any firm selling animal products within the EU; or of its foreign conduct pertaining even to transactions that were not in any way connected territorially to the EU. The contours of this concept may be clarified by reference to an example currently found in EU law.

EU Regulation 391/2009 establishes common rules and standards for ship inspection and survey organizations.[20] For an organization of this kind to be eligible to act as a 'recognised organization' on behalf of an EU Member State, it must be authorized by the European Commission.[21] In order to gain authorization, the

[19] *Ibid.*

[20] Regulation 391/2009 of 23 April 2009 on common rules and standards for ship inspection and survey organisations, OJ 2009 L 131/11.

[21] Recognized organizations act on behalf of flag states to certify that vessels registered by them are compliant with international conventions in the areas of safety at sea and the prevention of marine pollution.

organization must comply with the specified standards laid down in EU law.[22] This extends to the minimum criteria laid out in Annex I, which includes a multitude of far-reaching and sometimes quite specific governance and operational requirements. To give just one example, '[t]he recognised organisation must not be controlled by shipowners or shipbuilders, or by others engaged commercially in the manufacture, equipping, repair or operation of ships'.[23]

For the purposes of this discussion of firm-level territorial extension, it is highly relevant to note that the concept of an 'organization' (the firm) is defined very broadly in this regulation. It includes not only the parent entity but also 'its subsidiaries and other entities under its control, which jointly or separately carry out tasks falling under the scope of [the] Regulation'.[24] Moreover, the recognition process will 'encompass all legal entities that contribute to ensuring that the organisation in question provides cover for their services worldwide'.[25] To this end, the European Maritime Safety Authority (EMSA) conducts inspections of the component parts of recognized organizations including those which are situated in third country locations.[26] Recognized organizations, including third country entities, are required to ensure that their contracts with shipowners or ship operators make certification of compliance with international conventions conditional upon their 'not opposing the access of Commission inspectors on board the ship' for the purpose of verifying that applicable EU standards have been met.[27] The varying parameters of the concept of a firm, organization or entity in EU law will be discussed further later. The phenomenon of territorial extension in the EU's ship inspection regulation is summarized in Table 1.3.

Moving beyond firm-level territorial extension to country-level territorial extension, we see the EU using the existence of a territorial connection with its Member States to gain leverage over the content of third country law. Classically, with country-level territorial extension, access to the EU market will be denied for goods originating

Table 1.3 Territorial extension in the EU regulation of ship inspection and survey organizations

Instrument	Territorial trigger	Territorial extension
Regulation 391/2009 on ship inspection and survey organisations	Providing services as a 'recognised organisation' to an EU Member State	Assess compliance with a broad range of EU governance and operational requirements, including in relation to the foreign conduct of the organization, including its related third country entities

[22] Regulation 391/2009, note 20, Art. 3. [23] *Ibid.*, Annex I(A)(6).

[24] *Ibid.*, Art. 2(c). Further, according to Art. 2(d), '"control" means, for the purpose of point (c), rights, contracts or any other means, in law or in fact, which, either separately or in combination confer the possibility of exercising decisive influence on a legal entity or enable that entity to carry out tasks falling under the scope of this Regulation'.

[25] *Ibid.*, Art. 4(3).

[26] For details see the EMSA website: http://www.emsa.europa.eu/visits-a-inspections/assessment-of-classification-societies.html. (All website references in this chapter were last visited on 21 February 2019.)

[27] Regulation 391/2009, note 20, Art. 9(2).

in countries that are deemed to have inadequate laws in place. Because this implies that all goods coming from a non-conforming third country will be excluded from the EU market, 'innocent' products that have been produced in conformity with EU law are likely to be excluded as well.[28] Country-level territorial extension is common in financial regulation but is found in many other areas of EU law as well. This concept will be illustrated by reference to one example in financial regulation and one example in the environmental domain.

In the domain of financial regulation, the EU has adopted measures to mitigate the risk associated with over-the-counter (OTC) derivatives contracts and to increase their transparency.[29] To this end—following agreement within the G20—the EU determined that derivatives contracts should be cleared through a central counterparty (CCP) and reported to trade repositories.[30] A third country CCP is only allowed to provide clearing services within the EU if it has gained EU recognition. This recognition will in turn only be granted when the CCP's home country has been recognized as having EU-equivalent laws in place and where the EU has entered into a cooperation agreement with the relevant authorities of this third country.[31] Regardless of the prudential level at which an individual CCP actually operates, it will be precluded from providing services within the EU in the absence of recognition of this kind. This example is summarized in Table 1.4.

In the environmental domain, building on international standards, the EU has adopted a framework to prevent, deter and eliminate illegal, unreported and unregulated fishing.[32] This prohibits the importation of fishery products into the EU which have been obtained from illegal, unreported or unregulated (IUU) fishing.[33] In order to ensure the effectiveness of this prohibition, fishery products must be accompanied by a valid catch certificate if they are to be imported into the EU. EU authorities are required to refuse importation of fishery products where the catch

Table 1.4 Country-level territorial extension in financial regulation

Instrument	Territorial trigger	Territorial extension
Regulation 648/2012 on OTC derivatives trading, central counterparties and trade repositories	The provision of services within the EU market by third country entities	Third country must be recognized as having EU-equivalent laws in place

[28] For a discussion, see D. Regan, 'How to Think about PPMs and Climate Change', in T. Cottier, O. Nartova and S. Z. Bigdeli (eds), *International Trade Regulation and the Mitigation of Climate Change* (2009).

[29] Regulation 648/2012, note 14.

[30] *Ibid.*, Arts 4 (CCPs) and 9 (trade repositories). See also the G-20 2009 Pittsburgh Agreement at http://www.g20.utoronto.ca/2009/2009communique0925.html, esp. paras 10–16.

[31] This oversimplifies a complex regulatory framework. On third country CCPs see Regulation 648/2012, note 14, Art. 25. On trade repositories, see Art. 75. For a list of Commission implementing decisions recognizing equivalence under this and other aspects of this regulation, see https://ec.europa.eu/info/sites/info/files/emir-equivalence-decisions_en.pdf. For a detailed discussion, see Paul Davies, Chapter 4 in this volume.

[32] Council Regulation 1005/2008 of 29 September 2008 establishing a Community system to prevent, deter and eliminate illegal, unreported and unregulated fishing, OJ 2008 L 286/1.

[33] *Ibid.*, Art. 12.

Table 1.5 Country-level territorial extension in EU-IUU fishing

Instrument	Territorial trigger	Territorial extension
Regulation 1005/2008 establishing a Community system to prevent, deter and eliminate illegal, unreported and unregulated fishing	Import of fishery products into the EU	Exclusion of fishery products from non-cooperating third states from EU market

certificate has been validated by the authorities of a flag state which has been identified as a 'non-cooperating state'.[34] 'A third country may be identified as a non-cooperating third country if it fails to discharge the duties incumbent upon it under international law as flag, port, coastal or market state, to take action to prevent, deter and eliminate IUU fishing.'[35] Where a catch certificate has been validated by a non-cooperating third country, the related fisheries products will be excluded from the EU market regardless of how sustainable the fishing methods that were used to procure them were. The EU-IUU fishing example is summarized in Table 1.5.

E. The Relationship between the Different Levels of Territorial Extension

In the discussion in section 2.D, the treatments of the different levels of territorial extension have been separated: transaction, firm and country. In practice, however, it is very often the case that a single instrument will combine more than one of these types of territorial extension. Where this is the case, it is important to pay close attention to the relationship between the different levels of territorial extension. This is particularly so when it comes to country-level territorial extension, because this has the potential to be quite draconian due to its tendency to exclude 'innocent' products from the EU market. This is a point which will be returned to later.

In some instances, country-level territorial extension is the only possible route to secure compliance with EU law. Where a third country does not meet the country-level conditions laid down, products originating in that country will be deemed not to comply with EU law. This is the case in relation to both the examples of country-level territorial extension set out in section 2.D. In other instances, however, country-level territorial extension offers one possible route to secure compliance with EU law, but transaction-level and/or firm-level compliance also remains possible. A clear example of this can be seen in relation to the EU's decision to include GHG emissions from aviation in its emissions trading scheme.[36] Here, airlines were required to surrender emission allowances to cover each tonne of GHGs emitted during the entire course of an EU-departing and EU-arriving flight. This may be considered

[34] *Ibid.*, Art. 18(1)(g).

[35] *Ibid.*, Art. 31(3). The two-stage procedure for declaring a country a non-cooperating third country is laid down in Arts 32–33. Countries are first given a warning about the possibility of being included on this list ('yellow card') and may then be included on the list ('red card'). The list of countries that have been issued with either yellow cards or red cards can be found at https://ec.europa.eu/fisheries/sites/fisheries/files/illegal-fishing-overview-of-existing-procedures-third-countries_en.pdf.

[36] Directive 2008/101, note 2.

an example of transaction-level territorial extension, as compliance with EU law could be secured at the level of a single flight. No firm-level or country-level compliance was required. However, this measure also embodied an element of country-level territorial extension as it provided for the possible exemption of EU-arriving flights where these flights originated in a third country that had adopted EU-equivalent measures to reduce the climate change impact of flights.[37] Thus, for incoming flights, compliance could be achieved either at the level of an individual transaction (an individual flight in this example) or at the level of a third country. As such, this measure created two possible routes towards compliance for EU-arriving flights. Some other examples of transaction-level/country-level hybrids will be seen later.

F. Objectives of Territorial Extension

Although, by definition, territorial extension has an external dimension in that it makes compliance with EU law conditional upon conduct or circumstances abroad, it would be misleading to assume on this basis that it operates exclusively, or even principally, in pursuit of external as opposed to global or internal objectives.

Notwithstanding these high-profile examples and the intensity of the political reactions that they provoked, it is important to be aware that the vast majority of EU measures that give rise to territorial extension pursue objectives that are internal to the EU and are less prone to causing controversy.[38] Such measures aim, for example, to protect the competition on EU markets,[39] the stability of EU financial markets and institutions,[40] or the welfare, privacy, safety or security of EU citizens or (habitual) residents.[41] On some occasions, EU law even endeavours to protect the interests of EU persons when they are engaged in conduct outside the EU. For example, the provision of services by a third country entity to the third country branch of an EU firm has been equated with EU market access even though the services are provided outside the territory of the EU.[42]

[37] *Ibid.*, Art. 25a.

[38] See the interesting discussion in Silversmith, 'The Long Arm of the DOT: The Regulation of Foreign Air Carriers Beyond US Borders', 38 *Air & Space Law* (2013) 173. Although this examines territorial extension in US aviation law, it shows that there has been greater acceptance of measures that are motivated by aviation safety or security concerns, as opposed to economic or moral concerns. For example, the author points out that the dispute between the EU and the US concerning the disclosure of passenger name records (PNRs) centred upon privacy concerns rather than extraterritoriality because, in jurisdictional terms, this measure was viewed by most commentators as a 'reasonable self-protective measure' in the wake of the events of 9/11.

[39] See Giorgio Monti, Chapter 5 in this volume.

[40] See Paul Davies, Chapter 4 in this volume.

[41] See Christopher Kuner, Chapter 3 in this volume, regarding data protection. In terms of the safety/security of EU citizens, the EU's directives on aviation safety and aviation security are exemplary in this respect.

[42] Regulation 648/2012, note 14, Art. 25(2). The opposite may also be true in that EU persons may be excluded from enjoying the protection of EU law even when they are engaged in activities within the EU. For example, some measures deem that services provided within the territory of the EU are to be regarded as not having been provided within the territory of the EU where they are provided at the exclusive initiative of the person receiving the service. See, e.g., Regulation 600/2014 of 15 May 2014 on markets in financial instruments, OJ 2004, L 173/84, Art. 36(4) and recital 36. This is because these clients are regarded as professional investors and as not requiring the protection that the measure confers.

That the EU is frequently more concerned with the realization of objectives which are internal to the EU can be exemplified by reference to competition law. While the EU has been willing to extend the global reach of its competition laws to protect competition in the EU market from risks that originate abroad, it has only been willing to exercise its territorial jurisdiction over export cartels to the extent that these may have an appreciable impact on the EU market.[43] This remains the case regardless of the severity of the negative consequences that they may generate elsewhere. This focus on domestic, as opposed to global, welfare effects has been criticized.[44]

As will become particularly clear in the discussion of the approach of the Court of Justice of the European Union (CJEU) to appraising the legality of territorial extension, there are nonetheless occasions when the EU uses a territorial extension device to promote the achievement of an objective outside the EU. There are several examples of this in the area of animal welfare, including the example relating to the protection of animals at the time of killing that was highlighted earlier.[45] Occasional examples relating to environmental protection, public health and human rights may also be encountered.

The EU's regulation to prevent trade in goods that could be used for capital punishment, torture or other cruel, inhuman or degrading treatment in third countries offers a good example in this respect.[46] This prohibits the export from the EU of goods that have no practical use other than for the purposes of imposing capital punishment, torture or other cruel, inhuman, degrading treatment or punishment.[47] Prior authorization is required for the export of goods that could be used for one of these purposes and will be denied when there are reasonable grounds to believe they could be used in this way.[48] EU measures regulating the conduct of clinical trials in third countries are also illustrative from this point of view. If clinical trials conducted outside the EU are to be taken into account in the assessment of a marketing application for pharmaceutical products within the EU, these must comply with EU-equivalent requirements regarding good clinical practical and ethical principles.[49] Good clinical practice is not only intended to ensure that the data generated from clinical trials is reliable and robust, but also to ensure the protection of the rights, safety and wellbeing of subjects, including third country subjects, involved in clinical trials.

While recourse to territorial extension in pursuit of external objectives is often viewed as particularly problematic, this legislative technique can also be controversial when the EU aims to contribute to the attainment of global objectives. Although the

[43] For a discussion, see Giorgio Monti, Chapter 5 in this volume.

[44] See, e.g., C. Ryngaert, *Jurisdiction in International Law* (2nd edn, 2015).

[45] Council Regulation 1099/2009, note 18.

[46] Council Regulation 1236/2005 of 27 June 2005 concerning trade in certain goods which could be used for capital punishment, torture or other cruel, inhuman or degrading treatment or punishment, OJ 2005 L 200/1.

[47] *Ibid.*, Art. 3.

[48] *Ibid.*, Art. 4.

[49] Directive 2001/83 of 6 November 2001 on the Community code relating to medicinal products for human use, OJ 2001 L 311/67, Annex I(8), and Regulation 536/2014 of 16 April 2014 on clinical trials on medicinal products for human use, OJ 2014 L 158/1, Art. 2(2). For a good, early, discussion of some of the dilemmas surrounding the pursuit of external objectives, see Micklitz, 'EC Regulation of the Export of Dangerous Pharmaceuticals to Third World Countries: Some Prospects' 11 *Journal of Consumer Policy* (1998) 29.

validity of the EU's decision to include extraterritorial GHG emissions in its emissions trading scheme was upheld by the CJEU, it was widely condemned by third countries and even provoked the United States to adopt a 'blocking statute' which conferred authority on the Secretary of State for Transportation to prohibit US airlines from complying with the EU law.[50] The EU also faced intensive opposition from both Canada and the United States when it proposed to take the lifecycle emissions—including extraction phase emissions—of imported fuel into account for the purpose of assessing compliance with the EU's fuel intensity reduction targets.[51] When this external opposition gained support from a number of EU Member States, the European Commission's draft implementing act was dropped.[52]

G. The Relationship between Territorial Extension and the 'Brussels Effect'

While territorial extension (and to a lesser extent extraterritoriality) serves as an important tool to extend the global reach of EU law, it is not the only such tool. Indeed, assisted by the prospect of Brexit,[53] the concept of the 'Brussels Effect' has garnered considerable attention.[54] Building on David Vogel's earlier concept of the 'California Effect',[55] Anu Bradford coined the term the 'Brussels Effect' and drew a distinction between its *de jure* and *de facto* components.

The *de facto* Brussels Effect is said to occur when third country companies that are required to comply with EU standards when they are producing goods for the EU market decide to comply with these standards even when they are producing goods for their domestic and/or a third country market. 'This converts the EU rule into a global rule—the "de facto Brussels Effect." '[56] By contrast, the *de jure* Brussels Effect is said to occur when a third country legislature decides to incorporate the substance of EU standards into its domestic law. While Bradford offers many examples of the Brussels Effect in her article, her principal aim is to provide a hypothesis regarding when it will occur. To this end, she identifies some general conditions that must be met, as shown in Table 1.6.

The last condition included in Table 1.6, concerning the non-divisibility of standards, forms a very important part of Bradford's account of the Brussels Effect. Standards are considered to be non-divisible when there is a compelling reason for a third country to 'over-comply' with EU law by meeting its requirements even when

[50] European Union Emissions Trading Prohibition Act of 2011.

[51] Directive 2009/30 of 23 April 2009 as regards the specification of petrol, diesel and gas-oil and introducing a mechanism to monitor and reduce greenhouse gas emissions, OJ 2009 L 140/88, Art. 7a. The Commission relied on a report that suggested that the lifecycle emissions of fuel derived from 'tar sands' (bitumen) were 22% higher compared to conventional crude oil.

[52] Carbon Briefing, 'Who killed the EU's transport fuel standards?' (2013), available at https://www.carbonbrief.org/carbon-briefing-who-killed-the-eus-transport-fuel-standards.

[53] The proposed withdrawal of the UK from the EU following the referendum held in June 2016.

[54] Bradford, 'The Brussels Effect', 107 *Northwestern University Law Review* (2015) 1. Beattie, 'Why the "Brussels Effect" will Undermine Brexit Regulatory Push', *Financial Times*, 12 July 2017.

[55] For his most recent writing on this topic, see D. Vogel, *California Greenin': How the Golden State Became an Environmental Leader* (2018).

[56] Bradford, note 54, at 6.

Table 1.6 Conditions giving rise to the Brussels Effect

Condition	Definition
EU market power	The EU must enjoy a large domestic market relative to other available markets
EU regulatory capacity	The EU must enjoy a high level of regulatory expertise and resources to enforce its rules
EU preference for strict rules	The EU must exhibit a propensity to promulgate strict standards
EU predisposition to regulate inelastic targets	EU regulation must be aimed at regulating inelastic targets, such as consumer goods as opposed to capital markets, thus making it hard for third country companies to avoid the regulation by relocating their activities
Non-divisibility of standards	Third country producers must have an incentive to comply with EU standards not only when producing for the EU market but at all times

it is producing goods for its domestic market or a third country market. Bradford identifies three categories of incentives which she considers to be the drivers of non-divisibility of standards. These are economic non-divisibility, technical non-divisibility and legal non-divisibility of standards.[57]

Economic non-divisibility of standards is said to occur when it is less costly in economic terms for a company to harmonize production according to a single, strict, standard than it is to comply with a multitude of different, often less stringent, standards. Technical non-divisibility of standards occurs when the presence of a technical obstacle precludes companies from producing separate batches of goods for different markets. They are therefore compelled to comply with the strictest standards at all times. The concept of legal non-divisibility of standards is not defined by Bradford but is, rather, illustrated by reference to a single example. '[G]lobal mergers ... cannot be consummated on a jurisdiction-by-jurisdiction basis ... [and therefore] the most stringent antitrust jurisdiction gets to determine the fate of the transaction worldwide'.[58]

The goal here is not to offer a general appraisal of Bradford's theory of the Brussels Effect,[59] but rather to clarify the relationship between this notion and the concept of territorial extension which forms the principal focus of this chapter. As a starting point, it is important to note that there is no necessary relationship between territorial extension and the Brussels Effect. Some measures that generate the Brussels Effect may be imbued with territorial extension,[60] but many others will not. And similarly, not all measures that give rise to territorial extension will give rise to the Brussels Effect. Nonetheless, despite the absence of any inherent relationship between territorial extension and the Brussels Effect, it does appear that territorial extension

[57] *Ibid.*, at 17–19. [58] *Ibid.*, at 18.

[59] For a critical discussion of her mergers example, see Giorgio Monti, Chapter 5 in this volume.

[60] E.g. Bradford discusses the EU's decision to include GHG emissions from aviation in its emissions trading scheme as an example of the Brussels Effect and, as has already been observed in this chapter, this measure gives rise to both transaction-level and country-level (for EU-arriving flights) territorial extension (Bradford, note 54, at 30–31).

is a phenomenon that can sometimes serve to promote the emergence of the Brussels Effect. If this is accepted, it has implications for our understanding, and indeed the operation, of the Brussels Effect.

The argument that territorial extension may fuel the Brussels Effect proceeds in the following way. First, standards must be non-divisible for the Brussels Effect to occur. Second, certain types of territorial extension create legal non-divisibility of standards, thereby fuelling the Brussels Effect.

Firm-level territorial extension requires third country companies to comply with EU law even when they are not producing goods for the EU market, thereby generating legal non-divisibility of standards. For example, in the same way as it is not possible for a company to be merged for the purpose of EU law and unmerged for the purpose of US law, it is not possible for a company to operate in accordance with a particular EU-mandated code of conduct for the purpose of EU law and not operate in accordance with this same code of conduct for the purpose of US law.[61] Therefore, it is possible to argue that firm-level territorial extension may engender legal non-divisibility of standards and thereby fuel the *de facto* Brussels Effect.

Further, *country-level territorial extension* operates to make EU market access conditional upon the content of third country law.[62] Country-level territorial extension in EU legislation may be narrowly or broadly drawn. It was narrowly drawn in the EU's aviation emissions trading law, because EU-arriving flights could be exempted from the EU scheme in the event that a third country took steps to reduce the climate change impact of *EU-bound* flights.[63] Where country-level territorial extension is narrowly drawn in this way, there is no inevitability that it will contribute to the *de jure* Brussels Effect. Even if the United States were to regulate the GHG emissions of EU-bound flights, airlines would be unlikely to comply with this law when flying to other destinations.

Where, however, country-level territorial extension is more broadly drawn and makes EU market access conditional on the overall content of third country law, country-level territorial extension will operate to generate legal non-divisibility of standards and to fuel the emergence of the *de jure* Brussels Effect. To give an example that has already been referred to above, for a third country CCP to be authorized to clear derivatives transactions falling within the scope of EU law, it must be established or authorized in a third country that is considered to have EU-equivalent systems for anti-money-laundering and combating the financing of terrorism in place.[64] Once these systems are in place, they will govern third country CCPs regardless of to whom they are selling their services.

[61] This draws upon the example of Regulation 391/2009 on common rules and standards for ship inspection and survey organisations (note 20).

[62] EU requirements may also relate to the effectiveness with which law is enforced and may refer to standards drawn from international as well as national law. See the EU-IUU fishing regulation (note 32), Art. 31(3) for an example. See also Van der Marel, 'Problems and Progress in Combatting IUU Fishing', in E. J. Molenaar and R. Caddell (eds), *Strengthening International Fisheries Law in an Era of Changing Oceans* (2018).

[63] Directive 2008/101, note 2.

[64] Regulation 648/2012, note 14, Art. 25(1)(2)(d).

If it is accepted that territorial extension and the Brussels Effect are related in this way, this has important implications for our understanding and the operation of the Brussels Effect.

First, legal non-divisibility of standards deserves a much more prominent place in Bradford's account of the Brussels Effect. This is because there are many EU measures that give rise to firm-level, and broadly drawn country-level, territorial extension and which therefore serve to fuel the *de facto* or the *de jure* Brussels Effect. Indeed, the single example of legal non-divisibility of standards that Bradford provides fails to capture the 'legislated' as opposed to the contingent nature of this phenomenon. It may be that her mergers example should be viewed as an instance of technical as opposed to legal non-divisibility of standards (it is not technically possible for companies to be merged and not merged at the same time), and that the concept of legal non-divisibility of standards should be reserved for situations in which legal non-divisibility of standards is embodied in the substance of EU law.

Second, given that country-level territorial extension is very widespread in EU law, the *de jure* Brussels Effect will often precede the *de facto* Brussels Effect because country-level territorial extension renders compliance with EU law conditional upon the content of third country law. Thus, country-level territorial extension militates in favour of the *de jure* Brussels Effect, independent of third country companies that have previously embraced the *de facto* Brussels Effect bringing any pressure to bear. This is contrary to the picture that Bradford paints in her account.[65]

Third, there is a tension in Bradford's account of the Brussels Effect between the role of 'market forces' in generating the Brussels Effect and the active role of the EU in intentionally exporting its norms.

On the one hand, Bradford presents the Brussels Effect as arising due to the capacity of 'market forces' to generate 'involuntary incentives' for companies and countries to over-comply with EU standards.[66] While the EU plays a role in this, due to its large market, strict standards, focus on inelastic targets and regulatory capacity, the emergence of non-divisible standards remains out of its hands. Economic forces drive economic non-divisibility, technical forces drive technical non-divisibility, and contingent legal forces, which appear to arise independent of EU agency, drive the emergence of legal non-divisibility of standards.

On the other hand, for Bradford, the political economy of the Brussels Effect seems to be rooted in a regulatory competition perspective.[67] It is in the EU's interests to export its norms to third countries in order to preserve the competitive position of industry when competing within the EU or in third country markets.[68] But, if the emergence of non-divisibility of standards is out of the EU's hands, it is not clear what, if anything, the EU is doing to promote the export of its norms. As such, the concept of territorial extension can help to address this tension between market forces and regulatory competition that is present in Bradford's account. By incorporating firm-level or

[65] Bradford, note 54, at 8. [66] *Ibid.*, at 9.

[67] See, e.g., R. D. Keleman and D. Vogel, *Trading Places: The US and the EU in International Environmental Politics* (2018).

[68] Bradford, note 54, at 39 where Bradford notes '[a] concern for EU corporations' competitiveness offers a compelling explanation for the EU's global regulatory agenda'.

country-level territorial extension into the very substance of its laws, thereby taking steps to secure the presence of legal non-divisibility of standards, the EU may be viewed as taking an active step to ensure that the conditions for the emergence of the Brussels Effect are met. While I do not intend this observation to be taken as a straightforward endorsement of Bradford's regulatory competition perspective, it is clear that the presence of territorial extension in EU law can help Bradford's argument, taken on its own terms.

It is therefore a mistake to overlook the concept of territorial extension when developing an account of the Brussels Effect. Legal non-divisibility of standards is not a contingent feature of EU law, as Bradford's single mergers example might seem to suggest. It is, however, inherent in EU legislation giving rise to firm-level and country-level territorial extension when it is broadly drawn. Its presence will often reflect a choice that the EU legislature has made.

H. The Permissive Stance of the CJEU towards Territorial Extension

Despite some recent 'near misses',[69] the CJEU has not had occasion to pronounce on the lawfulness of measures which are conceived as extraterritorial, outside the field of competition law. As Giorgio Monti shows in Chapter 5 of this volume, in competition law the CJEU has endorsed a 'qualified effects test'.[70] As a result, the CJEU considers it to be lawful for EU law to apply to an anticompetitive agreement concluded outside the EU where it is foreseeable that this agreement will have an immediate and substantial effect within the EU.[71]

The CJEU has, however, contended with the phenomenon of territorial extension on a number of occasions, although it has not labelled it in this way. The CJEU has been willing to construe legislation as giving rise to territorial extension,[72] and

[69] See esp. Case C-209/13, *United Kingdom v. Council* (ECLI:EU:C:2014:283) concerning the United Kingdom's action for annulment of the Council's decision to authorize 11 Member States to establish enhanced cooperation among themselves to establish a financial transaction tax where the CJEU concluded that neither the counterparty principle nor the issuance principle formed part of the contested Decision authorizing enhanced cooperation and that therefore that the action should be dismissed; Case C-507/13, *United Kingdom v. European Parliament and Council* (ECLI:EU:C:2014:2481) where AG Jaaskinen rejected all of the pleas in law put forward by the United Kingdom and subsequently the UK exercised its prerogative to withdraw its application for annulment and was ordered to pay the costs; and Case C-308/06, *R. ex parte Intertanko v. Secretary of State for Transport* [2008] ECR I-4057 (ECLI:EU:C:2008:312), where the CJEU refused to assess the legality of an EU Directive regulating ship-source pollution, including on the high seas, on the basis that the European Community was not party to the MARPOL Convention and that the United Nations Law of the Sea Convention is not such as to confer rights on individuals. Though the directive in question could be considered to be extraterritorial, this issue was not raised before the CJEU.

[70] Case C-413/14 P, *Intel Corporation Inc. v. Commission* (ECLI:EU:C:2017:632), judgment of 6 September 2017.

[71] This is the same test that the General Court has endorsed in relation to third country mergers in Case T-102/96, *Gencor Ltd v. Commission* [1999] ECR II-753 (ECLI:EU:T:1999:65). As Monti shows in Chapter 5 in this volume, the CJEU has also endorsed an 'implementation test' that is capable of catching agreements concluded outside the EU. This was confirmed in *Intel*, note 70.

[72] See, e.g., Case C-592/14, *European Federation of Cosmetics Ingredients* (ECLI:EU:C:2016:703) and Case C-324/09, *L'Oreal v. Ebay* [2011] ECR I-6011 (ECLI:EU:C:2011:474) where the CJEU states that 'the mere fact that a website is accessible from the territory covered by the trade mark is not a sufficient basis for concluding that the offers for sale displayed are targeted at consumers in that territory' in interpreting the scope of application of EU consumer protection laws (at para. 64).

to do so even where the measure in question is not explicit in making compliance with EU law conditional upon conduct that takes place abroad. Consequently, no presumption against territorial extension operates in EU law.[73]

The CJEU has also been willing to uphold the validity of a measure giving rise to territorial extension. Famously, in the *Air Transportation of America* case, the CJEU ruled on the validity of the EU's directive including extraterritorial GHG emissions within the scope of its emissions trading scheme.[74] In assessing the compatibility of the EU measure with customary international law, the CJEU observed that the EU 'cannot' render its laws applicable to foreign country aircraft which are over-flying third countries or the high seas.[75] However, it went on to find that the EU directive did not infringe the principle of territoriality in customary international law because it only applied to aircraft that were physically present within EU territory.[76] Aircraft taking off from and landing at an airport within the EU should be regarded as being subject to the 'unlimited jurisdiction' of the EU and its Member States.[77] After all, the measure only applies to aircraft operators who have chosen to operate a commercial activity within the EU.[78]

The permissive stance of the CJEU is further reflected in three facets of its territorial extension case law, although as yet all three facets have never come together in a single case.[79]

First, while the CJEU did observe in the *Air Transportation of America* case that the EU's climate change objectives 'follow on from' international agreements,[80] the Court has not made the existence of international standards a precondition for the legality of territorial extension in EU law. For example, in cases involving animal welfare, the Court has laid emphasis upon the important place that this objective occupies within the EU legal order, without looking for evidence of broad multilateral recognition of it.[81]

[73] See Case C-424/13, *Zuchtvieh-Export GmbH v. Stadt Kempten* (ECLI:EU:C:2015:259). The CJEU's judgment stands in contrast to the Opinion of AG Bot in this case, who interpreted the legislation as applying only within EU territory, arguing that it is for the legislature and not the Court to decide to extend the extraterritorial reach of EU law and to make this extension 'subject to the establishment of an appropriate system of checks' (at paras 94–95). On the CJEU's permissive stance and the distinction between interpreting measures with territorial extension if not explicitly there and upholding the validity of measures designed with territorial extension in the environmental field, see I. Hadjiyianni, 'The Role of Domestic Courts in Global Environmental Governance: Judicial Review of Extraterritoriality by the Court of Justice of the European Union' (2018) *EUI Working Paper* MWP/RNS/2018. Also, I. Hadjiyianni, 'Domestic Courts as Transnational Actors: Review of the Territorial Scope of EU Environmental law by the Court of Justice of the EU' (forthcoming).

[74] Case C-366/10, *Air Transportation Association of America v. Secretary of State for Energy and Climate Change (ATAA)* [2011] ECR I-13755 (ECLI:EU:C:2011:864).

[75] *Ibid.*, para. 122. [76] *Ibid.*, para. 125. [77] *Ibid.*, para. 124.

[78] *Ibid.*, paras. 127–128.

[79] The three facets are (a) strongly unilateral; (b) in pursuit of an external objective; and (c) country-level territorial extension. In particular, the only example of country-level territorial extension discussed in this case law was concerned with an internal as opposed to a global or an external objective (EU data protection law aims to ensure data protection for individuals within the EU).

[80] *ATAA*, note 74, para. 128.

[81] E.g. Zuchtvieh, note 73, para. 35 where the CJEU emphasizes the existence of Protocol 33 on the protection and welfare of animals annexed to the EC Treaty and its case law recognizing animal welfare as a legitimate objective in the public interest.

Second, although the CJEU often makes an effort to construe the objectives pursued by legislation giving rise to territorial extension as at least partly internal to the EU, it has nonetheless shown itself to be willing to endorse external objectives as well. This is most apparent from the recent *Zuchtvieh* case. Here, the Court construed the relevant legislation as extending beyond EU borders. It did so despite the fact that there was no suggestion that the foreign conduct rendered subject to EU law would generate effects within the EU.[82] There was likewise no suggestion in this case that a failure to extend the geographical scope of EU law would compromise the EU's ability to achieve its objectives because this would enable individuals to circumvent it by moving their activities to the territory of a third country.[83]

Third, the CJEU has been willing to adopt a robust interpretation of legislation giving rise to *country-level* territorial extension. It favoured a strict interpretation of the adequacy standard laid down in Article 25(1) of the EU's data protection directive, which makes the transfer of personal data to a third country for processing conditional on that third country ensuring an adequate level of data protection.[84] While the Court accepted that a third country's level of protection could be considered to be adequate even if the means that it uses to ensure data protection differ from those of the EU, 'those means must nevertheless prove, in practice, effective in order to ensure protection essentially equivalent to that guaranteed within the European Union'.[85] For the European Commission to endorse as adequate the level of protection guaranteed by a third country, it must adopt a reasoned decision finding that the third country in question ensures a level of protection that is essentially equivalent to that of the EU.[86] Given the importance of the EU's data protection objective, and the grave threat posed to it by a transfer of data to a third country that does not ensure an adequate level of protection, the Court narrowed the Commission's discretion and insisted that the requirements underpinning an adequacy determination must be strictly applied.[87]

While the CJEU has taken a permissive stance to territorial extension, it is important to stress that it has also been sensitive to the danger that territorial extension can generate conflicts with third country laws. For example, in the *Zuchtvieh* case,[88] the CJEU read a conflict equivalence clause into the relevant EU legislation although this did not exist on the face of the text. This clause served to recognize that where the law or administrative practice of a third country 'verifiably and definitely

[82] Contrast with *Intel*, note 70, and *ATAA*, note 74.

[83] Contrast with *Cosmetics*, note 72, para. 42; Case C-131/12, *Google Spain SL and Google Inc. v. Agencia Española de Protección de Datos (AEPD) and Mario Costeja González* (ECLI:EU:C:2014:317); *Intel*, note 70;, and Case C-362/14 *Maximillian Schrems v. Data Protection Commissioner* (ECLI:EU:C:2015:650).

[84] *Schrems*, note 83, this has since been superseded by the General Data Protection Regulation, note 3. This is subject to other provisions in the directive.

[85] *Schrems*, note 83, para. 74. The Commission is required to revisit its adequacy determination periodically to verify whether its adequacy determination is still legally and factually justified (para. 76).

[86] *Ibid.*, para. 96. [87] *Ibid.*, para. 78.

[88] *Zuchtvieh*, note 73. Hadjiyianni argues that the Court's concern to avoid direct conflicts between laws is often the only engagement with the extraterritorial impacts of EU legislation interpreted with a broad geographical scope by the CJEU, which may not be sufficient (note 73 2018).

precludes full compliance' with EU law, compliance with EU-equivalent standards of animal welfare would be viewed as sufficient instead.[89]

Also, in the *Cosmetics* case, the Court followed the Advocate General in rejecting the maximalist reading of the relevant EU legislation that had been proposed by a number of Member States and by a third party intervener in this case.[90] The Court did not accept that the EU's marketing ban should be triggered whenever animal testing had been conducted to demonstrate the safety of a cosmetic ingredient, even where the testing had been carried out to satisfy the regulatory requirements of a third country. On the contrary, the Court concluded that the prohibition on animal testing should only apply when the results of the animal testing had been relied upon to prove the safety of cosmetic ingredients for the purpose of demonstrating compliance with EU law.[91] Thus, it would be open to a manufacturer to demonstrate the safety of cosmetics ingredients through recourse to animal testing in a third country that mandates such testing, while still being able to market the ingredients within the EU.

3. The Distinction between Extraterritoriality and Territorial Extension is not Intended to be a Normative Shortcut

It is important to stress that I developed the concept of territorial extension with a view to it serving as an analytical construct that could help us to map and understand the extraterritorial effect of EU law. Nonetheless, it is often the case that observers of this phenomenon are less interested in the 'is' than the 'ought'. Ought the EU to use territorial extension to expand the geographical scope of its laws? As a preliminary to considering this question, it should be stressed that the concept of territorial extension is not intended to serve as a normative shortcut in appraising the global reach of EU law.

The mere fact that the application of a measure is triggered by the existence of a territorial connection with the EU should not be regarded as sufficient to ground a conclusion that it was appropriate or even lawful for the EU to act in this way.[92] As Justice Scalia famously said:

[89] *Zuchtvieh*, note 73, para. 54.

[90] *Cosmetics*, note 72. AG Bobek was considerably more fulsome than the Court in explaining why the maximalist reading should be rejected. He stated that such a broad reading could lead to the EU's marketing ban being triggered by events that are 'unconnected... temporally, territorially and sectorally' to the act of placing of cosmetics ingredients on the EU market. He considered that this interpretation could lead to 'extreme results', forcing 'producers to choose between marketing an ingredient in the EU or in [another] jurisdiction that mandates animal testing' and creating 'de facto export or import bans'. He argued that if the legislature had intended such effects, 'one could legitimately have expected it to have chosen clearer wording to express that intent' (paras 60–73).

[91] *Ibid.*, para. 43.

[92] For an example of the CJEU rendering invalid a measure which rested upon a territorial connection, see Joined cases C-446/09 and C-495/09, *Koninklijke Philips Electronics NV v. Lucheng Meijing Industrial Company Ltd and others and Nokia Corporation v. Her Majesty's Commissioners of Revenue and Customs* [2011] ECR I-12435 (ECLI:EU:C:2011:796). This case was concerned with the seizure of pharmaceutical products in transit in EU Member States and the judgment of the Court was based on

it is a rare case of prohibited extraterritorial application that lacks *all* contact with the territory of the United States. But the presumption against extraterritorial application would be a craven watchdog if it retreated to its kennel whenever *some* domestic activity is involved in the case.[93]

The existence of a territorial connection cannot be considered conclusive, given that there will often be disagreement about what constitutes a territorial connection and such connections vary considerably in type and degree. The example of data protection is telling in this respect. Here, the EU is relying upon a novel and flimsy territorial connection, namely the fact that data processors are using computer equipment located within the EU; for example, by collecting data from EU-located computers by means of 'cookies', JavaScript, ad banners and spyware.[94]

Further, the answer to the question of whether a measure rests on a territorial basis will depend in significant part upon how the measure is framed. WTO litigation in the *EC—Seals* case is telling in this respect.[95] Here, the EU 'territorialized' its regulatory objective by arguing that the contested measure was at least in part 'aimed at addressing public moral concerns on the welfare of seals'.[96] This framing was challenged unsuccessfully by the complainants in the case who argued that the measure pursued several objectives, prominently including the extraterritorial objective of protecting the welfare of seals outside the EU.[97] The issue of framing was important in this case because there is still a certain degree of ambiguity in WTO law concerning the extraterritorial scope of the general exception included in GATT, Article XX.[98]

It is also the case that the mere fact that a measure gives rise to territorial extension should not be regarded as sufficient to condemn a measure out of hand. In some instances, this is at least as much a product of the technology of regulation as it is of a deeper shift in the nature of the EU's global ambitions. We can see this in the area of food safety regulation where a shift from a 'poke and sniff' method for detecting violations to a management-based approach (Hazard Analysis and Critical Control Point—HACCP) has resulted in the presence of territorial extension.[99] While the EU's regulatory objective remains unchanged (safe food in the EU's internal market), the proceduralized nature of management-based approaches has led to an 'off-shoring' of the steps necessary to achieve this objective.

its interpretation of EU legislation as opposed to public international law. See also WT/DS408 *European Union and a Member State—Seizure of Generic Drugs in Transit* for a taste of this controversy. A Panel has not been formed in this case.

[93] *Morrison v. National Australia Bank Ltd*, 561 U.S. 247 (2010), para. 2884.

[94] Directive 95/46, note 3.

[95] WT/DS400 & WT/DS401, *European Communities—Measures Prohibiting the Importation and Marketing of Seals*.

[96] *Ibid.*, para. 7.3. [97] *Ibid.*

[98] Recall para. 133 of WT/DS58, *United States—Measures Concerning the Importation of Shrimp and Shrimp Products* where the Appellate Body stated that '[w]e do not pass upon the question of whether there is an implied jurisdictional limitation in Article XX(g), and if so, the nature or extent of that limitation'.

[99] See Coglianese and Lazer, 'Management-Based Regulation: Prescribing Private Management to Achieve Public Goals', 37 *Law and Society Review* (2003) 691. In the area of food safety, management-based regulation uses HACCP regulation which relies on procedural tools and results in regulatory interventions at the point of production rather than the point of sale.

It is also the case that public international law sometimes sanctions recourse to territorial 'system boundaries'. The concept of a system boundary is used here to describe the manner in which responsibility for regulating conduct is apportioned between different states. This concept is used in the field of climate change, where there is considerable debate about whether a production-based or a consumption-based system boundary should be preferred.[100] As it currently stands, the climate change system boundary is principally territorial, in that it apportions responsibility to the state in which GHG emissions are generated.

However, some international treaties include non-territorial system boundaries, and therefore permit or even require states to regulate conduct beyond their territorial boundaries. To take a simple example of a non-territorial system boundary in public international law, the Tokyo Convention on Offences and Other Acts Committed on Board Aircraft 1963 confers criminal law jurisdiction on contracting states over offences committed on board foreign aircraft, while these aircraft are outside the territory of the state exercising jurisdiction in certain circumstances. This includes situations in which the commission of the offence beyond a state's territory has an effect within a state, is against the security of the state, or where the offence is committed by or against one of its nationals or permanent residents.[101]

Human rights also offer an important example of a system boundary that is at least in part non-territorial. Human rights treaties impose extraterritorial obligations on Parties in situations where they assert 'effective control' over territory or a person or situation.[102] As the human rights example indicates, contestation around the theme of extraterritoriality may be predicated upon a concern that a state is doing too little, extraterritorially, rather than too much.[103]

Ironically, given the fuss that sometimes accompanies EU measures that give rise to territorial extension, the presence of territorial extension can sometimes serve to make a measure less, rather than more, restrictive as far as third countries are concerned. Again, the EU seals regulation offers a compelling example. In the main, this measure takes the form of a classic import ban which does not give rise to territorial extension because it does not make importation conditional on the manner in which the product has been harvested or produced. The only aspect of this measure that results in its giving rise to territorial extension is the inclusion of the so-called 'Inuit exception'. This allows seal products to be placed on the EU market to the extent that they result from hunts that have been conducted using traditional methods by Inuit

[100] See Peters, 'From Production-based to Consumption-based National Emission Inventories', 65 *Ecological Economics* (2008) 13.

[101] Tokyo Convention, Art. 4(a), (b) and (c). See also Art. 4(d) and (e) for additional situations in which countries may assert jurisdiction. It is interesting to observe that several states may assert jurisdiction over the same crime and that the convention does not seek to establish an order of priority between states.

[102] Tzevelekos, 'Reconstructing the Effective Control Criterion in Extraterritorial Human Rights Breaches: Direct Attribution of Wrongfulness, Due Diligence and Concurrent Responsibility', 36 *Michigan Journal of International Law* (2012) 129.

[103] Augenstein and Kinley, 'When Human Rights "Responsibilities" become "Duties": The Extraterritorial Obligations of States that Bind Corporations', in D. Bilchitz and S. Deva (eds), *Human Rights Obligations of Business: Beyond the Corporate Responsibility to Respect?* (2013).

or other indigenous communities and which contribute to their subsistence.[104] An assessment of compliance with the Inuit exception necessitates an appraisal of conduct that takes place abroad, thereby injecting an element of territorial extension. Nonetheless, in this example, the presence of territorial extension serves to soften the stringency of the measure in recognition of the rights and needs of indigenous communities.

While the existence of a territorial connection was relied upon by the CJEU to ground its arguments relating to the validity of the EU's aviation directive, there are therefore good reasons to conclude that the distinction between extraterritoriality and territorial extension should not be viewed as constituting a normative shortcut.[105] This leaves the question of how to appraise the widespread presence of territorial extension in EU law. It is to this question that the chapter now turns, using environmental protection as a case study.

4. Appraising Territorial Extension in EU Environmental Law

It was noted earlier in this chapter that territorial extension has mainly been deployed to protect the EU—including its citizens, (habitual) residents, corporations and markets—from threats that originate outside the EU. We have seen examples in this chapter, and additional examples are discussed in the chapters that follow. For many commentators it seems axiomatic that it will be easier to justify measures when they pursue an objective that is internal to the EU. After all, who could possibly doubt the reasonableness of the EU extending the global reach of its laws in a bid to reduce the risk posed by aircraft when operating within the EU?[106] Or the reasonableness of applying EU food safety requirements to imported food?[107]

This privileging of measures that pursue internal objectives can be seen in much recent scholarship including, for example, in writings by Barbara Cooreman, Osin Suttle and Natalie Dobson.[108] At first glance, Cedric Ryngaert appears to be an outlier

[104] Regulation 1007/2009 of 16 September 2009 on trade in seal products (as amended), OJ 2009 L 286/36, Art. 3(1).

[105] Recalling the earlier discussion, in all fairness to the CJEU it cited the existence of effects within the EU and the fact that EU action followed on from an international agreement in reaching this conclusion.

[106] Regulation 2011/2005, note 5.

[107] Regulation 854/2004, note 4.

[108] See B. Cooreman, *Global Environmental Protection through Trade: A Systematic Approach to Extraterritoriality* (2017), see esp. at 131–138; O. Suttle, *Distributive Justice and World Trade Law: A Political Theory of International Trade Regulation* (2018). In Suttle's account, this is both because measures pursuing external objectives are more likely to be classified as external trade measures and require additional justification and because he sanctions recourse to external trade measures where these are necessary to protect peoples' capacity for self-determination, including the provision of essential public goods (at 26). N. L. Dobson, 'Extraterritoriality in International Law: The Case of EU Climate Protection' (2018) (PhD thesis, on file at the University of Utrecht), where she places considerable emphasis upon the fact that a problem causes substantial effects within the territory of the regulating state (at 262–263 summarizing the importance of the effects doctrine and the protective principle in grounding extraterritorial jurisdiction in relation to climate change). While Dobson discusses the relevance of the universality principle, she does not think this can ground the exercise of territorial extension in the absence of substantial internal effects. See also I. Hadjiyianni, *The EU as a Global Regulator for Environmental Protection: A Legitimacy Perspective* (2019 forthcoming), who argues that when EU

in this respect.[109] He argues that states should be entitled to exercise subsidiary jurisdiction extraterritorially, where a regulatory failure by the primary jurisdiction state has led to a diminution of global welfare.[110] This includes 'non-affected states', which he argues may in fact 'be better suited than affected states to represent... [the] global interest'.[111] It nonetheless remains uncertain even in Ryngaert's account whether it should be deemed to be reasonable for non-affected states to address *local* harms in third countries which do not result in a breach of an *erga omnes* norm or cause harm to other states or to the international community as a whole. This uncertainty is manifested in Ryngaert's discussion of territorial extension where even he exhibits scepticism towards measures that address 'a purely national situation' in a third country, such as animal welfare.[112] 'Arguably', he suggests, 'such measures should only pass muster if they protect values or interests that are globally recognized (e.g. are laid down in an international legal instrument)'.[113]

In this respect, Ryngaert also references the second factor that is viewed by many commentators as salient in appraising the appropriateness of territorial extension; namely the extent to which a measure is grounded in international law. For example, Suttle adopts a more permissive approach to external trade measures that serve to advance 'contingently shared goals and projects to which particular states have jointly committed themselves'.[114] Moreover, Cooreman has developed an elaborate framework to assess the degree to which a problem or a specific norm has received international recognition.[115] At its simplest, her framework leads to the conclusion that measures that serve to enforce treaty obligations between parties can be more readily justified than those that are unilateral in the sense that they 'find no support under international law, not even under soft law'.[116]

It is salient to note that Cooreman reaches the bald conclusion that unilateral measures that give rise to territorial extension can never be justified except where they seek to address an internal, as opposed to an external or global, concern.[117] Moreover, in the case of country-level territorial extension, she considers that measures

legislation applies on the basis of conduct abroad and has legal impacts beyond EU borders, sufficient mechanisms of accountability and participation should be in place to take due consideration of third country interests as well as to address distributive justice concerns that the EU's unilateral action towards developing countries may be raising.

[109] Ryngaert, note 44. See also E. Benvenisti, 'Legislating for Humanity: May States Compel Foreigners to Promote Global Welfare?' (1 February 2013), GlobalTrust Working Paper No. 2/2013, which mirrors Ryngaert's arguments in many respects. Benvenisti confines his arguments to global 'public bads' such as climate change. He explicitly excludes: 'This last emphasis on global public bads excludes legislation that extends extraterritorially but is designed to prevent adverse effects on the domestic jurisdiction rather than respond to global collective action failures' (footnote 9).

[110] Ryngaert, note 44, at 190 and 215 ff.

[111] *Ibid.*, at 230. There is a certain ambiguity in Ryngaert's position. See, e.g., his reference to 'other states that are harmed' being entitled to exercise subsidiary jurisdiction on behalf of the international community, at 229.

[112] *Ibid.*, at 98. [113] *Ibid.*, at 99.

[114] Suttle, note 108, at 26. Recall also that the CJEU not only placed emphasis upon the fact that climate change has effects within the EU in the *Air Transportation of America* case but also upon the fact that the EU action in this area followed on from the conclusion of international agreements.

[115] Cooreman, note 108, at 138–151.

[116] *Ibid.*, at 148. [117] *Ibid.*, at 270.

can only be justified if they serve to enforce customary international law or a treaty that is binding on affected countries; and even then such measures should never be permitted when they operate in pursuit of external objectives.[118]

In light of these observations, the area of environmental law offers a good lens through which to appraise territorial extension in EU law. As will be seen, environmental measures giving rise to territorial extension are very varied, both in terms of the objectives they pursue and the degree to which they find support in international law. By contrast to some of the other areas discussed in this volume, environmental measures giving rise to territorial extension operate principally in pursuit of external and/or global objectives as opposed to objectives that are internal to the EU. Equally, while many such measures pursue objectives that are recognized as important by international law and are based on standards laid down in international law, it is also possible to find examples of measures that are strongly unilateral. Several examples of country-level territorial extension can also be found in this domain.

This section will begin by offering a brief overview of territorial extension in EU environmental law. It will then proceed to cast light on the extent of the EU's global environmental footprint, because this is critical in considering the geographical scope of the EU's global environmental responsibilities. The chapter will then turn to consider the concept of complicity and exemplify how this concept can serve as a tool both to justify territorial extension and to articulate a critique of it.

A. Territorial Extension in EU Environmental Law

It is hardly surprising in view of the transboundary and global nature of many environmental problems that territorial extension is present in many areas of EU environmental law. EU environmental policy aims to achieve a high level of protection, while also contributing to the preservation, protection and improvement of the quality of the environment, encouraging the prudent and rational utilization of natural resources, and promoting measures at international level to deal with regional or worldwide environmental problems, in particular combating climate change.[119] Within the sphere of its competences, the EU is empowered both to cooperate with third countries and international organizations and to negotiate in international bodies and to conclude international agreements.[120]

While animal welfare is not included as one of the objectives of the EU's environmental policy, the Treaty on the Functioning of the European Union (TFEU) instructs the EU and its Member States to pay full regard to the welfare of animals in formulating and implementing a variety of EU policies including those relating to agriculture, fisheries, transport and internal market.[121] Following the European

[118] *Ibid.*, at 266–267.

[119] Taken largely verbatim from Art. 191 TFEU.

[120] Art. 191(4) TFEU.

[121] Art. 11 TFEU. This also states that animals are sentient beings and that the EU and Member States shall pay full regard to animal welfare 'while respecting the legislative or administrative provisions and customs of the Member States relating in particular to religious rites, cultural traditions and regional heritage'. This enshrines in the body of the TFEU an earlier Protocol annexed to the EC Treaty (No. 33) on protection and welfare of animals.

Table 1.7 Territorial extension in EU environmental law

Waste	Climate	Forests	Fish	Animal welfare
Hazardous waste exports (Reg. 1013/2006)	Aviation (Dir. 2008/101)	Timber (Reg. 2173/2005 and Reg. 995/2010)	Illegal, unreported and unregulated fishing (IUU) (Reg. 1005/2008)	Seal pups (Reg. 1007/2009)
				Leghold traps (Reg. 3254/91)
	Shipping (Reg. 2015/757)			
				Transport of live animals (Reg. 1/2005)
				Animal testing of cosmetics ingredients (Reg. 1223/2009)
	Biofuels (Dir. 2009/28, Arts 17–20 and Dir. 2009/30, Art. 7b)			Protection of animals at the time of killing (Dir. 1099/2009)
Waste electrical and electronic equipment (Dir. 2012/19)	Fuel quality (Dir. 2009/30, Art. 7a)			
	Carbon 'offsets' (Dir. 2003/87, Art. 11b(6)			
Ship recycling (Reg. 1257/2013)				
			Sustainable fishing (Reg. 1026/2012)	

Commission's example of drawing a link between environmental policy and animal welfare,[122] this chapter will treat animal welfare measures as falling within the scope of EU environmental law.

While not intended to be comprehensive, Table 1.7 identifies the principal EU legislative instruments that give rise to territorial extension in the environmental domain.

The EU makes recourse to a variety of different jurisdictional 'triggers' in this legislation. Most of these triggers are self-evidently territorial in nature, including EU market access,[123] export from the EU,[124] journeys starting and/or ending in the EU,[125] access to EU ports,[126] and operations within EU ports and EU waters.[127] In other examples, there is more room for discussion about whether the triggers can be conceived as territorial. For example, where the application of EU law is triggered by the fact that a vessel is registered within an EU Member State,[128] it can be argued that the EU is relying upon a territorial trigger—the legal presence of the vessel within a Member State—or a trigger that is more akin to nationality. Depending on how this, and other examples,[129] are conceived, it may be that this chapter has drawn the boundaries of the concept of territorial extension too broadly. However, this possibility simply reinforces the point made earlier, concerning room for disagreement about whether a territorial connection has been engaged.

As in other areas of EU law, territorial extension operates at different levels in the environmental domain. While the majority of the measures included in Table 1.7 only give rise to transaction-level territorial extension,[130] a small number give rise to country-level territorial extension. For example, in the aviation directive, incoming flights may be exempted from the requirement to surrender GHG emission allowances when the country from which the flight departed has itself adopted EU-equivalent measures to reduce the climate change impact of EU-bound flights.[131] Country-level territorial extension is present also in the timber regulation, in that timber originating in a country that has entered into a Voluntary Partnership Agreement with the EU is exempted from due diligence requirements that are

[122] Animal welfare is included on the Commission's environment website here as part of EU policy on nature and biodiversity, available at http://ec.europa.eu/environment/biodiversity/animal_welfare/index_en.htm.

[123] This includes the following examples: fuel quality, timber, IUU fishing, leghold traps and humane killing.

[124] This includes shipments of hazardous waste and the E-waste Regulation.

[125] This includes aviation, shipping and animal transportation.

[126] This includes IUU fishing.

[127] This includes IUU fishing.

[128] As in the ship recycling and IUU fishing regulations.

[129] The other triggers relied upon in the legislation included in Table 1.7 that are more uncertain in terms of their characterization as territorial triggers, would include eligibility to count towards fulfilment of obligations or targets in EU law (biofuels and carbon offsets) and eligibility to receive financial assistance from EU Member States (biofuels). Also, vessel registration in the ship recycling regulation and EU-IUU fishing can be viewed as giving rise to a nationality connection or as a territorial connection (legal presence within the state of registration).

[130] The language of transaction-level territorial extension does not capture well measures that apply to journeys arriving or departing the EU. The idea here would be that a single EU-arriving or EU-departing journey would count as a single transaction for the purpose of transaction-level territorial extension.

[131] Directive 2008/101, note 2, Art. 25a.

otherwise imposed by EU law.[132] In both of these examples, the legislation in question permits compliance at either a transactional or a third country level. The IUU fishing regulation is different in this respect. Here, country-level compliance is unavoidably required. Where a third country does not meet the standards laid down in the regulation, vessels flying its flag will be subject to a variety of different penalties, including a prohibition on importing fishery products into the EU.[133] Thus, in this example 'innocent products' caught by a vessel flying the flag of a 'guilty' country will be prevented from gaining access to the EU.[134]

It is also the case that EU environmental measures giving rise to territorial extension operate in pursuit of different kinds of objectives. These may be external to the EU, as in relation to the export of hazardous waste or the pursuit of animal welfare. However, most of these measures pursue global objectives such as avoidance of dangerous climate change, the protection of global biodiversity, or the sustainable exploitation of living aquatic resources.

In terms of their relationship with international law, there is a high level of variation between the different measures giving rise to territorial extension in EU environmental law. While some serve to enforce existing international law commitments,[135] others enforce instruments that are inherently non-binding or that have yet to enter into force.[136] While some pursue globally recognized objectives,[137] others pursue objectives that are more idiosyncratic.[138]

If one were to evaluate EU measures according to the factors that are widely considered to render them more problematic from a jurisdictional point of view, as discussed previously,[139] the animal welfare measures would be considered to be the most controversial. Although these measures only give rise to transaction-level rather than country-level territorial extension, they pursue external objectives in

[132] Regulation 995/2010 of 20 October 2010 laying down the obligations of operators who place timber and timber products on the market, OJ 2010 L 295/23, Art. 3.

[133] Regulation 1005/2008, note 32, Arts 31–38.

[134] Regan, note 28, at 102–103.

[135] This is partly true in relation to the waste shipment regulation and largely true in relation to the IUU fishing regulation. For the latter, imports of fishery products into the EU, or re-exports from an EU country, must be accompanied by a catch certificate, the aim of which is to prove that catches have been made in accordance with applicable laws, regulations and international (Regional Fisheries Management Organisations) conservation and management measures. Catch certificates are validated by the (third country) flag state and verified by the importing EU Member State. This verification entails an examination of the legality of the catch, the status of the vessel or fishing operator (vessels or operators linked with IUU fishing, e.g. because they appear on an RFMO (regional fisheries management organisation) or the EU blacklist, cannot land their catch), as well as the validating flag state's compliance with international fisheries laws and regulations more generally. See also Hadjiyianni, note 108, at chapter 1, mapping the variation of environmental measures giving rise to territorial extension, drawing attention to different degrees of unilateralism in the standards they embody.

[136] This is true in relation to the regulation of large hydropower projects in carbon offsets (non-binding international standards) and in relation to the waste shipment regulation and ship recycling (the Basel Ban Amendment and the Hong Kong Convention).

[137] This would include measures pertaining to hazardous waste exports, climate change, timber and IUU fishing.

[138] This would include measures which pursue animal welfare as an objective although even here, some relevant norms of international law exist and a number of important initiatives have been launched at the international level. See Peters, 'Global Animal Law: What it is and Why We Need it', 5 *Transnational Environmental Law* (2016) 9.

[139] Namely pursuit of an external objective, the presence of country-level territorial extension and strongly unilateral in nature as per the earlier discussion.

that they appear to aim to promote animal welfare in third countries, and they find quite limited support in international law.[140] While there are other environmental measures that also pursue external objectives, these tend to exhibit a much stronger grounding in international law.[141]

While there is one measure included in Table 1.7 that gives rise to *mandatory* country-level territorial extension,[142] this measure may be viewed as less problematic because it operates principally in pursuit of a global as opposed to an external objective and it is strongly grounded in international law. At the end of the day, what is perhaps most notable is that none of the measures included in the table simultaneously exhibit all three of the characteristics that tend to result in such measures being viewed as particularly problematic. Even the controversial aviation emissions trading directive that operated in pursuit of a global as opposed to an external objective, pursued an objective that that was recognized internationally as being very important, and rendered country-level territorial extension optional rather than required.

B. The EU's Global Environmental Footprint

The analysis that follows in this chapter rests upon three key factual claims. First, the EU is a major net importer of raw materials and of ecological assets that originate in third countries. This includes especially raw materials and ecological assets that are 'embodied' in imported products. Second, the EU uses more than its fair share of the world's raw materials and ecological assets. Third, the processes of extracting, harvesting or making products destined for the EU market, or managing with associated waste products, frequently cause severely negative impacts in third countries. In sum, the EU's global environmental footprint is both big and damaging.

1. *The EU is a Major Importer of Raw Materials and Ecological Assets*

Over recent years, a series of consumption-based indicators for sustainable development have been elaborated and continuously improved. The first is known as the 'material footprint' and is used as one of the indicators to measure progress in achieving Sustainable Development Goal 12 (SDG12), which relates to sustainable production and consumption.[143] A country's material footprint measures its total usage of raw

[140] Nonetheless, these animal welfare measures would fall further down this list if they were to be interpreted as pursuing an internal as opposed to an external objective relating to the protection of public morals. Note that the timber regulation enforces third country standards of legality, or standards that have been negotiated bilaterally between the EU and the third country in question in the context of the conclusion of a voluntary partnership agreement (VPA).

[141] This would be true, for example, of the EU's waste shipment regulation and the EU-IUU fishing regulation.

[142] This also requires compliance at the level of individual fishing vessels which is not easy to capture in the transaction-firm-country dichotomy applied here. Unless a vessel can be characterized as a firm—in the same way as a branch of a parent undertaking may be viewed as a firm narrowly conceived—this may suggest that this dichotomy needs to be further refined.

[143] For further details, see https://sustainabledevelopment.un.org/sdg12. This goal was reviewed at the High-Level Political Forum in 2018. See Eurostat, at http://ec.europa.eu/eurostat/statistics-explained/index.php/Material_flow_accounts_statistics_-_material_footprints. Material footprint is measured in metric tonnes.

materials to satisfy final demand within it.[144] Crucially, this includes raw materials that are not physically traded as commodities but which are embodied in products that are consumed within a country, be it at the production, transportation or disposal stage of the product's lifecycle. Not only is the EU's material footprint 'generally growing', but there has been a 'dramatic shift regarding the origin of [the] raw materials' consumed in the EU.[145] As a result of this shift, only 35 per cent of the raw materials that make up the EU's material footprint were extracted within the EU in 2011, as compared to 68 per cent in 1995.[146] Consequently, 'today [in 2011] around two-thirds of the raw materials that are directly and indirectly needed to satisfy European final demand is extracted in other world regions'.[147] The EU is more dependent upon other regions for its material footprint than any other region of the world.[148]

While SDG12 includes a country's material footprint as an indicator of sustainable consumption, it does not make recourse to the concept of an 'ecological footprint'. However, this consumption-based indicator is widely used within the EU and elsewhere.[149] The ecological footprint aims to measure how much biologically productive land and water is required to produce all the biological resources that the EU consumes and to absorb all of the waste that it generates.[150] While the European Environment Agency recognizes that there are data uncertainties when it comes to calculating the environmental pressures that are tied to consumption,[151] it states that 'the data do indicate that an increasing proportion of the environmental pressures linked to European demand occurs in other parts of the world'.[152] The Agency observes that a very significant percentage of the EU's environmental footprint is exerted outside EU borders; more than 50 per cent in the case of land use and around 40 per cent in the case of water.[153]

In terms of the EU's dependence on the global environment to meet its consumption demands, forests can be taken as a more specific example. The EU was the world's biggest importer of embodied deforestation between 1990 and 2008. While China has since overtaken the EU in absolute terms, the EU remains the biggest *per*

144 For background, see Wiedmann *et al.*, 'The Material Footprint of Nations' (2015) 112 *PNAS* 6271.

145 Giljum *et al.*, 'Identifying Priority Areas for European Resource Policies: An MRIO-based Material Footprint Assessment', 5 *Journal of Economic Structures* (2017) 1, at 1. This observes that there has been an increase in relation to three out of four of the types of raw materials included in the calculation (biomass, fossil fuels, minerals and metal ores) from 1995 to 2011, and a small decline in relation to fossil fuels.

146 *Ibid.* 147 *Ibid.* 148 *Ibid.*, at 20.

149 See European Environmental Agency, at https://www.eea.europa.eu/data-and-maps/indicators/ecological-footprint-of-european-countries#tab-data-references-used. Ecological footprint is measured in global hectares.

150 *Ibid.* This includes cropland, pasture, forest and fisheries. CO2 emissions are also included as part of the footprint.

151 European Environment Agency, 'Consumption', at https://www.eea.europa.eu/soer-2015/europe/consumption.

152 *Ibid.*

153 *Ibid.* Unfortunately the data are rather out of date, with the latest being from 2008. See also Wiedmann and Lenzen, 'Environmental and Social Footprints of International Trade' (2018) 11 *Nature Geoscience* 314, who note that more than 50% of the EU's total consumption of cropland, grazing land and forest land in 2007 took place in other countries (at 317).

capita importer.[154] Moreover, a recent report suggests that the EU is one of the largest importers of products derived from illegal deforestation. A little under one-quarter of agricultural commodities from illegal deforestation in international trade are said to be destined for the EU. This includes 27 per cent of soy, 18 per cent of palm oil, 15 per cent of beef and 31 per cent of leather.[155]

2. The EU Uses more than its Fair Share of the World's Raw Materials and Ecological Assets

The European Environmental Agency frames the key policy question underpinning the concept of an ecological footprint as: 'Are Europeans using more than their fair share of the world's resources?'[156] In this respect, it is notable that the EU's ecological footprint is more than double its biocapacity, and that it increased from 3.4 hectares per person in 1995 to 4.5 hectares per person in 2010.[157] For the world's two most populous regions—Asia-Pacific and Africa—the per capita ecological footprint is less than 2 hectares.[158] If every person in the world had the same ecological footprint as the average EU-28 resident, 2.6 Earths would be required to support these demands.

When it comes to the EU's material footprint, as with other parts of the world, this is closely correlated with its (very high) development status.[159] The EU's material footprint is more than twice the global average, more than four times that of countries with medium levels of human development, and more than eight times that of countries with low levels of human development.[160] The EU's material footprint has grown substantially from 1990 to 2008 and from this perspective there has been no 'decoupling' of growth and resource use in the EU.[161]

3. The Processes of Extracting, Harvesting or Making Products Destined for the EU Market, or Managing Associated Waste Products, Frequently Cause Severely Negative Impacts Globally and in Third Countries

It is commonplace to observe that international trade has brought about a significant displacement of environmental burdens from rich countries to poor

[154] For recent figures and an explanation of the methodology used to arrive at them, see FERN, 'Stolen Goods: The EU's Complicity in Tropical Deforestation' (2015), at http://fern.org/sites/default/files/news-pdf/Stolen%20Goods_EN_0.pdf.

[155] *Ibid.* [156] *Ibid.*

[157] European Environment Agency, at https://www.eea.europa.eu/data-and-maps/indicators/ecological-footprint-of-european-countries/ecological-footprint-of-european-countries-2.

[158] Nearly 5bn people live in these two regions, with 503m in the EU. The EU's is the second highest per capita ecological footprint (the US average is almost 7 tonnes compared to the EU's 4.5 tonnes). However, the EU has the biggest biocapacity deficit.

[159] UNEP, *Global Material Flows and Resource Productivity: An Assessment Study of the UNEP International Resource Panel* (2016).

[160] Based on the UNEP study, note 159, I am assuming for this purpose that the EU's material footprint is around 20 tonnes per person in 2010. More recent figures place this at 20.7 tonnes in 2017.

[161] Wiedmann *et al.*, note 144. Using these figures, this represents a growth of around 40%.

countries.[162] It has also been widely noted that this shift will often entail an overall exacerbation of environmental impacts 'because production in developing countries tends to be more ecologically insensitive and less socially regulated'.[163] A recent UNEP Report prepared by its International Resource Panel has confirmed this in relation to material use. This finds that global material productivity has declined since the year 2000 and that this has been '*caused* by a large shift of economic activity from very material-efficient economies such as Japan, the Republic of Korea and Europe to the much less-efficient economies of China, India and Southeast Asia'.[164] This report observes that material footprint is a good 'proxy' for environmental impacts and emphasizes that:

> Rising material use will result in climate change, higher levels of acidification and eutrophication of soils and water bodies, increased biodiversity loss, more soil erosion and increasing amounts of waste and air pollution. It will also have negative impacts on human health and quality of life. It will ultimately lead to the depletion of certain natural resources and will cause supply shortages for critical materials in the short and medium terms.[165]

An article published in *Nature Geoscience* takes us beyond the general and explains that a number of recent scientific advances have enabled us to better evaluate and concretize such claims.[166] New consumption-based indicators combined with more sophisticated global multi-region input-output (GMRIO) modelling and collaboration between database developers can generate better environmental and social 'footprint studies'.[167]

Drawing widely upon academic literature, the *Nature Geoscience* article illustrates this claim by reference to a number of different examples. It shows how air pollution has shifted from rich to poor countries and concomitantly spread over broader geographical areas over the last 50 years.[168] In 2007, almost one-third of fine particulate matter emissions were embodied in trade, including prominently in products exported from China and India to the EU. The article also illustrates how GMRIO modelling can shed light on the biodiversity impacts of international trade. These models are capable of yielding quite detailed results, suggesting for example that 'consumption in the European Union . . . has a hotspot of threats to marine species around islands in the Indian Ocean'.[169] Biodiversity footprint studies confirm that food consumption is the most importer driver of biodiversity loss globally and that this is exacerbated by international trade.[170]

The water footprint models being used today are likewise so sophisticated that they not only take the volume of water that is embodied in traded products into account, but also the water scarcity of the region from which the water has been drawn. When water use is weighted according to scarcity, as much as 80 per cent of the water consumed within the EU originates outside this region, 'with the largest pressure exerted in the Indus Delta'.[171] Similarly, a water footprint study covering nitrogen pollution

[162] See, e.g., S. Bringezu *et al.*, *Assessing Global Resource Use: A Systems Approach to Resource Efficiency and Pollution Reduction* (2017).
[163] Wiedmann and Lenzen, note 153. [164] UNEP, note 159, at 16. Emphasis added.
[165] *Ibid.*, at 18. [166] Wiedmann and Lenzen, note 153. [167] *Ibid.*, at 315.
[168] *Ibid.* [169] *Ibid.*, at 316. [170] *Ibid.* [171] *Ibid.*, at 317.

in 14 global regions has suggested that the EU and United States 'outsourced the largest amount of polluted water to other regions'.[172] And so the list of the negative global environmental impacts of EU (over-)consumption could go on.

Advances in the modelling of the spatial pathways leading to environmental degradation are accompanied by rich, contextual, studies that exemplify the pernicious environmental effects of the extraction, harvesting, production, recycling or disposal of products that are consumed in other parts of the world. Shocking films, such as *Plastic China* and *Darwin's Nightmare* have shone a spotlight on the EU.[173] Reports by non-governmental organizations (NGOs) serve similarly to illuminate the destructive global environmental effects associated with consumption that takes place within the EU. The Environmental Justice Foundation's hard-hitting reports are exemplary in this respect.[174]

Needless to say, the increasing availability of detailed information clarifying both the global and local environmental consequences caused by our careless and excessive consumption, does not obviate the need for political judgment about the nature of our individual and collective responsibilities. This information may help us to experience our wrongdoing and offer us guidance in considering how best to mitigate this. However, such is the 'phenomenology' of individual agency,[175] which leads individuals to downplay both the distant and the diffuse effects of their actions, that the appropriate 'locus of responsibility' may well turn out not to be the individual but rather the state.[176]

C. Is Complicity the New 'Effects'?

As discussed earlier, scholars frequently consider that it is more appropriate for states to extend the global reach of their laws when they are acting to guard against damaging internal effects. The existence of substantial internal effects is often cited as a factor making measures giving rise to territorial extension easier to defend. In the final part of this chapter, I will consider whether the concept of complicity might similarly provide a rationale for the EU to make recourse to territorial extension in order to mitigate the negative environmental impacts that it has contributed to, where these impacts are globally diffuse or even entirely confined to the territory of

[172] *Ibid.*

[173] Plastic China at https://www.plasticchina.org; Darwin's Nightmare, available at https://www.imdb.com/title/tt0424024.

[174] See by way of example, Environmental Justice Foundation, *White Gold: Uzbekistan, A Slave Nation for our Cotton* (2013).

[175] S. Scheffler, *Boundaries and Allegiances: Problems of Justice and Responsibility in Liberal Thought* (2002), at chapter 2.

[176] *Ibid.*, at 104–105, where Scheffler argues that the phenomenology of agency leads individuals to privilege acts over omissions and persons to whom they stand in a special relationship. He argues that the moral salience of a global perspective may militate in favour of rethinking the primary locus of responsibility. See similarly, Lichtenberg, 'Negative Duties, Positive Duties and the "New Harms"', 120 *Ethics: An International Journal of Social, Political and Legal Philosophy* (2010) 557, where she argues in favour of collective action to address 'new harms'. While she appears to see the individual as the principal locus of responsibility, she considers that the individual can be encouraged and enabled to do the right thing only with the help of the state.

a third country.[177] This inquiry was partly stimulated by the title of a report that was referred to above: 'Stolen Goods: The EU's Complicity in Illegal Tropical Deforestation'.[178] While included in the title of this report, the concept of 'complicity' is not defined within it.

For the purpose of this discussion, Chiara Lepora and Robert E. Goodin's understanding of the concept of complicity will be drawn upon.[179] They define what they call 'complicity simpliciter' as 'being implicated in another's wrongdoing'.[180] They therefore distinguish between agents which are principals or co-principals in wrongdoing (principal agents), and agents which are 'merely' complicit in wrongdoing that others carry out (secondary or complicit agents). Lepora and Goodin's account of complicity is particularly helpful for three reasons. First, they clearly identify the essential components of complicity. Second, they provide criteria for 'grading' complicity which can help in determining how much blame ought to attach to a complicit act. Third, driven in part by Lepora's practical experience as a doctor with Médecins Sans Frontières, they recognize that the moral wrongness of complicity will sometimes be outweighed by other considerations.[181] These three elements are explained in more detail in the following paragraphs.

1. *The Essential Components of Complicity*

For an act to count as a complicit act, three elements must be present. First, the action of the secondary agent must have the potential to contribute causally to something that the principal agent is doing. Second, the secondary agent must know that his or her action has the potential to contribute in this way. Third, he or she must know that what the principal agent is doing is wrong.[182] For the secondary agent to be deemed to know that the principal agent's action is wrong or that his own action has the potential to contribute to it, it is sufficient that he could and should have known. That is to say, the secondary agent 'should have invested enough time and effort to have found [these things] out'.[183] Where the secondary agent performs an action involuntarily, for example under duress, it will still count as a complicit act if

[177] Territorial extension can also be justified in other ways, not least by the argument that it serves to enforce existing international law standards or to serve as a catalyst towards their formation. In keeping with the latter, I have characterized the EU as a 'contingent unilateralist' in the past and there is evidence that this has borne some fruit in the area of climate change with specific regard to international aviation and international shipping. See Scott and Rajamani, 'EU Climate Change Unilateralism', 23 *European Journal of International Law* (2012) 469.

[178] See note 154. The relevance of the concept of complicity has been highlighted previously by several scholars in the context of the regulation of the harvesting or production of internationally traded goods. See, e.g., Charnovitz, 'An Analysis of Pascal Lamy's Proposal on Collective Preferences', 8 *Journal of International Economic Law* (2005) 449. However, it has generally been under-explored as a concept in this context and also used specifically in relation to regulations that are unlikely to bring about any change in behaviour in the target state. For example, Charnovitz observes that if a US ban on fur trade did not bring an end to the 'slaughter', its only benefit 'would be to prevent U.S. moral complicity'. Also, e.g., Regan, note 28, at 116 who also seems to conceive of complicity as most relevant where the measure does not change behaviour in the target state.

[179] C. Lepora and R. E. Goodin, *On Complicity and Compromise* (2013).

[180] *Ibid.*, at 41.

[181] *Ibid.*, at chapter 2.

[182] See generally, *ibid.*, at chapter 6.

[183] *Ibid.*, at 104.

it meets these three conditions. However, where the act is wholly involuntary, the secondary agent will not be regarded as blameworthy.[184]

2. *Criteria for 'Grading' Complicity*

Lepora and Goodin identify a number of criteria to assist in determining how much blame ought to attach to a complicit agent. Several of these criteria are multi-faceted, and they are combined in a rather intricate way. Nonetheless, broadly, the level of blame that attaches to a complicit agent will depend upon four factors. First, the 'badness factor'—how morally bad the principal wrongdoing is.[185] Second, the 'contribution factor'—whether the secondary agent's actions make a definitely causally essential or a potentially causally essential contribution to the principal agent's wrongdoing.[186] Third, the 'responsibility factor'—the secondary agent's action was entirely voluntary or more-or-less voluntary.[187] Fourth, the 'shared purpose factor'—the extent to which the secondary agent approves of the principal agent's wrongdoing and shares that agent's wrongful purpose.[188]

3. *Making an 'On Balance' Judgment about Whether it is Ethical to Engage in a Complicit Act*

Where the essential components of complicity are present, Lepora and Goodin consider that a secondary agent is *pro tanto* blameworthy for complicit acts that are carried out voluntarily. By the concept of *pro tanto* blame, they mean to suggest that there is a good moral reason for a secondary agent not to act in this way. Nonetheless, they accept that there may be competing reasons that lead to the conclusion that a complicit act is nonetheless 'on balance' the right thing to do.[189] Therefore, in order to determine the blameworthiness of a complicit act, it is not only necessary to 'grade' this act in accordance with the factors identified above, but also to balance the wrongdoing inherent in it with the good consequences which flow from it. Lepora and Goodin also recognize the relevance of distributive considerations, arguing that it will be easier to justify a complicit act where the good consequences caused by it accrue to the same persons who suffer the act's negative consequences.[190]

Lepora and Goodin's volume is enriched by reference to multiple practical examples in which they illustrate the process of balancing the wrongdoing inherent in complicity with the good consequences that may flow from it.[191] For example, they consider the position of NGOs which provide humanitarian assistance in refugee

[184] *Ibid.*, at 104–105 and 110. In this context, *pro tanto* blame means that there is a reason to act to avoid being considered blameworthy, but that this reason might be outweighed by other considerations, as will be discussed later.

[185] *Ibid.*, at 103–104. [186] *Ibid.*, at 106–107.

[187] *Ibid.*, at 104–105. Knowledge is also included in the responsibility factor but this is viewed as an all or nothing concept and is included in the essential components that determine whether complicity is present at all.

[188] *Ibid.*, at 107–109. [189] *Ibid.*, at 112–13. [190] *Ibid.*, at 112.

[191] *Ibid.*, at chapters 7 and 8.

camps, in which civilians are being used as human shields in conflict situations.[192] These NGOs may be considered to be complicit in wrongdoing when the aid that they provide serves to confer 'legitimacy, protection and material support' to those wrongly engaged in the abuse of civilians.[193] Nonetheless, depending upon the circumstances, the provision of humanitarian assistance may still be the right thing to do because of its positive impact for the survival and wellbeing of refugees. However, even in this situation, available steps should be taken to minimize the secondary agent's complicity in the wrongful act.

4. *Territorial Extension: Complicity as Justification and Complicity as Critique*

The implications of complicity for thinking through the scope and nature of the EU's moral responsibilities for reducing the scale and harmfulness of its global environmental footprint will need to be carefully worked through, both as regards the existence of complicity, and in relation to the question of whether and when complicity in wrongdoing can be justified as being necessary to achieve a greater good. In this sense, recognition of the relevance of this concept in this context sets an agenda for future research. However, even at this initial stage, it does appear that the concept of complicity can shed light on territorial extension in EU law, serving both as a basis for justification and as a basis for critique.

5. *Complicity as Justification*

By contrast to some previous writings on the negative global effects of consumption,[194] the discussion here will focus on the role of the EU as a complicit actor, rather than upon the possible complicity of individual consumers.[195] With a view to understanding how Lepora and Goodin's complicity framework may serve to justify territorial extension in EU environmental law, five key elements will now be accentuated (and in some cases reiterated).

First, a secondary agent may be considered to be complicit in wrongdoing as a result of an act that takes the form of an omission.[196] Thus, the failure of the EU to take available steps to prevent or minimize environmental wrongdoing in third

[192] *Ibid.*, at chapter 7. [193] *Ibid.*, at 147.

[194] See, e.g., D. T. Schwarz, *Consuming Choices: Ethics in a Global Consumer Age* (2010), esp. at chapter 4.

[195] The concept of complicity occupies a complex place in public international law. See M. Jackson, *Complicity in International Law* (2015). However, it is clear that international organizations as well as states incur obligations as secondary agents in relation to the activities of other states and/or international organizations. See Draft Articles on Responsibility of International Organizations for Internationally Wrongful Acts, Art. 14 and the ILC's Articles on the Responsibility of States for Internationally Wrongful Acts, Art. 16. Note that I do not intend to suggest that the conditions giving rise to a breach of these articles are present as I am focusing on the EU's moral rather than legal obligations in this discussion.

[196] Lepora and Goodin, note 179, at 45 and 52.

countries is capable of constituting complicity where the other relevant conditions are met.

Second, although Lepora and Goodin include a 'contribution factor' as an essential component of complicity, they construe this in a relatively open way.[197] According to their understanding, it would be enough if the EU's failure to take available steps to prevent or minimize environmental wrongdoing in third countries has the *potential* to make an essential contribution to that wrongdoing. This condition would therefore be satisfied even where there is a *possibility* that EU intervention would not in practice serve to prevent or mitigate wrongdoing; for example, because environmentally tainted products that would have been sold in the EU are diverted to other world markets instead.

Third, Lepora and Goodin's account is capable of accommodating the fact that the EU's failure to intervene can only contribute causally to future wrongdoing. They argue that connivance with past wrongdoing can serve to induce or incentivize future wrongdoing, and thereby make a potentially essential causal contribution to that future wrongdoing.[198] In keeping with this, the EU's passive stance in relation to past environmental wrongdoing may incentivize future wrongdoing by offering reassurance to those responsible for it that the EU will continue to desist from taking steps to prevent or minimize that wrongdoing.

Fourth, by choosing to focus on the responsibilities of the EU as a potentially complicit actor, as opposed to the responsibilities of individual consumers within the EU, it is more likely that Lepora and Goodin's knowledge conditions for complicity will be met. With the increasing sophistication of the environmental footprint studies discussed earlier, together with rich case studies compiled by academics and NGOs, there are many circumstances in which it can be argued that the EU could and should know of the existence of environmental wrongdoing on the one hand, and of its potential causal contribution to that wrongdoing on the other. Indeed, sometimes clear evidence of the EU's contribution to environmental wrongdoing in third countries can be seen as a result of studies that have been prepared on behalf of the EU.[199]

Finally, although Lepora and Goodin recognize that it may be far from straightforward to evaluate the 'badness' of a wrongful act, or the balance between the negative and positive consequences that flow from it, they consider that these matters are to be judged 'from the perspective of the actor, at the time of the action'.[200] The presence of complicity thus depends upon a secondary agent's own conception of

[197] *Ibid.*, at section 6.2.3.

[198] *Ibid.*, at 46. Connivance is considered to be a close 'conceptual cousin' to complicity *simpliciter* but can amount to complicity when it makes a potentially essential causal contribution to wrongdoing (at 44–47).

[199] See the European Commission studies on 'The Impact of EU Consumption on Deforestation' (2013) available at http://ec.europa.eu/environment/forests/impact_deforestation.htm. This finds that of the proportion of crops and livestock products traded internationally (33% and 8% respectively according to this study), 'the EU 27 imported and consumed 36% of crops and livestock products associated with deforestation in the countries of origin'.

[200] Lepora and Goodin, note 179, at 171.

wrongdoing.[201] Given that such agents will only be complicit in wrongdoing in the event that they make a potentially essential causal contribution to it, and are therefore active contributors to the wrongdoing rather than passive bystanders, it is reasonable that complicit agents should make their own judgment about whether particular behaviour should be considered to be wrong.

The question of the perspective from which the existence of wrongdoing should be assessed does not emerge as a key issue in Lepora and Goodin's account of complicity because the examples that they invoke involve principal acts which are unequivocally bad, and more often than not prohibited by law. There is little room for disagreement about the wrongfulness of murder, terrorism, torture or the practice of using civilians as human shields in conflict situations.

However, from the point of view of the discussion in this chapter, disagreements about which types of activities should be viewed as constituting environmental wrongdoing, and especially about how to balance the good and bad consequences of this wrongdoing, are frequent and intense. This is the case both in relation to aggregative harms where primary agents are judged to have consumed more than their fair share of a finite resource, and *malum in se* harms which are considered to be intrinsically wrong.[202] Particular controversy surrounds the setting of a threshold for wrongdoing in relation to aggregative harms because here the vague and contested principle of common but differentiated responsibilities and respective capabilities (in light of different national circumstances) comes into play.[203] The wrongness of a principal agent's actions should be assessed having regard to relevant circumstances, viewed from the perspective of this principle, prevailing within the country in which the principal agent operates.

The difficulties of balancing the negative and positive consequences of commercial activities can be illustrated by reference to the example of ship recycling at Alang-Sosiya in India.[204] Although an historic example, the discussion remains relevant to the implementation of the EU's ship recycling regulation. The activities at Alang-Sosiya have given rise to an 'ecological distribution conflict',[205] where several clashing 'languages of valuation' have emerged,[206] involving different trade-offs between competing interests and between different groups of people, including ship breakers, workers, villagers and fishing communities. National and international environmental and human rights NGOs, public authorities, ship breakers, villagers, fishing communities and to a lesser extent workers, jostled to promote the influence of their competing 'frames'.

201 This is also clear from some of the examples included in the book. For example, it is clear that it is for the doctors involved in a given activity to make their own moral assessment of the 'badness' of the procedure (e.g. female genital mutilation, *ibid.*, at 145) and the 'on balance' appropriateness of being involved nonetheless, in order to mitigate risks.

202 Lichtenberg, note 176.

203 For a discussion of the version of CBDR-RC contained in the Paris Agreement on Climate Change, see D. Bodansky, J. Brunnée and L. Rajamani, *International Climate Change Law* (2017), at chapter 7. For a discussion of its relevance to EU climate change unilateralism see note 177.

204 Demaria, 'Shipbreaking at Alang-Sosiya (India): An Ecological Distribution Conflict', 70 *Ecological Economics* (2010) 1.

205 *Ibid.* 206 *Ibid.*

While, in this example, there was considerable agreement that environmental damage, human rights abuses and threats to human health were 'bad', there was strong disagreement about how to strike an appropriate balance between the negative consequences and the positive consequences of ship recycling. The point is not simply that there would be winners and losers associated with every (non-)intervention by the EU, both within the EU and in third countries, but that negative and positive consequences may also be experienced within a single group. For example, ship-recycling workers are employed in deeply difficult and hazardous conditions, but for those among the mainly migrant workforce who avoid death or disability, these jobs offer a 'survival strategy', and enable them to remit money to their families back home.[207]

Given the existence of complex and multi-faceted disagreements of this kind, it is hardly surprising that the EU often seeks to ward off opposition by basing its environmental measures giving rise to territorial extension upon an 'objective standard' which is embodied in either third country or international law.[208] Equally, even where EU legislation is based on unilateral standards, this legislation is sometimes drafted in a manner that is intended to be responsive to future developments in international law, with the EU indicating a willingness to step aside, or to align its standards with international law, in the event of the conclusion of an international agreement. The aviation directive is exemplary in this respect.[209]

6. *Complicity as Critique*

While Lepora and Goodin's unpacking of the concept of complicity creates a framework that can serve to justify territorial extension in EU environmental law, this framework can also provide a springboard for critique. In so far as it can help to identify shortcomings in the EU's current approach, it can also assist in improving the practice of territorial extension by the EU. The capacity of the concept of complicity to constitute a critical vantage point to evaluate current EU policy forms an important part of the complicity-focused agenda for future research. To give a taste of the kind of critical insights that the concept of complicity can help to bring into view, three shortcomings will be tentatively illustrated here.

First, it is important to be attentive to the possibility that the EU may use territorial extension in a manner which is self-serving and in a way that is not commensurate with the extent of its wrongdoing as a complicit agent. A single example can illustrate this claim.

Territorial extension implies an appraisal of foreign conduct by reference to standards that are laid down in EU law. Where the application of EU law is triggered

[207] *Ibid.*, at 5–7.

[208] The language of 'objective standard' was used by the Appellate Body in the EC—Tariff Preferences report (DS246, para. 163). The AB observed that '[b]road-based recognition of a particular need, set out in the WTO Agreement or in multilateral instruments adopted by international organizations, could serve as such a[n] [objective] standard'.

[209] Directive 2008/101, note 2, Art. 25a indicating EU responsiveness in the face of the adoption of EU-equivalent measures by third country measures or the conclusion of a multilateral agreement.

by the existence of a territorial connection, EU law applies to that foreign conduct. In most of the examples given earlier,[210] the application of EU law served to level the regulatory playing field as far as competition between domestically-produced products and products that are imported into the EU were concerned. The question then arises as to whether the EU is similarly willing to extend the global reach of its laws when the effect of so doing is to impose an additional regulatory burden on goods exported from the EU to third country markets, or on EU undertakings when they engage in commercial activities, and perhaps environmental wrongdoing, abroad.

There is at least one area of EU law which suggests a negative answer to this question. As is well known, environmental wrongdoing by EU corporations in third countries is subject to the application of third country law when this wrongdoing gives rise to an action for non-contractual (tortious) liability which is heard in a Member State court. This is because under EU private international law, the applicable law will normally be the law of the country in which the damage occurred,[211] and exceptionally the law of the country in which the event giving rise to the damage occurred.[212]

It needs to be considered whether this disparity in the treatment under EU law of the foreign conduct of third country actors producing goods for sale in the EU market on the one hand, and the foreign conduct of EU corporations on the other hand, can be justified from a complicity point of view. This will depend upon whether the essential components of complicity are present, the degree to which the factors that render complicity more or less blameworthy are present, and an assessment of the balance between the negative and positive consequences of complicity. These are not the kinds of factors that EU private international law currently takes into account. Were it to do so, it seems highly probable that there are circumstances in which the EU's failure to take available steps to constrain environmental wrongdoing by EU corporations in third countries would constitute a complicit act.[213] As with the permitted importation of environmentally tainted goods into the EU, the criteria relating to responsibility (voluntariness and knowledge of wrongdoing and of contribution to wrongdoing) and contribution (a potentially essential causal contribution) would at least sometimes be met.

This, however, begs the question of whether it may be reasonable for the EU to reach a different 'on balance' judgment about the appropriateness of complicity depending upon whether it is regulating an elastic or inelastic target.[214] Faced with demanding regulation, it is more likely that an elastic target, such as a corporation, will change its nationality or alter its corporate form to avoid a harsh regulatory burden, creating a high likelihood of regulatory arbitrage. Therefore, the concept of complicity cannot provide an off-the-peg answer to the question of when it is appropriate for the EU to regulate foreign conduct, and what consistency in the treatment of different situations

[210] See *ibid.*, and the discussion of export cartels at note 51.

[211] Regulation 864/2007 of 11 July 2007 on the law applicable to non-contractual obligations (Rome II), Art. 4(1).

[212] *Ibid.*, Art. 79(1). See van Calster, 'The Role of Private International Law in Corporate Social Responsibility', 5 *Erasmus Law Review* (2014) 125 and Grusic, 'International Environmental Litigation in EU Courts: A Regulatory Perspective', 35 *Yearbook of European Law* (2016) 180.

[213] For examples of such wrongdoing, see the examples discussed in van Calster and Grusic, note 212.

[214] Recall the discussion of the conditions underpinning the 'Brussels Effect', at note 54.

demands in this respect. It does, however, provide a template that can help us to ask probing questions of the EU and to evaluate the answers we receive.

Second, in the lead-up to the adoption of measures giving rise to territorial extension in the environmental domain, the EU gives the impression of being insufficiently attentive to the negative third country consequences of its measures giving rise to territorial extension. In a manner that is not consistent with Lepora and Goodin's complicity framework, the EU does not appear always to balance carefully the negative and positive consequences of interventions, with a view to making an 'on balance' judgment about whether its role as a complicit agent may be justified, all things considered. Surprisingly perhaps, this is the case even where EU legislation expressly requires the Commission to evaluate the effects of implementing measures, including their social effects.

To give just one example, the EU's sustainable fishing regulation includes a novel provision that provides that when the Commission adopts implementing decisions, it must 'evaluate the environmental, trade, economic and social effects of those measures in the short and long terms and the administrative burden associated with their implementation'.[215] Having adopted measures, the Commission may later decide that the measures cease to apply '[o]n duly justified imperative grounds of urgency relating to unforeseen economic or social disruption'.[216] This provision would appear to hold promise in guarding against or mitigating disproportionately negative consequences for third countries.

The EU has only once introduced measures under the sustainable fisheries regulation. These related to the conservation of Atlanto-Scandian herring stock by the Faroe Islands and identified the Faroe Islands as a country allowing non-sustainable fishing. As a consequence, the EU imposed restrictions on the importation of fish caught under the control of the Faroe Islands,[217] and upon fishing vessels flagged in the Faroe Islands, fishing for herring or mackerel, using EU ports.[218]

As required under the sustainable fishing regulation, the Commission conducted an evaluation of the short- and long-term effects of these measures.[219] Aside from the environmental impacts, which were noted to be positive in terms of the measures' capacity to contribute to improving the sustainability of fish stocks, the Commission's evaluation appears to focus exclusively on the impact of the measures on the EU rather than on the third country in question.[220] For example, the

[215] Regulation 1026/2012 of 25 October 2012 on certain measures for the purpose of the conservation of ocks in relation to countries allowing non-sustainable fishing, OJ 2012 L 316/34, Art. 5(4).

[216] *Ibid.*, Art. 7(4).

[217] Commission Implementing Regulation 793/2013 of 20 August 2013 establishing measures in respect of the Faeroe Islands to ensure the conservation of the Atlanto-Scandian herring stock, OJ 2013 L 223/1. See esp. Art. 5.

[218] *Ibid.*, Art. 5. This prohibition shall not apply in cases of *force majeure* or distress within the meaning of Art. 18 of the 1982 United Nations Convention on the Law of the Sea for services strictly necessary to remedy those situations.

[219] *Ibid.*, recital 21.

[220] *Ibid.*, recital 26. See also Hadjiyianni, note 108, who argues that the Commission tends to frame third country impacts as beneficial for the third countries in question and in terms that serve the EU's own interests in convincing Member States of the need for EU action or in pre-empting international opposition.

Commission observed that in the longer term no shortage of supplies of herring was expected within the EU. Likewise, the Commission appears to have had the welfare of EU fleets in mind when it commented on the possible medium- to long-term benefits of the measures for fishing fleets. Likewise, the nature of the administrative burden of implementing the measure is assessed only in relation to the EU.

It was, in fact, only when conducting a proportionality assessment that the Commission observed that a more far-reaching import ban including fish meal and oil would be too burdensome; not only because it would impose a high administrative burden on the EU but also because 'it may affect sectors of the Faeroese fishing industry not directly related to the pelagic catching sector'.[221]

This emphasis upon EU as opposed to third country impacts is born out also in the impact assessment prepared prior to adopting the sustainable fishing regulation.[222] While this regulation—which was adopted with the mackerel dispute with Iceland and the Faroe Islands in mind—does observe the scale of the monetary losses that Iceland and the Faroe Islands would suffer as a result of an import ban, this was viewed in a positive light. It is, after all, only because of the severity of these economic consequences that the EU restrictions can be expected to induce export firms to lobby to secure continued access to the EU market.[223]

Thus, while the EU repeatedly expresses a commitment to ensure that measures adopted under the sustainable fisheries regulation are 'equitable',[224] it fails to define this concept and it does not appear to take this criterion seriously by evaluating the impact of EU measures on particular groups within third countries. There is, for example, no assessment of the negative impact of the EU measures on small-scale fisheries and associated downstream industries within the Faroe Islands; and, indeed, no assessment of how these impacts might be prevented or at least reduced.[225]

EU measures giving rise to territorial extension have the potential to generate negative economic consequences for third countries, including developing countries, and to threaten the economic security of vulnerable groups and individuals within those countries. This was clear from the earlier discussion of the ship recycling example. As things stand, 95 per cent of ships are recycled in Asia, predominantly in Bangladesh, Pakistan and India. The impact assessment accompanying the Commission's proposal for a ship recycling regulation contained a quite balanced overview of the advantages and disadvantages for developing countries of ship recycling that is undertaken in poorly regulated conditions.[226]

However, in its assessment of the impacts of the different options for regulation, there was very little emphasis upon negative third country effects. When 'social

[221] Commission Implementing Regulation 793/2013, note 217, recital 24.

[222] SEC(2011) 1576 final, 'Commission Staff Working Paper: Impact Assessment'.

[223] *Ibid.*, at 26–27.

[224] COM(2011) 888, point 3; Regulation 1026/2012, note 215, recital 5; Impact Assessment, note 222, at 36–37.

[225] For an overview of the difficulties faced by small-scale fisheries in the Faroe Islands, see Ólavur Waag Høgnesen, 'Small-scale fishing in the Faroe Islands', at http://www.coastalfisheries.net/wp-content/uploads/2013/06/The-Faroese-coastal-sector.pdf.

[226] SWD/2012/0047, Commission Staff Working Document Impact Assessment, Accompanying the document Proposal for a Regulation on ship recycling, at section 3.1.

impacts' in third countries were assessed, the emphasis was upon the reduction of fatal and non-fatal accidents among workers,[227] rather than upon the social implications of declining employment opportunities for vulnerable migrant groups. There was equally no discussion of the trade-offs between workers, villagers and fishing communities. The section on economic burdens included a discussion of the impacts on EU shipowners, the administrative burden for EU Member States, the impacts on consumers and on small and medium-sized enterprises in the EU, and the impact on the EU budget.[228] However, it did not appraise the likely economic impacts on developing countries and on specific groups within these. While there was recognition that all ship recycling facilities in third countries would have to be upgraded to comply with EU requirements, there was no discussion about how the costs of this upgrading would be met. This was viewed, instead, as presenting a potential compliance problem, in that it might result in some 'international opposition'.[229]

From the end of 2018, large commercial ships flying the flag of an EU Member State may only be recycled in a recycling facility that is included on a European list of recycling facilities.[230] In July 2018, only EU facilities have been included on this list.[231] The preamble to the Commission's implementing decision drawing up this list observes that its assessment of applications submitted in relation to third country recycling facilities is 'still ongoing' and that a decision will be reached once this assessment has been finalized.[232] Nonetheless, as things stand, no EU-flagged ship will be eligible to be recycled in a third country facility from the end of 2018. While the fact that there is nothing in the EU legislation to prevent shipowners from changing the registration of their vessel prior to selling the ship for recycling could alleviate the economic impacts on third countries,[233] this would be at the expense of the regulation's primary objective, which is to mitigate negative effects on human health and the environment.

Before concluding, this chapter will turn briefly to a third possible criticism of territorial extension in EU environmental law, as viewed from a complicity perspective. Thinking back to the overview of the EU's environmental footprint that was

[227] *Ibid.*, section 5.3.2.2. [228] *Ibid.*, section 5.3.3. [229] *Ibid.*, section 5.8.5.

[230] Regulation 1257/2013 of 20 November 2013 on ship recycling, OJ 2009 L 330/1, Art. 6(2).

[231] Commission Implementing Decision 2018/684 of 4 May 2018 amending Implementing Decision 2016/2323 to update the European List of ship recycling facilities pursuant to Regulation No 1257/2013, OJ 2018 L 116/47.

[232] *Ibid.*, recital 4.

[233] A proposal to introduce a financial mechanism to provide an incentive for non-EU ships to be recycled in EU-approved facilities was rejected by the European Parliament. The European Parliament Committee on Environment, Public Health and Food Safety had proposed an amendment introducing a financial levy, but this was defeated in a plenary vote of the European Parliament. According to this proposal, a financial levy would have been charged on all ships calling at EU ports and anchorages, other than those in respect of which a financial guarantee had been deposited as a guarantee that they would go to an EU-approved facility for recycling. The Committee was rightly concerned that without a financial incentive of this kind, the demands of the EU regulation could be circumvented by reflagging a ship outside the EU. While the Commission was charged with producing a report on the feasibility of a financial instrument to facilitate the safe and sound ship recycling of third country ships, there is no suggestion that the funds raised as a result of such an instrument would be used to provide financial assistance to ships recycling facilities situated in developing countries to assist them in upgrading their facilities to meet EU demands. For the report, see European Commission, 'Financial Instrument to Facilitate Safe and Sound Ship Recycling' (June 2016).

provided earlier, it is clear that this gives rise to two, closely related, problems. First, as the EU has become more dependent on other world regions for its ecological resources, this has led to a displacement of environmental burdens from the EU to third countries and in some cases to an exacerbation of these environmental burdens.[234] Second, put bluntly, on a *per capita* basis, individuals within the EU consume too much. Recall, the discussion of the EU's ecological footprint that suggested that 2.6 Earths would be required if every individual in the world had an ecological footprint equal to that of the average person within the EU.[235]

With that in mind, it is striking that with the arguable exception of the EU's aviation directive,[236] measures giving rise to territorial extension in EU environmental law focus on limiting the damaging effects of EU consumption globally and in third countries, rather than upon reducing overall consumption within the EU. Wrongdoing in EU environmental legislation giving rise to territorial extension tends to be understood in terms of intrinsic as opposed to aggregative harms; be it illegal deforestation, illegal, unreported or unregulated fishing, the non-environmentally sound management of waste or the non-humane killing of animals.[237] To the extent that quantitative as opposed to qualitative elements are included within EU environmental measures giving rise to territorial extension, these are framed as intensity standards rather than as absolute limits on EU consumption. An example will be seen later in the EU's fuel quality directive, which requires suppliers to reduce the lifecycle GHG emissions per unit of energy from fuel and energy supplied by 10 per cent by the end of 2020.[238]

This bias in environmental measures giving rise to territorial extension in favour of regulating the qualitative/efficiency aspects of third country production rather than the quantitative aspects of EU consumption, would be difficult to justify from a complicity point of view. Even if one continues to conceive of the EU as the putative complicit agent in both situations, the principal agent engaged in wrongdoing operates in a third country in relation to the qualitative aspects (a third country producer, for example), but within the EU as far as the quantitative aspects are concerned (EU consumers). In many situations, the EU is likely to be 'graded' more harshly for its complicity with the wrongdoing of EU consumers than it is for its complicity with the wrongdoing of third country actors which are providing goods or services for consumption within the EU.[239] The EU's causal role in relation to EU consumption as opposed to third country production is likely to be greater, as is its

[234] UNEP, note 159. [235] See text at note 158.

[236] The aviation directive (see note 2) does impose an absolute cap on international aviation emissions from the flights that are included within the emissions trading scheme. However, even in this instrument, the aviation sector is able to buy GHG emissions allowances to cover surplus emissions. To the extent that the price of aviation services should in principle rise (ignoring for a moment the fact that the price of allowances is too low to achieve this goal), this measure has the potential to reduce overall demand for international aviation services within the EU.

[237] See note 202 in relation to the distinction between intrinsic and aggregative harms. Quantitative thresholds may be laid down in third country or international law and play a role in determining, e.g., illegality, but the point here is that the EU does not seek itself to determine these quantitative thresholds in the main.

[238] Directive 2009/30, Art. 7a. See note 51.

[239] Recall Lepora and Goodin's criteria for grading complicity discussed in the text accompanying note 179.

knowledge of this causal contribution and of the wrongdoing for which EU consumers are responsible. This raises an important question, to be addressed in future research. Is this bias in favour of the qualitative as opposed to the quantitative dimensions of environmental wrongdoing, simply a reflection of current EU policy or intrinsic to some degree in the nature of territorial extension as a regulatory tool?

5. Conclusion

This chapter has explored a number of techniques that serve to extend the global reach of EU law, including extraterritorial 'triggers', territorial extension and the Brussels Effect. It has discussed the relationship between these tools, arguing that an understanding of territorial extension can shed light on the concept of legal non-divisibility of standards which forms a key element of the Brussels Effect.

The chapter has also engaged in the question of the justifiability of territorial extension in EU law by highlighting the quantitative and qualitative dimensions of the EU's large and damaging global environmental footprint. It has used this case study to explore the relevance of the concept of complicity in appraising territorial extension in EU law.

It is increasingly widely accepted that it is permissible for the EU to extend the global reach of its laws where foreign conduct causes substantial effects within the EU. This chapter has argued that the concept of complicity, as understood by Lepora and Goodin,[240] can serve to justify territorial extension even where such domestic effects are not present. Lepora and Goodin provide tools to assist in 'grading' complicity with wrongdoing and these tools can offer assistance to the EU in determining when it may be justified in extending the global reach of its law.

However, the chapter concluded by stressing that while the concept of complicity can sometimes provide a justification for territorial extension, it can also provide a springboard for critique. It can help to assess whether the EU is using territorial extension in a manner that is self-serving, to verify whether it is balancing the good and bad consequences of complicity in a rigorous, reasoned and appropriate manner and whether there is a danger that it is focusing unduly on third country wrongdoing at the expense of wrongdoing in the form of over-consumption within the EU.

[240] Lepora and Goodin, note 179, chapter 6.

2

Extending the Reach of EU Law

The EU as an International Legal Actor

Marise Cremona

1. Introduction: Law as the Structural Foundation of EU External Power

The enquiry into the reach of EU law beyond the territorial boundaries of the EU presented in this book requires us to consider the relation between law and EU external policy. This and subsequent chapters of this book will explore the ways in which, and for what purposes, the EU uses its external relations powers and its wide range of external instruments to extend the reach of EU law; and concomitantly the ways in which law shapes the EU's external action. The EU's external powers encompass a range of policy fields, both explicitly external (e.g. trade, development, the Common Foreign and Security Policy (CFSP)) and primarily internal (e.g. the internal market or the Area of Freedom, Security and Justice (AFSJ)), as well as those which naturally cross between internal and external (e.g. environmental policy); and a range of instruments (international agreements, financial instruments, unilateral measures, non-binding instruments such as Guidelines or dialogues). These powers and instruments may be deployed in ways which extend the impact of EU legislation beyond the boundaries of the EU. It may be said that the external instruments leverage the power of the EU so that its power to act internally is projected externally. Within the framework of its external policies and governed by EU constitutional law, the EU maintains a complex web of relations founded on and operating within international law, and these relations mediate between EU law and third countries and international organizations. The mediation may move in both directions: indeed, one of the aims of this chapter is to demonstrate that the EU takes part in a multi-layered process of unilateral, bilateral and multilateral normative interactions which cannot be categorized simply as either norm export or import.

Exploring this process will allow the fundamental character of the EU as an international actor and the centrality of law to the EU's international actorness to be seen more clearly. The EU derives its external power from law; it is constituted by law and

Extending the Reach of EU Law: The EU as an International Legal Actor. First Edition. Marise Cremona

operates through law. Its autonomous identity, both internally (with respect to its Member States) and externally (with respect to the rest of the world) is defined in terms of a *legal order*. Thus the EU's 'specific characteristics' include 'those relating to the constitutional structure of the EU', including the principle of conferral of powers and its institutional framework.[1] This legal structure establishes the EU's international capacity and external powers as distinct from those of its Member States, the institutional framework through which those powers are exercised, and the 'structured network of principles, rules and mutually interdependent legal relations linking the EU and its Member States, and its Member States with each other'[2] which enable and govern its external action.[3] Thus, in pursuing its interests and values as it is enjoined to do by Article 3(5) of the Treaty on European Union (TEU), the EU is constrained procedurally by its institutional legal framework and substantively by the need to ensure compliance with its own constitutional principles, including the protection of fundamental rights and the rule of law.[4] Even those areas of its external activity which may seem to be least subject to the control of the courts—such as the CFSP—are subject to these legal constitutional constraints.[5]

It is as a legal order that the EU relates to the outside world and the boundary between what is internal and what is external to that order is a legal one. The EU does not simply use law to project itself externally—choosing a legal tool among others in its toolbox—although this is certainly part of the picture. Rather, it is through law that the EU is able to *construct itself* as an autonomous and effective international actor. The aim of this chapter is to explore the nature of the symbiotic relationship between (EU and international) law and external action. The conclusion will be that the 'external reach of EU law' is thus a natural expression of the EU's international actorness.

If law defines the EU as an international actor, how is this reflected in its international action and what roles does law actually play? What kind of international legal actor is the EU? This chapter will look at three dimensions of the EU's 'actorness' which show three distinct—though overlapping—dynamics to the relationship between law and external action. These three dimensions do not aspire to be exhaustive in characterizing the EU as an international actor or the roles that law plays; they are, rather, both characteristic and distinctive, giving different perspectives to the law and external action dynamic. The specific examples—from the abolition of the death penalty, to association and trade agreements, and measures to combat money laundering—have been chosen to illustrate the variety of types of EU external action and policies, as well as to complement rather than duplicate the substantive policy fields discussed in the chapters that follow.

First, the role law plays in the construction of the EU's international legal presence as a Union of values can be examined. To what extent is law used to promote

[1] *Opinion 2/13* (ECLI:EU:C:2014:2454), para. 165. [2] *Ibid.*, para. 167.

[3] M. Cremona (ed.), *Structural Principles in EU External Relations Law* (2018).

[4] As far as international agreements are concerned, compliance with EU primary law (procedural or substantive) may be ensured either *ex ante*, via the prior opinion procedure of Art. 218(11) TFEU, or *ex post*, via an action for the annulment of the decision signing or concluding the agreement.

[5] Case C-263/14, *European Parliament v. Council* (ECLI:EU:C:2016:435).

EU values externally, and to what extent does law act as a constraint, ensuring that the EU upholds its values (including human rights norms) in its external relations? The Union has claimed that pursuit of values and interests can be reconciled: does its external action bear this out? If we look at the ways in which the EU engages with the creation of norms at the international level, what challenges does this pose for its claim to be a Union of values? Behind these questions the EU, with its commitment to legality, can be seen navigating between its own constitution and international legal principles.

Second, law mediates between the EU and its external partners. The EU uses law as a way of conducting its foreign policy, and of promoting its interests. Other actors do too, of course, but this is a distinctive dimension of EU external activity given expression in the Treaty mandate for external action: the EU is to 'seek to develop relations and build partnerships with third countries, and international, regional or global organisations which share [its] principles'.[6] It includes the employment of international agreements (bilateral and multilateral), as well as the use of external legal instruments (international law) and of its own legal norms as reference points or benchmarks in developing its relations with third countries. And these relations are consistently framed in terms of economic and legal integration; the building of the EU as an integration project has an external as well as an internal quality.[7] Law constructs the framework for integration-based relationships: 'integration through law' can be seen as an external relations enterprise. In constructing these relationships, law also defines the boundary between internal and external (indeed we may say that establishing that boundary is a necessary part of defining the EU's autonomous identity in relation to other actors) and thus also constrains the degree to which integration into EU structures is possible as well as the ways in which the EU can integrate itself into external, international, legal regimes.

Third, the EU is a regulatory actor with a commitment to 'multilateral solutions to common problems' and 'good global governance';[8] an actor engaged in shaping, importing and promoting international legal norms. The EU Treaties instruct the EU to contribute to the development of international law, in particular in the framework of the United Nations; law derived from multilateral cooperation is presented by the Treaties as an answer to global problems.[9] Thus, for example, the European Neighbourhood Policy (ENP) is an external policy framework within which, and with which, the EU seeks to address common problems and shared threats through law: promoting the ratification of key international conventions by ENP partners, supporting international institutions and the implementation and enforcement of ratified conventions, and enlisting the support of the ENP partners for the EU's own multilateral legal agendas.[10] The chapters on trade and sustainable development in the EU's more recent trade agreements are designed both to ensure that trade

[6] Art. 21(1) TFEU.

[7] As expressed in Art. 21(1) TEU: 'The Union's action on the international scene shall be guided by the principles which have inspired its own creation, development and enlargement'.

[8] Art. 21(1) and (2)(h) TEU.

[9] Art. 21(1) TEU.

[10] Cremona, 'Multilateralism and the ENP', in S. Poli (ed.), *The European Neighbourhood Policy—Values and Principles* (2016).

between the parties takes place in compliance with their international commitments on social and environmental protection,[11] and to promote those international standards more broadly. The Commission's claim is that '[b]asing trade policy on EU and universal values allows the EU to shape globalisation to promote sustainable development both at home and abroad, contributing to the UN Sustainable Development Goals and initiatives such as the Paris climate agreement'.[12]

These features of EU external policy have led some to characterize the EU as a *normative power*, a term coined by Ian Manners in an influential article written in 2002.[13] It is certainly a contested claim, not least because its meaning is not always clear.[14] Manners, for example, claimed that being a normative power entailed the power to define what is *normal*,[15] but has also linked it to the idea that the EU presents itself as an ethical power (supporting ethical values).[16] It is not my intention here to present the EU as—or to critique any claim that it may be—a normative power in this sense. I would simply say that law is the basis for establishing the EU as an autonomous international actor; that the development of norms at a global as well as a bilateral and regional level are among its objectives; and that it seeks to pursue its interests through normative means: through legal instruments, international law and international organizations. As this suggests, law plays a number of different roles. It may indeed operate as a constraint on action and on the EU's political choices; it may also, through the use of legal instruments, be a tool to be used in achieving political objectives; the creation and implementation of (international) legal norms is also one of the EU's external objectives. In the example of the abolition of the death penalty, which will be examined in section 2.C, we find examples of all these different roles for law, as well as seeing how they interact with other non-legal instruments, objectives and constraints.

The three dynamics just outlined illustrate different meanings that might be attributed to the notion of 'extending the reach of EU law' in the context of external relations, and in so doing they raise questions about the ambivalent role that law plays in these processes. As the idea of 'extending the reach of EU law' implies, these dynamics derive from the ways in which law mediates between the internal and the external. Indeed, 'law' itself is both internal (EU) and external (international), and in its external relations the EU is constrained by, and uses, both. The relationship between the two, as far as the EU is concerned, is governed by EU constitutional law, and the Treaty-proclaimed commitment to respecting and developing international

[11] *Opinion 2/15* (ECLI:EU:C:2017:376), paras 152 and 156.

[12] European Commission, Report on the Implementation of the Trade Policy Strategy 'Trade for All': Delivering a Progressive Trade Policy to Harness Globalisation, COM(2017) 491, 13 September 2017, at 9.

[13] Manners, 'Normative Power Europe: A Contradiction in Terms?', 20 *Journal of Common Market Studies* (2002) 235.

[14] See, e.g., Hyde-Price, '"Normative" Power Europe: A Realist Critique', 13 *Journal of European Public Policy* (2006) 217; Sjursen, 'The EU as a "Normative" Power: How Can this Be?', 13 *Journal of European Public Policy* (2006) 235.

[15] Manners, note 13, at 239–240.

[16] Manners, 'The Normative Ethics of the European Union', 84 *International Affairs* (2008) 65.

law is subject to gate-keeping by the Court of Justice.[17] In the words of one commentator, 'the EU has always been highly ambivalent towards international law, and has carved out an ethos to justify this: what matters—and has always mattered—is the protection of the integrity of the EU legal order and the autonomy of EU law'.[18] So EU law upholds the autonomy of the EU as an international actor with the ability to contribute to the development of international law, but at the same time the principles of EU law impose constraints on the EU's ability to participate in external regulatory regimes. The law structures the ways in which internal norms are projected externally and the two-way traffic between internal and external norms as the EU participates in external norm-generation. It provides the framework and instruments through which the EU establishes external relationships, but at the same time it establishes limits to those relations and the degree of integration compatible with the EU's autonomy. These ambivalences and tensions pose challenges for our attempt to understand the ways in which the EU is an international *legal* actor, with law at the foundation of its external power and the instrument through which, and in accordance with which, it expresses that power.

2. The Union of Values: Between EU and International Law in 'Upholding and Promoting' Human Rights Standards

A. Law and Power, Values and Interests

Article 3(5) TEU establishes the EU's external mission:

> In its relations with the wider world, the Union shall uphold and promote its values and interests and contribute to the protection of its citizens. It shall contribute to peace, security, the sustainable development of the Earth, solidarity and mutual respect among peoples, free and fair trade, eradication of poverty and the protection of human rights, in particular the rights of the child, as well as to the strict observance and the development of international law, including respect for the principles of the United Nations Charter.

The EU is to uphold and promote its values and interests. It is easy to see that the promotion of its *values* may involve the external reach of EU legal norms as well as the espousal and promotion of international norms, and later in this chapter we will look at some examples of this. Interests could be seen as essentially non-normative and concerned rather with power politics, operating in competition with 'values' as a driver of EU foreign policy. But a dichotomous opposition of law (values) against power (interests) is too simple. Interests and values may certainly be in tension but are not inevitably opposed to each other. Law may indeed be an expression of power. Tocci argues that an actor will shape its values according to its interests while at

[17] Art. 3(5) TEU; see Case C-266/16, *Western Sahara Campaign UK* (ECLI:EU:C:2018:118), discussed later.

[18] Klabbers, 'Straddling the Fence. The EU and International Law', in A. Arnull and D. Chalmers (eds), *The Oxford Handbook of European Union Law* (2015) 52, at 55. See also Klabbers, 'Völkerrechtsfreundlich? International Law and the Union Legal Order', in P. Koutrakos (ed.), *European Foreign Policy: Legal and Political Perspectives* (2011).

the same time an actor's values will help to shape its interests.[19] Thus interests (e.g. stability in the neighbourhood) influence the values to be promoted there (e.g. rule of law) and values (e.g. human rights) help to define and construct interests (e.g. combating terrorism). The interdependence of values and interests is an idea promoted by the EU Global Strategy presented by High Representative Mogherini in June 2016:

> Our interests and values go hand in hand. We have an interest in promoting our values in the world. At the same time, our fundamental values are embedded in our interests. Peace and security, prosperity, democracy and a rules-based global order are the vital interests underpinning our external action.[20]

The Global Strategy here represents values *as* interests: it is in the EU's interests to promote its values. This is of course a rhetorical statement intended to demonstrate that the agenda and policy priorities of the Global Strategy operationalize the 'mission statement' in Article 3(5) TEU.[21] There is certainly a danger that emphasizing the interdependence of values and interests will lead to the shaping of the EU's legal values according to its current political interests. As Kuner argues, '[i]t is thus important that the EU should not cloak the assertion of its political interests in the language of fundamental legal values, in order to keep a degree of integrity in the law that is resistant to changing political pressures'.[22] It is not difficult to find examples where the EU's values and interests may indeed conflict—the 2016 agreement with Turkey on the settlement of refugees being an obvious case.[23] But rhetoric is significant, and in recent EU practice we see, for example, a shift in the presentation of the ENP, with the earlier strong focus on shared values now more explicitly combined with a stress on the mutual interests of the EU and its ENP partners.[24] Likewise, a shift can be seen in the EU's most recent Trade Strategy, which puts the EU's values alongside its commercial interests, reflecting—it declares—the priorities of EU citizens:

> One of the aims of the EU is to ensure that economic growth goes hand in hand with social justice, respect for human rights, high labour and environmental standards, and health and safety protection. This applies to external as well as internal policies, and so also includes trade and investment policy.[25]

The presentation of values as interests, of interests as normative, suggests that the EU's external mission—its pursuit of power—is defined in terms of *milieu* goals.

[19] N. Tocci, 'Profiling Normative Foreign Policy: The European Union and its Global Partners', CEPS Working Document No. 279 (December 2007), at 3.

[20] European Union, 'Shared Vision, Common Action: A Stronger Europe A Global Strategy for the European Union's Foreign And Security Policy' (June 2016), at 13.

[21] See Editorial Comments, '"We Perfectly Know what to Work for": The EU's Global Strategy for Foreign and Security Policy', 53 *Common Market Law Rev* (2016) 1199; Smith, 'A European Union Global Strategy for a Changing World?', 54 *International Politics* (2017) 503.

[22] See Christopher Kuner, Chapter 3 in this volume, at section 7.B.

[23] The so-called 'EU-Turkey statement', European Council Press release 144/16, 18 March 2016. See further note 52 and Bernard Ryan, Chapter 6 in this volume, at section 4.

[24] See, e.g., the Joint Communication by the Commission and the High Representative, Review of the European Neighbourhood Policy, JOIN (2015) 50, 18 November 2015.

[25] European Commission, 'Trade for All—Towards a More Responsible Trade and Investment Policy', 14 October 2015, at 20.

Whereas possession goals are associated with competition and the exclusion of others, milieu goals:

> are of a different character. Nations pursuing them are out not to defend or increase possessions they hold to the exclusion of others, but aim instead at shaping conditions beyond their national boundaries.... [E]fforts to promote international law or to establish international organizations, undertaken consistently by many nations, are addressed to the milieu in which nations operate and indeed such efforts make sense only if nations have reason to concern themselves with things other than their own possessions.[26]

The EU's mission as framed in Articles 3(5) and 21 TEU is directed at the pursuit of *milieu* goals—at shaping the world around it. It is to do this, according to Article 21 TEU, by developing relations and building partnerships with third countries, and international, regional or global organizations which share 'the principles which have inspired its own creation, development and enlargement'—its values. There is thus a normative dimension to the promotion of both values and interests. As I have previously argued, the EU derives its power from and through law.

The EU is, therefore, profoundly committed to law and to the legality of its actions, both internally (constitutional legality) and externally (with respect to international law).[27] Two iconic statements of the Court of Justice encapsulate these two dimensions:

> [T]he obligations imposed by an international agreement cannot have the effect of prejudicing the constitutional principles of the EC Treaty, which include the principle that all Community acts must respect fundamental rights, that respect constituting a condition of their lawfulness which it is for the Court to review in the framework of the complete system of legal remedies established by the Treaty.[28]
>
> Under Article 3(5) TEU, the European Union is to contribute to the strict observance and the development of international law. Consequently, when it adopts an act, it is bound to observe international law in its entirety, including customary international law, which is binding upon the institutions of the European Union.[29]

Law, in the form of the EU's constitutional law, is a procedural and substantive constraint on EU external policy. By constraint is meant here not simply a limitation on, but rather a control over, the procedural framing of policy and the direction of policy content. In fact, I have argued elsewhere that EU law is primarily concerned with *structuring the process* of external policy formation, with the powers and inter-relations of the different actors, rather than with policy direction.[30] Nevertheless the EU's values—and in particular its commitment to the protection of human rights—operate as part of its constitutional law on a substantive as well as a procedural level:

[26] Wolfers, 'The Goals of Foreign Policy', in *Discord and Collaboration: Essays on International Politics* (1962), at 73, cited by Tocci, note 19, at 4.

[27] Cf. Tocci, note 19, at 6.

[28] Case C-402/05 P and C-415/05 P, *Kadi and Al Barakaat International Foundation v. Council and Commission* ('*Kadi I*') (ECLI:EU:C:2008:461), para. 285.

[29] Case C-366/10, *Air Transport Association of America* (ECLI:EU:C:2011:864), para. 101; see also Case C-266/16, *Western Sahara Campaign UK* (ECLI:EU:C:2018:118), para. 47.

[30] Cremona (ed.), note 3.

procedurally as a constraint on the process of policy formation and substantively in shaping the direction and content of EU external policy. Article 3(5) TEU requires the EU to promote the protection of human rights in its external relations and to 'uphold and promote its values', which as defined in Article 2 TEU include respect for human rights. Article 21(2) TEU requires the EU to safeguard its values as well as its fundamental interests through its external action, and to 'consolidate and support democracy, the rule of law, human rights and the principles of international law'. Although such statements may appear utopian, as constitutional norms they carry some weight in the procedural and substantive shaping of policy.[31] More specifically, the EU institutions are bound by the Charter of Fundamental Rights as well as by general principles of law when acting under external relations powers.[32]

The Strategic Framework on Human Rights and Democracy, adopted by the Council in June 2012, provides an overall framework for the integration of human rights into EU policies, including all external action, from trade and investment to development, security and defence.[33] If human rights objectives may (indeed, should) be pursued via policies such as trade and investment or development policy, and human rights protections should be built into policies such as migration and combating crime and terrorism, how might these expansive commitments be translated into practice? The Strategic Framework mentions a number of different external instruments—not all of them legal instruments—designed to promote human rights: human rights dialogues, the use of financial instruments to fund support for human rights education and training, the 'human rights clauses' in agreements with third countries, and economic and other sanctions in cases of human rights violations. To these we may add trade preferences linked to ratification and implementation of core conventions on human and labour rights through the GSP+ scheme,[34] and the possibility of the EU itself adhering to international human rights conventions, such as the UN Convention on the Rights of Persons with Disabilities.[35]

[31] J. Larik, *Foreign Policy Objectives in European Constitutional Law* (2016).

[32] *Opinion 1/15* (ECLI:EU:C:2017:592), discussed further later. O. de Schutter, 'The Implementation of the Charter of Fundamental Rights in the EU Institutional Framework', Study for the AFCO Committee of the European Parliament, PE 571.397 (November 2016), at 55–58.

[33] EU Strategic Framework and Action Plan on Human Rights and Democracy, 25 June 2012, Council doc. 11855/12, at 6.

[34] Regulation 978/2012 of 25 October 2012 applying a scheme of generalised tariff preferences, OJ 2012 L 303/1. Beneficiaries must meet 'vulnerability' criteria set out in the Regulation and must have ratified 27 core international conventions in the fields of human and labour rights, the environment and good governance; they must commit to implementation and accept the reporting requirements and monitoring imposed by those conventions as well as EU monitoring. The EU has engaged with the ILO in offering support for implementation to some beneficiary states. The core conventions include Convention on the Prevention and Punishment of the Crime of Genocide (1948); International Convention on the Elimination of All Forms of Racial Discrimination (1965); International Covenant on Civil and Political Rights (1966); International Covenant on Economic Social and Cultural Rights (1966); Convention on the Elimination of All Forms of Discrimination Against Women (1979); Convention Against Torture and other Cruel, Inhuman or Degrading Treatment or Punishment (1984); Convention on the Rights of the Child (1989).

[35] Council Decision 2010/48 of 26 November 2009, OJ 2010 L 23/35; the legal bases were Arts 13 and 95 EC (now Arts 19 and 114 TFEU).

In December 2001 the Council adopted a set of *Guidelines on Human Rights Dialogues*, and they were reviewed and readopted in January 2009.[36] These dialogues take place in a variety of contexts, some within a broader framework of political dialogue (such as those with the Western Balkans or ASEAN) as part of the 'mainstreaming' of human rights objectives into EU external policy as a whole;[37] others as dedicated human rights dialogues (such as those with China and Russia); as ad hoc dialogues via an EU delegation or Special Representative; or within the framework of multilateral human rights bodies. While not legal instruments, Human Rights Dialogues provide a framework within which the EU can promote adherence to international law norms. The Guidelines identify a number of substantive human rights issues (e.g. the death penalty, torture, children's rights, the rule of law) and prioritize the signing, ratification and implementation of international human rights instruments and cooperation with international human rights procedures and mechanisms.

The EU also engages in more general diplomatic promotion of its policies, using the CFSP common positions, Council Conclusions and Guidelines.[38] The Council has adopted Human Rights Guidelines on a number of specific issues, setting out EU policy and forming a basis for dialogue and the submission of resolutions and other initiatives in multilateral fora.[39] These include Guidelines on the death penalty, torture, children in armed conflict, the rights of the child, freedom of expression and freedom of religious belief, and international humanitarian law. The Guidelines have several purposes: they set out the EU's understanding of the specific rights at issue; they are intended to ensure the consistency of EU policy and serve as a public statement of its objectives; and they provide guidance to EU and Member State officials working in third countries and multilateral fora.[40] From this it may be seen that the Guidelines are directed at human rights compliance by third countries rather than by the EU itself.[41]

The borderline between promoting and upholding human rights is, however, not a bright line, in particular when considering the EU's own actions vis à vis third countries. Human Rights Impact Assessments, a mechanism designed to ensure that the human rights implications of EU policy proposals are taken into account,[42] are

[36] EU Guidelines on Human Rights Dialogues adopted by Economic and Financial Affairs Council of 13 December 2001; updated Guidelines adopted 19 January 2009, Council doc. 16526/08.

[37] 'Mainstreaming human rights across CFSP and other EU policies', Council doc. 10076/06.

[38] See Hoffmeister, 'The Contribution of EU Practice to International Law', in M Cremona (ed.), *Developments in EU External Relations Law* (2008).

[39] See further Wouters and Hermez, 'EU Guidelines on Human Rights as a Foreign Policy Instrument: An Assessment', in S. Poli (ed.), *Protecting Human Rights in the European Union's External Relations, Centre for Law of European External Relations*, CLEER paper 5/2016, at 63.

[40] See, e.g., the Guidelines on Freedom of Expression, adopted by the Foreign Affairs Council on 12 May 2014, paras 9 and 10.

[41] The Guidelines on International Humanitarian Law expressly state that 'measures taken by the EU and its Member States to ensure compliance with IHL in their own conduct, including by their own forces... are not covered by these Guidelines', Council doc. 16841/09, 1 December 2009.

[42] Note, however the view of Christopher Kuner, Chapter 3 in this volume, text at note 209, that 'impact assessment provisions in EU legislation concerning the Internet tend to consider only its impact with regard to the EU'.

a case in point.[43] The 2012 Action Plan which accompanied the Strategic Framework included a commitment to include human rights in Impact Assessments, including those carried out for trade agreements with 'significant economic, social and environmental impacts'.[44] Impact Assessments are referred to in the Commission's 2015 Trade Strategy,[45] and the European Parliament has strongly advocated the need for Human Rights Impact Assessments.[46] While this is a political commitment, it is not without effect. In February 2016 the European Ombudsman adopted a decision following a complaint that the Commission had not carried out a Human Rights Impact Assessment in respect of the trade agreement then under negotiation with Vietnam.[47] The Ombudsman's position is that good administration—which it is her role to supervise—includes observance of and respect for fundamental rights: 'In fact, where fundamental rights are not respected, there cannot be good administration'.[48] Thus, she said, citing Article 21 TEU, the EU institutions 'must always consider the compliance of their actions with fundamental rights and the possible impact of their actions on fundamental rights... [and this applies] also with respect to administrative activities in the context of international treaty negotiations'.[49] The Ombudsman found that the failure to conduct a Human Rights Impact Assessment was an instance of maladministration, stressing its distinctive role.[50]

[43] See further V. Kube, 'The EU's human rights obligations towards the wider world and the international investment regime' (2018) (PhD thesis on file at the EUI, Florence), chapter 5.

[44] Action Plan on Human Rights and Democracy, Council doc. 11855/12, 25 June 2012, point 1, at 12. This commitment was reiterated in May 2014 and again in the Action Plan adopted in April 2015 which is designed to build upon the Strategic Framework for the period 2015–2019: Council conclusions on a rights-based approach to development cooperation, encompassing all human rights, Foreign Affairs (Development) Council, 19 May 2014, Council doc. 10020/14, para. 8; Action Plan on Human Rights and Democracy (2015–2019) 'Keeping Human Rights at the Heart of the EU Agenda', Joint Communication from the Commission and the High Representative, 28 April 2015, JOIN (2015) 16 final, points 24 and 27. On impact assessment generally, see Commission Staff Working Document, Better Regulation Guidelines, 19 May 2015, SWD (2015)111, at 16–32. This requires an assessment of 'regulatory fitness' including the possibility of amendment to reduce 'Impact on human rights in the partner country in relation to its obligations arising from international treaties' (at 32).

[45] European Commission, 'Trade for All—Towards a More Responsible Trade and Investment Policy', 14 October 2015, at 13. See further DG Trade Guidelines on the analysis of human rights impacts in impact assessments for trade-related policy initiatives, 2 July 2015, tradoc 153591.

[46] E.g. European Parliament Resolution on a new forward-looking and innovative future strategy for trade and investment, A8-0220/2016, para. 13: the Parliament 'stresses that the EU has a legal obligation to respect human rights...; is of the opinion that the EU has a responsibility to make all necessary efforts to foresee, prevent and tackle any potential negative impact caused by its CCP by regularly conducting ex-ante and ex-post human rights and sustainability impact assessments, and consequently reviewing trade agreements as necessary'. See also EP resolution of 25 November 2010 on human rights and social and environmental standards in international trade agreements, OJ 2012 C 99E, at 31.

[47] Decision of the European Ombudsman in case 1409/2014/MHZ on the European Commission's failure to carry out a prior human rights impact assessment of the EU-Vietnam free trade agreement, 26 February 2016.

[48] Draft recommendation of the European Ombudsman in the inquiry into complaint 1409/2014/JN against the European Commission, 26 March 2015, para. 21. The complainants were the International Federation for Human Rights (FIDH) and the Vietnam Committee on Human Rights (VCHR).

[49] *Ibid.*, paras 21–22.

[50] 'Its role is preventive in the first place because when negative impacts are identified, either the negotiated provisions need to be modified or mitigating measures have to be decided upon before the agreement is entered into.' Decision of the European Ombudsman in case 1409/2014/MHZ, note 47, para. 25.

Other instruments used to promote human rights in Vietnam (such as the human rights clause in the Partnership and Cooperation Agreement; the trade and sustainable development chapter in the free trade agreement under negotiation; and the human rights dialogue with Vietnam) do not fulfil the same function.[51]

Even more recently, in January 2017, in the context of the agreement (or 'Statement') with Turkey on migration, the Ombudsman held that the obligation to take account of the human rights impact of an agreement applies also during its implementation, and does not depend on the agreement being legally binding.[52] She made recommendations as to the content of future progress reports by the Commission on the implementation of the agreement.

These instances show that the integration of human rights objectives into EU policy-making processes may be liable to *administrative* assessment and challenge. This is important but it does not affect the legality of the measure.[53] In section 2.B we turn to the way in which the commitment to uphold and promote human rights may affect the *legality* of EU action, as a matter of administrative or substantive law.

B. Human Rights Compliance as a Condition of Legality of EU Action

Compliance with fundamental rights is a condition of legality of all EU acts. Since the *Kadi I* judgment quoted earlier,[54] the principle has been reiterated in several post-Lisbon cases on external action, including the conclusion of international agreements.[55] *Opinion 1/15*, on a proposed agreement with Canada on the transfer by airlines to national security authorities of passenger name record (PNR) data, is an important milestone. It affirms that the Court's jurisdiction to assess the compatibility of an international agreement with the Treaties includes compliance with fundamental rights as part of EU primary law:

> A judgment on the compatibility of an agreement with the Treaties may... depend, inter alia, [on] the compatibility of an international agreement with the first subparagraph of Article 6(1) TEU and, consequently, with the guarantees enshrined in the Charter, since the Charter has the same legal status as the Treaties.[56]

[51] See the joint FIDH-VCHR observations on the Opinion of the Commission on the European Ombudsman's draft recommendation ref. 1409/2014/JN, 30 September 2015.

[52] Decision of the European Ombudsman in the joint inquiry into complaints 506-509-674-784-927-1381/2016/MHZ against the European Commission concerning a human rights impact assessment in the context of the EU-Turkey Agreement. The General Court held on 28 February 2017 in Case T-192/16, *NF v. European Council* (ECLI:EU:T:2017:128), that the agreement was in fact not an EU agreement but was concluded by the Member States acting collectively. This would not alter the Commission's obligations if it is given the task of implementing the agreement by the Member States: 'the Charter is addressed to the EU institutions, including... when they act outside the EU legal framework'; Joined Cases C-8/15 P to C-10/15 P, *Ledra Advertising v. Commission and European Central Bank* (ECLI:EU:C:2016:701), para. 67.

[53] See further Vianello, 'Guaranteeing the Respect for Human Rights in EU External Relations: What Role for Administrative Law?', in S. Poli (ed.), *Protecting Human Rights in the European Union's External Relations*, CLEER Papers 2016/5.

[54] See text at note 28.

[55] Case C-130/10, *European Parliament v. Council* (ECLI:EU:C:2012:472), paras 83–84; Case C-263/14, *European Parliament v. Council* (ECLI:EU:C:2016:435), para. 47.

[56] *Opinion 1/15*, note 32, para. 70.

For the first time the Court found a proposed international agreement to be incompatible with the Treaties on the ground that it failed to comply with the Charter of Fundamental Rights. The Court in fact made a point of using the Charter as its point of reference, in particular Article 8 on the protection of personal data, rather than Article 16 of the Treaty on the Functioning of the European Union (TFEU), on the grounds of its greater specificity.[57] Under the terms of the proposed agreement, personal data was to be transferred out of EU jurisdiction to a third country, and as had already been held in the *Schrems* case, EU law requires that such a transfer must 'ensure protection essentially equivalent to that guaranteed within the European Union'.[58] The Court set out in some detail what were the defects of the agreement from the perspective of the Charter and what would be needed to remedy them.[59]

The position, including the application of the Charter, is more complex where there is no similar legislative link to the EU. The EU's administrative commitment to conduct Human Rights Impact Assessments in the case of significant trade agreements has already been mentioned. Can this be translated into a generalizable legal obligation? What legal obligation is the EU under to take account of the impact of its international agreements on the human rights situation in a third country? And should the reference point be EU primary law (the Charter) or (or additionally) international human rights law (is the obligation internally or externally driven)? In the *Front Polisario* case, the General Court, Advocate General Wathelet and the Court of Justice each took a different approach to this question.[60]

In *Front Polisario*,[61] the applicant challenged the legality of the Council decision concluding an agreement with Morocco on trade in agricultural and fisheries products on grounds, inter alia, of breach of the EU's values (including fundamental rights) and breach of the principles governing the EU's external action.[62] It was argued that the agreement would *de facto* be applied by Morocco to the territory of Western Sahara, sovereignty over which is disputed. The General Court dismissed arguments based on the EU's international legal obligations, but held that assessing the human rights impact of a trade agreement is not only a matter of good administration (as the Ombudsman had found); it is also a procedural requirement enforceable via judicial review, derived from the obligation on the EU institutions to base

[57] *Ibid.*, para. 120.

[58] *Ibid.*, para. 134, citing Case C-362/14, Schrems (ECLI:EU:C:2015:650), paras 72–74. In later discussing the conditions under which interference with the Charter right may be permitted, the Court cites its recent case law on data protection, including *Schrems* and Case C-203/15 and C-698/15, *Tele2 Sverige and Watson and others* (ECLI:EU:C:2016:970); there is thus no suggestion that the external context affects the legal tests applied.

[59] *Opinion 1/15*, note 32, para. 232.

[60] Case T-512/12, *Front populaire pour la liberation de la saguia-elhamra et du rio de oro (Front Polisario) v. Council* (ECLI:EU:T:2015:953); Case C-104/16 P, *Council v. Front Polisario*, Opinion of AG Wathelet (ECLI:EU:C:2016:677); Case C-104/16 P, *Council v. Front Polisario*, judgment, (ECLI:EU:C:2016:973).

[61] Case T-512/12, *Front Polisario v. Council* (ECLI:EU:T:2015:953).

[62] The agreement, concluded by Council Decision 2012/497/EU, amended the existing association agreement between the EU and Morocco, thereby extending liberalization of trade in agricultural and fisheries products.

their decisions on an examination of all relevant facts. While emphasizing the wide discretion enjoyed by the Council in deciding to conclude such an agreement, the General Court nevertheless held that the exercise of that discretion is subject to review on grounds of a manifest error of assessment, and in particular a review of whether the Council has, before taking its decision, carefully and impartially examined all the relevant facts.[63] The effect of the agreement on the fundamental rights of the population of Western Sahara was a factor which should, the General Court held, have been taken into account. In particular, the Council should have examined the effects of production of goods for export to the EU under the agreement in the light of specific rights contained in the EU's Charter of Fundamental Rights, including human dignity, and the prohibition of slavery, forced labour and child labour. Its failure to do so led the Court to annul the decision insofar as it was deemed to approve the application of the agreement to the Western Sahara.

The judgment of the General Court was reversed on appeal by the Court of Justice on the ground that there was no legal basis for interpreting the EU-Morocco agreement as applicable to the territory of the Western Sahara.[64] The decision concluding it could therefore not be of direct and individual concern to the applicant, who as a result lacked standing to bring the action. Its reasoning on this point will be discussed later.[65] The Court did not, as a result, rule on whether the Council's duty to take account of all relevant facts included the requirement to assess the human rights implications of concluding the agreement. Advocate General Wathelet, who took the same view as the Court of Justice on the issue of the territorial scope of the agreement, nevertheless did discuss this question, concluding that the Council is indeed under such a duty.[66] The Advocate General based his reasoning on two propositions, both of which we have met before. First, the principle that 'compliance with the principles of the rule of law and human rights, as well as respect for human dignity, is required of all actions of the European Union'.[67] Second, that the EU must respect international law in the exercise of its powers.[68] From these, he concluded that 'the question of the conformity of the agreement at issue with international law must be taken into account in the prior examination of all the relevant facts to be conducted by the institutions before concluding an international agreement'.[69] Since, under international law, compliance with the peremptory norms of international law (*jus*

[63] Case T-512/12, *Front Polisario v. Council* (ECLI:EU:T:2015:953), para. 225: 'where an EU institution enjoys a wide discretion, in order to verify whether it has committed a manifest error of assessment, the Courts of the European Union must verify whether it has examined carefully and impartially all the relevant facts of the individual case, facts which support the conclusions reached'.

[64] Case C-104/16 P, *Council v. Front Polisario* (ECLI:EU:C:2016:973).

[65] The Court's ruling is of practical as well as legal significance in holding that the EU's Association Agreement with Morocco does not apply to the Western Sahara, since the practice of accepting products from the region as of Moroccan origin will have to be altered: see further below.

[66] C-104/16 P, *Council v Front Polisario*, Opinion of AG Wathelet (ECLI:EU:C:2016:677), paras 220–237.

[67] Citing Case C-263/14, *European Parliament v. Council* (ECLI:EU:C:2016:435), para. 47.

[68] Case C-162/96, *Racke* (ECLI:EU:C:1998:293), para. 45; Case C-402/05 P and C-415/05 P, *Kadi and Al Barakaat International Foundation v. Council and Commission* (ECLI:EU:C:2008:461), para. 291.

[69] Case C-104/16 P, Opinion of AG Wathelet (ECLI:EU:C:2016:677), para. 256.

cogens) and *erga omnes* obligations must be ensured,[70] this brings international human rights norms into play:

> it is clear that international law imposes a clear obligation on the European Union and its Member States not to recognise an illegal situation resulting from the infringement of principles and rules concerning fundamental rights and not to render aid or assistance in maintaining the situation created by that infringement. To that end, the EU's institutions and its Member States must examine the impact which the international agreement at issue could have on human rights.[71]

The Advocate General took issue, on the other hand, with the General Court's use of the EU's Charter of Fundamental Rights as a reference point, on the ground that the conditions for extraterritorial effect of Charter rights did not apply.[72] Thus, for the Advocate General, the obligation to uphold human rights in its external action was linked to the obligation to comply with international law, and the relevant standards were international law standards—a point which will be returned to later.[73]

It is important that both the General Court and the Advocate General cast the obligation in *procedural* terms: the duty is to take account of the human rights implications of EU external action, as part of the procedural duty of care—the duty to ensure that a policy decision is based on all relevant facts.[74] Although the Court of Justice did not discuss this aspect of the case directly, the case nevertheless represents a step forward in the operationalization of the human rights compliance obligation for the EU institutions. As the Advocate General pointed out, first, 'the Council does not deny that the general human rights situation in the other party to an international agreement is one of the elements to be taken into account at the time of the negotiation and the conclusion of the agreement'.[75] Second, (in his view) 'neither the Council nor the Commission nor any of the interveners put forward a convincing reason' why the EU institutions should *not* be required to examine the impact which the conclusion of an international agreement could have on the human rights situation in the other party to the agreement.[76] And third, although the Court of Justice did not see the need to affirm (or reject) this line of argument, its judgment brings the protection of human rights under international law into the picture in a different but significant way.

70 *Ibid.*, para. 259. 71 *Ibid.*, para. 269.

72 *Ibid.*, paras 270–272. The AG refers 'by analogy' to the case law of the European Court of Human Rights (ECtHR) on the extraterritorial effect of the ECHR, without explaining why this case law should be applied to the EU Charter. This issue is a debated one; see, e.g., Bartels, 'The EU's Human Rights Obligations in Relation to Policies with Extraterritorial Effects', 25 *European Journal of International Law* (2014) 1071; Moreno-Lax and Costello, 'The Extraterritorial Application of the EU Charter of Fundamental Rights: From Territoriality to Facticity, the Effectiveness Model', in S. Peers *et al.* (eds), *The EU Charter of Fundamental Rights: A Commentary* (2014).

73 Case C-104/16 P, Opinion of AG Wathelet (ECLI:EU:C:2016:677), para. 276.

74 Case T-512/12, *Front Polisario v. Council* (ECLI:EU:T:2015:953), para. 224; Case C-104/16 P, Opinion of AG Wathelet (ECLI:EU:C:2016:677), para. 278. See further I. Vianello, *EU External Action and the Administrative Rule of Law A Long-Overdue Encounter* (2016) (PhD thesis on file at the EUI, Florence).

75 Case C-104/16 P, Opinion of AG Wathelet (ECLI:EU:C:2016:677), para. 260.

76 *Ibid.*, para. 262.

In finding that the EU agreement with Morocco could not be interpreted as applying to the Western Sahara, the Court of Justice based itself on three principles of international law, binding on the EU as customary and/or *erga omnes* obligations.[77] The first of these was the principle of self-determination, which gives the Western Sahara a 'separate and distinct status', a status which then both determines the meaning to be given to the reference to the 'territory of the Kingdom of Morocco' in the agreement itself, and establishes that 'the people of Western Sahara must be regarded as a "third party" within the meaning of the principle of the relative effect of treaties'.[78] The Court refused to accept practice under the agreement and the evidence of its application *de facto* to products from Western Sahara as evidence of the Union's intention that the agreement would be legally applicable to this territory. It argued that such a conclusion 'would necessarily have entailed conceding that the European Union intended to implement those agreements in a manner incompatible with the principles of self-determination and of the relative effect of treaties'.[79] The Court thus relied on the international law principle of self-determination, 'a legally enforceable right *erga omnes* and one of the essential principles of international law',[80] in deciding on the correct interpretation of a Union agreement. And in assessing the legal significance of the Union's practice, the Court assumed that the Union did not intend to breach this international legal obligation, and that it intended to act legally with respect to international law-based rights.[81] The argument of the Council and Commission that there could be a pragmatic 'application without recognition' of the EU-Morocco agreement in Western Sahara was rejected by the Court, which insisted that the Union's international law obligations were to be taken seriously in interpreting both its international agreements and its practice.

So instead of building an argument based on the application of EU law-based (Charter) rights to the population of Western Sahara, the Court adopted a different route, basing itself on compliance with international law. This approach was confirmed in the *Western Sahara* case, which concerned the Fisheries Partnership Agreement between the EU and Morocco, a protocol to the Association Agreement on fisheries, and related EU legislation.[82] The implementation of these agreements by the UK was challenged by a UK-based non-governmental organization (NGO), arguing that they were illegal under EU law for breach of Article 3(5) TEU. The Court again held that the agreements could not be illegal for breach of international

[77] Case C-104/16 P, *Council v. Front Polisario* (ECLI:EU:C:2016:973), paras 87–107. The Court of Justice based its conclusion on three principles of international law: (i) the principle of self-determination, (ii) the principle codified in Art. 29 of the Vienna Convention that a treaty applies to the 'territory' of the parties, and (iii) the principle of the relative effect of treaties (*pacta tertiis nec nocent nec prosunt*), the Court taking the view that the agreement should not be interpreted so as to affect the position of a third party, *in casu*, the people of Western Sahara.

[78] *Ibid.*, para. 106. [79] *Ibid.*, para. 123.

[80] *Ibid.*, para. 98, citing East Timor, (*Portugal v. Australia*), judgment, ICJ Reports 1995, at 90, para. 29.

[81] Its interpretation of the operation of *jus cogens* has been both criticized and defended: Cannizzaro, 'In Defence of *Front Polisario*: The ECJ as a Global *Jus Cogens* Maker', 55 *Common Market Law Review* (2018) 569; Kassoti, 'The Council v. Front Polisario Case: The Court of Justice's Selective Reliance on International Rules on Treaty Interpretation', 2 *European Papers* (2017) 23.

[82] Case C-266/16, *Western Sahara Campaign UK* (ECLI:EU:C:2018:118).

law in relation to the Western Sahara because the Western Sahara was not part of the territory of Morocco to which these agreements applied.[83]

The judgment of the Court of Justice in these two cases can in this sense be seen as a complement to *Kadi I*: the former case based on the EU's own constitutional principles, the latter on international norms. As such it sheds further light on one of the most problematic aspects of the EU's engagement with international law: in insisting on the EU's legal autonomy, the Court of Justice has—it is argued—both made it difficult for the EU to participate in external regulatory systems, especially when they involve legal enforcement processes, and has even, despite the Union's declared commitment to the United Nations Charter, undermined the authority of the United Nations.[84] In *Kadi I* the Court insisted on a legality (fundamental rights) control of EU measures implementing a UN Security Council resolution. The judgment was welcomed by many for its defence of fundamental rights,[85] but it also led de Búrca, among others, to express concern at what was seen as a departure from the 'conventional presentation and widespread understanding of the EU as an actor which maintains a distinctive commitment to international law and institutions'.[86] De Búrca sees 'a significant dissonance between the pluralist, autonomy-driven approach of the ECJ on the one hand, and the official discourse of the political and institutional branches on the international role of the EU'.[87] Interestingly, a tension or dissonance between Court and political institutions can also be seen in *Front Polisario*, but in this case the argument of the Council and Commission that there could be a pragmatic 'application without recognition' of the EU-Morocco agreement in Western Sahara was rejected by the Court, which insisted that the Union's international law obligations were to be taken seriously in interpreting both its international agreements and its practice.

Front Polisario thus invites us to consider the relation between different sources of fundamental rights norms—internal and external. The critical reaction to *Opinion 2/13*, which found the draft agreement on the accession of the EU to the European Convention on Human Rights (ECHR) to be incompatible with the Treaties, points to the difficulty of reconciling the EU's legal autonomy and its ability to engage with external international regimes, even those designed to protect human rights. De Witte and Imamović, for example, conclude that 'the CJEU treats the ECtHR as a *foreign* court that threatens the authority which the CJEU has acquired in the course of time. [It] decided to cut off a new institutional route for the protection of fundamental rights which accession to the ECHR had promised to offer'.[88] The Court in

[83] *Ibid.*, paras 63–64.

[84] On this debate, see Odermatt, 'The Court of Justice of the European Union: International or Domestic Court?', 3 *Cambridge Journal of International and Comparative Law* (2014) 696.

[85] See, e.g., Ziegler, 'Strengthening the Rule of Law, but Fragmenting International Law: The Kadi Decision of the ECJ from the Perspective of Human Rights', 9 *Human Rights Law Review* (2009) 288.

[86] De Búrca, 'The European Court of Justice and the International Legal Order after *Kadi*', 51 *Harvard International Law Journal* (2010) 1.

[87] *Ibid.*, at 7.

[88] De Witte and Imamović, 'Opinion 2/13 on Accession to the ECHR: Defending the EU Legal Order against a Foreign Human Rights Court', 40 *European Law Review* (2015) 683, at 704. Among many other critiques, see Spaventa, 'A Very Fearful Court? The Protection of Fundamental Rights in the European Union after Opinion 2/13', 22 *Maastricht Journal of European and Comparative Law* (2015)

Opinion 2/13, citing *Kadi* as well as *Internationale Handelsgesellschaft*,[89] held that while fundamental rights 'recognised by the Charter' were at the heart of the Union's legal structure, '[t]he autonomy enjoyed by EU law in relation to the laws of the Member States and in relation to international law requires that the interpretation of those fundamental rights be ensured *within the framework of the structure and objectives of the EU*'.[90] The close connection between the Charter and the Convention, as internal and external sources of fundamental rights in the EU,[91] creates particular difficulties for an agreement intended to bridge that gap via accession to the Convention: the Court insisted on maintaining a clear distinction between internal jurisdiction over the structural relations between the EU and its Member States (its own exclusive preserve[92]) and external adjudication.

From this perspective, it is possible to assess the move found in *Front Polisario* from internal to external sources, starting from the General Court's reference to Charter rights, rejected by the Advocate General who instead argued that the institutions must ensure compliance with 'the very short list of peremptory norms of international law (*jus cogens*) and *erga omnes* obligations',[93] followed by the Court of Justice's reliance on an *erga omnes* obligation, the right to self-determination, as a crucial determinative factor in its interpretation of the territorial scope of an EU external agreement. The move is significant because whereas the Charter is part of EU primary law, the precise legal effect of a specific norm of international law within the EU legal order will be a matter for determination by the Court itself.

In *Front Polisario*, a conflict was avoided since the Court was able to interpret the EU's agreement in conformity with a higher norm of international law (*jus cogens*).[94] The judgment in *Western Sahara* is explicit that failure to comply with international law may be a ground of illegality of the EU act concluding an international agreement:

> the European Union is bound, in accordance with settled case-law, when exercising its powers, to observe international law in its entirety, including not only the rules and principles of general and customary international law, but also the provisions of international conventions that are binding on it...

35; Eeckhout, 'Opinion 2/13 on EU Accession to the ECHR and Judicial Dialogue—Autonomy or Autarky?', 38 *Fordham International Law Journal* (2015) 955.

[89] Case 11/70, *Internationale Handelsgesellschaft* (ECLI:EU:C:1970:114), para. 4, and Case C-402/05 P and C-415/05 P, *Kadi and Al Barakaat International Foundation v. Council and Commission* (ECLI:EU:C:2008:461), paras 281–285.

[90] *Opinion 2/13*, note 1, para. 170 (emphasis added); cf. Case 11/70, *Internationale Handelsgesellschaft*, note 89, para. 4.

[91] Art. 6(1) and (3) TEU; Art. 52(3) Charter of Fundamental Rights.

[92] The Court's insistence that 'the Member States have, by reason of their membership of the EU, accepted that relations between them as regards the matters covered by the transfer of powers from the Member States to the EU are governed by EU law to the exclusion, if EU law so requires, of any other law' (*Opinion 2/13*, note 1, para. 193), recalls its early ruling that as between the Member States the EU Treaties have superseded the GATT (Case 10/61, *Commission v. Italy* (ECLI:EU:C:1962:2)).

[93] Including '"the outlawing of acts of aggression, and of genocide, [and] the *principles and rules concerning the basic rights of the human person*, including protection from slavery and racial discrimination" and the right to self-determination'. Case C-104/16 P, *Council v. Front Polisario*, Opinion of AG Wathelet (ECLI:EU:C:2016:677), para. 259 (emphasis in original, footnotes omitted).

[94] Cannizzaro, note 81, at 579–580.

Consequently, the Court has jurisdiction, both in the context of an action for annulment and in that of a request for a preliminary ruling to assess whether an international agreement concluded by the European Union is compatible with the Treaties ... and with the rules of international law which, in accordance with the Treaties, are binding on the Union.[95]

This apparently straightforward summary of the relation between EU law and international law nonetheless reveals the complexity of the hierarchy of norms both within and between the two legal systems. In the first paragraph quoted above, the implications of Article 216(2) TFEU are spelled out; international agreements concluded by the EU are binding on the institutions in the exercise of their powers (including the enactment of legislation), and this superiority of international law over secondary EU law is extended to the rules and principles of general and customary international law. The second paragraph then draws conclusions from the fact that, as has long been recognized, 'international agreements concluded by the European Union pursuant to the provisions of the Treaties constitute, as far as the Union is concerned, acts of the institutions of the European Union'.[96] As such, they must comply with EU primary law, including the EU Treaties and the Charter of Fundamental Rights, and the Court here also refers to 'the rules of international law which, in accordance with the Treaties, are binding on the Union'. The latter would include peremptory norms of general international law (*jus cogens*).[97] By interpreting the agreements at issue in *Front Polisario* and *Western Sahara* in conformity with *jus cogens*, the Court avoided the possible invalidity of the concluding decision.[98] And since the validity of the Council decision concluding the agreements was not at issue the Court also avoided the need to address the question whether the relevant rules of international law meet the criteria it has developed when assessing the validity of Union acts in the light of international treaties and customary international law.[99]

In the decade since *Kadi I*, augmented by explicit commitments in the Lisbon Treaty, we have begun to see the working out in EU external relations law of what a commitment to constitutional and international fundamental rights legality entails. The need for substantive compliance has been asserted; a failure to comply with constitutional fundamental rights as expressed in the Charter has resulted in a declaration of incompatibility of a projected international agreement;[100] and the Court has applied a strong principle of conforming interpretation to ensure that existing

[95] Case C-266/16, *Western Sahara Campaign UK* (ECLI:EU:C:2018:118), paras 47–48. The Court references Case C-286/90, *Poulsen and Diva Navigation* (ECLI:EU:C:1992:453), para. 9; Case C-402/05 P and C-415/05 P, *Kadi and Al Barakaat International Foundation v. Council and Commission* (ECLI:EU:C:2008:461), para. 291; and *Air Transport Association of America*, note 29, paras 101 and 123.

[96] Case C-266/16, *Western Sahara Campaign UK* (ECLI:EU:C:2018:118), para. 45, citing Case C-162/96, *Racke* (ECLI:EU:C:1998:293), para. 41; and Case C-386/08, *Brita* (ECLI:EU:C:2010:91), para. 39.

[97] A treaty is void as a matter of international law if it conflicts with a peremptory norm of general international law: Vienna Convention on the Law of Treaties, Art. 53.

[98] Cannizzaro, note 81, at 584.

[99] See, e.g., *Air Transport Association of America*, note 29, paras 51–55 with respect to international treaties, and para. 107 with respect to customary international law.

[100] *Opinion 1/15*, note 32.

agreements are applied in conformity with binding international law norms. Some procedural principles are also starting to emerge, guiding the policy-making process even in fields of external action where traditionally the institutions have the widest discretion. Certainly not all questions have been answered: the precise nature of the procedural obligation, the conditions under which the validity of EU acts may be impugned on grounds of non-compliance with international law, the extent to which these conditions apply in cases involving peremptory norms of general international law, and the scope of application of Charter rights in relation to external action, might each be questioned.

Section 2.C will turn to one specific example—the abolition of the death penalty—to take a closer look at how 'upholding and promoting' fundamental rights becomes a practical part of EU external action. In particular, two questions will be addressed: what role is played by law? And to what extent does the promotion of human rights in EU external policy represent the promotion of the EU's own vision of human rights on the EU's own terms?

C. The Abolition of the Death Penalty

1. The Policy Context

Article 2 of the EU Charter of Fundamental Rights affirms the right to life and outlaws the death penalty. This might seem superfluous within the EU legal order given that all EU Member States are party to Protocol 13 ECHR which provides for the complete abolition of the death penalty. However, it provides a normative basis both for requiring candidates for EU membership to abolish the death penalty and for the EU's campaign for its more general abolition. The EU Strategic Framework on Human Rights and Democracy of 2012 includes the campaign against the death penalty among the EU's priorities.[101] The Guidelines on the Death Penalty, originally adopted in 1998 as the EU's first set of Human Rights Guidelines and most recently revised in 2013,[102] state that the EU objectives are 'to work towards universal abolition of the death penalty as a strongly held policy agreed by all EU Member States', to advocate for a moratorium on its use (with a view to eventual abolition), and to seek reductions in the number and type of offences for which it is applied. The EU also supports the UN's minimum standards for the imposition of the death penalty, including rights to a fair trial, right of appeal, the prohibition of the death penalty on minors and the insane, and the prohibition of public executions.[103]

[101] 'The death penalty and torture constitute serious violations of human rights and human dignity. Encouraged by the growing momentum towards abolition of the death penalty worldwide, the EU will continue its long-standing campaign against the death penalty. The EU will continue to campaign vigorously against torture and cruel, inhuman and degrading treatment.' EU Strategic Framework, note 33, at 7.

[102] 'EU demarches on the issue of the death penalty—Declaration', in Conclusions of the General Affairs Council, 29 June 1998; EU Guidelines on the Death Penalty, 12 April 2013, Council doc. 8416/13.

[103] United Nations Economic and Social Council Safeguards Guaranteeing Protection of Rights of those Facing the Death Penalty, ECOSOC Res. 1996/15, UN Doc E/CN.15/1996/15 (1996).

The EU's campaign against the death penalty has been carried out at both bilateral and multilateral levels. At the multilateral level, the EU is seeking to secure universal standards with respect to the death penalty and its eventual universal abolition. Since 1999 the EU has regularly proposed Resolutions in the UN General Assembly calling for a moratorium on the use of the death penalty, Resolution 62/149 eventually being adopted in December 2007,[104] and Resolution 67/176 in 2012.[105] Initiatives include declarations and *démarches* on the death penalty in international fora, as well as *démarches* in specific cases where the use of the death penalty violates international commitments or the minimum standards. As well as issuing public statements calling for adherence to these minimum standards in specific cases, the EU has filed *amicus curiae* briefs in two US Supreme Court appeals against the death penalty in cases involving juveniles and offenders with intellectual disability.[106] Bilaterally, the EU includes the death penalty in its regular political dialogue with third countries.[107] The EU also funds various activities, especially NGOs campaigning for abolition, through the European Instrument for Democracy and Human Rights.[108] The Human Rights Action Plan for 2015–2019 includes actions against the death penalty, adding to the types of advocacy already mentioned a focus on the EU's own actions: the need to 'mainstream safeguards against death penalty, torture and ill-treatment in EU activities, including in counter-terrorism and in crisis management'.[109] Some examples of these safeguards are given in the following paragraphs.

2. *Legal Norms Addressing the Death Penalty in Third Countries*

Although advocacy and diplomatic *démarches* form an important part of the EU's policy on the death penalty, it is also operationalized through specific legal instruments, involving different fields of EU external action. In other words, this policy is

[104] UNGA Resolution 62/149 on a Moratorium on the use of the death penalty, 18 December 2007, reaffirmed the following year in Resolution 63/168. In its 2008 Guidelines on the Death Penalty (Council doc. 10015/08) the EU says that '[t]he European Union actively participated in the cross-regional alliance which successfully led and guided this initiative through the General Assembly and all EU partners co-sponsored this initiative'.

[105] UNGA Resolution 67/176 on a Moratorium on the use of the death penalty, 20 December 2012, A/RES/67/176.

[106] US Supreme Court, *Atkins v. Virginia*, 536 US 304 (2002), in relation to an offender with intellectual disability; US Supreme Court, *Roper v. Simmons*, 2004 WL 1619203 (US), in relation to juvenile offenders; see further Hoffmeister, note 38, at 115–117.

[107] E.g., the EU-Egypt Action Plan includes under the head of 'enhanced political dialogue and reform', not only dialogue on the death penalty but a commitment to ensure the possibility of legal recourse against the death sentences in all courts 'in accordance with the UN Safeguards guaranteeing protection of the rights of those facing the death penalty' (OJ 2008 L 230/19, at para. 2.1.1(b)).

[108] Regulation 235/2014 of 11 March 2014 establishing a financing instrument for democracy and human rights worldwide, OJ 2014 L 77/85. Art. 2(1)(b)(i) of this financial instrument includes the death penalty among its explicit human rights objectives: '. . . abolition of the death penalty and the establishment of moratoria with a view to its abolition and, where the death penalty still exists, advocacy for its abolition and the observance of international minimum standards'.

[109] Action Plan on Human Rights and Democracy (2015–2019), 'Keeping Human Rights at the Heart of the EU Agenda', Joint Communication from the Commission and the High Representative, 28 April 2015, JOIN (2015) 16 final, point 15.

implemented not only through the human rights financial instrument already mentioned, but also impacts EU trade policy, justice and home affairs and even the CFSP.

(a) Trade Policy: Export Controls

The EU prohibits the export and import of 'goods which have no practical use other than for the purpose of capital punishment or for the purpose of torture and other cruel, inhuman or degrading treatment or punishment', including for example electric chairs, automatic drug-injection apparatus and chemicals for lethal injections.[110] The export and import of other goods which could be used for these purposes requires authorization. The EU Regulation refers to Article 2 of the Charter of Fundamental Rights, but it also mentions in its preamble Article 5 of the Universal Declaration of Human Rights, Article 7 of the International Covenant on Civil and Political Rights and Article 3 of the ECHR as well as the UN Convention against Torture and the UN Standard Minimum Rules for the Treatment of Prisoners.

(b) Justice and Home Affairs: Prohibition on Extradition

The EU Charter of Fundamental Rights requires extradition of a suspect to a requesting jurisdiction to be blocked if there is a real risk that that person may be subject to the death penalty:

> No one may be removed, expelled or extradited to a State where there is a serious risk that he or she would be subjected to the death penalty, torture or other inhuman or degrading treatment or punishment.[111]

This provision has been implemented in the extradition treaty between the US and the EU, which contains a clause permitting the requested state to make non-application of the death penalty a condition of extradition; the request for extradition may be denied if the requesting state does not accept the condition.[112]

(c) CFSP: Incorporating Human Rights Standards in EU Agreements

As mentioned earlier, the current Human Rights Action Plan for 2015–2019 expressly refers to the need to include safeguards against the death penalty in EU activities, including within the CFSP. An example of this can be seen in the agreements the EU has made with Mauritius and other third countries in the context of its military mission 'Atalanta', a Common Security and Defence Policy naval mission designed to contribute to the deterrence, prevention and repression of piracy off the coast of Somalia.[113] The UN Security Council resolution to which the EU's mission is a response calls for cooperation between states in the prosecution of responsible

[110] Council Regulation 1236/2005 of 27 June 2005 concerning trade in certain goods which could be used for capital punishment, torture or other cruel, inhuman or degrading treatment or punishment, OJ 2005 L 200/1.

[111] Art. 19(2) Charter of Fundamental Rights.

[112] Agreement on extradition between the United States and the EU, OJ 2003 L 181/27, Art. 13.

[113] EU NAVFOR Somalia—Operation Atalanta, Council Joint Action 2008/851/CFSP, OJ 2008 L 301/33. Piracy is defined by Art. 101 of the UN Convention on the Law of the Sea.

persons 'consistent with applicable international law including international human rights law',[114] and the EU's Joint Action establishing the mission provides that persons detained who are suspected of piracy may be transferred to another state for prosecution, if that state consents, and provided that 'the conditions for the transfer have been agreed with that third State in a manner consistent with relevant international law, notably international law on human rights, in order to guarantee in particular that no one shall be subjected to the death penalty, to torture or to any cruel, inhuman or degrading treatment'.[115] As a result the EU has entered into several agreements with states in the region which are prepared to accept suspected pirates detained for prosecution.[116] The Preamble to the Agreement with Mauritius references international human rights instruments (including the International Covenant on Civil and Political Rights and the Convention against Torture); Article 4 establishes general due process standards for the detention and trial of suspected pirates, and Article 5 prohibits the death penalty:

> No transferred person shall, in accordance with Mauritius Abolition of Death Penalty Act, be charged with an offence that carries the death penalty, be sentenced to death or be the subject of an application of the death penalty.[117]

Similar provisions are included in the agreements concluded by the EU with third countries that are contributing to Operation Atalanta.[118]

The agreement between the EU and the Central African Republic (CAR) on the transfer to the CAR of persons detained by the EU military operation EUFOR RCA also provides that in cases where a transferred person is at risk of the death penalty 'such a penalty shall neither be sought, imposed nor carried out by the CAR with respect to that person', and if such a person is transferred to a third party the CAR shall ensure that the death penalty 'shall not be sought, imposed or carried out with respect to that person'.[119]

The campaign against the death penalty thus harnesses a wide range of external activities, from political advocacy and diplomatic pressure to legally binding export controls and restrictions on extradition. In the agreements on the transfer of

[114] UN Security Council Resolution 1816 (2008).

[115] Council Joint Action 2008/851/CFSP, Art. 12(3).

[116] Agreements have been concluded with Mauritius, Kenya, Seychelles, Tanzania and the Central African Republic. See further Bosse-Platière, 'Le volet judiciaire de la lutte contre la piraterie maritime en Somalie: les accords de transferts conclus par l'Union européenne avec les États tiers', in *Les différentes facettes du concept juridique de sécurité Mélanges en l'honneur de Pierre-André Lecocq* (2011).

[117] Agreement between the European Union and the Republic of Mauritius on the conditions of transfer of suspected pirates and associated seized property from the European Union-led naval force to the Republic of Mauritius and on the conditions of suspected pirates after transfer, concluded by Council Decision 2011/640/CFSP, OJ 2011 L 254/1.

[118] See, e.g., Agreement between the European Union and Montenegro on the participation of Montenegro in the European Union military operation to contribute to the deterrence, prevention and repression of acts of piracy and armed robbery off the Somali coast (Operation Atalanta) OJ 2010 L 88/3, Annex, Art. 4.

[119] Agreement between the European Union and the Central African Republic concerning detailed arrangements for the transfer to the Central African Republic of persons detained by the European Union military operation (EUFOR RCA) in the course of carrying out its mandate, and concerning the guarantees applicable to such persons, OJ 2014 L 251/3.

suspected persons, the EU seeks to impose constraints on the law enforcement and death penalty policies of third countries. As well as providing policy tools, the law also provides the normative basis for EU policy. It finds its justification in provisions of the EU Charter, which themselves reflect regional and international norms, and the EU is engaged in both promoting the universal acceptance of those international norms, and in advocating the UN-sponsored minimum standards. We have here, therefore, an example of the interaction between internal and external sources of human rights law, and the use by the EU of legal instruments both to ensure its own compliance and to promote international legal norms.

D. Conclusions

The activities examined in this section appear to be normative more than interest-driven. But, as discussed earlier, the EU sees a normative agenda (the global promotion of human rights) as in its interest and also part of its self-identification as an international actor: in the eyes of the EU, successes in its death penalty campaign demonstrate its effectiveness and influence.

It is now accepted by the EU political institutions, the Ombudsman and the Court of Justice that fundamental rights compliance is a condition of legality of EU external action, although how that obligation should be put into practice is still in question. In *Opinion 1/15* the Court for the first time assessed in detail the provisions of a projected international agreement from the point of view of compliance with the EU's Charter of Fundamental Rights, giving it effect as part of EU primary law. It is an important milestone, but note that the agreement fell within the scope of application of EU secondary legislation on data protection (a Charter right), and the agreement was itself clearly an attempt (albeit inadequate) to ensure fundamental rights compliance. The trade and fisheries agreements at issue in the *Polisario Front* and *Western Sahara* cases lack this specific link to Charter-based fundamental rights. Although the General Court based itself on the Charter, the Court of Justice referred to peremptory norms of international law, including the right to self-determination. It regarded compliance with an international *erga omnes* obligation as determinative in its interpretation of an EU international agreement.

Although the General Court's judgment was not upheld on appeal, the Court of Justice did not repudiate the suggestion that the EU should at least investigate the human rights impact *in third countries* of its external actions, including its trade policy, and this is indeed the position espoused by the Ombudsman, seeing it as a matter of good administration. The reaction to both the General Court and Court of Justice judgments in *Polisario Front* demonstrates that values and interests do not always pull in the same direction.[120] The Council and Commission will need to

[120] As a response to the General Court ruling, Morocco suspended diplomatic relations with the EU (later resumed once the Council appealed the judgment). The CJEU ruling in December 2016 was hailed as both a defeat and a victory for the Front Polisario: a defeat in that the challenge to the decision concluding the agreement was ultimately unsuccessful but a victory in that the ruling was seen as a blow to Morocco's claim of sovereignty over Western Sahara and thus a pyrrhic victory for Morocco (see, e.g., Gehring, 'EU Law Analysis', 23 December 2016, available at http://eulawanalysis.blogspot.com/2016/12/eumorocco-relations-and-western-sahara.html; A. Eriksson, *EU Observer*, 23 December

ensure that the EU's policy of non-recognition of the Moroccan claim to Western Sahara, based on the right of self-determination, is given effect in the implementation of its agreements with Morocco. In this way, international norms impact not only the validity and interpretation but also the application of EU agreements.

The abolition of the death penalty provides an example of the EU 'promoting and upholding' human rights, using a variety of soft and hard instruments. Although some of the EU's action is political rather than legal (dialogues, *démarches*), law plays a number of roles here: as a constraint on EU external policy-making, shaping its political action (the EU's Charter commitment to prohibition of the death penalty shapes its UN priorities, its export policy, and the terms of its agreements with third countries); as an instrument (the use of treaties and financial and trade instruments, as well as the use of international legal norms as reference points); and as an objective (the furtherance of international human rights law).

And here the complex interrelationship between EU values, international law and the 'external reach' of EU law can also be seen, making it impossible to give a simple answer to the question: whose norms is the EU promoting? The constraint that operates not only to shape policy but even as a condition of legality of EU acts is derived from EU constitutional law, in particular the Charter of Fundamental Rights. The sources of those EU constitutional norms of course include broader European and international human rights law and these are the sources referred to by the EU in its external policy on the death penalty, in its own legislation as well as in its Guidelines and international agreements; it promotes the ratification and implementation of these international instruments. The EU is thus using its own legal (external relations) power to promote international legal norms. One dimension of the 'external reach of EU law' is the EU's policy of seeking to extend to third countries its own acceptance of the legal constraints imposed by international human rights law.

3. The EU as an Integration Project: 'Integration through Law' as an External Enterprise

Integration has been the basis of the EU's own development (and enlargement) and in a real sense the EU sees progress in its relations with third states—and especially with its neighbours—as progress in integration.[121] And the EU's mode of integration, externally as well as internally, is through law; the law of integration mediates between the internal and the external, extending the reach of the EU *acquis* through international agreements while maintaining the distinction between the two. This 'integration through law' is one of the most powerful tools in the EU's external relations toolbox and is used to develop close relations with neighbours, reflecting a mix

2016, available at https://euobserver.com/foreign/136401). (All website references in this chapter were last visited on 6 February 2019.)

[121] Further on this, see Cremona, 'Enlargement as Foreign Policy—A Research Agenda', in H. A. Ikonomou, A. Andry and R. Byberg (eds), *European Enlargement across Rounds and Beyond Borders* (2017).

of values and interests and even creating a new legal space. And yet the EU's legal identity also ensures that the boundary between inside and outside remains distinct. Non-members may become almost-members (and members may become non-members) but there are legal constraints on the integration that the EU can embrace in its international relationships, and the law calibrates these distances.

Two examples, concluded 20 years apart and in very different contexts, will be compared: the European Economic Area (EEA) Agreement of 1994 and the Association Agreement with Ukraine concluded in 2014. Neither of these agreements envisages an 'accession track' for the partner countries; they are not explicitly designed to prepare countries for accession to the EU, but rather to provide an advanced form of 'integration without membership'. They thus provide important test cases of the EU's ability to create successful integration-based relations with its regional neighbours.[122] The legal regimes they create are derived from the international agreements on which they are based: this is not a case of extraterritorial application of the EU *acquis*. It is, instead, the creation of a new legal relation or *acquis*—for example 'EEA law'—which to some extent reflects EU law, and which will be implemented through the domestic legal orders of the contracting parties. Against the background of this convergence of norms between the partner countries and the EU, the parties agree to reciprocal market integration, the degree of integration reflecting the degree of norm convergence. To some extent the legal techniques used in the EEA and Ukraine agreements are similar, but the two agreements pose different questions when considering what exactly it means to 'extend the *acquis*' to third countries and the flexibility of the EU's external 'law of integration'.

A. Almost—but not quite—Internal: The European Economic Area

The EEA Agreement was negotiated with seven EFTA states (Austria, Finland, Iceland, Liechtenstein, Norway, Sweden and Switzerland) in the early 1990s.[123] The agreement was a response to the EFTA states' concern over the future of their trading relations with the EU (then EC) in the light of the EU's ambitious single market programme, launched in 1986. The EEA was designed to provide an advanced form of integration into the single market, without membership of the EU, without participation in external policy (such as external trade policy), and without the closer forms of political and economic integration that were to follow (including EU citizenship, the AFSJ and of course Economic and Monetary Union).

At present the non-EU (EFTA) parties to the EEA are Iceland, Lichtenstein and Norway.[124] The impetus behind the EEA is the desire of a number of close neighbours to take part in EU economic integration while remaining outside the EU itself. But the EEA itself may be said to possess an integration momentum: although

[122] Cf. Art. 8 TEU, which calls upon the EU to 'develop a special relationship with neighbouring countries, aiming to establish an area of prosperity and good neighbourliness, founded on the values of the Union and characterised by close and peaceful relations based on cooperation'.

[123] Agreement on the European Economic Area, OJ 1994 L 1/3.

[124] Switzerland decided not to conclude the EEA and instead has a series of bilateral agreements with the EU. Austria, Finland and Sweden joined the EU.

for a few states the compromise reflects established political preferences, what was originally seen as a long-term alternative became for several a route to EU membership. Much has been written about the EEA's history and legal character.[125] This chapter will focus on the nature of the integration offered by the EEA and the challenges it poses to the boundary between internal and external in EU law.

The EEA is based on the twin principles of homogeneity and dynamism.[126] Homogeneity means that the EEA and its Annexes 'mirror' provisions of primary and secondary EU law (notably on the four freedoms). The homogeneity of the EEA is selective: it does not encompass the whole of the EU *acquis*. And some non-EEA integration, including Schengen, is covered by side agreements, thereby helping to maintain a high degree of homogeneity in connected aspects of EEA law, such as the free movement of persons. Dynamism refers to the continuous updating of the Annexes to the EEA so that they continue to 'track' developments in EU secondary law. The Annexes include secondary legislation which, defined in terms of the EEA *acquis*, is 'EEA relevant'. The procedure for amending the Annexes is political, combining a joint EFTA/EU committee structure and national decision-making, and can be protracted; it can be difficult in practice to agree on the boundaries of what is 'EEA relevant'.[127] In theory, if the Joint Committee does not take a decision to adopt a specific amendment, the Annex as a whole—and thereby the EEA rules in this sector—can be suspended,[128] but this has never (so far) been triggered.

According to Article 6 EEA Agreement the provisions of the EEA are to be interpreted in conformity with the rulings of the EU Court of Justice prior to the signature of the agreement. Subsequent case law is to be 'kept under review' by the Joint Committee[129] and provision is made for exchanges of information between the EFTA and EU Courts '[i]n order to ensure as uniform an interpretation as possible of this Agreement'.[130] In addition, the EFTA Agreement establishing the EFTA Court and Surveillance Authority requires the EFTA Court to take 'due account' of 'relevant rulings' of the EU Court of Justice.[131] The picture which emerges is of an EEA legal order which is distinct from EU law but which shares certain of its characteristics. Central to that EEA legal order is the objective of ensuring equality of treatment of individuals and economic operators throughout the EEA.[132] Let us look at a couple of examples from the EFTA Court and the EU Court of Justice.

[125] See, e.g., Haukeland Fredriksen and Franklin, 'Of Pragmatism and Principles: The EEA Agreement 20 Years On', 52 *Common Market Law Review* (2015) 629; Rye, 'Integration from the Outside: The EC and EFTA from 1960 to the 1995 Enlargement', in H. A. Ikonomou, A. Andry and R. Byberg (eds), *European Enlargement across Rounds and Beyond Borders* (2017).

[126] Preamble to EEA Agreement, note 123, 4th recital.

[127] Haukeland Fredriksen and Franklin (note 125, at 658) give the example of Regulation 1007/2009 on trade in seal products, which in 2015 had still not been included in the EEA Annexes.

[128] Art. 102(5) EEA, note 123.

[129] Art. 105 EEA, note 123; in deference to the concerns of the CJEU expressed in *Opinion 1/91*, Protocol 48 provides that 'Decisions taken by the EEA Joint Committee under Articles 105 and 111 may not affect the case-law of the Court of Justice of the European Communities'.

[130] Art. 106 EEA, note 123.

[131] Art. 3(2) Agreement on the EFTA Court, available at http://www.eftacourt.int/the-court/jurisdiction-organisation/surveillance-and-court-agreement/.

[132] Cf. the reference in its preamble to the EEA being established on 'the basis of equality and reciprocity and of an overall balance of benefits, rights and obligations for the Contracting Parties'.

The EFTA Court's approach to treaty interpretation has been influenced by the need, where possible, to ensure equality of rights between EU and EFTA nationals. In *Sveinbjörnsdóttir*, for example, the EFTA Court held that the doctrine of state liability (the *Francovich* doctrine[133]) applies in the EEA context.[134] The EFTA Court affirmed both the existence of an EEA legal order—'the EEA Agreement is an international treaty *sui generis* which contains a distinct legal order of its own'[135]—and the importance of equality of rights in that order, linked to the homogeneity objective:

> The Court finds that the homogeneity objective and the objective of establishing the right of individuals and economic operators to equal treatment and equal opportunities are so strongly expressed in the EEA Agreement that the EFTA States must be obliged to provide for compensation for loss and damage caused to an individual by incorrect implementation of a directive.[136]

Here is an example of the EFTA Court developing its own version of one of the 'unwritten principles' of EU constitutional law. Even more striking, perhaps, is the way in which the EFTA Court has responded to changes in EU primary law, which have not been reflected in amendments to the EEA. The most important of these changes for the EEA are the Charter of Fundamental Rights and the creation of EU citizenship—especially given the latter's close connection with free movement of persons. When Directive 2004/38 (the so-called 'citizen's directive') was incorporated into the EEA Annexes, the Joint Committee adopted a declaration affirming that EU citizenship 'has no equivalent' in the EEA. This has posed a challenge to the EFTA Court in its attempts to interpret the directive for the EEA in the light of EU case law, and the EFTA Court has shown remarkable ingenuity in managing to maintain homogeneity.[137] For example, the EFTA Court held in *Gunnarsson* that Article 7 of Directive 2004/38 (on the right of residence) can be interpreted to impose obligations on a home state,[138] despite the fact that in similar cases the EU Court of Justice has applied the EU Treaty provisions on citizenship—Articles 18 and 21 TFEU, which of course do not exist in the EEA Agreement—rather than the directive.[139] *Gunnarsson* demonstrates the distinction between homogeneous interpretation of a specific piece of legislation (Directive 2004/38) and homogeneity of result, in terms of individual rights. In *Gunnarsson* the EFTA Court prefers the latter at the cost of the former.

What about the EU Court of Justice? A recent judgment strikingly illustrates the degree to which the EEA creates an integrated legal space as well as echoing the EFTA Court's concern for equality of treatment. Tellingly, it concerns the EU institutional structures within which the EEA operates. In *United Kingdom v.*

[133] Case C-6/90 and 9/90, *Francovich and Bonifaci* (ECLI:EU:C:1991:428).

[134] Case E-09/97, *Sveinbjörnsdóttir v. Iceland* [1998] EFTA Ct Rep 95.

[135] *Ibid.*, para. 59. [136] *Ibid.*, para. 60.

[137] See further Fløistad, 'Associated, Adapted and (almost) Assimilated: The European Economic Area Agreement in a revised EU constitutional framework for welfare services' (2016) (PhD thesis on file at the EUI, Florence).

[138] Case E-26/13, *Gunnarsson* [2014] EFTA Ct Rep 254, paras 77–81.

[139] E.g., Case C-224/02, *Pusa* (ECLI:EU:C:2004:273).

Council,[140] the Court had to decide the correct legal basis in the EU Treaties for a Council decision on the position to be taken by the EU within the EEA Joint Committee concerning an amendment to one of the EEA Annexes, bringing it into line with amended EU legislation on coordination of social security for migrant workers. The possibilities were Article 79(2)(b) TFEU (which provides for the adoption of measures defining 'the rights of third-country nationals residing legally in a Member State'), suggested by the UK; and Article 48 TFEU (on social security for migrant EU workers), which was the legal basis actually proposed by the Commission and adopted by the Council—and challenged by the UK. Alternatively, Article 217 TFEU (the legal basis for Association Agreements, of which the EEA Agreement is one) was suggested by Advocate General Kokott.

Given that the EEA Agreement is an external agreement, one might have imagined that either Article 217 TFEU or Article 79(2)(b) TFEU would be appropriate. Indeed, Article 79(2)(b) TFEU is the basis for Regulation 1231/2010, which extends EU social security Regulations to third country nationals legally resident within the EU.[141] However, the Court disagreed. It explicitly contrasted the EU's immigration policy, of which Article 79 TFEU forms part, with the EEA Agreement. In contrast to Article 79, the EEA Agreement is based on reciprocity and equality of treatment: the inclusion of the new social security regulations in the EEA Annex would establish a social security regime not only for EFTA nationals in the EU but also for EU nationals in the EFTA state parties—thus throughout the EEA legal space.

This equality of treatment throughout the EEA would also be jeopardized were Article 79 to be used since this provision falls within the opt-out from the AFSJ established for the UK and Ireland by Protocol 21 and Denmark by Protocol 22. Were the UK and/or Ireland to opt out of the EFTA decision, this (the Court said) would 'undermine the realisation of the objectives pursued by that agreement' by giving rise to two parallel regimes for the coordination of social security.[142] This reasoning is striking given the fact that the UK (not Ireland) did in fact opt out of Regulation 1231/2010, which was based on Article 79(2)(b) TFEU. As a result the UK was able to opt out of the internal EU measure extending the social security regime to third country nationals within the EU but could not opt out of the decision taken in the EEA Joint Committee which would extend this regime throughout the EEA. The differentiation within the EU as regards the treatment of third country nationals represented by the UK and Irish opt-out is not reflected in the external EEA regime; on the contrary, the Court put emphasis on the commitment to homogeneity under the EEA.

Instead of Article 79(2)(b) TFEU, the Court found that Article 48 TFEU was the appropriate legal basis, despite the fact that it concerns the coordination of social security *within* the EU for the benefit of *EU nationals*. It argued that 'the law

[140] Case C-431/11, *United Kingdom v. Council* (ECLI:EU:C:2013:589).

[141] Regulation 1231/2010 of 24 November 2010 extending Regulation (EC) No 883/2004 and Regulation (EC) No 987/2009 to nationals of third countries who are not already covered by these Regulations solely on the ground of their nationality, OJ 2010 L 344/1.

[142] Case C-431/11, *United Kingdom v. Council* (ECLI:EU:C:2013:589), para. 65.

governing the EU internal market is to be extended as far as possible to the EEA, with the result that nationals of the EEA States concerned benefit from the free movement of persons under the same social conditions as EU citizens'.[143] So the Court rejected one externally oriented legal basis (Article 79(2)(b) TFEU) and did not refer to the other (Article 217 TFEU). Instead, it opted for the internal legal basis (Article 48 TFEU) despite its apparent personal and territorial limitations. In doing so it brackets together the EEA and internal policy:

> it is only in the sphere of the internal policies and actions of the European Union or of the external actions relating to third countries which can be placed on the same footing as Member States of the European Union... that Article 48 TFEU empowers the European Union to adopt measures in this area.[144]

This views the EEA as creating a reciprocity-based legal space, an extension of the internal market, rather than simply an export of EU law to third countries.[145] The Court's reference to the problem of the UK and Irish opt-out also follows this logic—this would not be simply a difference in treatment of third country nationals within the EU, which can be accommodated (cf. the opt-out to Regulation 1231/2010, already mentioned), but a disruption to the unity of the EEA (EU + EFTA) as a legal space.

There are, however, limits to this assimilation which make it clear that the EEA legal space is not the EU. Despite being (in the words of the Court itself) 'placed on the same footing as Member States', the EFTA parties to the EEA are *not* Member States and do not participate in the EU's decision-making institutions, although they may influence policy in a consultative capacity.[146] And the Court has maintained a distinction between the EEA Agreement and internal EU law. In the case in which it famously referred to the EC Treaty as the 'constitutional charter' of the Community, it insisted on a two-pillar institutional structure with an EFTA Court and Surveillance Authority separate from the European Commission and Court of Justice, as necessary to preserve the autonomy of EU law.[147] Despite the objective of homogeneity, the Court emphasized the separate nature of the EEA, with its own objectives and characteristics, and was clearly concerned that the attempt to mirror certain provisions of the EC Treaty in an external agreement with less ambitious integration objectives would have consequent effects on the autonomous development of EU law.

Likewise, from an EFTA perspective, EU law does not *as such* take effect in the EFTA states and the EEA does not require that its provisions, or the Annexes, have direct effect. The legal boundary remains clear, as does the institutional. The EFTA Surveillance Authority and EFTA Court are formally independent of the EU's institutions although in practice they follow the decisions of the European Commission

[143] *Ibid.*, para. 58.

[144] Case C-81/13, *United Kingdom v. Council* (ECLI:EU:C:2014:2449), para. 59, distinguishing the Association Agreement with Turkey.

[145] Rennuy and Van Elsuwege, 'Integration without Membership and the Dynamic Development of EU Law: *United Kingdom* v *Council (EEA)*', 51 *Common Market Law Review* (2014) 935, at 945.

[146] Arts 99–101 EEA, note 123.

[147] *Opinion 1/91* (ECLI:EU:C:1991:490), para. 21.

and Court of Justice closely.[148] The EEA was shaped deliberately to accommodate the EFTA states' concerns about sovereignty and the EU's own requirements of autonomy would not allow the legal boundary to shift in the sense of accepting an external input into law-making structures.

The essential distinction between membership and non-membership derives from the autonomy of EU law: law is used to calibrate the relationship, to establish both the degree of integration into the EU system, and its boundaries. Although the EEA appears as a form of 'partial membership', the EU institutions (including the Court) maintain control over the development of the law. The EEA demonstrates both integration as an aim of external policy realized through legal instruments, and the limits to that integration. The creation of EEA law is a delicate balance between the EU and the EFTA Courts and we should perhaps not be surprised to find that it is the EFTA Court which seeks to create homogeneity—or equality—of individual rights within the EEA legal space, whereas the position of the Court of Justice is more ambiguous. On the one hand we have seen the Court declaring that the EFTA parties are 'placed on the same footing' as EU Member States; on the other hand we are still in the realm of external relations; outsiders may become close to being insiders but the Court of Justice will ensure that the distinction between the two is maintained, incidentally protecting its own position as exclusive interpreter of EU law.[149]

B. Conditionality-based Integration: The Ukraine Association Agreement

In proposing 'integration through law' as a model of EU external policy we should bear in mind not only the different levels of (and limits to) the integration achieved but also that this integration may have different ultimate objectives. There is a clear contrast between the EFTA states and the states of the Eastern Partnership (EaP)/ European Neighbourhood Policy (ENP) (Ukraine, Georgia, Moldova), who have signed very far-reaching Association Agreements with the EU. Despite the limits to integration through the EEA just discussed, there was never any real doubt that those EFTA states that wished to take the next step would be able to accede to the EU; the same is certainly not true of Ukraine. But neither is the Ukraine Agreement presented as a static alternative to membership—as a *finalité* in its own right. Here, it might be significant that Article 217 TFEU (the basis for Association Agreements) was chosen as a legal basis, alongside Article 37 (CFSP) and there is no mention of Article 8 TEU. Association Agreements are open-ended in their potential; they have been used as pre-accession instruments, although of course they may have other objectives and have often been concluded with countries that are not eligible for, or do not want, EU membership (the EEA Agreement is also an Association Agreement). Article 8 TEU, on the other hand, may be said to envisage a specific end-goal or *finalité*: an area of prosperity and good neighbourliness distinct from membership of the Union.[150] Its place in the TEU underlines this, placed as it is among the 'common provisions' in Title I and not among the external relations provisions.

[148] See further Fløistad, note 137.

[149] Art. 344 TFEU.

[150] See note 122.

The decisions concluding the Ukraine Association Agreement (UAA) do not refer to Article 8 TEU, but in the agreement itself there are many references to integration. It speaks of 'gradual rapprochement' and 'increasingly close cooperation' between the EU and Ukraine; 'ever-closer integration', but with no explicit mention of membership of the EU.[151] In the Preamble the Parties confirm 'that the European Union acknowledges the European aspirations of Ukraine and welcomes its European choice' and affirm 'that this Agreement will not prejudice and leaves open future developments in EU-Ukraine relations'. An undefined future prospect is also held out in the Foreign Affairs Council Conclusions of 10 February 2014: 'The Council expresses its conviction that this Agreement does not constitute the final goal in EU-Ukraine cooperation.'[152] In addition, it has been pointed out that many phrases in the Preamble echo the Copenhagen accession criteria and even Article 49 TEU,[153] and more generally the ENP has borrowed and adapted methodologies and instruments developed by the EU for the Central and Eastern European enlargement.[154]

There is therefore a deliberate ambiguity here as to the final objective of the proposed integration process; on the one hand the relationship is not defined in terms of Article 8 (neighbourhood but not membership), but on the other hand—and unlike the Association Agreements with the states of the Western Balkans, for example[155]—accession is not established as a shared goal. This carries the risk of on the one hand creating false expectations, and on the other creating an image of an inherently absorptive model of integration.

The Association Agreement with Ukraine contains what is called a 'deep and comprehensive free trade agreement' (DCFTA) and requires a substantial degree of sectoral alignment to the EU *acquis*—but without offering free movement of persons. In the case of Ukraine, as with the EEA, law structures the relationship with the EU, not only in the Association Agreement itself, but also through the technique of legal integration, of approximation to the EU (legal) *acquis*. Legal integration draws Ukraine towards the EU (integration with the internal market) and the extension of the *acquis* certainly has an integration purpose. But the aim of integration is not the same as for the EEA, and there are important differences in the methodology.

[151] EU-Ukraine Association Agreement, OJ 2014 L 161/3.

[152] Council Conclusions on Ukraine, 10 February 2014, doc. 6264/14.

[153] Van der Loo, Van Elsuwege and Petrov, 'The EU-Ukraine Association Agreement: Assessment of an Innovative Legal Instrument' (2014), EUI Working Papers LAW 2014/09, at 10.

[154] See, e.g., Tulmets, 'Adapting the Experience of Enlargement to the Neighbourhood Policy: The ENP as a Substitute to Enlargement?', in P. Kratochvil (ed.), *The European Union and Its Neighbourhood: Policies, Problems and Priorities* (2006). Kelley, 'New Wine in Old Wineskins: Promoting Political Reforms through the New European Neighbourhood Policy', 44 *Journal of Common Market Studies* (2006) 29. Cremona, 'The European Neighbourhood Policy: More than a Partnership?', in M. Cremona (ed.), *Developments in EU External Relations Law* (2008).

[155] In June 2000 the European Council referred to the countries of the Western Balkans for the first time as 'potential candidates' for EU membership. The phrase appears in the preambles to the Stabilisation and Association Agreements and in the preamble to Regulation 231/2014 of 11 March 2014 establishing an Instrument for Pre-accession Assistance (IPA II) OJ 2014 L 77/11, recital 6. See, e.g., the Stabilisation and Association Agreement with Bosnia and Herzegovina, which recognizes in its preamble 'its status as a potential candidate for EU membership', OJ 2015 L 164/2.

A key aim is stated in Article 1 UAA: the use of integration to help Ukraine transition into a functioning market economy. This is the use of EU law as a model for modernization.[156] However, the UAA is also designed to serve EU interests in its neighbourhood, notably support for its foreign policy and security objectives. The Preamble to the UAA reflects clearly the political and economic interests of the EU, with references to an 'ever-closer convergence of positions on bilateral, regional and international issues of mutual interest' as well as the 'common values on which the European Union is built' (note that the values are 'common' but also specifically identified with the EU). As the EU has extended its own integration to cover the CFSP and the AFSJ, so these elements are included also in the UAA, going beyond the 'economic transition' purpose of the agreement. The comprehensive provisions on foreign policy cooperation include commitments from Ukraine to align itself to EU foreign policy, including on weapons of mass destruction and arms control, and to cooperate on migration, border management, counter-terrorism and organized crime—all manifestly serving the EU's interests. Giusti points to 'the risks of over-emphasizing the normative aspects (exporting values, principles and legislation) of the EU's actorness' which 'might lead to an underestimation of the power politics and geopolitical implications of certain external policies such as the EaP [Eastern Partnership]'.[157] She concludes that 'the EaP is also an interest-oriented policy although drawing from the normative heritage of the EU'.[158]

The political chapters of the UAA (including the CFSP) were signed by the EU in March 2014 while Ukraine was still not in a position to sign the agreement as a whole;[159] at the same time unilateral trade preferences were adopted by the EU as a transitional measure to bridge the gap before the full DCFTA could come into force. Once a new President had been elected the agreement as a whole was signed, in June 2014, most of it being subject to provisional application.[160] Provisional application was delayed until 1 January 2016 in order to allow space for a settlement between Ukraine and Russia.[161] But before coming into full force, the UAA as a mixed agreement needed to be ratified by all Member States. A referendum on ratification held by the Netherlands in 2015 was negative, and resulted in further delay before the agreement could come into full force.[162] The reasons for the Netherlands-induced delay are complex but, among others, reflect the ambiguity of the integration model

[156] M. Cremona and G. Meloni (eds), 'The European Neighbourhood Policy: A Framework for Modernisation?', EUI Working Paper 2007/21.

[157] Giusti, 'The EU's Transformative Power Challenged in Ukraine', 21 *European Foreign Affairs Review* (2016) 165, at 166.

[158] *Ibid*., at 176.

[159] Council Decision 2014/295/EU of 17 March 2014 on the signing, on behalf of the European Union, and provisional application of the Association Agreement between the European Union and the European Atomic Energy Community and their Member States, of the one part, and Ukraine, of the other part, as regards the Preamble, Article 1, and Titles I, II and VII thereof, OJ 2014 L 161/1.

[160] Two decisions were needed for signature on the EU side because of the UK opt-out, one of them dealing with a single provision: Art. 17 UAA, on the treatment of workers legally employed in the territory of the parties, the EU decision being based on Art. 79 TFEU (cf. the EEA case discussed earlier). Council Decision 2014/668/EU of 23 June 2014, OJ 2014 L 278/1; Council Decision 2014/669/EU of 23 June 2014, OJ 2014 L 278/6.

[161] Council Decision 2014/691/EU of 29 September 2014, OJ 2014 L 289/1.

[162] The agreement finally came into force on 1 September 2017; see OJ 2017 L 193/1.

already mentioned.[163] This political ambiguity is not in itself negative; it allows for an openness on both sides, a flexibility as to the ultimate relationship which will of course depend on many factors, including the conditionality which is a feature of the agreement discussed later. But it sits somewhat uneasily with the regime of legal integration established by the UAA.

Like the EEA, the UAA uses Annexes to codify the EU *acquis* covered by the agreement, but with significant differences. The Annexes themselves are based on the EU *acquis*, but the EU-Ukraine Association Agenda, which establishes the immediate priorities, also contains many references to international instruments and standards.[164] This is in line with the 'modernisation' or 'transition' objective of the UAA, as well as reflecting the EU's interest in promoting multilateral governance instruments.[165] The Association Council (a joint institution) may take decisions to amend the Annexes so as to keep pace with the EU *acquis*, building in a degree of dynamism.[166] The Annexes vary considerably in the level of detail they contain; some give full lists of legislation with timetables for implementation; others are much less specific.

An important feature of the UAA integration methodology is its use of conditionality, as its Preamble recognizes:

> the political association and economic integration of Ukraine with the European Union will depend on progress in the implementation of this Agreement as well as Ukraine's track record in ensuring respect for common values, and progress in achieving convergence with the EU in political, economic and legal areas.[167]

Conditionality is thus integral to the agreement (and the ENP of which the agreement forms a part) and provides a structure for its implementation and the operation of the DCFTA in particular. It takes two different forms.

First, there is the standard 'common values' conditionality, mentioned in the preambular paragraph just quoted and reflected in Articles 2 and 3 UAA. Article 2

[163] As do the agreed formulae for resolving the impasse. A Decision of the Heads of State or Government of the 28 Member States of the European Union, meeting within the European Council, on the Association Agreement was adopted on 15 December 2016. This states that 'as a common understanding' the UAA while 'aiming to establish a close and lasting relationship between the parties to the Agreement based on common values... does not confer on Ukraine the status of a candidate country for accession to the Union, nor does it constitute a commitment to confer such status to Ukraine in the future'. While the UAA establishes security cooperation, it 'does not contain an obligation for the Union or its Member States to provide collective security guarantees or other military aid or assistance to Ukraine'. And while the UAA objectives include 'enhancing the mobility of citizens', the Agreement 'does not grant to Ukrainian nationals or Union citizens, respectively, the right to reside and work freely within the territory of the Member States or Ukraine'. According to para. 24 of the European Council Conclusions, the Decision has a somewhat odd status given that it purports simply to explain what the agreement does and does not do: 'The European Council notes that the Decision... is legally binding on the 28 Member States of the European Union, and may be amended or repealed only by common accord of their Heads of State or Government. It will take effect once the Kingdom of the Netherlands has ratified the agreement and the Union has concluded it. Should this not be the case, the Decision will cease to exist.'

[164] EU-Ukraine Association Agenda, endorsed by the EU-Ukraine Association Council 16 March 2015, Council doc, St6978/15

[165] See further section 4.

[166] Art. 463 UAA, note 151.

[167] Preamble UAA, note 151.

is an 'essential elements' clause, referring to 'democratic principles, human rights and fundamental freedoms' as well as to the ECHR and other international human rights instruments.[168] More unusually, and an indication of the specific political context in which the agreement was signed, reference is also made to 'the principles of sovereignty and territorial integrity, inviolability of borders and independence, as well as countering the proliferation of weapons of mass destruction' as essential elements of the agreement. The essential elements clause is accompanied by a procedural provision for 'appropriate measures', including suspension, in case of violation.[169] In addition, Article 3 UAA lists a number of principles as 'enhancing' and 'underpinning' the relationship, but without attaching any specific sanction to their breach. These include the principles of a free market economy, the rule of law, good governance, the fight against corruption, transnational organized crime and terrorism, the promotion of sustainable development and effective multilateralism. Again, a mix of EU values (e.g. the rule of law) and interests (e.g. the fight against organized crime and terrorism) can be seen.

The second form of conditionality is the market access conditionality included in the DCFTA, linking market opening to progress in legal approximation and implementation of specified measures.[170] The 'further market opening' envisaged varies from sector to sector, but includes, for example, further agreements on conformity assessment and determinations of equivalence for SPS standards. Annex XVII on regulatory approximation in services, including financial and telecommunication services, is closest in approach to the EEA, even including an equivalent to Article 7 EEA.[171] A Trade Committee will add new EU legislation to the appendices of this Annex, to be implemented by Ukraine. When it is accepted by the EU that Ukraine has achieved 'full enactment and complete and full implementation of all applicable provisions' for a sector, then the Trade Committee may decide that 'the Parties shall grant each other internal market treatment with respect to the services sector(s) concerned'.[172] Once internal market status in a sector has been agreed under Annex XVII, Ukraine is under an obligation to give effect to new EU laws which are added

[168] On 'essential elements' clauses, see Commission Communication on the inclusion of respect for democratic principles and human rights in agreements between the Community and third countries, 23 May 1995, COM(95)216 final; approved by Council 29 May 1995. For a discussion of their evolution, see Cremona, 'Human Rights and Democracy Clauses in the EC's Trade Agreements', in N. Emiliou and D. O'Keeffe (eds), *The European Union and World Trade Law after the GATT Uruguay Round* (1996); Reidel and Will, 'Human Rights Clauses in External Agreements of the EC', in P. Alston (ed.), *The EU and Human Rights* (1999); E. Fierro, *The EU's Approach to Human Rights Conditionality in Practice* (2003); L. Bartels, *Human Rights Conditionality in the EU's International Agreements* (2005).

[169] Art. 478 UAA. A reminder of this clause is included in the Decision of Heads of State or Government of 15 December 2016 mentioned in note 163.

[170] Art. 475(5) UAA.

[171] Annex XVII concerns regulatory approximation in financial, telecommunications, postal, courier, and international maritime transport services. Art. 2 provides for the legal acts listed in the Annex appendices to be 'made part of Ukraine's internal legal order', specifying the type of legal effect for acts equivalent to EU regulations, directives and decisions; cf. Art. 7 EEA. Annex XVII also contains a clause on homogeneity of interpretation (Art. 6) which extends to post-signature case law, in other words without the prior-to-signature time limit found in Art. 6 EEA; the clause only applies to Annex XVII but there are other interpretative provisions elsewhere in the agreement (e.g. the chapter on competition).

[172] UAA Annex XVII, Art. 4(3).

to the Annex by decision of the Trade Committee, and that implementation will be assessed by the EU: only in exceptional circumstances may the Trade Committee agree a temporary derogation from the transposition obligation.

While the EU Courts have interpreted clauses of the EEA on the four freedoms as being directly effective within the EU,[173] the DCFTA section of the UAA (Title IV) is declared not to be directly effective.[174] This denial of direct effect is a characteristic of recent EU trade agreements.[175] Enforcement of the agreement is thus via arbitration rather than the ordinary courts; here again we have a contrast with the emphasis on individual rights in the EEA. Nor is there any equivalent in the UAA to the EFTA Court, but from the point of view of legal integration there is a significant provision on arbitration under the DCFTA with respect to 'disputes concerning the interpretation and application of a provision of this Agreement relating to regulatory approximation . . . or which otherwise imposes upon a Party an obligation defined by reference to a provision of EU law'. In such cases, where a question of the interpretation of EU law arises, the arbitration panel is to request a binding ruling from the EU Court of Justice.[176] The interpretation of the UAA and its annexes is thus even more closely linked to EU law, brought within the jurisdiction of the EU Court of Justice not only as part of the EU legal order,[177] but extending to bilateral dispute settlement with implications also for Ukraine. The provision is designed to safeguard the position of the Court of Justice, complying with the conditions imposed on external dispute settlement by the principle of autonomy.[178] But it also emphasizes the degree to which conditionality-based integration is based on regulatory approximation to the EU legal regime.

C. Conclusions

The EEA illustrates clearly the integration model of EU foreign policy. Law is a key component given its central role within EU integration (integration through law). The EEA creates a legal space in which the equality of treatment of EEA citizens has

[173] See, e.g., Case T-115/94, *Opel Austria* [1997] ECR II-39 (ECLI:EU:T:1997:3); Case C-452/01, *Ospelt* [2003] ECR I-9743 (ECLI:EU:C:2003:493). The EFTA Court has interpreted the EEA agreement as not requiring direct effect as far as the EFTA parties are concerned: Art. 7 and Protocol 35 EEA; Case E-4/01, *Karlsson* [2002] EFTA Ct Rep 240, para. 28. See further Haukeland Fredriksen and Franklin, note 125.

[174] Somewhat oddly, the statement is placed in a footnote to the heading of chapter 14, on dispute settlement. There is also a statement denying direct effect to the UAA as a whole in the Council decisions concluding the UAA; although these latter are only unilateral declarations by one party and would not necessarily be conclusive, it is hard to envisage the CJEU setting them aside.

[175] See further M. Cremona, 'A Quiet Revolution: The Common Commercial Policy Six Years after the Treaty of Lisbon', SIEPS Papers 2017:2, at 53–56; Semertzi, 'The Preclusion of Direct Effect in the Recently Concluded EU Free Trade Agreements', 51 *Common Market Law Review* (2014) 1125.

[176] Art. 322(2) UAA. The provisions on regulatory approximation in the DCFTA referred to are Chapter 3 (Technical Barriers to Trade), Chapter 4 (Sanitary and Phytosanitary Measures), Chapter 5 (Customs and Trade Facilitation), Chapter 6 (Establishment, Trade in Services and Electronic Commerce), Chapter 8 (Public Procurement) and Chapter 10 (Competition).

[177] Agreements concluded by the EU are a part of EU law and subject to the interpretative jurisdiction of the Court of Justice as far as the EU is concerned; for a recent statement of this principle, see Case C-266/16, *Western Sahara Campaign UK* (ECLI:EU:C:2018:118), paras 45–46.

[178] In relation to the EEA, see earlier, note 147 and accompanying text.

been prioritized by both the EU Court of Justice and the EFTA Court, including, in the case of the latter, great efforts to preserve equality of treatment despite divergent primary law.

The limits of 'external integration' can also be seen—the essential distinction between membership and non-membership which derives from the autonomy of EU law. Law, including the autonomy principle, establishes the degree of integration into the EU system and constrains its boundaries. Although the EEA appears as a form of 'partial membership', the EU institutions (including the EU Court of Justice) maintain control over the development of the law. It works as a result of the intense pragmatism of the EFTA parties. The EEA is a strong example of the EU's milieu goals: it has extended the single market so that it is more attractive and economically powerful, while retaining ultimate control over the legal construction of that market.

The EEA is a strong example of the use of law to create a situation of joint ownership. It is striking that despite implementation problems, there has never been recourse to suspension or dispute settlement. There is no EFTA-EU enforcement procedure except that predicated on reciprocity, which has never been used. The EU has not used (public) rewards or threats towards the EFTA states but has relied on negotiation within the Joint Committee.[179]

The ENP, and the UAA as the most far-reaching instrument of the ENP, have often been presented as epitomizing the EU as a normative power. The UAA is certainly normative in its use of law and legal integration to structure the relationship—not only the agreement itself but the ongoing process that it envisages, penetrating deeply into the Ukrainian legal order. This integration is an instrument in the pursuit of their diverse (but—the parties hope—compatible) interests by both the EU and Ukraine. For Ukraine, it is an expression of its 'European identity' and its 'European choice' (as expressed in the UAA preamble) as well as a way of leveraging economic transformation. For the EU, the UAA also represents its milieu goals: a way of gaining support for its foreign policy world-view, as well as—which was one of the original aims of the ENP—an instrument to create greater security and stability through prosperity in its neighbourhood. Although the UAA reflects the interests of both Ukraine and the EU, the inbuilt operation of conditionality makes it difficult to see the agreement as an example of joint ownership, a joint enterprise in creating a shared legal space. This is particularly true of the DCFTA part of the agreement (the part in which we see more clearly the translation of EU norms into Ukrainian law). Those aspects of the UAA which are concerned with political cooperation are less dominated by conditionality.

It is tempting to portray the integration represented by the EEA and UAA through 'exporting' the EU *acquis* as an instance of EU law operating beyond EU boundaries.

[179] Contrast the case of Switzerland, when the Swiss referendum in February 2014 threatened to undermine the Free Movement of Persons agreement, and the Swiss government postponed the ratification of the Protocol designed to extend the agreement to Croatia. The EU reacted by suspending the negotiation of agreements with Switzerland on participation in Horizon 2020 and Erasmus+. For the moment there is stalemate, but it appears that the Swiss government is anxious to avoid a suspension of the agreement and is trying to find an accommodation.

But it is not so straightforward. These agreements do not entail that EU law *as such* takes effect in the EFTA states or Ukraine. They, rather, envisage a wholesale domestic legal implementation of a set of norms modelled on EU law. The absence of direct effect makes this clear. The legal boundary remains clear, as does the institutional. Giusti makes the point that 'the balance between preserving the integrity of [the EU's] institutional/legal boundary and extending its transactional boundary is very delicate'.[180] The EEA was shaped deliberately to accommodate the EFTA states' concerns about sovereignty and the EU's own requirements of autonomy would not allow the legal boundary to shift inwards, in the sense of accepting an external input into law-making structures, or even shared institutions (such as a court) which might affect internal EU law. These examples of highly integrated agreements are of course all based on acceptance by the third state of alignment to EU-derived norms. It is important to realize that this not just the result of the EU's political and economic leverage, although that certainly plays a part.[181] It is also the result of the constraints imposed by the EU's own legal order, and raises the question of the extent to which the EU is able to create a successful non-enlargement model of integration which incorporates the EU's own principle of equality.[182]

4. The EU as a Regulatory Actor: The Making and Implementation of International Norms

A. Competence and the Internal–External Dynamic

Third, and finally, we turn to the EU's commitment to the development of international law and to good global governance. It was argued at the start of this chapter that the EU's identity is defined through its ability to create and shape the law. This chapter is concerned with the EU's external actorness, its external relations, and therefore with its ability to create and shape international law. Through its general external objectives, as defined in Articles 3(5) and 21 TEU, the EU is committed to contributing to the international legal order: to the development of international law, promoting rule-based multilateral solutions to common problems, and to good global governance. Put another way, law is a primary tool of the EU's soft power and so becomes its objective.[183] In its foreign relations the EU is increasingly engaged with international law-making activities via international conventions, and its international agreements are full of references to international norms and standards.

[180] Giusti, note 157, at 171.

[181] See the discussion of the 'Brussels Effect', in Chapter 1 in this volume, applied in the context of unilateral instruments.

[182] Cf Art. 4(2) TEU: 'The Union shall respect the equality of Member States before the Treaties.'

[183] On soft power, see J. Nye, *Soft Power: The Means to Success in World Politics* (2004); on soft power and the EU, see Hill, 'Cheques and Balances: The European Union's Soft Power Strategy', in M. Cox and I. Parmar (eds), *Soft Power and Hegemony in US Foreign Affairs: Theoretical, Historical and Contemporary Perspectives* (2010) 182; Smith, 'Is the European Union's Soft Power in Decline?', 113 *Current History* (2014) 104. It should be noted that soft power does not equate to 'soft law': although soft law is by no means irrelevant (see later, at note 210), soft power may be based on hard law.

In this dynamic we see a synergy, a close inter-relation, between internal and external norm-making and between unilateral, bilateral, regional and multilateral norm-making. In this section these inter-relationships will be explored. External agreements are seen as a way to ensure EU economic and security interests: this is the pursuit of a milieu goal: ensuring that as many countries as possible accept global norms and that those norms are at least compatible with and at best reflect the EU's own approach to economic governance and security (and its relationship to fundamental rights).

This section will look at the example of criminal law, and more specifically the law relating to money laundering and terrorist finance, to explore the interaction between EU law and international norms. In this field, which is part of the EU's AFSJ, the interdependence of the internal and the external is both a matter of pragmatic fact and built into the legal nature of the policy. The threats identified by the Internal Security Strategy (ISS) adopted in March 2010 (terrorism, serious and organized crime, cyber-crime, natural and man-made disasters) are not threats which respect the EU's external borders.[184] Unsurprisingly, the ISS argues that internal security cannot exist without an external dimension: external and internal dimensions of security are interdependent and a 'global security approach' with third countries is advocated.[185] The Strategic Guidelines for justice and home affairs, adopted by the European Council in June 2014, argued that 'an effective EU counter-terrorism policy is needed, whereby all relevant actors work closely together, integrating the internal and external aspects of the fight against terrorism'.[186] The European Agenda on Security, a Commission Communication of May 2015, again stresses the need to bring together external and internal dimensions.[187]

The EU Treaties do not contain any express external powers in relation to criminal law, counter-terrorism or organized crime. And yet the EU has been active in concluding agreements in this field, both bilateral and multilateral, under the doctrine of implied powers.[188] As a condition for implying an external power from an internal competence, the external action must be designed to achieve the objectives established by the Treaty—in this case, the Union's internal security.[189] In general the EU finds it easier to justify, and to engage in, external norm-making in the AFSJ

[184] Internal Security Strategy 'Towards a European Security Model', adopted by the European Council, 25–26 March 2010, see Council doc. 7120/10. For an assessment, see F. Trauner, 'The Internal-external Security Nexus: More Coherence under Lisbon?' European Union Institute for Security Studies, Occasional Paper 89, March 2011.

[185] Internal Security Strategy, note 184, at 16.

[186] European Council, Strategic Guidelines on Freedom, Security and Justice, Council doc. EUCO 79/14, 26–27 June 2014, para. 10.

[187] Commission Communication, European Agenda on Security, COM (2015) 185 final, 28 April 2015.

[188] That is, on the basis of case law deriving from Case 22/70, *Commission v. Council* (AETR), (ECLI:EU:C:1971:32), and now additionally from Art. 216(1) TFEU.

[189] The aims of the Area of Freedom, Security and Justice are set out in Art. 67(3) TFEU. As expressed by AG Mengozzi in *Opinion 1/15*: 'the external dimension of the AFSJ is functional and instrumental having regard to the objectives set out in those provisions. Accordingly, while the construction of the AFSJ may require external action on the part of the Union, an agreement must, if it is to be able to be regarded as falling within the AFSJ, have a close link with freedom, security and justice within the union, that is to say, a direct link between the purpose of safeguarding the internal security of the Union

if there is an internal policy in place, and there will tend to be a close relation between the internal policy and the external action. This is not to say that the EU does not sometimes find itself strongly influenced by external actors (e.g. the US) in developing its approach. The PNR agreements and legislative initiatives are an example where external commitments have preceded internal legislation, and perhaps precisely for this reason have been influential in directing the internal response.[190] However, even in cases where the initial initiative has been external, a dynamic is emerging whereby internal norms (such as data protection) influence the external relationship.[191]

Even before gaining (implied) external competence related to internal security, the then EC concluded international agreements related to criminal law and money laundering, including the Vienna Convention on drug trafficking and the Palermo Convention on organized crime, on the basis of the common commercial policy, internal market and even development cooperation powers. The negotiation and conclusion of the Palermo Convention by the EC illustrates some of the competence constraints on the EU, in particular before the Treaty of Lisbon, when criminal and police cooperation still fell under the 'third pillar' of the TEU (Justice and Home Affairs). The EC Treaty legal bases used to conclude the Convention were establishment, services, internal market and development.[192] It is a mixed agreement, and the criminal law aspects were covered by the 'third pillar' and negotiated by the Member States coordinated via a third pillar Joint Position.[193] The EC declaration of competence mentions its competence in relation to the internal market, money laundering and anti-corruption, and refers to specific articles of the Convention dealing with money laundering, anti-corruption, development and technical assistance, and public procurement. Two of the Convention Protocols, on trafficking of persons and on smuggling of migrants respectively, were also concluded by the Community.[194] A third Protocol, on illicit manufacturing and trafficking of firearms, was signed by the Community in respect of certain provisions only, which fell

and the police and/or judicial cooperation which is developed outside the Union'. Opinion of AG Mengozzi in *Opinion 1/15* (ECLI:EU:C:2016:656), 8 September 2016, para. 102.

190 Papakonstantinou and de Hert, 'The PNR Agreement and Transatlantic Anti-terrorism Cooperation: No Firm Human Rights Framework on Either Side of the Atlantic', 46 *Common Market Law Review* (2009) 885; Pawlak, 'The External Dimension of the Area of Freedom, Security and Justice: Hijacker or Hostage of Cross-pillarization?', 31 *Journal of European Integration* (2009) 25; Argomaniz, 'When the EU is the "Norm-taker": The Passenger Name Records Agreement and the EU's Internalization of US Border Security Norms', 31 *Journal of European Integration* (2009) 119. For a discussion of the appropriate legal basis for external PNR agreements and the importance of EU data protection, see now *Opinion 1/15*, note 32.

191 See, e.g., Cremona, 'Risk in Three Dimensions: The EU-US SWIFT Agreement on the Processing and Transfer of Financial Messaging Data', in T. Tridimas and H.-W. Micklitz (eds), *Risk and EU Law* (2015).

192 Council Decision 2004/579/EC of 29 April 2004, OJ 2004 L 261/69.

193 Joint Position 99/235/JHA of 29 March 1999 on the proposed UN Convention against organised crime, OJ 1999 L 87/1.

194 However, there is an additional complexity here too: each Protocol has been concluded by means of two separate Council Decisions. The first decision is based on Arts 179 and 181a TEC (development cooperation and cooperation with third countries): Council Decision 2006/618/EC of 24 July 2006, OJ 2006 L 262/44; the second is based on Title IV TEC: Council Decision 2006/619/EC of 24 July 2006, OJ 2006 L 262/51. In the latter case, the Decision states in recital 5 that 'the UK and Ireland are not bound by this Decision to the extent that it concerns the exercise of an external power by the

within Community competence,[195] the Council also adopting a Common Position under the third pillar agreeing a common approach of the Member States to certain issues within the negotiations, such as the definition of a firearm.[196]

As EC and then EU competence has evolved, so too has the relation between internal and external norms, and between EU action at multilateral and bilateral levels, as the following discussion of measures relating to money laundering will show.

B. Money Laundering

1. International Norms and EU Law

International measures aimed at money laundering have evolved and broadened their targets since the 1988 Vienna Convention which focused on the proceeds of drug trafficking.[197] The 1990 Council of Europe Convention on money laundering covered the proceeds of serious and organized crime more generally,[198] as did the 2000 UN Convention against Transnational Organised Crime (the Palermo Convention).[199] More recently, the recommendations issued by the Financial Action Task Force (FATF) link money laundering to terrorist financing, as does the Council of Europe Convention of 2005 on Laundering, Search, Seizure and Confiscation of the Proceeds from Crime and on the Financing of Terrorism.[200] The EU has followed these developments in its successive directives on money laundering, including serious crime in the 1990s and terrorist financing in the third directive in 2005.[201]

As Mitsilegas points out,[202] the EU was concerned to ensure that the Palermo Convention would be consistent with existing Community/Union law, such as the definition of organized crime adopted in a 1998 Joint Action.[203] The 1999 Joint

Community in fields where its internal legislation does not bind the UK and/or Ireland'. Denmark is similarly not bound.

[195] Council Decision 2001/748/EC, OJ 2001 L 280/5, adopted with a legal basis of Arts 95 and 133 TEC (internal market and trade policy powers). According to the Commission's proposal to sign the Protocol, those issues within Community competence included the marking of firearms, record-keeping, import, export and transit licensing, border controls, brokers, and deactivation of firearms, COM(2001) 397.

[196] Council Common Position 2000/130/JHA of 31 January 2000, OJ 2000 L 37/1.

[197] United Nations Convention against Illicit Traffic in Narcotic Drugs and Psychotropic Substances, Vienna 1988; the Convention entered into force in 1990 and now has 189 parties, including the EU and all its Member States.

[198] Convention on Laundering, Search, Seizure and Confiscation of the Proceeds from Crime, ETS 141.

[199] United Nations Convention against Transnational Organized Crime, Palermo, 2000, entered into force 2003.

[200] Council of Europe Convention on Laundering, Search, Seizure and Confiscation of the Proceeds from Crime and on the Financing of Terrorism, CETS 198.

[201] Mitsilegas, 'The European Union and the Rest of the World: Criminal Law and Policy Interconnections', in M. Evans and P. Koutrakos (eds), *Beyond the Established Legal Orders—Policy Interconnections between the EU and the Rest of the World* (2011).

[202] *Ibid.*, at 154.

[203] Joint Action 98/733/JHA on making it a criminal offence to participate in a criminal organisation in the Member States of the European Union, OJ 1998 L 351/1.

Position mentioned earlier,[204] intended to coordinate the Member States' negotiating positions, had as one of its general purposes 'to avoid incompatibility between the proposed convention and instruments drawn up in the Union', and the Member States were to ensure 'that the provisions of the draft convention relating to the obligation to criminalise particular activities are consistent in particular with Articles 1 and 2 of Joint Action 98/733/JHA'.[205] In relation to money laundering more specifically, again the Member States were to ensure that provisions relating to criminal assets 'should not be inconsistent with, and should take account of' the EU's existing Joint Action on money laundering and should be consistent with FATF recommendations.[206] In fact, the text of the Palermo Convention on the definition of organized crime does follow the pre-existing EU position; subsequent internal EU law, including a 2008 Framework Decision which replaced the 1998 Joint Action, then took Palermo as a benchmark.[207] The conclusion of the international instrument was a reason to update internal EU law, and the opportunity was taken to move from a Joint Action to a Framework Decision, which had stronger legal force.[208]

This interplay between international instruments and EU law can also be seen where the international instruments are not legally binding, but are so-called 'soft law' in the form of recommendations. The FATF, covering money laundering and terrorist finance, was established by the G7 in 1989, under the auspices of the OECD, and all 15 pre-2004 EU Member States are members.[209] The FATF has issued 40 recommendations on money laundering and eight special recommendations on terrorist finance. These have been (and are) very influential on successive EU money laundering directives and other legislation.[210] The Preamble to the Fourth Money Laundering Directive, adopted in 2015, for example, states:

> Union action should continue to take particular account of the FATF Recommendations and instruments of other international bodies active in the fight against money laundering and terrorist financing.... the relevant Union legal acts should, where appropriate, be aligned with the International Standards on Combating Money Laundering and the Financing of Terrorism and Proliferation adopted by the FATF in February 2012 (the 'revised FATF Recommendations').[211]

Just as the EU seeks to ensure compatibility between externally-derived norms and EU law, so EU-level implementation of international norms through directives is

[204] See note 193.

[205] Joint Position 99/235/JHA, note 193, Art. 1(2).

[206] *Ibid.*, Art. 1(5) and (6). The Joint Action referred to is Joint Action 98/699/JHA of 3 December 1998, OJ 1998 L 333/1. On FATF, see later.

[207] Council Framework Decision 2008/841/JHA on the fight against organised crime, OJ 2008 L 300/42.

[208] Mitsilegas, note 201, at 158–159.

[209] FATF members also include the USA, Russia, China, Brazil, India, Japan, Korea and Turkey. The 12 post-2004 EU Member States are members of MONEYVAL, a Council of Europe body.

[210] Mitsilegas, note 201, at 177, points out that the FATF standards have been accepted uncritically by the EU, with virtually no policy discussion. As he concludes, ' "soft law" has perhaps proved to have harder teeth than the multilateral conventions in the field'.

[211] Directive 2015/849 of 20 May 2015 on the prevention of the use of the financial system for the purposes of money laundering or terrorist financing, OJ 2015 L 141/73, recital 4. See also Regulation 2015/847 of 20 May 2015 on information accompanying transfers of funds, OJ 2015 L 141/1.

designed to ensure harmonized enforcement. In its February 2016 Communication on terrorism financing,[212] the Commission proposed to introduce new legislation which would implement, at EU level, FATF recommendations and the Council of Europe Convention on terrorist financing,[213] in particular through a directive on criminal offences and sanctions for money laundering linked to terrorist offences and other serious criminal offences. The proposed directive, it argues, would be 'an important step towards EU ratification' of the Council of Europe Convention, 'the most comprehensive international convention on money laundering'.[214] Thus, especially where an international instrument covers areas where competence is shared with the Member States, EU ratification may be seen (inter alia) as a means, through EU internal law, of ensuring that Member State and EU implementation are convergent.[215] EU implementation also (in principle) guarantees compliance with EU law more generally, and in particular fundamental rights.[216] The Fourth Money Laundering Directive, for example, is designed to ensure that implementation of FTAF Recommendations complies with EU data protection law.[217] So although the implementation of FATF recommendations has been undertaken with little internal policy debate, it has also sought to comply with the EU's internal norms. This point will be returned to later, in the conclusion to this section.

This context of money laundering legislation also demonstrates the ways in which the EU extends the reach of its legislation towards third countries. The Fourth Money Laundering Directive contains provisions designed to identify third countries which have 'strategic deficiencies' in their national anti-money laundering and terrorist-finance regimes that 'pose significant threats to the financial system of the Union'. These 'high-risk third countries'—identified by the Commission under delegated powers—are subject to enhanced due diligence requirements.[218] In addition, the Directive requires branches and subsidiaries of EU companies in third countries to apply EU standards where possible, thereby providing a good illustration of firm-level territorial extension, as discussed by Joanne Scott in Chapter 1 of this volume.[219]

[212] Communication from the Commission to the European Parliament and the Council on an Action Plan for strengthening the fight against terrorist financing, COM(2016) 50, 2 February 2016.

[213] See note 200.

[214] Proposal for a Directive of the European Parliament and of the Council on countering money laundering by criminal law, COM(2016) 826 final, 21 December 2016, at 4.

[215] Currently criminal sanctions are covered by Framework Decision 2001/500/JHA on money laundering, the identification, tracing, freezing, seizing and confiscation of instrumentalities and the proceeds of crime, OJ 2001 L 182/1 (partially replacing Joint Action 98/699/JHA, see note 206).

[216] It might also be noted that Joint Position 99/235/JHA, note 193, on the negotiation of the Palermo Convention, provided in Art 1(4) that the draft convention 'should provide appropriate safeguards for the protection of human rights'.

[217] Directive 2015/849, note 211, recital 43 and Arts 40–44. Of course such compliance may be disputed; for an example of a recent opinion of the EU Data Protection Supervisor (EDPS), see Summary of the Opinion of the European Data Protection Supervisor on a Commission Proposal amending Directive 2015/849/EU and Directive 2009/101/EC, OJ 2017 C 85/3. On data protection more generally, see Christopher Kuner, Chapter 3 in this volume.

[218] Directive 2015/849, note 211, Arts 9 and 18.

[219] 'Money laundering and terrorist financing are international problems and the effort to combat them should be global. Where Union credit institutions and financial institutions have branches and subsidiaries located in third countries in which the requirements in that area are less strict than those of the Member State, they should, in order to avoid the application of very different standards within the

Alongside these unilateral measures, which are primarily designed to further the better functioning of the EU's own regime, the EU also endeavours to promote international norms on money laundering, including the FATF recommendations, within the framework of its bilateral relations.

2. *The Bilateral Agenda*

The Action Plan annexed to the Commission's 2016 Communication on the financing of terrorism includes an external dimension.[220] It refers to technical assistance, cooperation with third countries over the EU's terrorist listings, and compliance support to third countries with respect to implementing UN Security Council Resolution legal requirements and FATF recommendations. Bilateral agreements—not only those with EU neighbours—increasingly include references to money laundering, terrorist finance and sometimes even to FATF recommendations. For example, Article 20 of the UAA provides not only for cooperation in combating money laundering and terrorism financing; it also makes reference to FATF standards, even though Ukraine is not a member of FATF: the Parties are to 'ensure implementation of relevant international standards, in particular those of the FATF and standards equivalent to those adopted by the Union'.[221] The Ukraine Association Agenda includes implementation of the Palermo Convention and other UN and Council of Europe Conventions, implementation of FATF standards and EU anti-money laundering legislation.[222]

Beyond the EU's neighbourhood, the EU-Philippines Partnership and Cooperation Agreement includes among its aims cooperation in combating terrorism and cooperation in the area of justice and security, including 'illicit drugs; money laundering; combating organised crime and corruption'.[223] A specific provision on combating terrorism[224] puts EU-Philippines cooperation in a multilateral context, referring to the UN Global Counter-Terrorism Strategy,[225] as well as the EU-ASEAN Joint Declaration on Cooperation to Combat Terrorism of 28 January 2003, and the implementation of relevant UN Security Council Resolutions,[226] and 'working towards an early agreement on the Comprehensive Convention on International Terrorism'. The provision on money laundering and terrorist financing[227] refers to

institution or group of institutions, apply to those branches and subsidiaries Union standards or notify the competent authorities of the home Member State if the application of such standards is not possible.' Directive 2015/849, note 211, preamble para. 48; see further Art. 45. For an example of state-level territorial extension, see Regulation 2015/847, note 211; under Art. 24 Member States may be authorized by the Commission to negotiate agreements to treat money transfers with a specific third country as if they are transfers within that Member State, on condition (inter alia) that 'the country or territory concerned requires payment service providers under its jurisdiction to apply the same rules as those established under [the] Regulation'.

220 COM(2016) 50, note 212.

221 Art. 20 UAA, note 151.

222 EU-Ukraine Association Agenda 2015, note 164, paras 3.5 and 7.9.

223 Framework Agreement on partnership and cooperation between the European Union and its member states, of the one part, and the Republic of the Philippines, of the other part, COM(2013) 925 final (Annex), Art. 2.

224 *Ibid.*, Art. 10.

225 UN General Assembly Resolution 60/28 of 8 September 2006.

226 Including UN Security Council Resolutions 1373, 1267, 1822 and 1904.

227 EU-Philippines Agreement, note 223, Art. 22.

technical and legal assistance aimed at the development of regulation and 'the adoption of appropriate standards... equivalent to those adopted by the Union and the international bodies active in this area, such as the Financial Action Task Force (FATF)'. Again, there is a reference to (and promotion of) the FATF standards as an international standard, even though the Philippines is not a member.

These references to international standards are not limited to agreements with transition or developing economies. The EU's Free Trade Agreement with South Korea, for example, contains a provision on financial governance, committing the parties to the implementation of 'internationally agreed standards for regulation and supervision in the financial services sector'.[228] These standards include the Basle Committee principles on banking supervision, OECD and G20 agreements on exchanges of information on tax matters, and the 40 FATF recommendations on money laundering and nine Special Recommendations on terrorist financing.

C. Conclusions

These examples illustrate a dynamic relationship between international instruments and internal EU law, and between the unilateral, multilateral and bilateral dimensions of EU external policy. The language of 'exporting' or 'importing' norms does not do justice to the complex interactions between these different levels of EU regulatory activity. Where the EU participates in multilateral agreements and norm-creating structures it will try to ensure that these follow an approach which is at least compatible with existing EU internal legislation. Internal norms 'uploaded' to the international level in this way gain in hierarchical authority within the EU legal order since international law obligations take precedence over secondary law; they are therefore in a sense 'locked in'. The EU also justifies participation in an international convention (although it might have internal law in place already) so as to encourage take-up of the convention among third countries, as well as arguing that its own legislative implementation gives added legal value: by translating the convention's provisions into EU law they acquire stronger force in the legal systems of Member States and may be implemented more quickly than would the international convention itself. Implementation at EU level should also ensure compliance with internal EU norms, including fundamental rights (see later).

The EU will then take these international norms as a baseline in its relations with third countries, encouraging them to adhere to and implement international conventions, putting resources into capacity-building and including references to them in hard and soft law instruments, such as bilateral treaties and Association Agendas. In this way, internal (EU) regulatory choices may be uploaded to the international level via multilateral conventions, and bilateral relations are then used to promote these multilateral norms. The global impact of EU law may involve not only the promotion of the EU's own 'home-grown' norms, but also include international norms to which the EU has contributed, and/or wishes to promote. These processes serve the EU's interest in promoting international rule-making and, as we have

[228] EU-Korea Free Trade Agreement, OJ 2011 L 127/6, Art. 7.24.

argued, the EU sees this objective as important to its international identity as well as in its internal and external security interest. They do, however raise questions as to their impact on the EU's commitment to its values, especially fundamental rights. We will here raise two issues, one internal, and one external.

The EU would like to say that in importing international norms and implementing them at EU level it can ensure compliance with its own human rights standards. But is this really true? At the time of conclusion of the SWIFT agreement with the US on the exchange of financial information, concerns were expressed as to its compliance with EU data protection standards.[229] The Court of Justice has recently decided that the proposed PNR agreement with Canada does not fully comply with EU data protection standards,[230] and the adoption of the (internal) PNR directive was delayed by the European Parliament over data protection concerns.[231] The *Schrems* case illustrates the difficulty of assessing 'equivalence' of rights protection in a third country, and the need to keep it under review,[232] as does Advocate General Sharpston in the different context of counter-terrorism sanctions.[233] It is surely not a coincidence that these cases all involve the EU adopting measures whose original impetus was external, albeit subjecting them to a degree of internal adjustment. From this perspective, the very detailed analysis and set of prescriptions which the Court was prepared to undertake in *Opinion 1/15* in relation to the compliance of the EU-Canada PNR agreement with EU data protection standards is important, although it might not be so easily replicable in cases where the internal EU standards are less detailed.

Second, the problems that may occur when the EU engages in international standard-setting or norm creation should be addressed. If an international instrument (e.g. one which includes commitments to adopt criminal sanctions) does not contain human rights or due process safeguards, the EU will tend to reassure its public by affirming that any implementation within the EU will necessarily have to comply with the EU's own human rights protections. So as long as the agreement does not *compel* action which is non-human rights compliant, the EU claims that there is no problem. So, for example, when the EU negotiated the controversial Anti-Counterfeiting Trade Agreement (ACTA), the Commission argued that the agreement provided enough flexibility for the EU to be able to implement it in such a way as to be compatible with the Treaties and the Charter.[234] The Parliament's Legal Service opinion agreed with this assessment, finding that ACTA did not impose any

[229] See, e.g., Cremona, 'Risk in Three Dimensions', note 191.

[230] *Opinion 1/15*, note 32.

[231] Directive 2016/681 of 27 April 2016 on the use of passenger name record (PNR) data for the prevention, detection, investigation and prosecution of terrorist offences and serious crime, OJ 2016 L 119/132. See literature cited at note 190.

[232] Case C-362/14, *Schrems* (ECLI:EU:C:2015:650). On this point see Christopher Kuner, Chapter 3 in this volume.

[233] Case C-599/14 P, *Council v. LTTE (Tamil Tigers)*, Opinion of AG Sharpston (ECLI:EU:C:2016:723), paras 62–67; see also the Court's judgment in the same case, (ECLI:EU:C:2017:583), paras 22–38.

[234] See further Cremona, 'The EU's International Regulatory Policy, Democratic Accountability and the ACTA: a Cautionary Tale', in M. Cremona and T. Takács (eds), *Trade liberalisation and standardisation—new directions in the 'low politics' of EU foreign policy*, CLEER Working Paper 2013/6; EUI AEL Working Paper 2014/01.

obligations that were incompatible with EU fundamental rights.[235] Certainly the EU may—and indeed would be required to—insert due process requirements into its own legislation and ensure that it complies with fundamental rights, but these safeguards were not written into the agreement itself. There were general provisions on due process and proportionality, and references to freedom of expression, fair process and privacy, but these were not defined. So, although the ACTA would have permitted such 'good practice' it did not require it: it did require the adoption of enforcement provisions while failing to specify clearly the concomitant safeguards.

This permissive rather than prescriptive approach to fundamental rights may not be so problematic for parties with solid fundamental rights protection in their own domestic constitutional laws, and courts that would not hesitate to accord priority to those rights when assessing the implementation of an international obligation.[236] But not all states have such protection and this raises broader questions over the use of international treaties to regulate at a global level, especially where the regulation concerns the liability of individuals. Putting the question rather crudely: if the EU seeks to 'upload' its preferred regulatory standards to the international level, encouraging their adoption by third countries, including transitional economies, should it not also seek to build in fundamental rights protection? However, were it to do so, this might risk every international regulatory instrument becoming a human rights treaty, with all that would follow in terms of multiplicity of standards and enforcement bodies.

5. Conclusions

This chapter has set out to explore the nature of the relationship between law and external action. The relationship is symbiotic in the sense that law is both a foundation for (a source of) the EU's ability to act externally and an instrument of that action. It is through law that the EU constructs itself as an autonomous international actor and one of its general external objectives is the development of international law. A number of examples have been used to demonstrate that these features of EU external action and the inherent centrality of law to the EU as an international actor are not simply rhetorical statements in the Treaties, but are translated into a wide variety of external policy-making. It is in this sense that it can be claimed that the 'external reach of EU law' is a natural expression of the EU's international actorness. It is through its own constitutional law that the EU has an external reach, and the reach of its law, through its external instruments, impacts on third countries and international legal regimes. The EU's own legal regime is shaped by, and helps to

[235] In July 2011 the EP Legal Service was asked for an opinion on the compatibility of the ACTA with the Treaties, general principles of EU law and the existing *acquis*, including the ECHR and the Charter of Fundamental Rights; a further request was made on 4 October 2011. The two opinions of October and December 2011 were later made public by the Legal Affairs Committee: SJ-0501/11 of 5 October 2011 and SJ-0661/11 of 8 December 2011.

[236] Cf. Joined Cases C-402/05 P and C-415/05 P, *Kadi and Al Barakaat International Foundation v. Council and Commission* [2008] ECR I-6351 (ECLI:EU:C:2008:461); Case C-584/10 P, *European Commission and others v Yassin Abdullah Kadi* ('*Kadi II*') (ECLI:EU:C:2013:518).

shape, international legal rules. This synergistic relationship can create tensions between these different functions of law—or, it could be said, between the constitutional law which creates the EU and international law which the EU helps to create and which it is committed to respect.

This chapter has looked at three dimensions of the EU's 'actorness' which show three overlapping dynamics to the relationship between law and external action and different dimensions to the external reach of EU law. These three dynamics all concern, in different ways, the interaction between EU law and international law.

First, the EU's own self-definition as a Union of values and how that determines and shapes its external action was explored. Law operates as an instrument to promote EU values externally; it operates as a constraint, ensuring that the EU upholds its values (including human rights norms) in its external relations; and it is also an objective of its external action as it seeks to build support for international norms. The EU's values, as expressed in the Treaties, reflect (and indeed include respect for) international norms, and it promotes its values both as belonging to the EU and as universal in reach and application. Within the EU, these values are operative as part of EU constitutional law, internalized and domesticated. The Court's concern to assert the identity (autonomy) of the EU, as expressed by the Court of Justice in *Opinion 2/13*, requires that 'the interpretation of those fundamental rights [must] be ensured within the framework of the structure and objectives of the EU'.[237] As a result, the EU finds it difficult to accept external adjudication of these EU/ international norms within the EU legal space.

The norms that govern the EU's engagement with third countries—as applied by the Court of Justice—may nonetheless be external. In *Front Polisario*, we see the Court of Justice taking account of customary international law and international *erga omnes* obligations in interpreting an EU international agreement. And in the EU's campaign against the death penalty, we saw a range of instruments deployed both to ensure that the EU was not indirectly furthering the use of the death penalty through its exports, and to support its campaign to universalize the abolition of the death penalty and thereby the creation of a new *erga omnes* norm. In this dimension, the external reach of EU law is identified with the EU's policy of seeking to extend to third countries its own acceptance of the legal constraints imposed by international human rights law.

Second, the chapter turned to look at the EU as an integration project, and the process of 'integration through law' as an external relations enterprise. Here, the use of bilateral and regional agreements to further the external reach of EU law, in the sense that third countries accept EU-derived legal norms, can clearly be seen. Not, however, as EU law operating directly in their own legal systems, but as domestic law, or in the case which represents the most advanced form of integration, as a distinct regional legal order (EEA law). The EU's interests and end-goal in engaging in these integration projects are varied and sometimes problematically uncertain. Law draws third states towards the EU, even to the extent of becoming 'virtual Member States'. But virtual members are not members and the law also, again in defence of

[237] *Opinion 2/13*, note 1, para. 170.

the EU's separate identity (autonomy), ultimately measures the distance between internal and external. The EU faces a challenge in attempting, outside the pre-enlargement context, to develop a successful model of integration without membership which creates a genuinely shared and reciprocal legal space based on equality.

Third, the EU is an international regulatory actor, engaging in shaping, importing and promoting international legal norms. A few examples taken from the development of international hard and soft law on money laundering, illustrated the multi-layered interactions between internal EU law, multilateral law and bilateral relationships. Although this dynamic is certainly one facet of the external reach of EU law, the traffic is not all in one direction: the EU implements the norms it helps to shape. The iterative and multi-layered nature of the process raises questions about the degree to which the EU can protect its own values when implementing norms derived externally, and the extent to which it can be said to have a responsibility, in contributing to the development of international standards, to ensure fundamental rights compliance not only within the norms themselves but also in their implementation by third countries.

3

The Internet and the Global Reach of EU Law

Christopher Kuner

1. Introduction

Since becoming available for widespread use in the mid-1990s, the Internet has 'contributed to a shrinking of the world and to an interconnectedness of legal orders that has never been as intense in legal history'.[1] During the same period, EU law has become a global normative power that exerts its influence over a variety of phenomena,[2] including the Internet.

The relationship between EU law and the Internet is one of mutual influence. On the one hand, EU law has influenced the development of the Internet, and impacted countries and parties outside the EU's borders. On the other hand, the Internet raises important questions about the application, scope and normative values of EU law. In many ways the Internet is the ideal vehicle for examining the ambitions of EU law in an increasingly complex and globalized world.

The Internet is based on technical protocols rather than legal rules. It was established as a distributed network not under the control of a single state,[3] and operates based on open standards that allow networks around the world to connect with each other. The Internet also makes it possible for anyone to create content or offer products and services without permission from a central authority. This open, independent structure has been one of the keys to its success.

[1] Basedow, 'The Law of Open Societies—Private Ordering and Public Regulation of International Relations', 360 *Recueil des cours/Collected Courses of the Hague Academy of International Law* (2012) 9, at 471.

[2] Some of the leading scholarly examinations of this topic include Bradford, 'The Brussels Effect', 107 *Northwestern University Law Review* (2013) 1; Gilardi, 'Transnational Diffusion: Norms, Ideas, and Policies', in W. Carlsnaes, T. Risse and B. Simmons (eds), *Handbook of International Relations* (2012) 453, available at http://www.fabriziogilardi.org/resources/papers/gilardi_handbook_IR_v2.pdf; Scott, 'Extraterritoriality and Territorial Extension in EU Law', 62 *American Journal of Comparative Law* (2014) 87; Scott, 'The New Extraterritoriality', 51 *Common Market Law Review* (2014) 1343; De Witte and Thies, 'Why Choose Europe? The Place of the European Union in the Architecture of International Legal Cooperation', in B. Van Vooren, S. Blockmans and J. Wouters (eds), *The EU's Role in Global Governance* (2013) 23; Young, 'The European Union as a Global Regulator? Context and Comparison', 22 *Journal of European Public Policy* (2015) 1233. (All website references in this chapter were last visited on 22 February 2019.)

[3] For a brief description of the Internet, what it is, and how it operates, see Internet Society, 'The Internet: How it Works', available at https://www.internetsociety.org/internet/how-it-works.

However, these same factors complicate the relationship between EU law and the Internet. The Internet is not an enterprise, government, public authority, product, technology or institution of the type that is normally the subject of influence by EU law. Furthermore, instruments of 'soft law' (e.g. contractual arrangements between private parties) play a crucial role in the way the Internet is used.[4] This demonstrates how its governance and regulation can be regarded as an example of pluralism and global legal hybridity.[5]

This chapter will examine the influence that EU law has over the Internet and parties outside the EU's territorial boundaries that use and are affected by the Internet. The global reach of EU law is manifested in different types of actions taken by the EU and its Member States, such as asserting EU values and interests in international organizations and the conclusion of international treaties; influencing the adoption of legislation in third countries; and requiring compliance with EU law with regard to activities carried out by parties in third countries.

The Internet has an impact on many areas of EU law, only a few of which can be examined here. There will be a particular focus on data protection, which is one of the areas where the global reach of EU law has been asserted most aggressively. Data protection is also strongly anchored in EU law, and has been strengthened in recent years through the Treaty of Lisbon,[6] the elevation of the EU Charter of Fundamental Rights[7] (the Charter) to the status of binding primary law,[8] the enactment of Article 16 of the Treaty on the Functioning of the European Union (TFEU),[9] and several ground-breaking judgments of the Court of Justice of the European Union (CJEU).

The Internet also presents EU law with important challenges. Because of the fragmented and global nature of Internet governance and regulation, the Internet is not subject to the direct control of EU law. The relationship between the EU institutions and the Member States also plays an important role in determining the limits and efficacy of EU action regarding the Internet.

An examination of the interaction between EU law and the Internet raises a number of important normative questions regarding the relationship between the EU's legal values and its political or policy interests; the implications of asserting EU values as universal values; ensuring that EU values apply to the Internet in practice as well as in theory; determining the territorial limits to the application of EU law; and the responsibilities that EU law has towards third countries. It also seems that, just as EU law influences the Internet, the Internet may be changing EU law. Finally, one may ask why the EU asserts its values and interests so strongly with regard to the Internet.

[4] See L. Bygrave, *Internet Governance by Contract* (2015), at 6 (Kindle edition); C. Marsden, *Internet Co-Regulation* (2011).

[5] See P. Schiff Berman, *Global Legal Pluralism* (2012), at 177–178 (Kindle edition).

[6] Treaty of Lisbon, OJ 2007 C 306/1.

[7] Charter of Fundamental Rights of the European Union, OJ 2010 C 83/389.

[8] Consolidated Version of the Treaty on European Union (TEU), OJ 2012 C 326/13, at Art. 6(1).

[9] Consolidated Version of the Treaty on the Functioning of the European Union (TFEU), OJ 2012 C 326/47. See H. Hijmans, *The European Union as Guardian of Internet Privacy: The Story of Art 16 TFEU* (2016).

2. The Internet and its Governance

A. What is the Internet?

Defining the Internet is more difficult than it might seem. A definition that is often cited was articulated in 1995 by the US Federal Networking Council (FNC):

> 'Internet' refers to the global information system that (i) is logically linked together by a globally unique address space based on the Internet Protocol (IP) or its subsequent extensions/follow-ons; (ii) is able to support communications using the Transmission Control Protocol/Internet Protocol (TCP/IP) suite or its subsequent extensions/follow-ons, and/or other IP-compatible protocols; and (iii) provides, uses, or makes accessible, either publicly or privately, high level services layered on the communications and related infrastructure described herein.[10]

This definition focuses on the Internet's use of the TCP/IP suite[11] in order to differentiate it from other networks. However, different networks, not all of which employ TCP/IP, may be connected to transfer data at least in part via the Internet.[12] The term 'Internet' is often used not just in relation to a particular protocol or technology, but to refer to the interconnection of electronic communications networks around the world, including the technical infrastructure that they use. Because Internet technologies and their use change so quickly, it seems best to adopt a broad definition that includes not only networks that run based on TCP/IP, but also the global communications infrastructure that underlies the Internet.[13] Understood in this way, the Internet can be defined to include the broad range of infrastructure, content, applications, hardware and other phenomena that determine both the purpose of the Internet and how it operates in practice.[14] Thus, the Internet will be considered here to constitute the 'network of networks' that includes the totality of global communications networks, infrastructure and content that are connected to it and transmitted on it.

B. How is the Internet Governed?

The Internet functions based on a multi-layered governance model, as illustrated by Table 3.1 (note that the bullet points included in each layer of the table are only examples).

[10] FNC Resolution of 24 October 1995, available at http://people.ucalgary.ca/~bakardji/Internet/definition.html.

[11] The TCP/IP suite is a set of communications protocols widely used to transmit data packets on the Internet. See http://www.pcmag.com/encyclopedia/term/52614/tcp-ip.

[12] For a discussion of the factors involved in defining what constitutes the Internet, see Bygrave, note 4, at 14–17 (Kindle edition).

[13] *Ibid.*, at 15 (Kindle edition).

[14] Solum, 'Models of Internet Governance', in L. Bygrave and J. Bing (eds), *Internet Governance: Infrastructure and Institutions* (2009) 48, at 48–49, stating that '[i]n the broad sense, the Internet is a complex entity that includes the hardware and software technical infrastructure, the applications, and the content that is communicated or generated using those applications'.

Table 3.1 Internet governance layers

Social Layer
- Trust and identity
- Human rights applied to the Internet
- Internet governance principles (e.g. net neutrality)

Content Layer
- Data protection
- Intellectual property rights
- Cybercrime
- SPAM

Logical Layer
- Internet naming and numbering
- Protocols & other standards

Infrastructure Layer
- Connectivit ly and universal access

Source: Adapted from Cerf, Ryan and Senges, 'Internet Governance is our Shared Responsibility', 10 *I/S: A Journal of Law and Policy for the Information Society* (2014) 1, at 10.

In this model, the infrastructure layer comprises the networks through which data travels on the Internet; the logical layer contains the code and mechanisms by which the Internet operates; the content layer contains the information that is transmitted through it and the legal rules that govern such information; and the social layer deals with 'practices that define paramount rights and principles associated with "social conduct" online'.[15] This chapter will mainly be concerned with the third layer (i.e. the content layer), though EU law may impact all four.

The instruments of EU primary law do not specifically mention the Internet. However, the various layers of governance set forth in Table 3.1 are subject to regulation by the EU insofar as there is EU law in the respective area (e.g. telecommunications networks are subject to telecommunications regulation).

The fragmented governance structure of the Internet limits the EU's ability to regulate it. The Internet is accessible globally, and most of the infrastructure on which it runs, the organizations that maintain it, and the individuals that use it are located outside the EU. Moreover, as a global communications infrastructure the Internet is of interest to countries all over the world, which may exercise their own legal and regulatory power over it, potentially leading to legal conflicts.

A number of international entities and organizations play an important role in the functioning and governance of the Internet. In 2006, the United Nations Secretary-General established the Internet Governance Forum (IGF), a forum for dialogue on issues of policy related to Internet governance that includes participation from stakeholders in all sectors, including governments, the private sector, civil

[15] Cerf, Ryan and Senges, 'Internet Governance is our Shared Responsibility', 10 *I/S: A Journal of Law and Policy for the Information Society* (2014) 1, at 9.

society, academia and the technical community.[16] Several organizations also play a crucial role in setting technical standards for the Internet, such as the Internet Engineering Task Force (IETF),[17] the World Wide Web Consortium (W3C)[18] and the Internet Corporation for Assigned Names and Numbers (ICANN).[19] However, none of these are 'regulators' in the sense of being public authorities mandated with enforcing a set of laws or legal rules.

The growing social, economic and political importance of the Internet has led to its increased regulation,[20] which can cause legal conflicts and complicate the application and enforcement of the law. The difficulty of applying and enforcing any regulatory system (not just EU law) to the Internet rests on the fact that its operation involves a highly fragmented universe of actors, norms, procedures, processes and institutions, including many non-state entities (such as private companies, non-governmental organizations, academic institutions, standards organizations and others). Their activities have resulted in the adoption of contracts, technical standards, guidelines and best practices that differ from legislation and legal regulation traditionally enacted by governments, but that still have had a profound effect on how the Internet functions, as Bygrave explains:

> [T]he governance structure for the Internet has been formed largely outside a treaty or other legislative framework that is Internet-specific. Contracts provide the legal bricks and mortar for much of the present structure, and they do so often without a direct basis in legislation. Concomitantly, the governance structure is relatively unencumbered by dirigiste ideology and has permitted a fairly high degree of self-regulation. While tentacles of government control are increasingly visible, private sector bodies have usually been allowed—and often encouraged—to lead the design and management of the Internet. Governments have acted more as facilitative partners of these bodies than as heavy-handed regulators, at least in Western democracies. In other words, governance has been exercised to a large degree by contractually based, co-operative networks rather than decree.[21]

Jurisdictional rules in many legal systems are based on the principle of territoriality, i.e. that jurisdiction obtains over acts committed within the territory of the country in question.[22] However, the Internet complicates application of the territoriality principle, since it can be difficult to determine the place where a particular online action occurs.[23] This leads to uncertainty concerning applicable law and jurisdiction, which is reflected in the challenges that the Internet presents to EU law.

[16] See http://www.intgovforum.org/multilingual/content/about-igf-faqs.

[17] See http://www.ietf.org. [18] See https://www.w3.org.

[19] See https://www.icann.org.

[20] See J. Goldsmith and T. Wu, *Who Controls the Internet? Illusions of a Borderless World* (2008); Schiff Berman, note 5, at 28–29 (Kindle edition), stating that countries around the world have enacted 'laws purporting to regulate almost every conceivable online activity, from gambling to chat rooms to auction sites, and seeking to enforce territorially based rules regarding trademarks, contractual relations, privacy norms, "indecent" content, and crime, among others'.

[21] Bygrave, note 4, at 2 (Kindle edition).

[22] See, e.g., C. Ryngaert, *Jurisdiction in International Law* (2nd edn, 2015), at 49 (Kindle edition).

[23] See, e.g., Michaels, 'Territorial Jurisdiction after Territoriality', in P. J. Slot and M. Bulterman (eds), *Globalisation and Jurisdiction* (2004) 105, at 106.

3. The EU and the Member States

Both the EU and the Member States are active in Internet-related issues, and the relationship between them helps determine the scope of EU law.

At the EU level, the making of law and policy is fragmented among the institutions. To give a few examples, in the European Commission different Directorates-General take the lead in work on Internet issues such as net neutrality,[24] data protection[25] and intellectual property rights.[26] Other EU institutions, such as the European Economic and Society Committee[27] and the European Parliament,[28] are also deeply involved in Internet issues. There are Internet-related initiatives pursued jointly by various EU institutions; an example is the Communication concerning the 'Cybersecurity Strategy of the European Union',[29] which was published jointly in 2013 by the European Commission and the High Representative of the EU for Foreign Affairs and Security Policy (the High Representative). As discussed throughout this chapter, there are numerous legislative initiatives in the EU and judgments of the CJEU dealing with the Internet. While it is not an EU institution, the European Court of Human Rights has also issued numerous judgments concerning the Internet.[30]

The Member States exercise influence through the Council's role in enacting EU law and policy (e.g. the Council is tasked with identifying the EU's 'strategic interests' in the context of external action[31]) and by pursuing their own legal and regulatory initiatives. A few examples of such national initiatives include the 'Digitale Agenda 2014–2017' of the German Federal Government,[32] the 'Agenda Digitale Italiana' of the Italian government[33] and the 'Digitales Österreich' initiative of the Austrian government.[34] Legislatures, courts and regulators in all Member States have been active in Internet-related issues.

[24] See https://ec.europa.eu/digital-single-market/en/open-internet-net-neutrality, work on which is led by DG CONNECT.

[25] See https://ec.europa.eu/info/law/law-topic/data-protection_en, work on which is led by DG JUST.

[26] See https://ec.europa.eu/growth/industry/intellectual-property_en, work on which is led by DG GROW.

[27] See https://www.eesc.europa.eu/en/policies/policy-areas/digital-change-and-information-society.

[28] See, e.g., the work of the European Parliament Committee on Civil Liberties, Justice and Home Affairs, http://www.europarl.europa.eu/committees/en/LIBE/home.html.

[29] European Commission and High Representative of the European Union for Foreign Affairs and Security Policy, 'Joint Communication to the European Parliament, the Council, the European Economic and Social Committee and the Committee of the Regions, Cybersecurity Strategy of the European Union: An Open, Safe and Secure Cyberspace', JOIN(2013) 1 final, 7 February 2013, http://ec.europa.eu/newsroom/dae/document.cfm?doc_id=1667. See Schaake and Vermeulen, 'Towards a Values-based European Foreign Policy to Cybersecurity', 1 *Journal of Cyber Policy* (2016) 75.

[30] See European Court of Human Rights, Research Division, 'Internet: Case-law of the European Court of Human Rights, Updated: 2015', https://www.echr.coe.int/Documents/Research_report_internet_ENG.pdf.

[31] TEU, note 8, at Art. 26(1). See P. Eeckhout, *EU External Relations Law* (2011), at 485–486 (Kindle edition).

[32] See https://www.digitale-agenda.de/Webs/DA/DE/Home/home_node.html.

[33] See http://www.agid.gov.it/agenda-digitale/agenda-digitale-italiana.

[34] See https://www.digitales.oesterreich.gv.at.

Shared competence between the EU and the Member States is the general rule,[35] and the Internet is not mentioned in Article 3 TFEU, which lists the Union's exclusive competences, so it is an area of shared competence. This conclusion is supported by the fact that some areas listed in Article 4(2) TFEU as examples of shared competence are particularly important with regard to the Internet, such as the internal market and consumer protection.

However, certain areas of EU law related to the Internet may fall primarily within the competence of the EU, as can be seen by the example of data protection. The Member States may act with regard to areas of shared competence only to the extent that the EU has not done so,[36] and data protection, which the EU first regulated on a horizontal basis in Directive 95/46/EC,[37] has now been harmonized via Regulation 2016/679 ('the GDPR'), which replaced the Directive.[38] The Regulation on Privacy and Electronic Communications[39] proposed by the Commission in January 2017 (the ePrivacy Regulation proposal) would also result in harmonization of data protection issues related to the Internet. This means that the Member States may not act with regard to data protection issues that fall within the scope of harmonizing EU legislation. The Member States may not undertake obligations with third countries that affect common rules laid down by the EU,[40] suggesting that, in practice, the conclusion of international agreements concerning data protection lies exclusively in the competence of the EU.[41] There are also limits on the ability of the Member States to participate in law-making initiatives in international fora even in the absence of exclusive competence of the EU,[42] in light of the duty of sincere cooperation that applies in cases of shared competence.[43]

With regard to the negotiation of international treaties relating to the Internet, in most cases the Commission should negotiate on behalf of the EU after being nominated by the Council,[44] except for treaties relating exclusively or principally to the Common Foreign and Security Policy, which should be negotiated by the High

[35] See TFEU, note 9, at Art. 4(1); A. Rosas and L. Armati, *EU Constitutional Law: An Introduction* (2012), at 23 (Kindle edition).

[36] TFEU, note 9, at Art. 2(2).

[37] Directive 95/46 of 24 October 1995 on the protection of individuals with regard to the processing of personal data and on the free movement of such data, OJ 1995 L 281/31.

[38] Regulation 2016/679 of 27 April 2016 on the protection of natural persons with regard to the processing of personal data and on the free movement of such data, and repealing Directive 95/46/EC (General Data Protection Regulation), OJ 2016 L 119/1.

[39] Proposal for a Regulation of the European Parliament and of the Council concerning the respect for private life and the protection of personal data in electronic communications and repealing Directive 2002/58/EC (Regulation on Privacy and Electronic Communications), COM(2017) 10 final, 10 January 2017.

[40] See Case 22/70, *Commission v. Council (AETR/ERTA)* [1971] ECR 263 (ECLI:EU:C:1971:32). The GDPR, note 38, affirms this principle with regard to data protection in recital 102, stating that 'Member States may conclude international agreements which involve the transfer of personal data to third countries or international organisations, as far as such agreements do not affect this Regulation or any other provisions of Union law and include an appropriate level of protection for the fundamental rights of the data subjects'. See also Eeckhout, note 31, at 71–76 (Kindle edition).

[41] See Hijmans, note 9, at 468–470.

[42] See De Witte and Thies, note 2, at 32–33.

[43] See TEU, note 8, at Art. 4(3).

[44] See TFEU, note 9, at Art. 218(3); Eeckhout, note 31, at 195–196 (Kindle edition).

Representative.[45] This latter case would apply in an area such as cybersecurity insofar as it relates to defence, as this would seem to fall under the Common Security and Defence Policy,[46] which is an integral part of the Common Foreign and Security Policy.[47]

Many important discussions between governments, countries and other stakeholders take place in the work of international organizations. Both the EU and the Member States participate in organizations such as the Council of Europe, the Organisation for Economic Co-operation and Development (OECD), various UN agencies, standards-setting bodies, entities dealing with Internet governance, and others.

The relationship between the EU and its Member States with regard to the Internet is marked by both cooperation and tension. On the one hand, the EU seeks to promote cooperation between the EU institutions and the Member States with regard to Internet issues. This can be seen in the European Commission's 2014 Communication on Internet governance, where it is stated that '[t]he Commission invites the Council and Parliament, the Economic and Social Committee, the Committee of the Regions, as well as Member States, to agree on a common vision as highlighted in this Communication and to defend it jointly in the forthcoming international debates'.[48]

At the same time, the division of competences between the EU and the Member States can lead to disputes between them. For example, during negotiation of the EU Directive on Electronic Signatures,[49] the German government sought to have it cover only digital signatures using asymmetric cryptography (as in the original version of the German Digital Signatures Act[50]), and not the broader category of electronic signatures,[51] which led to a dispute between it and the Commission as to the scope of the Directive. There were also disputes between the Member States and the European Commission during the drafting and enactment of the GDPR.

I have witnessed the tension between the EU and its Member States in international organizations such as the Council of Europe in its modernization of Convention 108,[52] and the United Nations Commission for International Trade Law

[45] TFEU, note 9, at Art. 218(3).

[46] See P. Koutrakos, *The EU Common Security and Defence Policy* (2013), at 85 (Kindle edition). See also Cybersecurity Strategy of the European Union, note 29, at 11–12.

[47] TEU, note 8, at Art. 42(1).

[48] Communication from the Commission to the European Parliament, the Council, the European Economic and Social Committee and the Committee of the Regions, 'Internet Policy and Governance: Europe's role in shaping the future of Internet Governance', COM/2014/072 final, 12 February 2014, available at https://eur-lex.europa.eu/legal-content/EN/TXT/PDF/?uri=CELEX:52014DC0072&from=EN.

[49] Directive 1999/93 of 13 December 1999 on a Community framework for electronic signatures, OJ 2000 L 13/12.

[50] *Signaturgesetz vom l. August 1997* (BGBl. I S. 1870, 1872), amended by *Signaturgesetz vom 16. Mai 2001* (BGBl. I S. 876) and Artikel 4 des *Gesetzes vom 17. Juli 2009* (BGBl. I S. 2091).

[51] See Bundesregierung der Bundesrepublik Deutschland, 'Anmerkungen der Bundesregierung zu dem Entwurf der Europäischen Kommission einer EG-Richtlinie über elektronische bzw. Digitale Signaturen', 8 April 1998, at 1.

[52] Convention for the Protection of Individuals with regard to Automatic Processing of Personal Data, opened for signature on 28 January 1981, in force 1 October 1985, ETS 108. Regarding the work

(UNCITRAL) in its work concerning the UNCITRAL Model Law on Electronic Signatures[53] and the UNCITRAL Convention on Electronic Communications.[54] In particular, disputes have arisen between the European Commission and the Member States when both have been participating in the work of an international organization and the Commission has asserted its right to negotiate on behalf of the EU regarding a matter that was the subject of present or pending EU legislation. When such disputes break into the open in the work of international organizations, it weakens the influence of EU law by showing cooperation between the EU institutions and the Member States in a bad light, and allowing third counties to assert themselves at the expense of a disunited EU.

4. The Internet and the Values of EU Law

A. Introduction

The EU is an autonomous legal entity based on values, the promotion of which is one of its aims,[55] and it is obliged to uphold and promote them in its dealings with the wider world.[56] The Treaty on European Union (TEU) contains a list of values by which the EU is to be guided on the international scene, including 'democracy, the rule of law, the universality and indivisibility of human rights and fundamental freedoms, respect for human dignity, the principles of equality and solidarity, and respect for the principles of the United Nations Charter and international law'.[57]

The extension of these values to the Internet has occurred in conjunction with the development of EU law over the last 20 years. One of the first times when the EU dealt with Internet legal issues in an international context was at the ministerial conference on 'Global Information Networks' held in Bonn on 6–8 July 1997,[58] which was jointly organized by the European Commission and the German government and included representatives of the Commission, the Member States, the US government, other third country governments, international organizations, and the private sector. The final 'Ministerial declaration', published at the conclusion of the conference, contained hardly any mention of actions to be taken specifically by the EU.[59] During the next few years, the EU largely focused on Internet-related

of the Council of Europe to modernize the Convention, see https://www.coe.int/en/web/data-protection/convention108/modernised.

[53] See http://www.uncitral.org/uncitral/en/uncitral_texts/electronic_commerce/2001Model_signatures.html.

[54] United Nations Convention on the Use of Electronic Communications in International Contracts 2005, 2898 UNTS, Registration No. 50525. See Killian, 'The Electronic Communications Convention: A European Union Perspective', in A. H. Boss and W. Killian, *The United Nations Convention on the Use of Electronic Communications in International Contracts: An In-Depth Guide and Sourcebook* (2008) 407.

[55] TEU, note 8, at Arts. 2 and 3(1). See also T. Tridimas, *The General Principles of EU Law* (2nd edn, 2006), at 15, finding that the values of the EU represent the EU legal order.

[56] TEU, note 8, at Art. 3(5) and Art. 21(3).

[57] *Ibid.*, at Art. 21(1). See also Hijmans, note 9, at 33.

[58] See http://www.echo.lu/bonn/conference.html.

[59] See http://www.echo.lu/bonn/final.html.

issues relevant to the internal market, through the enactment of instruments such as the Directive on Electronic Commerce[60] and the Directive on Electronic Signatures.[61] It was only following the entry into force of the Treaty of Lisbon in 2009 and the resultant elevation of the Charter to the status of primary law that EU law was given the tools to assert its values and interests at a global level regarding the Internet,[62] as can be seen in the post-Lisbon judgments of the CJEU which rely on the TEU, the TFEU and the Charter to assert the global reach of EU law. The following sections consider the values of EU law that are implicated with regard to the Internet.

B. The Autonomy of EU Law

EU law views itself as an autonomous legal system,[63] which refers to 'the separateness and autonomy of the EC from other legal systems and from the international legal order more generally, and the priority to be given to the EC's own fundamental rules'.[64] The autonomy of EU law means that even obligations imposed by international agreements cannot prejudice the constitutional principles of EU law.[65]

The pluralistic and fragmented nature of the Internet can lead to legal conflicts and situations where different norms cover the same actors or conduct, without the existence of clear rules to determine which has priority. Such situations impact the autonomy of EU law, since they may create a risk that non-EU norms could prevail over the fundamental values of EU law, a possibility that the CJEU has rejected in Internet-related cases.[66] An example of a potential conflict is provided by Article 44 GDPR, which states that onward transfers of personal data from an international organization to a third country or another international organization shall take place only if the other provisions of the GDPR and the conditions laid down in Chapter V are complied with.[67] However, many international organizations enjoy privileges and immunities under public international law, and may expect that the further transfer of data they receive from the EU will be subject to international law or their own internal rules, not EU law.

[60] Directive 2000/31 of 8 June 2000 on certain legal aspects of information society services, in particular electronic commerce, in the Internal Market, OJ 2000 L 178/1.

[61] See note 49. [62] See Hijmans, note 9.

[63] See, e.g., *Opinion 2/13* (ECLI:EU:C:2014:2454), 18 December 2014; Joined Cases C-402 and 415/05P, *Kadi* [2008] ECR 1–6351 (ECLI:EU:C:2008:461).

[64] de Búrca, 'The European Court of Justice and the International Legal Order After Kadi', 51 *Harvard International Law Journal* (2010) 1, at 23.

[65] See *Kadi*, note 63, at para. 285.

[66] See Case C-362/14, *Schrems* (ECLI:EU:C:2015:650), 6 October 2015, at paras 84–87, criticizing the EU-US Safe Harbour Arrangement as giving US law primacy over EU fundamental rights in situations where they conflict. See also Kuner, 'Reality and Illusion in EU Data Transfer Regulation Post-*Schrems*', 18 *German Law Journal* (2017) 881.

[67] See Kuner, 'International Organizations and the EU General Data Protection Regulation: Exploring the Interaction between EU Law and International Law', 16 *International Organizations Law Review* (2019) (forthcoming).

C. The Rule of Law

The rule of law is one of the values upon which the EU is founded.[68] While the meaning of the term is open to interpretation,[69] it includes requirements such as: actions by governments or public authorities are limited by rules; such rules are fixed and set in advance; and judicial review and access to courts are available if the rules are violated.[70]

As one of the central values of the EU, the rule of law is a benchmark for EU action with respect to third countries, and is a value that the EU seeks to export beyond the borders of the Union.[71] The CJEU has emphasized the need to respect the rule of law with regard to data processing on the Internet, as can be seen in its *Schrems* judgment, where it stressed the importance of upholding the rule of law with regard to legislation limiting the effective right to judicial protection contained in Article 47 of the Charter.[72] Thus, upholding the rule of law with regard to the Internet is a key concern of EU law.[73]

D. Fundamental Rights

Fundamental rights are a value upon which the EU is founded,[74] and they play an important role in the relationship between EU law and the Internet. First, the EU's action on the international scene must be guided by fundamental rights,[75] which includes action affecting the Internet. Second, fundamental rights place limits on the action that the EU may take, and oblige it to protect the rights of EU individuals. Fundamental rights must be respected whenever EU law applies,[76] as the CJEU has stressed in various judgments dealing with Internet-related issues of data protection,[77] online copyright infringement[78] and the retention of telecommunications data.[79] The CJEU has also found that a draft international agreement of the EU could not be concluded in its current form since it was adopted under the wrong legal basis and it did not comply with the standards of the Charter.[80] The CJEU's main concern

[68] TEU, note 8, at Art. 2.

[69] See Kochenov, 'The EU Rule of Law: Cutting Paths through Confusion', 2 *Erasmus Law Review* (2009) 5, at 9.

[70] Rosas and Armati, note 35, at 46 (Kindle edition).

[71] Pech, 'Rule of Law as a Guiding Principle in the EU's External Action', Centre for the Law of EU External Relations, CLEER Working Papers 2012/13, http://www.asser.nl/media/1632/cleer2012-3web.pdf, at 13.

[72] See *Schrems*, note 66, at para. 95.

[73] See Hijmans, note 9, at 27–31.

[74] See TEU, note 8, at Art. 2. See also Art. 6(1) TEU, stating that fundamental rights have the same legal value as the Treaties.

[75] *Ibid.*, Art. 21(1).

[76] See Case 617/10, *Åkerberg Fransson* (ECLI:EU:C:2013:105), 26 February 2013, at para. 21.

[77] See, e.g., *Schrems*, note 66; Case C-131/12, *Google Spain* (ECLI:EU:C:2014:317), 13 May 2014.

[78] Case C-160/15, *GS Media BV* (ECLI:EU:C:2016:644), 8 September 2016, at para. 31.

[79] Joined Cases C-293/12 and C-594/12, *Digital Rights Ireland and Seitlinger* (ECLI:EU:C:2014:238), 8 April 2014; Joined Cases C-203/15 and C-698/15, *Tele2 Sverige AB* (ECLI:EU:C:2016:970), 21 December 2016.

[80] *Opinion 1/15* (ECLI:EU:C:2017:592), 26 July 2017. See Kuner, 'International Agreements, Data Protection, and EU Fundamental Rights on the International Stage: *Opinion 1/15*', 55 *Common Market Law Review* (2018) 857.

seems to be to prevent the evasion of fundamental rights protection,[81] which can be seen as an 'anti-evasion trigger' for the application of EU law.[82]

5. Interaction between EU Law and the Internet

A. Introduction

Some topics of EU law are by their nature 'external', while others are inherently 'internal' but have global reach.[83] The Internet merges the distinction between these two categories, since 'in a globalized economy, everything has an effect on everything'.[84] The discussion in this section will thus cover several areas of EU law that directly focus on the Internet (such as Internet governance), as well as others that routinely raise Internet-related issues (such as data protection), in order to show how the EU exerts its influence on Internet-related developments.

B. Internet Governance

The term 'Internet governance' refers not only to the technical management of the Internet, but also to law and policy in a host of areas dealing with communication and information policy. This is reflected in the definition used by the European Commission in its 2014 Communication on Internet governance, which defines the term broadly and emphasizes its pluralistic nature.[85] One of the EU's main objectives in Internet governance is to have the law apply to the Internet just as it does to the offline world,[86] as has also been advocated by the UN Human Rights Council.[87]

An example of EU action to promote its values regarding Internet governance concerns the domain name system (DNS), which functions as a kind of address book that translates domain names to Internet protocol addresses so that computers connected to the Internet can communicate with each other.[88] Domain name registrars maintain a register of the owners of domain names that can be queried online by searching the WHOIS servers, which contain a substantial amount of data about

[81] See *Schrems*, note 66, at paras 84–87, suggesting that EU fundamental rights are violated when protections under EU law are overridden by US law enforcement requirements.

[82] See Scott, 'The New Extraterritoriality', note 2, at 1359–1360.

[83] See Rosas and Armati, note 35, at 237 (Kindle edition); Cremona and Micklitz, 'Introduction', in M. Cremona and H.-W. Micklitz (eds), *Private Law in the External Relations of the EU* (2016) location 1427, at location 1451 (Kindle edition).

[84] Michaels, note 23, at 123.

[85] See Communication from the Commission, 'Internet Policy and Governance', note 48, at 2, stating: 'Internet governance is broadly understood to refer to the development and application by Governments, the private sector and civil society, in their respective roles, of shared principles, norms, rules, decision-making procedures, and programmes that shape the evolution and use of the Internet.'

[86] *Ibid.*

[87] UN Human Rights Council, 'The Promotion, Protection, and Enjoyment of Human Rights on the Internet' (29 June 2012), UN Doc A/HRC/20L.13, at 2, stating that 'the same rights that people have offline must also be protected online . . .'.

[88] See https://www.internetsociety.org/issues/domain-name-system-dns/.

registered domains, their registrants, and the servers used. Placing this data on the Internet via the WHOIS protocol has led to criticism by the former Article 29 Working Party (the body of EU and Member State data protection authorities (DPAs), now replaced by the European Data Protection Board).[89] These criticisms have, in some cases, resulted in ICANN granting waivers to registrars in the EU with regard to the conditions for data access and retention contained in the Registrar Accreditation Agreement (RAA), which controls how they store and make available WHOIS data, in order to allow the registrars to take EU data protection requirements into account.[90]

The EU institutions may cooperate to assert the values of EU law in Internet governance. For example, the Communication published jointly by the European Commission and the High Representative of the EU for Foreign Affairs and Security Policy Communication in 2013 concerning the 'Cybersecurity Strategy of the European Union'[91] urges that the EU develop 'a coherent international cyberspace policy' that promotes 'EU core values' in cooperation with 'relevant international partners and organisations, the private sector and civil society', and that this be mainstreamed into EU external relations and the Common Foreign and Security Policy.[92]

C. Data Protection

Data protection law, which subjects the processing of personal data to a set of defined rules in order to protect the fundamental rights of individuals, has become an important tool for regulating the Internet. Much of the EU's influence in data protection occurs through the extraterritorial application of EU law. There are different varieties or degrees of extraterritoriality, which range from the direct application of EU law to parties or conduct in third countries, to 'territorial extension', meaning the application of a measure triggered by a territorial connection but with the regulator required as a matter of law to take into account conduct or circumstances abroad.[93] With regard to EU data protection law, it is less important to categorize the exact form of extraterritoriality used, than to recognize that it exerts its influence in different ways on persons and activities in third countries.

The extraterritorial application of EU data protection law through the use of private international law is discussed later, in section 5.E. A further example of extraterritoriality is provided by rules of EU data protection law restricting the transfer of personal data to third countries. Article 45 GDPR allows data transfers to third countries when an adequate level of data protection is provided in the country, based on EU legal standards. The European Commission is empowered to issue a formal decision that a third country provides an adequate level of protection,[94] based on a

[89] Article 29 Working Party, 'Opinion 2/2003 on the application of the data protection principles to the WHOIS directories' (WP 76, 13 June 2003), at 4. See Bygrave, note 4, at 120 (Kindle edition).

[90] Bygrave, note 4, at 121 (Kindle edition).

[91] Cybersecurity Strategy of the European Union, note 29.

[92] *Ibid.*, at 14–16.

[93] See Scott, 'Extraterritoriality and Territorial Extension of EU Law', note 2, at 90.

[94] There are currently 13 European Commission adequacy decisions in force, covering Andorra; Argentina; the Canadian Personal Information Protection and Electronic Documents Act (PIPEDA);

determination that the foreign legal system in question offers a level of protection 'essentially equivalent' to that under EU law.[95] When an adequacy decision has not been issued, Article 46 GDPR permits transfers of personal data if 'appropriate safeguards' are provided, such as when contractual clauses have been signed between the data exporter in the EU and the data importer outside the EU obliging both to provide protections for the data,[96] and Article 47 GDPR allows transfer when the party transferring the data has implemented binding corporate rules (BCRs, i.e., legally binding internal data processing rules applied by a group of undertakings or enterprises engaged in a joint economic activity). In addition, derogations (such as when the data subject has consented to the transfer) may allow the transfer of personal data.[97]

EU data protection law makes the processing of personal data transferred to third countries conditional on the external application of EU standards.[98] In the case of adequacy decisions, this occurs through a formal evaluation of third country standards by the Commission (an example of 'country-level' territorial extension[99]), whereas in the case of appropriate safeguards (or 'adequate safeguards' as they were called under Article 26(2) of Directive 95/46/EC) the parties that receive data exported from the EU are obliged to apply protections based on EU law when they process data in third countries[100] (an example of 'firm-level' territorial extension[101]).

Switzerland; the Faroe Islands; Guernsey; Israel; the Isle of Man; the Japanese Act on the Protection of Personal Information; Jersey; New Zealand; the EU-US Privacy Shield; and Uruguay. See https://ec.europa.eu/info/law/law-topic/data-protection/data-transfers-outside-eu/adequacy-protection-personal-data-non-eu-countries_en. In January 2017 the Commission announced that it will 'actively engage with key trading partners in East and South-East Asia, starting from Japan and Korea in 2017, and, depending on progress towards the modernization of its data protection laws, with India, but also with countries in Latin America, in particular Mercosur, and the European neighbourhood which have expressed an interest in obtaining an "adequacy finding" '. Communication from the Commission to the European Parliament and the Council, 'Exchanging and Protecting Personal Data in a Globalised World', COM(2017) 7 final, 10 January 2017, at 8. In January 2019 the Commission adopted an adequacy decision covering the Japanese Act on the Protection of Personal Information. See Commission Implementing Decision of 23.1.2019 pursuant to Regulation (EU) 2016/679 of the European Parliament and of the Council on the adequate protection of personal data by Japan under the Act on the Protection of Personal Information, C(2019) 304 final (not yet published in the Official Journal).

95 The CJEU articulated this standard in *Schrems*, note 66, at para. 73.

96 See, e.g., Commission Decision 2010/87/EU of 5 February 2010 on standard contractual clauses for the transfer of personal data to processors established in third countries under Directive 95/46/EC of the European Parliament and of the Council, OJ 2010 L 39/5, Clauses 5(a), 5(d)(i) and 5(e).

97 See GDPR, note 38, at Art. 49.

98 See Mills, 'Private International Law and EU External Relations: Think Local Act Global, or Think Global Act Local?', 65 *International and Comparative Law Quarterly* (2016) 541, at 573–574.

99 See Scott, 'Extraterritoriality and Territorial Extension of EU Law', note 2, at 107.

100 See, e.g., Commission Decision 2004/915/EC of 27 December 2004 amending Decision 2001/497/EC as regards the introduction of an alternative set of standard contractual clauses for the transfer of personal data to third countries, OJ 2004 L 385/74, Clause II(h), requiring the data importer to process personal data exported from the EU in accordance with one of the following, at its option: (1) the data protection law of the country (i.e. the EU Member State) where the data exporter is established; (2) the relevant provisions of a Commission adequacy decision when the data importer is based in a country where such decision applies; or (3) a set of data protection principles contained in the contract and based on EU law. See also Article 29 Working Party, 'Working Document Setting up a Framework for the structure of Binding Corporate Rules' (WP 154, 24 June 2008), at 10, providing that '[i]n any event data shall be processed in accordance to the applicable law as provided by the [*sic*] Article 4 of the Directive 95/46/EC and the relevant local legislation'.

101 See Scott, 'Extraterritoriality and Territorial Extension of EU Law', note 2, at 107.

The GDPR also introduces new data transfer mechanisms based on the application of EU data protection standards in third countries.[102]

The application of EU data protection law to third countries is also illustrated by the fact that Member State DPAs have several times asserted their enforcement authority to investigate whether parties in third countries comply with EU law with regard to data transferred from the EU. The first such case occurred in 1996, when Citibank consented to an on-site audit of its data processing facilities in the US, conducted by the Berlin Data Protection Commissioner's office.[103] The Spanish Data Protection Agency has also conducted an audit of a third party data processor located in Colombia regarding compliance with Spanish legal requirements for data transfers,[104] and the Italian Data Protection Authority has obtained the consent of Google to audit the company's compliance with EU data protection law on its premises in California.[105]

EU data protection law also exercises global influence through the adoption by third countries of data protection laws based on the EU model. Dozens of countries worldwide have enacted laws based on the model of Directive 95/46/EC,[106] leading it to be called 'by far the most influential international policy instrument' in the field of data protection.[107] Among the developments that can be traced to the influence of EU law are the adoption of data protection laws in Central and Eastern European countries that have acceded to the EU, the passage of federal privacy legislation in Canada in 2000, and the growth of privacy laws in Asian countries.[108] The influence of EU data protection law can also be seen in the adoption of data protection acts in some African countries[109] and the implementation of privacy standards and seal programs in the private sector.[110]

This influence has been caused in part by the perceived economic benefit that can accrue to countries that enact laws based on the Directive, and are then able to import personal data under an EU adequacy decision[111] (though whether adequacy

[102] GDPR, note 38, at Arts 40(3) and 42(2), providing that codes of conduct and certification mechanisms based on EU standards may serve as a legal basis for data transfers.

[103] C. Bennett and C. Raab, *The Governance of Privacy: Policy Instruments in Global Perspective* (2006), at 98.

[104] See Agencia Española de Protección de Datos, 'Report on International Data Transfers: Ex officio Sectorial Inspection of Spain-Colombia at Call Centres', July 2007.

[105] Essers, 'Google agrees to Italian privacy authority audits in the US', PC World, 20 February 2015, available at http://www.pcworld.com/article/2887192/google-agrees-to-italian-privacy-authority-audits-in-the-us.html.

[106] See, e.g., Bradford, note 2, at 22–26; L. Bygrave, *Data Privacy Law: An International Perspective* (2014), at 208 (Kindle edition), stating 'the overwhelming bulk of countries that have enacted data privacy laws have followed, to a considerable degree, the EU model...'; Greenleaf, 'The Influence of European Data Privacy Standards outside Europe: Implications for Globalization of Convention 108', 2 *International Data Privacy Law* (2012) 68.

[107] Bennett and Raab, note 103, at 93.

[108] *Ibid.*, at 117.

[109] See, e.g., République du Sénégal, loi sur la protection des données à caractère personnel, exposé des motifs, http://www.centif.sn/loi_caractere_personnel.pdf, at 1; Traça and Embry, 'An Overview of the Legal Regime for Data Protection in Cape Verde', 1 *International Data Privacy Law* (2011) 1.

[110] Bennett and Raab, note 103, at 172.

[111] See New Zealand Privacy Commissioner, 'Privacy Amendment Important for Trade and Consumer Protection' (26 August 2010), available at https://www.privacy.org.nz/news-and-publications/statements-media-releases/updated-media-release-30-8-10-privacy-amendment-important-for-trade-

decisions actually lead to economic growth has not been independently verified). The fact that EU data protection law is based on a set of clearly structured instruments also makes it attractive to third countries, which often find it easier to use an existing text as a model rather than draft new legislation from scratch.

D. International Agreements

There are few legally binding international agreements or treaties dealing specifically with the Internet.[112] One example, the UNCITRAL Convention on Electronic Communications (the Convention),[113] shows how the relationship between the EU and its Member States influences the EU's approach to the conclusion of international agreements.

Both the European Commission and numerous Member States participated in the negotiation of the Convention.[114] Early in the drafting, concerns were expressed by the Commission about the effect that the Convention could have on the EU *acquis communautaire*,[115] particularly the EU E-Commerce Directive 2000/31/EC.[116] In response to these concerns, the following 'disconnection clause' was incorporated into the Convention:

1. A regional economic integration organization that is constituted by sovereign States and has competence over certain matters governed by this Convention may similarly sign, ratify, accept, approve or accede to this Convention. The regional economic integration organization shall in that case have the rights and obligations of a Contracting State, to the extent that that organization has competence over matters governed by this Convention. Where the number of Contracting States is relevant in this Convention, the regional economic integration organization shall not count as a Contracting State in addition to its member States that are Contracting States.
2. The regional economic integration organization shall, at the time of signature, ratification, acceptance, approval or accession, make a declaration to the depositary specifying the matters governed by this Convention in respect of which competence has been

and-consumer-protection, quoting the New Zealand Privacy Commissioner as follows regarding amendments to the New Zealand Privacy Act: 'An EU adequacy finding is also likely to satisfy data export requirements of other countries. I believe New Zealand businesses are already losing some trading opportunities through a gap in our privacy laws. This change will allow New Zealand to compete on a secure basis for international data business.' See also Bennett and Raab, note 103, at 113–114. New Zealand was found adequate by the Commission in 2013 (Commission Implementing Decision of 19 December 2012 pursuant to Directive 95/46/EC of the European Parliament and of the Council on the adequate protection of personal data by New Zealand, OJ 2013 L 28/12).

[112] Examples include the Council of Europe Convention on Cybercrime 2001, ETS No. 185; the WIPO Copyright Treaty 1996, 2186 UNTS 121 (2004); and the WIPO Performances and Phonograms Treaty 1996, 2186 UNTS 203 (2004). See also Uerpmann-Wittzack, 'Internetvölkerrecht', 47 *Archiv des Völkerrechts* (2009) 261.

[113] See UNCITRAL Convention on the Use of Electronic Communications, note 54.

[114] See UNCITRAL, Working Group IV (Electronic Commerce), Forty-first session, New York, 5–9 May 2003, Provisional List of Participants, UN DOC A/CN.9/WG.IV/XLI/INF.1.

[115] See Killian, note 54, at 408.

[116] Directive 2000/31 of 8 June 2000 on certain legal aspects of information society services, in particular electronic commerce, in the Internal Market, OJ 2000 L 178/1.

transferred to that organization by its member States. The regional economic integration organization shall promptly notify the depositary of any changes to the distribution of competence, including new transfers of competence, specified in the declaration under this paragraph.

3. Any reference to a 'Contracting State' or 'Contracting States' in this Convention applies equally to a regional economic integration organization where the context so requires.
4. This Convention shall not prevail over any conflicting rules of any regional economic integration organization as applicable to parties whose respective places of business are located in States members of any such organization, as set out by declaration made in accordance with article 21.[117]

The Convention entered into force in 2013, but thus far neither the EU nor any of the Member States have signed or ratified it.[118] The reason for this lies in the EU's unhappiness with the final version of Article 17(4), which requires either regional organizations (i.e. the EU) or their State members (i.e. the EU Member States) to make declarations under Article 21 in order to opt out of application of the Convention to parties located in other State members.[119] The Commission demanded that this wording be replaced by a formulation under which EU law would automatically take precedence over the Convention without the need for declarations to be made.[120]

E. Private International Law

Rules of EU law on applicable law and jurisdiction (referred to here as private international law) can have external effect even when they are adopted mainly to further internal goals, since they impact disputes or relationships that have connections with third countries.[121] Private international law has thus become 'the key to the private law of global affairs in a multi-jurisdictional world'.[122]

Data protection law is a useful paradigm for examining the territorial scope of EU law under private international law as it relates to the Internet. Data protection in EU law is a self-contained area with regard to applicable law and jurisdiction, since they are determined by data protection instruments such as the GDPR rather than those dealing with private international law, at least insofar as administrative enforcement of the law by the DPAs is concerned.[123] Under the GDPR, the territorial scope of application of data protection law has been expanded to include the processing of the personal data of individuals in the EU by a data controller or data

[117] UNCITRAL Convention on the Use of Electronic Communications, note 54, at Art. 17.

[118] See http://www.uncitral.org/uncitral/en/uncitral_texts/electronic_commerce/2005Convention_status.html

[119] See Killian, note 54, at 411–414.

[120] *Ibid.*

[121] See Mills, note 98, at 542.

[122] Basedow, note 1, at 35.

[123] See Case C-230/14, *Weltimmo* (ECLI:EU:C:2015:639), 1 October 2015, at paras 23, 51–52, finding that for the purposes of data protection law, Directive 95/46 (the predecessor of the GDPR), Art. 4 determined choice of law and Art. 28(6) determined jurisdiction.

processor not established in the EU where the processing activities are related to the offering of goods or services to such individuals or the monitoring of their behaviour.[124] The GDPR will thus extend the geographic reach of EU law to apply directly to the Internet activities of many parties in third countries. The ePrivacy Regulation proposal would also apply to providers of electronic communications services not established in the EU when they provide such services to end users in the EU.[125]

The broad jurisdictional scope of EU data protection law on the Internet can be seen in two judgments of the CJEU. In *Google Spain*,[126] the CJEU found that EU data protection law granted individuals a right to suppress links to search engine results, even though the servers on which the search engine operated were based outside the EU. The French data protection authority (the CNIL) has interpreted the judgment to apply to searches performed on websites in all domains globally[127] (this issue is currently the subject of litigation in the CJEU[128]). And in *Schrems*, the CJEU found that the transfer of personal data to a third country was subject to EU data protection law.[129]

F. Other Areas

EU law has extended its global reach regarding the Internet to other fields as well, only two of which will be considered here.

In *L'Oréal v. eBay*, the CJEU applied EU trade mark law to the sale on an Internet auction site of a trade-marked product in a third country when such sale was targeted at customers in the EU.[130] The CJEU thus extended the reach of EU law to third countries when failing to do so would have an impact on the effectiveness of EU rules.[131] And in May 2016 a number of leading Internet companies (including Google, Facebook, Twitter and Microsoft) agreed to apply EU rules on hate speech to their online services, following pressure from the EU Member States and the European Commission.[132]

[124] GDPR, note 38, Art. 3(2). [125] ePrivacy Regulation proposal, note 39, at Art. 3(1).

[126] See *Google Spain*, note 77, at paras 42–61. See also Kuner, 'The Court of Justice of the EU Judgment on Data Protection and Internet Search Engines: Current Issues and Future Challenges', in B. Hess and C. M. Mariottini (eds), *Protecting Privacy in Private International and Procedural Law and by Data Protection* (2015) 19, at 27–31.

[127] See CNIL, 'Right to be delisted: the CNIL Restricted Committee imposes a €100,000 fine on Google', 24 March 2016.

[128] Request for a preliminary ruling from the Conseil d'État (France) lodged on 21 August 2017—*Google Inc. v. Commission nationale de l'informatique et des libertés (CNIL)* (Case C-507/17), 2017 OJ C 347/22.

[129] See *Schrems*, note 66, at paras 45–46.

[130] Case C-324/09, *L'Oréal SA and Others v. eBay International AG and Others* [2011] ECR I-6011 (ECLI:EU:C:2011:474).

[131] See Jääskinen and Ward, 'The External Reach of EU Private Law in the Light of *L'Oréal versus eBay and Google and Google Spain*', in M. Cremona and H.-W. Micklitz (eds), *Private Law in the External Relations of the EU* (2016) location 4843, at location 5123 (Kindle edition).

[132] See D. Robinson, 'Web Giants Sign Up to EU Hate Speech Rules', *Financial Times*, 31 May 2016, available at https://www.ft.com/content/e8fb1690-26fc-11e6-8ba3-cdd781d02d89#axzz4ACePo5cX, noting that '[t]he move comes after EU ministers demanded that the bloc work with IT companies

6. Mechanisms of Global Reach

A. Introduction

EU law uses different mechanisms to exert its global reach. The EU has generally viewed this as a one-way street in which EU standards are exported to third countries rather than vice versa, leading to what has been called a 'Europeanization' of Internet regulation.[133] Sometimes the EU's global reach mechanisms are exercised intentionally, whereas in other situations they may apply as an afterthought or as part of some other phenomenon. These mechanisms are often intermingled, so that it can be difficult to determine which one applies in a particular case; for example, the adoption of EU standards seemingly based on a voluntary decision by a third country may in fact be motivated by behind-the-scenes political pressure. In some cases, both third countries and the EU may not want to reveal the extent of the influence that EU law has had. But sufficient evidence exists to allow classification of the different mechanisms.

B. Emulation and Learning

One approach can be referred to as learning from EU law, or emulating it in domestic or international law-making. This can occur for various reasons, such as affinities in legal culture that make the EU example attractive to a third country, or the fact that EU law tends to be contained in neatly packaged legal instruments.

This emulation is encouraged by EU external action policy, which seeks to promote the adoption of EU law through means such as financing technical assistance projects that allow experts from the EU to work with third countries.[134] For example, in 2011 such assistance was given by the EU to Mauritius, focusing on 'ensuring the data protection accreditation of Mauritius with the European Union'.[135]

In certain areas EU law has become the leading model that other countries and international organizations seek to emulate; data protection is a good example of this. Dozens of data protection laws in all regions of the world have been inspired by the EU model,[136] and international organizations such as the Office of the United Nations High Commissioner for Refugees (UNHCR)[137] and the International

to "counter terrorist propaganda" during an emergency meeting in the aftermath of the Brussels terror attacks' and '[t]his push to codify the handling of illegal hate speech online has been led in Brussels by Vera Jourová, the commissioner responsible for justice'.

133 Kowalik-Bańczyk and Pollicino, 'Migration of European Judicial Ideas concerning Jurisdiction over Google on Withdrawal of Information', 17 *German Law Journal* (2016) 315, at 335.

134 See Communication from the Commission, 'Exchanging and Protecting Personal Data in a Globalised World', note 94, at 12. See also Pech, note 71, at 19.

135 See http://eeas.europa.eu/delegations/mauritius/eu_mauritius/development_cooperation/technical_cooperation/index_en.htm.

136 See note 106.

137 UNHCR, 'Policy on the Protection of Personal Data of Persons of Concern to UNHCR', May 2015, available at http://www.refworld.org/docid/55643c1d4.html. See Beck and Kuner, 'Data Protection in International Organizations and the new UNHCR Data Protection Policy: Light at the

Committee of the Red Cross (ICRC)[138] have also turned to EU law as an important source of inspiration when adopting data protection policies and guidelines. In 2017 the ICRC and the Brussels Privacy Hub also published a handbook on data protection and humanitarian action based on a number of internationally recognized data protection standards, including those of EU law.[139] As such policies become more widely adopted, they may lead to the gradual crystallization of international law based on EU standards.[140]

Courts in third countries have also been influenced by judgments of the CJEU in cases involving the Internet. This influence has resulted in the export of European law, which has been described thus:

> European judges 'export' European ideas outside Europe. Put differently, European courts' rulings, which are extensively quoted in an attempt to increase the legitimacy and persuasiveness of their own rulings, inspire and influence non-European Union judges.[141]

An example is the CJEU's *Google Spain* judgment, where it recognized the so-called 'right to be forgotten'.[142] This judgment has served as inspiration for courts in third countries, such as Canada[143] and Japan.[144]

EU legal standards have also influenced private sector practices in third countries and international organizations, as can be seen in the example of data protection.[145] The influence of EU data protection law in the private sector is based on factors such as the need to conform to EU standards in order to compete in Europe; the power of the European market; the importance of privacy in the public consciousness; and the need to ensure that EU law is not undermined by lower standards elsewhere.[146] As EU data protection law is used as the standard for private sector data transfer mechanisms such as BCRs and standard contractual clauses, its influence extends

End of the Tunnel?', EJIL: *Talk!*, 31 August 2015, available at http://www.ejiltalk.org/data-protection-in-international-organizations-and-the-new-unhcr-data-protection-policy-light-at-the-end-of-the-tunnel/#more-13568.

138 ICRC, 'ICRC Rules on Personal Data Protection' (January 2016), available at https://shop.icrc.org/publications/international-humanitarian-law/icrc-rules-on-personal-data-protection.html.

139 C. Kuner and M. Marelli (eds), *Handbook on Data Protection in Humanitarian Action* (2017), available at http://brusselsprivacyhub.eu/publications/dataprotectionhandbook.html. See also Kuner and Marelli, 'Creating International Frameworks for Data Protection: The ICRC/Brussels Privacy Hub Handbook on Data Protection in Humanitarian Action', *EJIL: Talk!*, 13 July 2017, available at https://www.ejiltalk.org/creating-international-frameworks-for-data-protection-the-icrcbrussels-privacy-hub-handbook-on-data-protection-in-humanitarian-action.

140 With regard to the development of rules of customary international law as a process of 'crystallization', see H. Thirlway, *The Sources of International Law* (2014), at 66 (Kindle edition).

141 Kowalik-Bańczyk and Pollicino, note 133, at 333.

142 *Google Spain*, note 77, at paras 62–99.

143 See Kowalik-Bańczyk and Pollicino, note 133.

144 See Miyashita, 'The Right to be Forgotten, from the Trans-Atlantic to Japan', in D. Svantesson and D. Kloza (eds), *Trans-Atlantic Data Privacy Relations as a Challenge for Democracy* (2017) 321.

145 See K. Bamberger and D. Mulligan, *Privacy on the Ground* (2015), at 65, noting, with regard to a survey of company privacy officers in the US, that 'respondents explained that European law plays a large role in shaping such company-wide privacy policies'.

146 Bradford, note 2, at 24–26; Shaffer, 'Globalization and Social Protection: the Impact of EU and International Rules in the Ratcheting Up of US Privacy Standards', 25 *Yale Journal of International Law* (2000) 1, at 81–88.

beyond the parties that have adopted them. For example, both BCRs[147] and standard contractual clauses[148] allow the parties to them to transfer data on to other parties (so-called onward transfers) only if the protections under their provisions continue to apply. This results in companies and organizations in third countries gradually adopting the protections for the data contained in the original data transfer instruments, thus creating a 'web' of protection for the data based on EU law. Private sector entities in third countries often apply EU data protection standards even when they are not legally required to do so, since it is easier and less expensive to adopt a single set of standards globally.[149] International organizations have also used the GDPR as a source of inspiration when they adopt data protection policies and procedures.[150]

C. International Negotiation

The EU participates in a number of international fora dealing with Internet law and regulation. This includes UN-based organizations concerned with Internet governance, such as the IGF; other multilateral organizations, such as the Council of Europe and the OECD; international legal harmonization organizations, such as UNCITRAL; and many others. The EU exercises its influence in the scope of such participation, which includes promoting its values and interests. This can lead to tension with other regions, as can be seen in the example of data protection, where there is often competition between the EU and the US to advance their respective views.[151]

The EU's participation in international negotiations is also motivated by political factors. For example, during the negotiation of the GDPR, I observed the EU using its influence in the Council of Europe to prevent amendments to Convention 108 from being approved, based on the perception that this would 'steal the thunder' of the EU if reformed data protection rules were adopted at the international level before the EU adopted its GDPR. This shows how EU action can be motivated in part by the desire to successfully realize its internal legislative projects and to overshadow similar multilateral projects.

[147] See, e.g., Article 29 Working Party, 'Explanatory Document on the Processor Binding Corporate Rules' (WP 204 rev. 01, 22 May 2015), at 7, stating 'a member of the Processor's group may subcontract its obligations under the Service Agreement (Art. 17 of the Directive) to an external sub-processor (outside of the group) only by way of a written agreement with the external sub-processor which provides that adequate protection is adduced according to Articles 16, 17 of Directive 95/46 and which ensures that the external sub-processor will have to respect the same obligations as are imposed on the member of the Processor's group according to the Service Agreement and sections 1.3, 1.4, 3 and 6 of the working document 195'.

[148] See, e.g., Commission Decision 2010/87 of 5 February 2010 on standard contractual clauses, note 96, at Art. 1(e), requiring that sub-processors who receive data from the original data processor must carry out processing in accordance with the standard contractual clauses.

[149] Shaffer, note 146, at 80.

[150] See Kuner, note 67, at 28.

[151] See, e.g., Greenleaf, note 106, at 73, describing attempts by the US government and US companies 'to use their combined economic and political influence to limit the development of data privacy laws in other countries'.

D. Coercion and Conditionality

Coercion involves pressuring third countries to adopt certain policies through conditionality, i.e. by making access to resources or benefits conditional on compliance with the EU's policy requirements.[152] Coercion need not necessarily be viewed negatively, as a polity may legitimately make the granting of legal and political benefits contingent on the meeting of certain conditions. Indeed, the EU makes accession conditional on accepting and implementing the *acquis communautaire*, which constitutes a form of coercion.[153]

An example of this 'carrot and stick' approach is the use of adequacy decisions issued by the European Commission confirming that a third country offers an adequate level of data protection based on EU standards. The EU also uses this approach in other areas such as private international law, trade law and environmental standards.[154] The 'carrot' in this approach is the offer of extending preferential status to third countries once their data protection standards are certified as being 'essentially equivalent' to those of EU law, which is considered to grant economic benefits by allowing personal data to be transferred freely to such countries. The 'stick' is the fact that EU law permits the free flow of data to third countries only when they adopt EU standards.

Passing judgment on whether the law of third countries is adequate based on EU standards risks entangling legal analysis with unrelated political factors. For example, in July 2010 the government of Ireland delayed an EU adequacy decision for Israel based on alleged Israeli government involvement in the forging of Irish passports.[155] The process of negotiating data protection adequacy assessments has also created political tensions with third countries.[156]

Pressure from the EU has led commercial actors to change their behaviour. For example, providers of Internet data storage services have located their data centres in the EU in order to escape restrictions on international data transfers under EU law. As one news story puts it, global technology giants 'are racing to store their data on the Continent as new laws and privacy concerns drive investment decisions'.[157] Data storage companies also market their services based on having infrastructure in

[152] Gilardi, note 2, at 13 (all citations to online version).

[153] Regarding EU accession as a form of coercion see *ibid.*, at 14.

[154] See Mills, note 98, at 542–543.

[155] See Ihle, 'Ireland blocks EU data sharing with Israel', *JTA*, 8 July 2010, available at http://www.jta.org/2010/07/08/news-opinion/world/ireland-blocks-eu-data-sharing-with-israel. Israel later received an adequacy decision from the European Commission. Commission Decision 2011/61 of 31 January 2011 pursuant to Directive 95/46/EC of the European Parliament and of the Council on the adequate protection of personal data by the State of Israel with regard to automated processing of personal data, OJ 2011 L 27/39.

[156] See Stoddart, Chan and Joly, 'The European Union's Adequacy Approach to Privacy and International Data Sharing in Health Research', 44 *Journal of Law, Medicine & Ethics* (2016) 143 (concerning tensions with Quebec); Mucci, Cerulus and Von Der Burchard, 'Data fight emerges as last big hurdle to EU-Japan trade deal', *POLITICO*, 9 December 2016, available at http://www.politico.eu/article/eu-japan-trade-deal-caught-up-in-data-flow-row-cecilia-malmstrom.

[157] Cerulus, 'It's raining cloud storage in Europe', *POLITICO*, 24 November 2016, at 20, available at http://www.politico.eu/pro/its-commission-vs-the-market-on-data-flows.

the EU,[158] and global companies have aligned their privacy policies with the GDPR.[159]

E. Blocking Recognition of Third Country Legal Measures

EU law may block recognition of third country legal measures that conflict with its own values. This is a method of extending the global reach of EU law, since it is based on an assertion of EU values in relation to legal measures taken by a third country.

An example of this is Article 48 GDPR, which limits the enforceability of decisions of third country courts and administrative authorities in the EU, and reads as follows:

> Any judgment of a court or tribunal and any decision of an administrative authority of a third country requiring a controller or processor to transfer or disclose personal data may only be recognised or enforceable in any manner if based on an international agreement, such as a mutual legal assistance treaty, in force between the requesting third country and the Union or a Member State, without prejudice to other grounds for transfer pursuant to this Chapter.[160]

This provision is similar to so-called 'blocking statutes'[161] that protect parties in the EU from what are viewed as exorbitant jurisdictional assertions by third countries. For example, French law prohibits the disclosure to foreign public authorities (such as courts or administrative authorities) of data or information if this would impair the important interests of France.[162]

7. Normative Questions

A. Introduction

EU law does not use a comprehensive, overarching normative approach to exercise its global reach regarding the Internet, which is not surprising in light of the Internet's relative novelty, the wide variety of EU institutions and legal instruments that deal with it, and the fragmented landscape of norms and actors involved in its governance and regulation. This accords with the view that the manifestations of the global impact of EU law vary based on their significance and difficulty of realization.[163]

[158] See Martin-Jung, 'Wir sind NSA-Frei', *Frankfurter Allgemeine Zeitung*, 16 November 2016, at 26, in which the European head of Fujitsu states, regarding the company's cloud storage services, that '[w]e are located in Germany and have a German infrastructure, we are free of the NSA...' (author's translation).

[159] See Communication from the Commission, 'Exchanging and Protecting Personal Data in a Globalised World', note 94, at 2.

[160] GDPR, note 38, Art. 48.

[161] Regarding blocking statutes in general, see Basedow, note 1, at 334–342; Cooper and Kuner, 'Data Protection Law and International Dispute Resolution', 382 *Recueil des cours/Collected Courses of the Hague Academy of International Law* (2017) 9, at 142–146.

[162] Loi no 80–538 du 16 juillet 1980 relative à la communication de documents ou renseignements d'ordre économique, commercial ou technique à des personnes physiques ou morales étrangères.

[163] See Young, note 2, at 1237.

However, in recent years the EU has extended its reach to Internet activities beyond its borders, as demonstrated by the growing number of legislative and regulatory initiatives adopted (e.g. the GDPR), and the increased willingness of the CJEU to assert EU values in its case law dealing with Internet-related topics (e.g. *Google Spain* and *Schrems*). In this regard, the Internet has served as a vehicle allowing EU law to assert itself globally. This increasing global reach of EU law, as it concerns the Internet, raises some important normative questions.

B. Values or Interests?

In its external action the EU must uphold and promote its 'values', which the TEU lists as 'human dignity, freedom, democracy, equality, the rule of law and respect for human rights, including the rights of persons belonging to minorities'.[164] These are described later in the TEU as the principles which the EU 'seeks to advance in the wider world',[165] and together represent the core values of EU law.

However, the EU is also guided by its political interests. Thus, in its external relations the EU is required to uphold and promote its 'interests',[166] to define and pursue its 'common policies and actions',[167] and to safeguard its 'fundamental interests'.[168] The Council is also obliged to identify the EU's 'strategic interests' in the context of external action.[169] Primary law does not define these terms or state whether there is any difference between them.

The influence of legal values when the EU exerts its global reach can be seen in the judgments of the CJEU in Internet-related cases, and in EU legislation such as the GDPR. An example of the EU asserting its political interests can be seen in the following statement by the European Commission concerning the adoption of adequacy decisions covering the level of data protection in third countries:

> Under its framework on adequacy findings, the Commission considers that the following criteria should be taken into account when assessing with which third countries a dialogue on adequacy should be pursued:
>
> (i) the extent of the EU's (actual or potential) commercial relations with a given third country, including the existence of a free trade agreement or ongoing negotiations;
>
> (ii) the extent of personal data flows from the EU, reflecting geographical and/or cultural ties;
>
> (iii) the pioneering role the third country plays in the field of privacy and data protection that could serve as a model for other countries in its region; and
>
> (iv) the overall political relationship with the third country in question, in particular with respect to the promotion of common values and shared objectives at international level.[170]

[164] TEU, note 8, at Art. 2.

[165] *Ibid.*, at Art. 21(1). [166] *Ibid.*, at Art. 3(5). [167] *Ibid.*, at Art. 21(2).

[168] *Ibid.*, at Art. 21(2)(a). [169] See note 31.

[170] Communication from the Commission, 'Exchanging and Protecting Personal Data in a Globalised World', note 94, at 8.

The CJEU stated in *Schrems* that the Commission's discretion with regard to the adequacy of protection ensured by a third country 'is reduced', and that its review of the requirements stemming from EU data protection law and the Charter should be 'strict'.[171] It seems that the EU would like to have its cake and eat it too by having one institution (the CJEU) insist on strict legal standards for adequacy decisions, while another (the Commission) prioritizes discussions with third countries based on political factors. The entanglement of EU legal values with the EU's political interests can also be seen in the way the CJEU has defined the territorial scope of EU law on the Internet in terms of the policy objectives that the law seeks to pursue.[172]

There is a natural interdependence between the EU's legal values and its political interests,[173] and law and politics can be viewed as 'structurally coupled systems',[174] since legal values are adopted as a product of political decisions. However, this does not mean that there is not a distinction between the values that the EU has enshrined in the constitutional instruments that form the basis of its legal order, and the political priorities of the day. When, intentionally or unintentionally, political interests are presented as legal values or vice versa, there is a risk that legal values will be diluted to fit a particular political agenda, or that political viewpoints will be reduced to the exercise of technical steps by bureaucrats and experts.[175] An example of the former can be seen in the assertion of EU legal values as universal values, as discussed later, which is clothed in legal language but is clearly based on a political project.

It is thus important that the EU should not cloak the assertion of its political interests in the language of fundamental legal values, in order to keep a degree of integrity in the law that is resistant to changing political pressures. As the EU increasingly asserts its global reach regarding Internet-related issues, it should be more honest about differentiating between its legal values and political interests, when each applies, and for what reasons.

C. EU Law as Universal Values

The EU increasingly asserts its values as universal, global standards for the Internet. This can be seen in the words of some of the leading figures involved in the adoption of the GDPR:

–Former EU Commissioner Viviane Reding: 'Europe must act decisively to establish a robust data protection framework that can be the gold standard for the world'.[176]

[171] *Schrems*, note 66, at para. 78.

[172] See Francq, 'The External Dimension of Rome I and Rome II: Neutrality or Schizophrenia?', in M. Cremona and H.-W. Micklitz (eds), *Private Law in the External Relations of the EU* (2016) location 3283, at location 3814 (Kindle edition).

[173] See Marise Cremona, Chapter 2 in this volume.

[174] Peters, 'Compensatory Constitutionalism: The Function and Potential of Fundamental International Norms and Structures', 19 *Leiden Journal of International Law* (2006) 579, at 609. See also A. Bianchi, *International Law Theories* (2016), at location 1701–1748 (Kindle edition).

[175] See M. Koskenniemi, *The Politics of International Law* (2011), at 149–151 (Kindle edition).

[176] See Reding, 'A data protection compact for Europe', 28 January 2014, available at http://europa.eu/rapid/press-release_SPEECH-14-62_en.htm. See also Kuner, 'The European Union and the Search for an International Data Protection Framework', 2 *Groningen Journal of International Law* (2014) 55, at 57.

–MEP Jan-Philipp Albrecht, Rapporteur in the European Parliament for the GDPR: The GDPR will change 'nothing less than the whole world as we know it'.[177]

–An unnamed EU official: 'With these proposals, the EU is becoming the de facto world regulator on data protection'.[178]

In a newspaper interview following the *Schrems* judgment, CJEU President Koen Lenaerts left no doubt about the leading role that he believes EU law should play in the wider world:

> Europe must not be ashamed of its basic principles: The rule of law is not up for sale. It is a matter of upholding the requirements in the European Union, of the rule of law, of fundamental rights. If this is also affecting some dealings internationally, why would Europe not be proud to contribute its requiring standards of respect of fundamental rights to the world in general?[179]

EU law has arisen in a unique constitutional and institutional context,[180] which gives rise to a paradox: if EU law is unique and fundamentally different from other legal systems, how can its standards be replicated elsewhere, and how can third countries be expected to adopt them? Many third countries have adopted legislation close to the EU model in areas such as data protection, but few have been found to provide a level of protection that is essentially equivalent to that provided under EU standards. Whether a norm is based on a fundamental legal value or a political interest also affects the ability to assert it as being universal, since it would be unreasonable to expect third countries to accept the EU's political interests as universal values.

When a legal system strives for its standards to be accepted as universal values, it is inevitably engaged in a hegemonic struggle in which it seeks to have its own special interests identified with the general interest.[181] The EU is engaged in such a struggle with regard to the assertion of its values and interests concerning the Internet, as can be seen in data protection, where efforts to promote the spread of EU law are portrayed as encouraging third countries and international organizations to adopt strong data protection standards.[182] The risk is that this may lead not to genuine, disinterested universalism, but to 'false universalism, the universalism of Empire'.[183]

[177] Albrecht, 'How the GDPR Will Change the World', 3 *European Data Protection Law Review* (2016) 287, at 287.

[178] See Vogel, 'Reding seeks Overhaul of Data Protection Rules', *European Voice*, 15 December 2011, available at http://www.europeanvoice.com/article/reding-seeks-overhaul-of-data-protection-rules.

[179] Popp, 'ECJ President on EU Integration, Public Opinion, Safe Harbor, Antitrust', *The Wall Street Journal*, 14 October 2015, available at http://blogs.wsj.com/brussels/2015/10/14/ecj-president-on-eu-integration-public-opinion-safe-harbor-antitrust/tab/print/.

[180] See, e.g., Rosas and Armati, note 35, at 4 (referring to 'the unique nature of the EU as a legal and constitutional order') (Kindle edition).

[181] See Koskenniemi and Leino, 'Fragmentation of International Law? Postmodern Anxieties', 15 *Leiden Journal of International Law* (2002) 553, at 561–562.

[182] See Communication from the Commission, 'Exchanging and Protecting Personal Data in a Globalised World', note 94, at 10, where the Commission states that it will 'work with and assist countries interested in adopting strong data protection laws and support their convergence with EU data protection principles'; at 12, where the Commission supports the 'swift adoption' of the modernized text of Council of Europe Convention 108 since the Convention 'will reflect the same principles as those enshrined in the new EU data protection rules and thus contribute to the convergence towards a set of high data protection standards'; and at 16, stating that the EU will actively engage with third countries to explore adequacy findings 'with a view to fostering regulatory convergence towards the EU standards…'.

[183] See Koskenniemi, 'International Law in Europe: Between Tradition and Renewal', 16 *European Journal of International Law* (2005) 113, at 116.

The promotion of EU law as a set of universal values can also backfire when it leads third countries to insist that the EU comply with their own legal requirements. This can involve, for example, third countries allowing data transfers to the EU only when it provides adequate protection under their standards.[184] Third countries may also require that any decision on the adequacy of their data protection system be mutual (i.e. they may also issue a decision as to whether they find the EU's level of data protection to be adequate); for example, in July 2018 the EU and Japan agreed to issue mutual adequacy decisions about each other's data protection systems.[185]

D. Theory and Practice

There is an important distinction between the spread of EU legal values and their protection in practice. For example, the fact that EU data protection law has influenced the adoption of legislation around the world does not necessarily mean that this has led to a higher level of data protection on the Internet. Determining the extent to which EU values are reflected in practice on the Internet would require a large-scale empirical study that has yet to be conducted.

EU law focuses on the application of its norms to the Internet in a legal sense (e.g. the application of EU law to Internet-related activities, or the adoption by third countries of law based on EU models), rather than on an evaluation of whether the legal values that the EU seeks to export are upheld in practice. An example of this phenomenon can be seen in the ePrivacy Regulation proposal,[186] Article 3(2) of which requires parties not established in the EU that provide electronic communications services (i.e. many types of websites, Internet services that use connected devices, etc.) to users in the EU to designate a 'representative in the Union' in writing. The proposed Regulation describes the duties of representatives, but contains no details about how they should be appointed, what liability they have, and other important practical points. There are well over one billion websites on the Internet,[187] not even counting the many other types of services covered by the proposal, and the resources necessary for establishing and policing a system for the appointment and registration of representatives on such a huge scale would seem to be far beyond the capabilities of any EU or Member State institution. Article 3(2) thus seems to be a textbook example of regulatory overreaching, i.e. of law being applied so broadly that it stands little chance of being enforced.[188]

[184] See, e.g., Angola, Law no. 22/11 on the Protection of Personal Data, Art. 33; Economic Community of West African States (ECOWAS), Supplementary Act A/SA.1/01/10 on Personal Data Protection within ECOWAS (16 February 2010), Art. 36; Japanese Act on the Protection of Personal Information (as amended 2015), Art. 24; Macau Special Administrative Region (MSAR) of the People's Republic of China, Personal Data Protection Act (Act 8/2005), Art. 19. See also C. Kuner, *Transborder Data Flows and Data Privacy Law* (2013), at 65–66.

[185] See, e.g., European Commission, 'The European Union and Japan agreed to create the world's largest area of safe data flows', 17 July 2018, available at http://europa.eu/rapid/press-release_IP-18-4501_en.htm, stating that the EU and Japan have 'agreed to recognize each other's data protection systems as "equivalent"'.

[186] ePrivacy Regulation proposal, note 39.

[187] See http://www.internetlivestats.com/total-number-of-websites/.

[188] See Bygrave, note 106, at vi (Kindle edition).

In order for the application of EU law to be meaningful, it must be effective in practice as well as applying on paper, as the CJEU has recognized. For example, the CJEU in *Schrems* emphasized that protections for personal data transferred from the EU to third countries must 'prove, in practice, effective in order to ensure protection essentially equivalent to that guaranteed within the European Union'.[189] EU law should put greater emphasis on whether the values that underlie its legal standards are fulfilled in practice. An example of such an approach is the requirement in the GDPR that regular periodic reviews be conducted of Commission decisions on the adequacy of data protection in third countries and international organizations.[190]

E. The Territorial Scope of EU Law

The Internet raises questions about how the EU should act with regard to conduct that occurs outside its borders but has an effect within them. It is easier to state that EU law should be given wide territorial application when important public policy interests are at stake[191] than to determine the limits of its application.

The EU adopts a schizophrenic attitude to the territorial application of its law. On the one hand, the EU and its Member States often insist on limits to jurisdiction based on sovereignty when jurisdictional assertions by third countries are involved; this can be seen, for example, in the insistence by the EU and the Member States on using the Hague Convention on the Taking of Evidence Abroad in Civil or Commercial Matters (the Hague Evidence Convention)[192] as the exclusive means for discovery of evidence abroad,[193] and in the enactment in some Member States of so-called blocking statutes that restrict compliance with third country discovery requests.[194] On the other hand, judgments such as *Google Spain* and *Schrems* demonstrate that the EU applies its law broadly to actions by third countries when this is necessary to defend its own substantive legal standards.[195]

The CJEU's current approach to defining the territorial scope of EU law on the Internet is based largely on the policy objectives that the law seeks to pursue. For example, the result of the CJEU's *Google Spain* judgment has been described as follows: 'the (territorial) scope of application of EU secondary law is determined by its policy objectives: a direct correlation can be established between the achievement of EU policies and the potential need to cover situations located in third states'.[196] The less guidance provided by the legislator as to the territorial scope of law, the higher the risk that courts will be left to determine it based on their interpretation of the

[189] *Schrems*, note 66, at para. 74. See also para. 39 (referring to the need for 'effective and complete' protection); para. 41 (referring to the importance of ensuring the 'effectiveness' of monitoring of compliance with the law by DPAs); and paras 81, 89, 91 and 95 (in which the CJEU stresses the need for protection of the fundamental right to data protection to be 'effective').

[190] See GDPR, note 38, Art. 45(3).

[191] See Jääskinen and Ward, note 131, at location 5246 (Kindle edition).

[192] Signed at The Hague, 18 March 1970, 847 UNTS 231.

[193] See Article 29 Working Party, 'Working Document 1/2009 on pre-trial discovery for cross border civil litigation' (WP 158, 11 February 2009), at 14. See also GDPR, note 38, Art. 48.

[194] E.g. in France. See Loi no 80–538 du 16 juillet 1980, note 162.

[195] See Cremona and Micklitz, note 83, at location 1523 (Kindle edition).

[196] See Francq, note 172, at location 3814 (Kindle edition).

EU's policy objectives of the moment.[197] This risks sacrificing the coherence and consistency of EU law, and may result in the presentation of political interests as legal values, as has already been discussed.

EU law is still searching for a paradigm for its application to Internet-related activities that is based on firm legal principles, secures the rights of EU individuals, and avoids jurisdictional overreach.[198] That some territorial limits to the application of EU law must exist is indicated by the CJEU's judgment in *Air Transport Association of America*,[199] where it found that EU law should not apply to aircraft registered in third countries that fly over third countries or the high seas, but that it can exercise jurisdiction when an aircraft arrives or departs from a Member State.[200] This judgment indicates the broad outlines of a jurisdictional approach to the Internet as well, i.e. to avoid applying EU law to parties and situations outside its borders that have no contact or connection with the EU, but to extend its application to situations that have effect in the EU or on EU individuals. Such an approach can also be seen in the tendency of DPAs to prioritize the protection of individuals with a substantial connection to the EU.[201]

It will be up to the CJEU to define a paradigm for the territorial application of EU law as cases involving the Internet are brought before it or referred to it. This will depend on resolving difficult questions such as what constitutes a sufficient contact or connection to justify the assertion of EU law, and what it means for conduct to have 'effects' regarding the EU.

F. Responsibilities towards Third Countries

In examining the global reach of EU law, the focus has invariably been on the influence and power exercised by the EU. But along with influence and power goes responsibility, and this raises the question of whether the EU has responsibilities to third countries that adopt its standards.

EU law has been willing to exert its influence on third countries, but less inclined to learn from them. For example, the following has been stated regarding the judicial dialogue between the EU courts and courts in third countries:

[197] Jääskinen and Ward, note 131, at location 5253.

[198] For one proposal for such an approach, see D. Jerker B. Svantesson, *Solving the Internet Jurisdiction Puzzle* (2017).

[199] Case C-366/10, *Air Transport Association of America* [2011] ECR I-13755 (ECLI:EU:C:2011:864).

[200] *Ibid.*, at paras 122–127.

[201] See, e.g., Article 29 Working Party, 'Guidelines on the implementation of the Court of Justice of the European Union judgment on "Google Spain and Inc. v. Agencia Española de Protección de Datos (AEPD) and Mario Costeja González" C-131/12' (WP 225, 26 November 2014), at 3, stating, with regard to the exercise of a request for de-listing under the *Google Spain* judgment, '[i]n practice, DPAs will focus on claims where there is a clear link between the data subject and the EU, for instance where the data subject is a citizen or resident of an EU Member State'. See also Peguera, 'In the Aftermath of Google Spain: How the "Right to be Forgotten" is Being Shaped in Spain by Courts and the Data Protection Authority', 23 *International Journal of Law and Information Technology* (2015) 325, at 341, describing a case in which the Spanish DPA dismissed a claim because the claimant was not an EU resident and did not have a clear link with the EU.

> The European courts seem more inclined 'to teach' rather than 'to learn' when discussing the protection, *erga omnes* (towards everyone), of European constitutional values, even beyond the reaches of Europe. In other words, the European judicial dialogue remains European-value-based even when globalized.[202]

There is a growing realization that 'as agents of humanity, sovereigns are obligated to take other-regarding considerations seriously into account in formulating and implementing policies…'.[203] It seems reasonable to conclude that this principle should also apply when one legal system exercises influence over others, particularly when it seeks to have its values adopted as global standards. The global reach of EU law should not be purely a matter of the EU seeing how far it can extend its influence towards third countries, but should subject it to responsibilities as well. These responsibilities are especially compelling with regard to developing countries, towards which there is a well-documented history of hegemony on the part of European legal systems.[204]

The EU's responsibilities towards third countries can be seen in the example of EU data protection law. Many of the third countries that have enacted legislation based on EU law are developing countries with limited resources, and enacting a legal framework for data protection based on EU standards with all that entails can be a significant burden for them.[205]

If EU law is to be the 'de facto standard for the world', then the EU has a moral responsibility towards other countries that adopt it. Recognizing such a responsibility is ultimately in the EU's own interest, since it would provide additional incentives for other countries to adopt EU law. The increased interaction with third countries produced by such measures could also benefit the EU by illuminating areas where it could learn from them.[206]

This moral responsibility is already reflected in some provisions of EU law. The TEU requires the EU to foster 'the sustainable economic, social and environmental development of developing countries, with the primary aim of eradicating poverty',[207] and the Internet can be seen as a vehicle for fostering economic and social development. At the level of secondary legislation, Article 50(d) GDPR provides that the Commission and the DPAs should 'promote the exchange and documentation of personal data protection legislation and practice, including on jurisdictional conflicts with third countries'. However, impact assessment provisions in EU

[202] Kowalik-Bańczyk and Pollicino, note 133, at 333.

[203] Benvenisti, 'Sovereigns as Trustees of Humanity: On the Accountability of States to Foreign Stakeholders', 107 *American Journal of International Law* (2013) 295, at 300.

[204] See, e.g., M. Koskenniemi, *The Gentle Civilizer of Nations* (2001), at chapter 2; A. Mbembe, *Critique of Black Reason* (2017) (Kindle edition); Nunn, 'Law as a Eurocentric Enterprise', 15 *Law and Inequality* (1997) 323.

[205] See Madhub, 'The Pioneering Journey of the Data Protection Commission of Mauritius', 3 *International Data Privacy Law* (2013) 239, at 241–242.

[206] Communication from the Commission, 'Exchanging and Protecting Personal Data in a Globalised World', note 94, at 12, stating that 'the EU can benefit from the exchange of best practices and the experience of other systems with new challenges for the protection of privacy and emerging legal or technical solutions, including as regards enforcement, compliance tools (e.g. certification mechanisms, privacy impact assessments) or the protections for certain specific data sets (e.g. children's data)'.

[207] TEU, note 8, at Art. 21(2)(d).

legislation concerning the Internet tend to consider only its impact with regard to the EU.[208] Further measures should be enacted to assess the impact of EU legislation on third countries, particularly developing countries; to provide information on EU legal developments of particular relevance to them (e.g., via an Internet portal); and to solicit input from third countries regarding the impact of EU law on them.

Finding that the EU has certain responsibilities towards third countries that are influenced by its law also raises the question of whether it is setting standards on others that it is not prepared to live up to itself. In a legal sense, the standards of EU law and those of third country law are two different matters, but in a moral sense, the legitimacy of EU law is undermined if the EU is viewed as holding third countries to higher standards than it obliges itself to meet.

An example can be seen in the *Schrems* judgment, where the CJEU held the conclusion of adequacy decisions by the European Commission regarding the level of data protection in third countries to a high standard, particularly regarding access to data by third country intelligence authorities. However, Article 4 TEU grants competence for national security to the Member States, and there is widespread sharing of information by intelligence agencies of the Member States with third countries such as the US, both under the 'Five Eyes'[209] intelligence-sharing network (which includes Australia, Canada, New Zealand, the UK and the US), and under bilateral arrangements between the US and Member States such as France[210] and Germany.[211] Thus, there are substantial gaps in legal protection against intelligence surveillance under EU law, which undermines the moral legitimacy of criticisms of third country standards. It would increase the influence of EU law on the international stage if the EU were to ensure that it can itself satisfy the standards that it expects third countries to meet.

G. Is the Internet Changing EU Law?

A final question is whether the Internet is also changing EU law. The increased rapidity and volume of international communications on the Internet have led to an increase in international disputes and increased contact between the EU and foreign

[208] E.g. periodic reviews of Commission data protection adequacy decisions are limited to assessing the continued existence of an adequate level of data protection in the relevant third country and whether the decisions are being implemented in a discriminatory way (i.e. discriminatory against the EU). See, e.g., Commission Decision C (2003) 1731 of 30 June 2003 pursuant to Directive (EC) 95/46 of the European Parliament and of the Council on the adequate protection of personal data in Argentina, OJ 2003 L 168/19, Art. 4; Commission Implementing Decision of 21 August 2012 pursuant to Directive 95/46/EC of the European Parliament and of the Council on the adequate protection of personal data by the Eastern Republic of Uruguay with regard to automated processing of personal data, OJ 2012 L 227/11, Art. 4.

[209] Regarding the Five Eyes alliance, see G. Greenwald, *No Place to Hide* (2014), at locations 1581, 1854–1900 (Kindle edition).

[210] See Root, 'French intelligence involved in NSA spying in France', *Bloomberg News*, 29 November 2013, available at http://www.bloomberg.com/news/articles/2013-11-29/french-intelligence-involved-in-nsa-spying-in-france-monde-says.

[211] See 'Geheimdienst-Kooperation: BND leitet seit 2007 Daten an die NSA weiter', *SPIEGEL ONLINE*, 8 August 2013, available at http://www.spiegel.de/netzwelt/netzpolitik/geheimdienste-bnd-leitet-seit-2007-daten-an-die-nsa-weiter-a-915589.html.

legal systems. These factors may cause changes in EU law, as can be seen in the growing need for the CJEU to take foreign law into consideration in the course of answering questions of EU law.

The CJEU's role is to serve as 'the ultimate authority for deciding any question concerning the interpretation or validity of EU law',[212] and in theory it does not pass judgment on the law of third countries.[213] In the interview he gave following the *Schrems* judgment, CJEU President Koen Lenaerts stated about the judgment: 'We are not judging the U.S. system here, we are judging the requirements of EU law in terms of the conditions to transfer data to third countries, whatever they be.'[214]

However, it is surely disingenuous to claim that the *Schrems* case did not involve evaluation of third country legal standards. The judgment is based on an examination of US intelligence gathering practices and their effect on fundamental rights under EU law, as can be seen, for example, in the CJEU's mention of studies by the European Commission finding that US authorities were able to access data in ways that did not meet EU legal standards in areas such as purpose limitation, necessity and proportionality.[215] The need to review third country standards is logically inherent in an evaluation of whether a Commission decision based on those standards results in protection that is essentially equivalent to that under EU law.

The CJEU's review of third country standards can also be seen in the opinions of Advocate General Bot in *Schrems*,[216] and Advocate General Mengozzi in *Opinion 1/15*,[217] a case based on a request for an opinion by the European Parliament concerning a draft agreement between the EU and Canada for the transfer of airline passenger name records. The opinion of Advocate General Bot contains an evaluation of questions of US law, such as the scope of the supervisory powers of the US Federal Trade Commission (FTC).[218] In his Opinion, Advocate General Mengozzi indicated that some provisions of Canadian law had been brought before the CJEU[219] and that some of the contentions of the parties required interpretation of issues of Canadian law.[220] The CJEU also referred to issues of Canadian law in its final Opinion.[221]

[212] G. Beck, *The Legal Reasoning of the Court of Justice of the EU* (2012), at 225 (Kindle edition).

[213] See *Opinion 1/15*, Opinion of Advocate General Mengozzi (ECLI:EU:C:2016:656), 8 September 2016, at para. 163, stating 'the Court cannot express a view on the legislation or the practice of a third country…'. The Grand Chamber of the Court issued its judgment in the case on 26 July 2017 (ECLI:EU:C:2017:592).

[214] Lenaerts interview, note 179.

[215] See *Schrems*, note 66, at para. 90. See also at para. 93, where the CJEU seems to imply that data transferred to the US are subject to undifferentiated storage, access and use.

[216] *Schrems*, Case C-362/14, Opinion of Advocate General Bot, 23 September 2015 (ECLI:EU:C:2015:627).

[217] See note 213.

[218] *Schrems*, Opinion of Advocate General Bot, note 216, at paras 207–208.

[219] *Opinion 1/15*, Opinion of Advocate General Mengozzi, note 213, at para. 320, stating: 'However, there is no reference in the agreement envisaged to the existence of that administrative appeal to the Canadian Privacy Commissioner, nor is its existence apparent from any provision of Canadian law brought to the knowledge of the Court.'

[220] *Ibid.*, at para. 156, mentioning a contention by the Council and the Commission that the international agreement in question between Canada and the EU 'reflects the obligation which the Canadian Constitution imposes on all Canadian public authorities to comply with a court order'.

[221] *Opinion 1/15*, note 80, at paras 66 and 177.

In *Schrems*, the CJEU virtually ordered national courts to make preliminary references to it of cases involving the adequacy of data protection in third countries,[222] and the Commission has indicated that in the future it will consider issuing additional adequacy decisions.[223] This indicates that the CJEU is likely to be faced with an increasing number of cases that require an evaluation of foreign law in order to determine whether it meets EU legal standards. In addition, *Opinion 1/15* was not a preliminary reference but a request for an opinion submitted by the European Parliament under Article 218(11) TFEU, demonstrating the variety of cases in which the CJEU may need to deal with the law and legal standards of third countries.

Since in a reference for a preliminary ruling the determinations of national courts will generally be accepted by the CJEU without further inquiry,[224] and intervention in such references is not possible,[225] there is a risk that a judgment could be based on an insufficient evaluation of foreign law. This could occur, for example, when the evidence concerning foreign law is delivered only by a single party and is uncontested,[226] a situation that has been criticized in private international law scholarship as a 'false application of foreign law'.[227] However, the CJEU's Opinion procedure does allow the use of expert opinions and further investigation,[228] and in cases under that procedure it could consider taking evidence from individuals and groups with an expert knowledge of the relevant foreign law.

8. Final Thoughts: Why the Internet?

Bradford has argued that the EU's external regulatory influence has emerged 'largely as an inadvertent by-product of its internal goal to create and strengthen the single market'.[229] However, as this chapter has shown, the EU tends to assert itself as a global regulatory power consciously and deliberately with regard to the Internet. This means that the EU seeks to have its own legal standards adopted by third countries and at the international level, and asserts its regulatory authority towards activities in third countries that affect its interests and those of individuals within its

[222] *Schrems*, note 66, at paras 64–65.

[223] See Communication from the Commission, 'Exchanging and Protecting Personal Data in a Globalised World', note 94, at 8.

[224] See K. Lenaerts, I. Maselis and K. Gutman, *EU Procedural Law* (2014), at location 15562 (Kindle edition).

[225] *Ibid.*, at location 23573 (Kindle edition).

[226] This is what happened in the *Schrems* judgment of the Irish High Court that resulted in the referral to the CJEU, where the evidence considered by the High Court concerning US law was in effect uncontested. See *Maximilan Schrems and Data Protection Commissioner*, 18 June 2014, 2013 No. 765JR.

[227] See Jänterä-Jareborg, 'Foreign Law in National Courts: A Comparative Perspective', 304 *Recueil des cours/Collected Courses of the Hague Academy of International Law* (2003) 181, at 233.

[228] See Consolidated Version of the Rules of Procedure of the Court of Justice of 25 September 2012, Arts 196–200.

[229] Bradford, 'Exporting Standards: The Externalization of the EU's Regulatory Power via Markets', 42 *International Review of Law and Economics* (2015) 158, at 158.

borders. One may ask why the EU would promote the influence of its own standards and ideas so strongly with regard to the Internet?

The first reason relates to the legal factors described in this chapter, including in particular the Lisbon Treaty and the enhanced legal status of the Charter of Fundamental Rights, as well as the Internet-related judgments of the CJEU that have been issued in the last few years. The Internet has assumed increased importance in almost every area of life, so that there are few areas of EU law that are not affected by it. The nature of how the Internet functions means that activities carried out in the EU have an effect in third countries and vice versa, thus creating a high potential for interaction between EU law and activities implicating third countries.

But just as significant have been the legal, political and social factors that have combined to cause EU law relating to the Internet to interact with the wider world in a way that might not be seen in many other areas of law. This has occurred as both the EU and Europe in a broader sense have been faced with an increasing number of political, economic and social challenges. Regulation of the Internet has proved a convenient vehicle through which the EU can assert itself on the world stage without having to take coordinated action geo-politically in a way that would exceed its current capabilities. By focusing on the Internet, the EU has been able to use its strengths in law and regulation, areas where it is a superpower, to make itself heard globally.

The Internet has led both to an opening of EU law (as in the expanding role of the CJEU in dealing with questions of foreign law), and to a tendency to take EU standards as the measure of all things (as when the EU attempts to have its own standards accepted universally). The question is whether EU law will allow interfaces with other legal systems, or retreat into the historical European tendency to focus on itself that Mbembe has described:

> [T]hroughout its history, European thought has tended to conceive of identity less in terms of mutual belonging (cobelonging) to a common world than in terms of a relation between similar beings—of being itself emerging and manifesting itself in its own state, or its own mirror.[230]

EU law has had significant influence on the Internet, but the Internet has also influenced the development of EU law. In coming years the EU will have to confront an increasing number of challenges posed by the Internet, such as how to define the territorial scope of EU law to Internet-related activities; what responsibilities the EU should have towards third countries that are influenced by the assertion of its legal standards; and how to evaluate issues of foreign law in the work of the CJEU. Thus, the relationship between EU law and the Internet will continue to evolve, to reflect both the values and interests of the EU, and the nature of the Internet as a social and legal phenomenon.

[230] Mbembe, note 204, at location 314 (Kindle edition).

4

Financial Stability and the Global Influence of EU Law

*Paul Davies**

1. Introduction

A. Finance as a Global Industry

Financial activities might be seen as a good context in which to examine the global influence of EU law, simply because finance has become, over the past few decades, a global industry. This development, it can be said, gives EU rule-makers a strong incentive to promote the extra-EU impact of their rules. However, it is not obviously true that the global nature of an industry generates such incentives for rule-makers. Many other industries, whether aimed at producing goods or services, now occur on a global basis, for example, vehicle manufacturing, but the incentive to extend national or regional rules cross-border appears to be much less in those cases. By and large, the law-makers in jurisdiction A seem able to live with manufacturing activities in jurisdiction B being governed by B's rules alone, though B's rules may give rise to occasional irritations to the rule-makers in A.[1]

There are two, interrelated ways in which global finance is arguably different from other global industries. First, its business model is more fragile; second, the probability of contagion from failure in one jurisdiction to other jurisdictions is very much higher.

1. The Fragility of Business Models

On the first difference, it is widely accepted that the business model of banking—a central part of the financial industry—is fragile. The core banking activity consists of making illiquid, medium- to long-term loans on the back of funding which is

* This chapter was completed in June 2017, with only limited subsequent additions.

[1] This statement is not inconsistent with the argument that, under certain specific conditions, *markets* may 'export' standards from one jurisdiction to another. See Bradford, 'Exporting Standards: The Externalization of the EU's Regulatory Power', 42 *International Review of Law and Economics* (2015) 158. As she points out, this export effect is largely an 'inadvertent byproduct' of the creation of a single market and occurs only under certain conditions, which she explores in her article. By contrast, the focus in this chapter is on legislators' and regulators' incentives to give external effect to their rules.

Financial Stability and the Global Influence of EU Law. First Edition. Paul Davies © Paul Davies 2019.
Published 2019 by Oxford University Press.

short-term and 'information insensitive'.[2] Information insensitivity means not simply that the bank's legal repayment obligation in relation to, for example, a deposit is fixed at the full amount of the funds deposited, but also that the depositors do not expect the value of the deposit to vary with the state of the bank or the wider economy. Unlike, for example, long-term bonds, where the bond-holder's legal entitlement to repayment in full exists only at the maturity of the bond and where there is, in the interim, a secondary market for the bonds in which their value does vary on the basis of economic factors, a depositor[3] is entitled to and expects to receive the full value of the deposit from the bank at any time or on short notice (though equally no more than the amount deposited, plus any interest due).

Since depositors know (at least after the crisis of 2007–2009) that this entitlement may not be met in all circumstances, they have an incentive to initiate correlated withdrawals (i.e. to 'run' on the bank), if they suspect that repayment may become doubtful in the future.[4] This would not be a major problem for the bank, if it could realize its assets (the loans) at full value and at short notice, but it cannot, mainly because the loans are difficult for outsiders to value and the outsiders are therefore subject to opportunism (adverse selection) on the part of the banks when selecting the loans to be sold or used as collateral. So, the outsiders discount the value of even 'good' loans. Of course, a run makes the depositors collectively worse off, for it ensures the collapse of the bank into insolvency, whereas without the run the bank might have been able to work its way out of its difficulties. However, the 'first movers' are incentivized to run by a 'safety first' strategy and, if a run starts, everyone else is likely to join in.[5] Thus, banking is based on confidence—not a confidence trick perhaps, but certainly confidence that withdrawals will be driven by depositors' consumption needs, not by their fears about the stability of the bank.[6]

It is widely accepted that the banks' business model is inherently fragile, but banks are only part of the global financial system. Today, financial markets are a more important source of finance than banks for large borrowers, at least in many jurisdictions. Are institutions operating in financial markets fragile in the same way as banks are? It appears that these institutions also often operate on the basis of short-term funding, involving promises to repay at par, to support their business activities, for example, investment banks that fund securities acquisition on the basis of repo

[2] That financing has traditionally been retail deposit finance, which can be withdrawn at no or short notice, but in recent years that source has been supplemented with wholesale funding, notably via commercial paper, with very short-term maturities, which can be withdrawn by not being rolled over. It was the initial withdrawal of wholesale funding which brought down the UK bank, Northern Rock, at the beginning of the financial crisis. The retail run on the bank followed only once the withdrawal of wholesale funding became public knowledge: H. S. Shinn, Risk and Liquidity (2010), chapter 8.

[3] Or holder of short-term commercial paper.

[4] M. Ricks, *The Money Problem* (2016), chapters 2 and 3.

[5] If the multiple short-term funders could coordinate their activities, they might agree to withdraw only on a 'normal' basis, but they cannot do so at a sensible cost.

[6] Much of bank regulation is thus aimed at preserving the confidence of short-term funders in the capacity of their banks to repay, for example, through deposit guarantee schemes, capital and liquidity requirements and access to central bank liquidity resources. See Armour *et al.*, *Principles of Financial Regulation* (2016), chapters 13–15. However, none of these mitigating techniques can guarantee bank solvency, except at the risk of undermining the transformation function of banks, which is where their social value lies.

transactions or securitization conduits that are funded by commercial paper. Before the crisis, this model was considered to be less risky in many situations than the traditional banking model because it was thought that the market assets acquired by investment banks could be liquidated quickly at good values to replace funds withdrawn by short-term funders. However, the recent crisis showed that previously liquid markets may dry up rapidly in the face of uncertainty.[7] Thus, mismatch between the liability and the asset sides of the balance sheet appeared in the 'shadow' banking sector[8] as much as in the traditional commercial banking sector.

The social case for ensuring the safety and soundness of traditional banks is a strong one. Banks are still crucial sources of funding for households and small businesses, despite the growth of non-bank substitutes since the crisis.[9] A principal reason for the bail-out of banks by states in the financial crisis was the calculation that, although expensive, bail-out would be less costly than the loss of economic output that the reduction in lending capacity would bring about if the banks were allowed to fail. However, the costs of bail-outs are certainly large enough to give states an overriding interest in the safety and soundness of banks, not just as deposit-takers and lenders but across the full range of their financial activities.

First, the largest and globally important banks are now involved in market activities as well as core banking. Losses on the market side of the business may affect the viability of the bank as a whole. A possible regulatory strategy is to attempt to keep the banks out of market activities and from holding market assets. Short, however, of a policy of requiring separate (beneficial) ownership of commercial banking and other bank activities—a policy which has not appealed to policy-makers post-crisis—this strategy has only limited traction.[10] Second, if commercial and investment banks hold assets in common, then, even without any ownership or contractual links, a fire-sale of assets by an investment bank to meet the demands of its short-term funders may threaten (or may be perceived by depositors to threaten) the viability of commercial banks by driving down the value of assets held on the latters' balance sheets.

On this argument, there may be a case for regulating even intermediaries who have made no promise to repay their funders at par. Thus, fund managers (of retail funds) promise immediate liquidity to investors, but only on the basis that investors

[7] Gorton and Metrick, 'Securitized Banking and the Run on Repo', 104 *Journal of Financial Economics* (2013) 425.

[8] Shadow banking is an imprecise term but the interpretation which stresses the analogy with traditional banking is favoured in this chapter. See Z. Pozsar *et al.*, 'Shadow Banking', Federal Reserve Bank of New York Staff Report No. 458 (February 2012).

[9] This is especially true in Europe: Langfield and Pagano, *Bank Bias in Europe: Effects on Systemic Risk and Growth* (2015) ECB working paper 1797.

[10] The much-discussed 'Volcker rule' in the US excludes banks only from proprietary trading in market assets; it does not reintroduce the full division between commercial and investment banking ownership which was once a feature of US regulation under the Glass Steagall Act of 1932 (which fell into desuetude and was later repealed). The UK's ring-fencing structure (Independent Commission on Banking, *Final Report*, September 2011; Financial Services (Banking Reform) Act 2013) makes a more far-reaching distinction between core and non-core banking activities, but allows both types of activity to be carried on under common ownership. It aims therefore not so much to reduce the probabilities of bank failure, as to make the resolution of a failed core bank easier (thus reducing the need for a bail-out).

are entitled to their pro rata share of the current market value of the fund. However, heavy withdrawals by investors may drive down the price of the asset class which the fund has to sell to meet its liquidity demands and that may affect the viability of other institutions which hold that class of assets, in particular banks—even though, again, there may be no contractual or ownership links between the funds and the banks. Equally, non-retail investment funds, notably hedge funds, may invest on a leveraged basis, which exposes them to the need to sell assets so as to reduce margin calls in times of market volatility, even if these funds do not offer daily liquidity. So, systemic risk regulators have an incentive to constrain to some degree the build-up of risk in investment funds because of the 'spill over' impact upon banks and other institutions.[11]

Third, a final reason for promoting the safety and soundness of investment banks is that they, too, provide some socially valuable economic services, such as facilitating the access of large companies to the equity and bond markets to raise finance. The loss of these services for a period of time or from some providers is likely to have adverse economic consequences, though perhaps not on the scale of a widespread withdrawal of credit.

Overall, therefore, the recent crisis revealed the inter-linked nature of financial institutions, whether operating as lenders on their own account, as acquirers of financial assets or as intermediaries in the financial markets. By extension, it showed the ease with which problems with one group of institutions can spread to another group, even in the absence of ownership or contractual links between those two groups.

2. *Contagion across Borders*

The above analysis does not explain fully the incentives for legislators to extend their rules to other jurisdictions. If the above analysis applied only jurisdiction by jurisdiction, one would have a strong argument for regulating banks and financial markets, but not for extending that regulation cross-border. As the financial crisis which began in 2007 itself shows, however, the very essence of a modern financial crisis is its capacity to spread contagion across borders.

In fact, the recent crisis is a very instructive example of the point. As is well known, the crisis had its origins in decisions by US banks to make home loans to 'sub-prime' US borrowers, i.e. borrowers whose expected capacity to repay the loan was lower than was normally required to induce the bank to advance the funds. Yet this piece of financial mismanagement came within an ace of bringing down the financial system, not only of the US, but also that of Western Europe, as well as causing perturbations in the rest of the world. Why was the impact of the crisis not substantially confined within the US, where the initial lenders and borrowers were located, in the same way as, some decades earlier, the impact of the US 'savings and loans crisis',

[11] Financial Stability Board (FSB), *Policy Recommendations to Address Structural Vulnerabilities from Asset Management Activities*, 12 January 2017. A similar analysis could be developed in relation to the non-insurance, non-traditional activities of insurance companies: Armour *et al.*, note 6, chapter 22.

which was also a housing crisis, had been confined? Answering that question tells us something about the interrelationship between banking activities and market activities; about the globalization of financial markets; and about the fragility of banking at the wholesale level.[12]

The bank/market interrelationship provides the first part of the answer. The development of securitization techniques permitted the lenders to dispose of the loans to market investors. In essence, securitization involved the transfer of 'bundles' of loans to independent entities ('structured investment vehicles' (SIVs)) which, on the one hand, used money raised from market investors to pay for the loans and, on the other, used the cash flows from the loans to meet the obligations under the debt securities issued to the market investors to raise the purchase finance. Having sold the loans in this way, the originators could re-invest the funds in further loans. In principle, securitization is a beneficial activity, because it provides a source of market finance for banks' lending activities and makes banks less dependent on short-term deposit or wholesale funding. For this reason the EU authorities have recently sought to revive the European securitization market, which has been moribund since the financial crisis.[13] The risks are also clear: lenders have less incentive to monitor the quality of the loans they make if they do not hold them to maturity, as under the traditional model; market investors may find it difficult to assess the value of the loans underlying the securities they purchase; and the sponsors of the SIV (typically large investment banks) may take advantage of this opacity to mis-sell products. All these downsides revealed themselves in the run-up to the crisis.[14] The broader point is that securitization means that bank lending and financial market activities are linked. In this way, problems in bank lending can feed through into securities markets.[15]

Whilst securitization provides the link to the financial markets, it does not by itself explain the global impact of the sub-prime lending by US banks. If the market investors had all been US institutions, the problem would have remained a US one. But they were not. Since the removal of capital controls in the early 1970s, capital markets have become global. The investors in the securities issued by the SIV were

[12] The question of why the US banks made the loans in the first place, especially as under the US system (unlike in Europe) there is no personal obligation to repay a housing loan, has been left aside. The lender's security is simply the house. If borrowers are required to put no or little equity into the initial acquisition and can 'just return the keys' if they get into repayment difficulty, they are as much incentivized to act opportunistically as lenders who securitize the loan subsequently. The answer to the question of why the loans were made at all seems to lie in some combination of US governmental pressure and lender bets that there would not be correlated falls in value across the whole of the US housing market.

[13] Commission Proposal for a Regulation on Securitisation, COM(2015) 472 final; Regulation 2017/2401 of 12 December 2017, OJ 2017 L 347/1 and Regulation 2017/2402 of 12 December 2017, OJ 2017 L 347/35; Bavoso, 'Good Securitisation, Bad Securitisation and the Quest for Sustainable EU Capital Markets', 30 *Butterworths Journal of International Banking and Financial Law* (2015) 221; Krahnen and Wilde, 'Skin-in-the-Game in ABS Transactions: A Critical Review of Policy Options' (2017) (available on ssrn.com/abstract=2916633).

[14] See, e.g., Gerding, 'Disclosure 2.0: Can Technology Solve Overload, Complexity, and Other Information Failures?', 90 *Tulane Law Journal* (2016) 1143, at section II.C.1–3.

[15] Just as, in the example of investment funds given earlier, problems in the securities markets can feed through into banking.

global—or at least heavily non-American. Whilst the 10 largest originators of the loans were all US banks, the 12 largest sponsors of the SIVs included some large European investment banks: Deutsche Bank, Barclays, ABN Amro and UBS.[16]

However, the puzzle of the global financial crisis still remains. The sub-prime loan portfolio, although large, was only a small proportion of global financial assets. Since securitization and globalization had spread these loans across the international investment community, absorption of the default losses should have been easier, not more difficult, than if the loans had not been so distributed. However, there were two pieces of information which were lacking. No one knew with certainty where the debt instruments issued in support of the securitizations had ended up (for example, were they heavily concentrated in particular financial institutions?) nor how the securities should now be valued in the presence of the unexpected event of a correlated decline in housing prices across the US.[17] In particular, there was a fear that globally important banks were heavily exposed to these securities.[18] The response of banks throughout the US and Europe was to hoard liquidity by reducing lending to other banks, so that the interbank lending market began to dry up, and also reducing lending to households and businesses. Less lending to other banks reduced the risk of non-payment by those banks and less lending to households and businesses reduced the funding needs of the banks, so that they could more easily withstand the drying up of the interbank market and more easily meet withdrawal demands made by retail and wholesale depositors. This created the 'credit crunch' which was a central feature of the crisis. In this way, contagion from the sub-prime crisis reached banks which had not engaged in sub-prime lending or the securitization process[19] and, even more importantly, businesses and households in the 'real' economy. It was probably the contagion effect of the crisis in the real economy which was the biggest inducement for states to bail out banks.[20]

[16] Jaffee *et al.*, 'Mortgage Origination and Securitization in the Financial Crisis', in V. Acharya and M. Richardson (eds), *Restoring Financial Stability* (2009) 81, Tables 1.2 and 1.4. Of course, the US investment bank sponsors of SIVs, such as Citigroup, Merrill Lynch, Goldman Sachs, Lehman Bros, J P Morgan, Bear Stearns and Bank of America would also have had a wide international clientele. (Three of these did not survive the crisis as independent entities.) Significantly, only Citigroup and Bank of America appear on the list of the 10 largest originators, showing the degree to which loan origination and securitization of the loans had become specialized activities.

[17] An additional uncertainty related to the viability of the protection against default by SIVs which risk-averse market investors had secured via credit default swaps, which are discussed later.

[18] The major banks were not just sellers of securitizations to lesser institutions. They took some of the securitizations onto their own books as investors themselves; they might have either legal or reputational obligations to the SIVs they sponsored if these defaulted on their obligations to their investors (i.e. the SIVs were not truly 'off balance sheet' as far as the sponsors were concerned); and when the crisis struck, sponsors were stuck with exposures to the SIVs which had not yet completed the securitization process (in particular, the banks were financing SIVs which had not yet issued securities to the general market).

[19] E.g., Northern Rock, see note 2, which had not engaged in the UK equivalent of sub-prime lending but had securitized some of its loans and had financed itself to an unusual extent with short-term wholesale funding, found that funding withdrawn as concerns about the value of mortgage-backed securities mounted.

[20] H. S. Scott, *Connectedness and Contagion* (2016).

B. Implications for Regulation

It is now possible to see how the global financial industry creates issues for national or regional regulation which other global industries do not replicate. First, the 'negative externalities' of the collapse of a large bank or other financial institution are of an order of magnitude greater than the collapse of a large manufacturer. The collapse of General Motors, which nearly occurred in the aftermath of the financial crisis, would have caused economic disruption in those foreign countries where it had manufacturing plants, but that disruption would have been confined to the car industry and would not have spread in any meaningful way to unconnected industries, unlike the 'credit crunch', which was economy-wide. Second, regulators in all exposed jurisdictions have an intense interest in the quality of each other's regulation. In a global financial industry there can be no guarantee of financial stability 'in one country' or 'region': controlling the risks arising in one jurisdiction (jurisdiction A) is not adequate protection for jurisdiction A's economy if risks from other jurisdictions can be easily transmitted to it. In the financial crisis, regulators outside the US discovered (too late) that they had a strong interest in the way the US regulated bank lending for real estate purchases and the process of securitizing those loans.[21] But the flow could equally have been the other way.

There are three broad strategies available for handling this set of problems. The first is to reverse globalization and retreat into national or regional silos which can be regulated effectively by the relevant national or regional regulator. This policy has not proved attractive to states in the aftermath of the crisis, though elements of it can be detected in the post-crisis structure of regulation, as we shall see, and could become more prevalent in the future. To be fully effective, such a policy would require the reintroduction of controls over the movement of capital across borders, so that financial transactions and institutions would be cabined within jurisdictions.[22] The reluctance to reverse globalization in a thoroughgoing way stems no doubt from an appreciation of the likely costs of so doing, i.e. loss of access to deep and liquid financial markets, loss of competition in the provision of services, and a reduction in inward investment.

Second, a jurisdiction might seek to impose its rules extraterritorially. That jurisdiction's rules would thus apply not only to those doing business in the jurisdiction but also to the worldwide activities of those operating in the jurisdiction, even if the activity in question occurs wholly or partly outside the jurisdiction in question.[23] Probably, only the US is a large enough market to contemplate this approach as a general strategy. On the one hand, access to the US market has a sufficiently strong

[21] Gerding, 'Bank Regulation and Securitization: How the Law Improved Transmission Lines Between Real Estate and Banking Crises', 50 *Georgia Law Review* (2015) 1. And on the (lack of) regulation of credit default swaps, see Stout, 'Derivatives and the Legal Origin of the 2008 Credit Crisis', 1 *Harvard Business Law Review* (2011) 1.

[22] Institutions in different jurisdictions might be subject to common ownership, but their operations would be ring-fenced within each jurisdiction.

[23] Some dispute whether such an extension is an example of extraterritoriality: Scott, 'Extraterritoriality and Territorial Extension in EU Law', 62 *American Journal of Comparative Law* (2014) 87, at 91–92; cf. C Brummer, *Soft Law and the Global Financial System* (2nd edn, 2015), at 34–45.

'pull' force, so that a significant number of non-US institutions will accept the extra burdens of complying with US as well as non-US rules, in order to gain access to the US market. On the other, the US market is sufficiently developed that US customers may not suffer if some non-US institutions withdraw from it.

However, it is not a comprehensive solution. Those who conduct business wholly outside, for example, the US, with counterparties who have chosen not to access the US markets, escape the rule. This is an inevitable restriction, since there is no practical way of enforcing US rules in this situation. These activities may constitute a minor part of the global financial markets at present, but they might develop in the future and this strategy might add to the incentives to develop competing centres (i.e. to escape US hegemony). Further, it is a strategy which invites retaliation in kind from other financial centres, which may respond by applying their rules on a similarly expansive basis. The result may be a reduction in cross-border financial activity. Institutions which comply with both sets of regulations may incur a compliance cost which makes them uncompetitive with institutions which comply with only one set (by confining their operations to a single jurisdiction). Alternatively, the two sets of rules may be in some respects incompatible so that institutions are forced to choose among regulatory sets and thus the jurisdiction in which they will operate. In either case, a strategy which aims to subject global financial activity to a single set of rules may result in bringing about a retreat from globalization.[24]

Given the disadvantages of a thoroughgoing extraterritorial application of jurisdictional rules, there is a strong incentive for a jurisdiction to qualify it in one of two ways. The first is to adopt a restricted form of extraterritoriality. Continuing with the example of the US, this might involve exempting transactions occurring outside the US by a foreign bank which has operations in the US, provided that the US presence is not used to implement the transaction in question. This qualification takes some of the sting out of the extraterritorial argument, since the rule then applies fully only to the worldwide activity of US institutions—though, equally, it may subject US institutions to a competitive disadvantage and so be unattractive for that reason. In addition, it deals less effectively with the spread of cross-border financial contagion than unqualified extraterritoriality. For example, a non-US institution might be brought down by engaging in an activity wholly outside the US which is prohibited to US institutions and its failure might have a significant impact in the US via the associated collapse of its operations in the US.[25]

The second qualification is to supplement the extraterritorial rule with an exception based on recognition of the other jurisdiction's rules. A transaction outside

[24] Nevertheless, Coffee has argued strongly that this strategy has a good chance of success, at least in relation to OTC derivatives, if the US and the EU jointly seek to impose common rules on the rest of the world: Coffee, 'Extraterritorial Financial Regulation: Why E.T. Can't Come Home', 99 *Cornell Law Review* (2014) 259. So, even here, unilateral action by one jurisdiction is not enough.

[25] The extraterritorial effect of the Volcker rule, banning trading by banks in securities on their own account, is shaped in this way, i.e. foreign banks operating in the US can engage in this activity provided the transactions take place wholly outside the US: Coffee, *ibid.*, section II.

jurisdiction A, which would otherwise be caught by A's rules, is exempted if it is subject to the rules of jurisdiction B where A regards B's rules as equivalent, although not identical, to its own. This approach might be accompanied by a requirement for mutual recognition, i.e. recognition by B of A's rules as equivalent in the converse situation. Or, without a formal requirement for mutual recognition, this situation may result from B's adoption of the same policy as A. Mutual recognition can be regarded as a bilateral way of coordinating national regulatory strategies, by reducing differences in approach.

The third strategy is to seek to coordinate the laws of the important financial jurisdictions at supranational level so that discrepancies among jurisdictions are minimized, ideally before national regulation is put in place. This has been the predominant strategy adopted since the financial crisis. In some cases an international standard-setter was already in operation, whose rule-making activities could be reinvigorated. The principal example[26] is the Basel Committee on Banking Supervision (BCBS), essentially a group of central bank governors, which before the crisis had already produced and later revised a substantial rulebook on bank capital and liquidity requirements. BCBS provided a ready forum for upgrading the regulation of banks. More important, the leading economies, constituted as the 'Group of Twenty' (G20), reinvigorated the Financial Stability Forum as the Financial Stability Board (FSB) in 2009. The FSB has subsequently devoted substantial effort to the development of regulatory principles across the financial spectrum. Since the FSB was a creation of the crisis and has been required to act in a wide range of areas, its principles tend to be less detailed and precise than the rules produced by the BCBS. Both FSB and BCBS are, however, alike in being organizations of regulators. Both are given some degree of democratic legitimacy by reporting to the G20, which consists of the heads of government of the member countries.

The rules and principles produced by the BCBS and the FSB have been criticized on the basis that they constitute 'soft' law rather than binding international law, so that compliance levels can be expected to be low. However, as Brummer has argued, it is easy to over-emphasize the compliance contrast between 'hard' and 'soft' international law, since in both cases the incentives for compliance are similar.[27] These incentives, essentially reputational and market access benefits, are reinforced in the case of international financial soft law by the 'peer review' systems which both the BCBS and the FSB require their members to participate in. A more convincing criticism is directed at the substance of the standards adopted at international level. Since the standard-setters operate largely by consensus, conflicts of national regulatory philosophy or even of simple national interest cannot always be overcome through consultation and debate. This may result in the adoption of less-than-robust standards at international level or the glossing over of differences of view through high-level formulations which allow for implementation in a variety of ways. In the former case, some states may opt to implement higher standards, either across the

[26] There were two other international standard setters (IOSCO in the area of securities regulation and IAIS in the area of insurance) but their pre-crisis rule books were much less developed.

[27] Brummer, note 23, at chapter 3.

board or for particular types of financial institution. Normally, this is perfectly in accord with the international standards, which purport to be only minima.[28] In both cases, however, a lower level of regulatory coordination is generated.

It follows that the second and third strategies are not mutually exclusive. Whereas international coordination under the third strategy reduces the scope for the second strategy, it does not rule it out completely. A 'super-equivalent' national or regional regulator or one which has simply interpreted the international standard in a particular way may seek to impose its choices on the worldwide activities of institutions which do business in its territory. And, of course, the third strategy may not be comprehensive, so omitted topics will be open to the full second strategy treatment. Even with the frenetic international activity post the crisis, the FSB's agenda has not embraced all possible regulatory responses.

2. The External Influence of EU Law

From the previous analysis, there emerge two main channels of influence for EU law on the development of global financial regulation. The first is by way of input into the coordination process which occurs at international level (the third strategy) and the second is by way of the application of EU law to activities outside the EU (the second strategy) and especially via the 'recognition' pathway of the second strategy.[29] Where recognition is a unilateral act by jurisdiction A vis-à-vis jurisdiction B's rules, then A influences B's rules, since B has an incentive to follow at least the broad outlines of A's rules in order to obtain recognition. With mutual recognition, whether formal or informal, jurisdictions seek mutually to influence each other's rules. In either case, recognition provides a method of bilateral coordination, which does not have the jurisdictional scope of multilateral coordination but which may be able to achieve coordination at a more detailed level because fewer jurisdictional conflicts have to be resolved.

The first level of influence is discussed next, in section 2.A, and the second in section 2.B. As a preliminary point, what is discussed here is the influence of EU institutions and law, not the influence of the laws and institutions of individual Member States. In other words, the question discussed is the external influence of the EU, not of 'Europe', on global financial law.

[28] Thus, there was controversy when the EU sought to implement the Basel III capital rules as maxima, but the heat was removed from the debate by the explicit provisions in Basel III (the so-called 'Pillar 2' provisions) which envisage lower level regulators increasing the capital standards for particular categories of banks or for individual banks whose soundness is in doubt and which also became part of the EU framework. Contrast Regulation 575/2013 of 26 June 2013, OJ 2013 L 176/1, Art. 1 and Directive 2013/36 of 26 June 2013, OJ 2013 L 176/338, Arts 97 and 104. Both the ECB and the Bank of England have made extensive use of the Pillar 2 provisions.

[29] Moloney has argued that in the future, notably post-Brexit, ESMA and other agencies may be able to play a role in the extension of EU law globally: Moloney, 'International Financial Governance, the EU, and Brexit: The "Agencification" of EU Financial Governance and the Implications', 17 *European Business Organization Law Review* (2016) 451.

A. Influence on International Standards

The influence of the EU on the development of international standards in the post-crisis period was low.[30] A number of reasons can be pointed to for this conclusion. First, the EU does not have an exclusive right of representation, as against the Member States, in either the G20/FSB or the BCBS. On the contrary, the EU as an institution is a latecomer (or late-ish comer) to both these parties since these bodies were initially constituted without a formal EU presence.[31] The governments and central bank governors of France, Germany, Italy and the UK have direct representation on the G20/FSB (along with the EU Commission and European Central Bank (ECB)), while those countries plus Belgium, Luxembourg, the Netherlands, Spain and Sweden are directly represented on the BCBS (along with the ECB, with the Commission as an observer). With such heavy Member State representation, it is difficult for the Commission or the ECB to present a unified view, if the represented Member States differ among themselves, and is arguably unnecessary if they do not.

Second, the EU has rarely enjoyed 'first mover advantage'. The state which first produces what is perceived to be a workable solution to a financial regulatory problem is in a good position to have it adopted by others, even if other workable solutions are in principle available, simply because of the benefits of a common international regulatory framework.[32] The EU legislative process is necessarily cumbersome as compared with national procedures. Thus, whereas the US had the comprehensive 248-page Dodd-Frank Act[33] on the statute book by 2010, there was

[30] The following analysis is broadly consistent with Quaglia's conclusions, based on the notion of 'regulatory capacity' (Quaglia, 'The European Union, the USA and International Standard Setting by Regulatory Fora in Finance', 19 *New Political Economy* (2014) 427). Overall, she is a bit more optimistic, probably because her research question focuses on the influence of 'Europe' (i.e. both the EU and its leading financial states) in comparison with the US, rather than the specific contribution of the EU bodies to standard setting in international fora.

[31] The BCBS was established in 1974 by the G10 group of industrial nations which did not (and still does not) include the EU in membership. The European Commission became (and still is) an observer member of the BCBS in 1987, but the ECB became a full member in 2014 with the establishment of the Single Supervisory Mechanism (SSM). Goodhart remarks that the attendance of the European Commission representatives in the early years 'was sporadic, with no one coming from the EC on about one third of the subsequent meetings...' (C. Goodhart, *The Basel Committee on Banking Supervision* (2011), at 73). The G20 was originally the 'group of six', founded in 1975, although the EU was included in its meetings from 1977 onwards.

[32] This proposition begs the question of what will be perceived to be a workable solution. Not all innovations are imitated elsewhere. Examples are the Volcker rule in the US and the ring-fencing of retail banks in the UK (note 10), neither of which has been followed closely outside their home jurisdictions. However, even these produced a response from the EU in the shape of a Commission proposal for a (rather different) Regulation on structural measures for banks, COM(2014) 43 final, which, as yet, has not been translated into legislation and may well not be. The failure of the US and UK initiatives to set a trend probably reflects strong path dependency in the US (divorce of commercial and investment banking was a remedy applied in the US in the 1930s, which was not adopted elsewhere) or economic realities not shared elsewhere (UK with a large banking sector relative to its economic size, a characteristic shared by Switzerland, which has also introduced some innovations not followed elsewhere).

[33] Wall Street Reform and Consumer Protection Act (Pub.L. 111–203, H.R. 4173). Of course, its implementation required many thousands more pages of agency rule-making, so that actual implementation of the legislation came later. Nevertheless, in terms of international influence, the structure laid out in the Act was more influential than the subsequent rule-making, which was too technical for many

nothing equivalent to be found at EU level. Leaving aside insurance reform (the impulse for which pre-dated the financial crisis), the only pieces of legislation at EU level by the end of 2010 were a first crack at credit-rating agencies[34] (three more pieces of legislation on this topic were to follow) and an initial stab at reforming the prudential requirements for banks.[35] There was also the institutionally important establishment in 2010 of the European system of financial supervisions (the European Banking Authority, the European Securities and Markets Authority and the European Insurance and Occupational Pensions Authority), which filled an EU-level gap which other leading jurisdictions had necessarily filled many years, if not decades, previously.[36]

Although the body of EU financial regulatory law today is undoubtedly substantial, it has rarely set the pace but rather followed initiatives taken largely at international level, where, as we have seen, the EU institutions were not well placed to make a unified EU voice influential. Of course, not all EU financial law was a simple adoption of norms from international level. In some cases, the EU has struck out on its own, but without significant impact on the approaches adopted in the international fora. For example, the Directive on Alternative Investment Fund Managers,[37] in so far as it went beyond the international consensus by more disclosure by hedge funds and private equity, did not find followers, perhaps because it was perceived to be driven by concerns other than for financial stability.[38] The FSB, by contrast, proceeded more slowly and focused on all funds (UCITS as well as hedge funds and private equity) and on their potential to affect systemic risk.[39] Again, in its third iteration of the regulation of credit rating agencies, the EU imposed rotation requirements and liability rules.[40] Neither is to be found in the main international standards document, which, in this case, has been issued by IOSCO.[41] Nor did the EU initiatives have impact 'laterally' on the Securities Exchange Commission (SEC) of the US, which was effectively the worldwide regulator of credit rating agencies before the crisis. This lack of influence can probably be explained on the basis that

policy-makers to take on board. It is an interesting question what will happen if the US repeals or amends parts of this Act in the future. It is unlikely that the international standard setters will simply follow the US changes, at least in relation to regulation that has been adopted at international level.

[34] Regulation 1060/2009 of 16 September 2009 on credit rating agencies, OJ 2009 L 302/1.

[35] Directive 2010/76 of 24 November 2010, OJ 2010 L 329/3 (known as 'CRD III'). The 2010 Directive was in any event aimed at transposing Basel Committee on Banking Supervision (BCBS) reforms, familiarly known as Basel II.5, rather than a distinctly EU initiative.

[36] The EU structure, although well adapted to the political needs of the EU, was somewhat old-fashioned in having separate bodies to oversee banking, securities markets and insurance. As the earlier account of the financial crisis shows, one of its great lessons was the recognition of the need for integration of these three categories of financial activity.

[37] Directive 2011/61 of 8 June 2011, OJ 2011 L174/1.

[38] Ferran, 'After the Crisis: Regulation of Hedge Funds and Private Equity in the EU', 12 *European Business Organization Law Review* (2011) 379.

[39] FSB, 'Policy Recommendations to Address Structural Vulnerabilities from Asset Management Activities' (January 2017).

[40] Regulation 1060/2009, note 34, Arts 6b and 35a, as inserted by Regulation 462/2013 of 21 May 2013, OJ 2013 L 146/1.

[41] International Organization of Securities Commissions (IOSCO), Code of Conduct Fundamentals for Credit Rating Agencies (2015).

there was an EU-specific reason for these regulatory initiatives—the sovereign debt downgrades during the euro crisis—which did not affect US debt nor, more generally, the ratings of non-euro countries.[42]

B. Influence via Recognition

1. Introduction

Overall, therefore, the evidence for post-crisis EU external influence via international regulatory authorities is limited. Is the evidence for influence via recognition procedures stronger? This section proceeds via an in-depth analysis of the one case so far where the boundaries of mutual recognition were explored in the course of a long and acrimonious debate between the US and the EU over their respective systems for the clearing of over-the-counter (OTC) derivatives through what are termed central counterparties (CCPs) in EU terminology or Derivatives Clearing Organizations (DCOs) in US terminology.

The recognition mechanism in EU financial instruments is known as 'equivalence'. By and large, equivalence provisions are to be found in those instruments dealing with 'wholesale' financial services but not in those dealing with 'retail' services (i.e. those in which the counterparty is normally a professional or a corporate, but not those where the counterparty is normally a consumer).[43] Thus, in retail services a third country institution normally has to obtain access permission from the individual EU Member State in which it wishes to operate, and that decision is broadly one for that Member State, except that the relevant EU instrument normally provides that the Member State may not grant access on terms more favourable than those available to institutions located in other Member States of the EU. By contrast, wholesale financial instruments normally contain an equivalence provision. This operates at EU (not Member State) level and requires decisions by the Commission and the relevant EU regulator, in our case normally the European Securities and Markets Authority (ESMA). Under these provisions, which vary in detail from instrument to instrument, the Commission and ESMA may give permission for an institution based in a third country to provide the relevant financial service in the EU on the basis of its home-country rules, provided these have been assessed as equivalent to the EU rules.

This division between the approaches to third country provision of financial services in the retail and wholesale spheres can be explained on a couple of grounds. The first is a 'political economy' explanation. In many Member States domestic providers of retail financial services are well established. They may take the view that they have no interest in increasing the level of competition from providers from outside the EU, especially as they are increasingly subject to competition from providers operating within the EU but located in other Member States, under the 'passporting' provisions for retail services. Their opposition may carry sway with their national

[42] Brummer, note 23, at 290–297.
[43] Ferran, 'The UK as a Third Country Actor in EU Financial Services Regulation', 3 *Journal of Financial Regulation* (2017) 40.

government and influence that government's approach in the EU legislative process. By contrast, wholesale financial services are relatively under-developed in the EU, except in the UK. The UK has, however, traditionally taken an 'open' approach to cross-border competition, while other Member States may be under more domestic pressure to resist outside competition.

Another, and not inconsistent explanation, relates to the dynamics of securing agreement among the Member States in the EU's legislative process. As in all financial regulation, there is a tension between the promotion of competition and of financial stability. In this case, admission of third country institutions will increase competition, to the benefit of the users of the services, but may increase the risks to financial stability arising from the admission of institutions operating under different rules, especially in the case of wholesale financial services. France and Germany have tended to put more emphasis on the risks to financial stability by admitting third country institutions, while the UK has recognized the benefits to competition of admitting them. As Quaglia has argued,[44] the equivalence provisions provide a way of squaring this circle, appearing both to provide a method of assessing the quality of a third country's rules and supervision and a method of entry for third country institutions. There is, therefore, some degree of ambiguity as to how the equivalence provisions will operate (whether more protective or more inclusive), which will be resolved in the process through which the Commission and ESMA exercise the discretion vested in them.

Not all third country providers need to rely on equivalence. If the third country provider is content to establish a subsidiary in the EU and be subject to the EU rules in relation to that subsidiary, even though these may differ from the rules in the parent's jurisdiction, equivalence is beside the point. In this case, the third country provider turns itself into an EU provider for the purpose of delivering the services within the EU. Thus, the three main rating agencies provide rating services within the EU via EU subsidiaries, which comply with the additional EU regulatory requirements,[45] whilst their US parents are subject to less demanding regulation in relation to their US services. The EU additions are factored in as a cost of doing business in the EU, just as stricter exhaust emission requirements in the US as compared to the EU are a cost of doing business in the US.

The need for equivalence arises in two situations in particular. The first is where the third country provider wishes to provide the services into the EU from a company based outside it and subject to the third country rules. Without an equivalence determination, this will not be permitted by the EU authorities. Second, although the third country provider does not wish to offer services within the EU, it may be caught by the extraterritorial impact of EU laws, for example, where those rules apply to services provided to EU citizens anywhere in the world.

The potential for EU external influence through the equivalence regime depends in large part on the strength of the desire of (i) third country institutions to provide

[44] Quaglia, 'The Politics of "Third Country Equivalence" in Post-Crisis Financial Services Regulation in the European Union', 38 *West European Politics* (2015) 1.

[45] See ESMA, *CRA Authorisation*, available at https://www.esma.europa.eu/supervision/credit-rating-agencies/risk. (All website references in this chapter were last visited on 09 February 2019.)

services in the EU or to EU persons on the basis of home-country rules and (ii) of EU institutions to provide services outside the EU but subject to home (in this case, EU) rules. However, the business requirements of institutions are not the only factor to which regulators and governments respond. Governments in particular may have political objectives, to which they are prepared to sacrifice the gains that could be obtained from increased cross-border provision of financial services. Those objectives may be financial market objectives (such as the promotion of financial stability) or they may lie outside the area of financial market regulation.

2. *Central Counterparties*

(a) Background

Central counterparties emerged as a way of handling the risks attached to derivatives. A derivative (or 'swap' in US terminology) is simply a type of contract whose aim is to reallocate the risks attached to some underlying commodity, asset or transaction (and upon which the contract is 'derivative'). Suppose an essential input for a company is priced in a currency which is not the currency in which the company normally operates and in which it reports its profits (for example a non-US airline buying fuel priced in dollars). In order to manage the risk attached to fluctuations in the price of the dollar, the airline could enter into a derivative with a bank, whereby the airline pays a periodic fee to the bank and the bank agrees to pay money to the airline if and to the extent that the price of the dollar rises above a level which is fixed by the contract. This may be advantageous to both parties. The company obtains some protection against a risk it is not well placed to handle, whilst the bank earns revenues from its expertise in handling such risks and the fact that it can spread its exposures by maintaining a 'balanced book' of contractual commitments, with some going one way and some the other.[46] The US term 'swap' thus focused on what the parties agree to do under the derivative contract.[47]

In the financial crisis, a rather different form of derivative—the credit default swap (CDS)—played a central part. Our account of securitization (see earlier) was incomplete, because it failed to describe an important feature of the bonds (notes) that the SIV sold to the market to obtain the financing needed to acquire the loans. There was rarely just one class of bonds issued, but rather multiple classes with

[46] Alternatively, the airline could enter into a contract with its fuel supplier for the provision of fuel in the future at a fixed price. However, the fuel supplier may be no better placed than the airline to handle the risks attached to currency fluctuations.

[47] 'A swap is a type of derivative instrument that consists of a contract between counterparties, the terms of which provide that each party makes a series of payments to the other at fixed dates in the future. One stream of payments is determined by an uncertain variable—such as a future interest rate, price of an underlying commodity or stock, or, as in a credit default swap, a default of the reference obligation. The second stream of payments is typically fixed, agreed upon by the swap counterparties.' Greene and Potiha, 'Examining the Extraterritorial Reach of Dodd-Frank's Volcker Rule and Margin Rules for Uncleared Swaps—A Call for Regulatory Coordination and Cooperation', 7 *Capital Markets Law Journal* (2012) 271, at 275. This definition also suggests that there are some derivative contracts which would not count as swaps.

different rights attached. This feature is known as 'tranching'.[48] The bond classes were ranked, so that the more senior the class the greater the priority it had over the revenues from the underlying loans, but equally the lower the interest rate to which it was entitled, because these bonds were less risky than more junior classes. The idea was to offer securities which would be attractive to different categories of investor, with different risk/reward profiles, thus increasing the capacity of the market to absorb these bonds.

The purchasers of the most senior tranches were generally very risk averse. They would buy the bonds only if they were rated A+++ and, in addition, they would often take out a CDS on the bond. With this derivative, the protection buyer would agree to make periodic payments to the protection seller, and, in exchange, the protection seller would agree to perform the obligations of the bond issuer (i.e. the SIV) if the issuer itself failed to do so. Thinking that the chances of default on the A+++ tranches were close to infinitesimally small, one US insurer in particular (AIG) sold large quantities of CDSs on these bonds at very low prices. These were, of course, all 'one way' commitments—no balanced book. When it appeared that borrower defaults threatened repayments even of the senior bonds, those who had bought protection required AIG, as they were contractually entitled to do, to post collateral against AIG's own default, i.e. assets the protection buyers could seize in the event of AIG's own failure to perform. Unable to produce sufficient assets of the required quality and facing bankruptcy, AIG was bailed out by the US government.

The AIG bail-out was one of the most expensive carried out in the financial crisis, involving a disbursement of some US$180bn.[49] One reason for the size of the bail-out was that, although a CDS looks like an insurance contract, US law and the laws of most jurisdictions do not class it as such. Consequently, the protection buyer did not need to have an insurable interest (for example, holding the bonds whose performance was guaranteed by the CDS). The CDS could be and was used as a speculative instrument, as a way of shorting the bonds issued by the SIV. The US government bailed out AIG, probably not so much because it was in itself a systemically important institution, but because the counterparties, i.e. the large commercial and investment banks which held substantial quantities of the CDSs, were systemically important. It probably did not improve the temper of the US government officials involved that some of the investment banks whose protection purchases were underwritten by US taxpayers were European banks.[50]

(b) Reform

In the aftermath of the financial crisis an international consensus on how to deal with derivatives quickly emerged. It was embodied in the G20 Pittsburgh summit

[48] Showing that not all the specialized words in this area are of English origin. Under the Commission's proposals a securitization is not covered by the Regulation if it does not have the tranching feature: Commission Proposal for a Regulation on Securitisation, COM(2015) 472 final, Art. 2.

[49] The events leading up to the bail-out are chronicled in V. Acharya *et al.*, *Regulating Wall St* (2011), at 277–285. However, the US government recouped its cash outlay by selling on AIG after acquiring it: Sender, 'AIG: An Improbable Profit', *Financial Times*, 22 October 2012.

[50] Acharya, note 49, at 282 lists Société Générale, Deutsche Bank, UBS, Deutsche Genossenschaftsbank, Barclays and Rabobank as major recipients of the bail-out funds.

declaration of September 2009[51] and had three elements, all designed to modify the previous practice in which most derivatives were regarded as private bilateral contracts, albeit private contracts concluded within the context of a sophisticated master agreement developed by a trade association, the International Swaps and Dealers Association. First, and least controversial, there was to be transparency about exposures under derivatives contracts by requiring derivative transactions to be reported to trade depositories, to which regulators would have access. During the crisis, exposures under CDSs had been wholly unclear since derivative transactions, as private contracts, were not subject to reporting requirements.

Second, the aim was for the majority of derivative contracts to be centrally cleared. Central clearing means the transaction ceases to be a bilateral contract, because a clearing institution inserts itself between the seller and the buyer under the derivative, becoming the buyer to every seller and the seller to every buyer. This has long been standard procedure when a security is bought and sold on an exchange. Applied to derivatives, clearing means the parties to a derivatives contract cease to be reliant on the performance of the economic counterparty and become instead reliant of the performance of the CCP. During the crisis, CCPs were thought to have performed well—they had dealt with defaults smoothly and, most importantly, without requiring public funds. So, they became the favoured core reform for derivatives transactions.

However, before the crisis only a small proportion of derivative transactions had been traded on exchanges and thus centrally cleared as an inherent part of exchange trading. Developing trading arrangements for securities is an expensive business for exchanges and the cost is justified, in their eyes, only if a high volume of transactions results. Thus, only standardized versions—developed by the exchange, not the parties—of the most popular derivatives contracts, notably foreign exchange swaps, were traded on exchanges. Most remained, as it was put, 'over-the-counter' instruments, i.e. their terms were customized by and for the parties through some sort of negotiation process. However, even without exchange trading, at the beginning of the century some clearing houses had begun to develop clearing facilities for OTC derivatives. Yet, the majority of derivatives contracts were not cleared prior to the crisis, whether through exchanges or directly by clearing houses. The aim of the reforms was to expand the first (exchange-traded) and, especially, the second (cleared but not exchange-traded) categories of derivative, and to shrink the third category (bilateral contracts). There was to be a stick and a carrot. Some categories of derivatives were to be required to be cleared. Those which formally could remain bilateral were to be discouraged by imposing additional capital requirements against exposures under these contracts.[52] This was the third element in the reforms.

[51] G20 Information Centre, *G20 Leaders Statement: The Pittsburgh Summit*, available at http://www.g20.utoronto.ca/2009/2009communique0925.html.

[52] D. Duffie, A. Li and T. Lubke, 'Policy Perspectives on OTC Derivatives Market Infrastructure' Federal Reserve Bank of New York Staff Reports, no. 424 (2010); Culp, 'OTC-Cleared Derivatives: Benefits, Costs, and Implications of the "Dodd-Frank Wall Street Reform and Consumer Protection Act"', 20(2) *Journal of Applied Finance* (2010) 1.

Just as a derivative contract does not cause the risks attached to the underlying asset or transaction to disappear but transfers them from the protection buyer to the protection seller, so central clearing does not cause the risks of default on the derivative contract to disappear, but rather transfers them from the protection seller to the CCP. This elaborate shuffling of risks makes sense only if the risks end up with a person better able to bear them than the original risk-holder.

Clearing houses are a private-ordering solution to the risks arising from trading securities. Sometimes they are free-standing, sometimes part of a larger financial group also containing an exchange. Their names are not as well known as those of stock exchanges, to which they may be attached.[53] Traditionally, they have been formed and owned by the largest financial firms active in securities markets in order, in effect, to guarantee each other's trades. From the point of view of the clearing house, it must be confident it can handle the risks arising from derivative contracts. The clearing house will, in particular, be unwilling to clear highly customized contracts, because it is not well equipped to deal with the resulting risks. Recognizing this, the reforms did not seek to require all derivative contracts to be cleared but proceeded on the basis that some residual classes of contract would not be acceptable to the clearing houses and so had to be dealt with, from a stability point of view, by imposing capital surcharges on those financial institutions exposed to risk as a result of the absence of clearing.[54]

More important from a financial stability point of view, what central clearing of derivatives represented was an enormous concentration of risk in the clearing houses rather than its dispersal across a large number of private parties. It could be argued that, if AIG was an example of the financial stability risks associated with the issuance of a large quantity of CDSs by a single financial institution, greater concentration of risk was precisely the wrong way to go.[55] However, reformers argued that central clearing houses represented an easier regulatory target than dispersed market participants and the performance of the clearing houses in the crisis suggested that they had already developed protective techniques which regulation could enhance to provide the necessary level of financial stability.[56]

In terms of financial resources to meet the risks of cleared derivatives, CCP regulation developed three elements. First, when the trade is taken by the CCP, the parties to the trade must provide high-quality 'margin' or collateral (normally cash or near cash) to cover the loss that the CCP is likely to suffer in extreme conditions in the period between a party's default on its obligations to the CCP and the CCP's

[53] The biggest clearing house in Europe is LCH.Clearnet.

[54] E.g., it was reported in February 2017 that three-quarters of interest rate swaps (a very popular form of derivative) has been shifted into central clearing, but the remaining uncleared segment still had a value of US$110tn: Stafford, 'Derivatives "Big Bang" catches market off guard', *Financial Times*, 2 February, 2017.

[55] For scepticism on the value of the reforms see Griffith, 'Substituted Compliance and Systemic Risk: How to Make a Global Market in Derivatives Regulation', 98 *Minnesota Law Review* (2014) 1291.

[56] When Lehman Bros failed, it had a notional amount of US$9tn in swaps in LCH.Clearnet, a central counterparty, but the CCP was able to auction them off in the market without incurring losses greater than the margin that the CCP had required Lehman to post with the CCP before default: Culp, note 52, at 13.

ability to dispose of the contract by selling it into the market. Second, only a small number of well-reputed financial institutions may become members of the CCP. Other financial institutions participating in the derivatives markets access the CCP via the members. Derivatives participants which are not members provide collateral to the members when contracting with them and the members pass (some or all) of that collateral on to the CCP when dealing with it.[57] Members are required to contribute to a guarantee fund held by the CCP to absorb losses not covered by the collateral. Finally, the CCP itself must meet certain capital requirements (i.e. 'own funds') which can absorb losses if the default fund is exhausted.[58]

(c) The Extraterritorial Problem

The sharpness of the jurisdictional clash between the EU and the US over the regulation of CCPs was generated by two main features of CCPs. First, the provision of margin through cash or near cash is costly for derivative parties because of the opportunity costs involved. A CCP which can reduce those costs will therefore have a competitive advantage. Regulation stands in the way of competition through the simple reduction of margin requirements. However, regulation does often permit netting, i.e. 'the netting of positive position values in some derivative types against negative position values in others'.[59] This is especially valuable for financial institutions which are parties to a large volume of derivatives contracts (typically the members of a CCP), some of which will put the risk one way and some the other. However, netting requires 'mutuality', i.e. common counterparties. Netting possibilities are thus maximized if a contracting party concentrates its derivative contracts on one or a very small number of CCPs and concentration is facilitated if a CCP clears multiple classes of derivatives. However, it is also the case that netting tends to reduce the levels of collateral in the hands of the CCP.

Second, the clearing of derivatives is the archetypal piece of detached financial infrastructure which does not need to occur in any of the jurisdictions in which the parties reside or in the jurisdiction whose law is used to govern the contact. Referring to the statistics on CDSs, Yadov and Turing remark '[p]ut another way, CDS traders conduct business with counterparties outside of their own jurisdiction at more than four times the rate than they do with those at home'.[60] More graphically, the authors give the following example of a swap transaction:

> Consider, for example, a Swiss bank that enters into a fixed-floating interest rate swap on a notional principal amount expressed in British Pounds, where its counterparty is the New York branch of a Japanese bank. Such a transaction may be documented under New York law and supported by collateral that includes German Government bonds held in

[57] When the member trades on its own account, it will, of course, also provide collateral to the CCP. As discussed later, the issue of how much participant-provided collateral ends up with the CCP was discovered to be an important issue during the EU/US debates over recognition.

[58] Duffie *et al.*, note 52, at 7–9 and Appendices A and B for more detail about the order in which these resources would be used in different loss situations.

[59] *Ibid.*, at 14.

[60] Yadov and Turing, 'The Extraterritorial Regulation of Clearinghouses', 2 *Journal of Financial Regulation* (2016) 21, at 22. By contrast, those who buy a security over an exchange (including an exchange-traded derivative) have to use the clearing house employed by that exchange.

> Euroclear (which is located in Belgium and operates under Belgian law).... Since there may be no obvious geographical link between the transaction and its originators and any particular clearinghouse, clearinghouses and market participants are likely to have a choice (subject to overriding legal rules) as to whether and where to conduct clearing activities.[61]

Putting these two points together, a number of conclusions can be drawn. First, cost pressures will lead to the emergence of only a small number of globally active CCPs, in the absence of regulatory rules pushing the other way, as has indeed been the case.[62] Second, national or regional regulators face a strong threat of regulatory arbitrage on the part of CCPs. CCPs are likely to migrate to the jurisdictions which enable them to offer their services to clients on the cheapest basis. Third, for contagion-avoidance reasons regulators face a strong incentive to adopt an extraterritorial approach, i.e. to apply national rules to local persons involved in clearing derivative transactions, no matter where in the world the clearing occurs. Fourth, given that all regulators face this incentive, a clash of jurisdictions is likely, as indeed happened between the EU and the US.

3. The Clash between the EU and the US

Since the US was first into the field with the regulation of derivatives, it was the first to face the extraterritoriality issue. Title VII of the Dodd-Frank Act made extensive changes to the regulation of derivatives in the US, mainly through amendments to the Commodities Exchange Act. The two crucial requirements made it unlawful for 'any person' (i) in those now common cases where clearing was required, to engage in a swap without clearing it on a CCP (DCO) registered under the Act[63] or (ii) to act as a 'swap dealer'[64] (typically a bank) or a 'major swap participant'[65] unless registered with the Commission.[66] The prudential requirements thought to be necessary to ensure the stability of central clearing were applied partly to the CCPs and partly to the dealers and participants. The focus of this chapter is on CCPs.

From an extraterritorial point of view, the central issue was how the Commission would define 'any person'. Essentially, Dodd-Frank passed the issue on to the Commodity Futures Trading Commission (CFTC) by extending the scope of the regulation to activities which 'have a direct and significant connection with activities in, or effect on commerce of, the United States'—a traditional formulation—or which contravened rules made by the CFTC in order to prevent the evasion of any

[61] *Ibid.*, at 23.

[62] The largest appear to be: Chicago Mercantile Exchange, Eurex, Euronext.Liffe, LCH.Clearnet, Chicago Board of Trade and the New York Mercantile Exchange.

[63] Commodity Exchange Act, section 2(h).

[64] Those who make a market in swaps or regularly enter into swaps with counterparties in the ordinary course of their business: *ibid.*, section 1(a)(49).

[65] A person, other than a dealer, who maintains a substantial position in swaps, other than for the purpose of hedging commercial risk (*ibid.*, section 1(a)(33)).

[66] *Ibid.*, section 4(s).

provision of the Act.[67] The CFTC decided to apply its rules to persons entering into derivatives contracts anywhere in the world, unless the bank party to the contract was not a US person and neither was the counterparty.[68] In other words, in principle, the US regulation would be inapplicable only where neither party to the contract was a US person and the contracting occurred outside the US. In that situation, and that situation alone, the swap could be cleared through a CCP not registered in the US and not subject to the CFTC's clearing rules, for example, on margining.

However, the CFTC also developed an exception to this wide-ranging territorial rule, involving a notion of 'substituted compliance'—a form of recognition—under which compliance with foreign rules would replace compliance with the US rules.[69] In particular, a foreign CCP might obtain registration in the US, but then operate on the basis of its home state rules where these fell within the concept of substituted compliance. To the extent this was possible, the CCP would be subject to a single set of rules and could clear derivatives on the same basis, whether or not these involved US persons. Substituted compliance is, however, a limited form of recognition. It does not exempt foreign CCPs from the need to register with the CFTC and thus from the supervision and enforcement activities of the CFTC. Substituted compliance involved deference on the part of the US authorities to foreign rules but not to foreign supervision.[70]

The EU legislation came later than Dodd-Frank, but was clearly inspired, in terms of its extraterritorial impact, by the provisions of that Act. Assuming an obligation to clear, Article 4 of Regulation 648/2012[71] on OTC derivatives, CCPs and trade repositories (commonly referred to as the European Market Infrastructure Regulation—EMIR) in principle requires parties to clear all OTC contracts. It then defines the parties so as to include contracts between an EU financial institution and 'an entity established in a third country that would be subject to the clearing obligation if it were established in the Union' and, echoing Dodd-Frank rather precisely, contracts:

> between two entities established in one or more third countries that would be subject to the clearing obligation if they were established in the Union, provided that the contract has a direct, substantial and foreseeable effect within the Union or where such an obligation is necessary or appropriate to prevent the evasion of any provisions of this Regulation.

[67] Dodd-Frank, section 722(d), inserting language into section 2(i) of the Commodity Exchange Act (7 U.S.C. § 2(i)).

[68] Greene and Potiha, note 47, at 280.

[69] Unlike in the EU, the recognition scheme was developed by the agency rather than being set out in the parent legislation (i.e. the Dodd-Frank Act or the Commodity Exchange Act).

[70] Jackson distinguishes between 'first' and 'second generation' substituted compliance. Under the 'first generation' version, developed by the SEC before the financial crisis but never brought into force, there would have been deference to foreign supervision and enforcement as well: Jackson, 'Substituted Compliance: The Emergence, Challenges, and Evolution of a New Regulatory Paradigm', 1 *Journal of Financial Regulation* (2015) 169. The CFTC does have a limited power to exempt foreign CCPs from registration, but only where they do not clear for US customers but only for their US members or affiliates: Commodity Exchange Act, section 5(b)(h).

[71] Regulation 648/2012 of 4 July 2012, OJ 2012 L 201/1.

To complete the circle, the Article requires clearing to be via a CPP authorized under the Regulation.

Like the CFTC regulations, EMIR provides for the recognition of third country rules under certain conditions. The first step is for the Commission to adopt an Implementing Act which needs to reach three conclusions about the third country set-up: first, that CCPs authorized in the foreign country are subject to legally binding rules which are 'equivalent' to the EU provisions; second, that CCPs authorized in the foreign country are subject to effective supervision and enforcement; and, third, that the third country provides an equivalent system of recognition for the rules of countries which are third countries in relation to the foreign country (i.e. including the EU).[72] The EU version of recognition differs from the US one in two main ways. First, it is a full system of recognition: if a third country system is recognized, then the EU relies on that country's supervision and enforcement, as well as upon its substantive law.[73] Second, it is, by virtue of the third requirement, a system of mutual recognition, since the third country must provide an equivalent for other countries, whereas substituted compliance is a unilateral act of the CFTC and does not turn on whether the third country has adopted a substituted compliance or any other recognition system in favour of the US. In relation to EU recognition of the US arrangements, mutuality is an immediate problem since, as we have seen, substituted compliance relates only to the substantive rules and not to supervision.

The scene was thus set for a classic mutual recognition debate. The cost of no mutual recognition was the fragmentation and segmentation of derivatives markets and increased costs for parties to derivatives contracts. To avoid being caught up in two sets of jurisdictional rules, derivative parties would be incentivized to contract only with persons from their own jurisdiction and to clear through a CCP registered in that jurisdiction. Indeed, there was evidence that this began to occur.[74] Alternatively, some form of mutual recognition would be achieved, but at the cost of some loss of control by jurisdictional regulators over activities which potentially affected the financial stability of their countries.

In February 2016 the Commission and the CFTC did reach political agreement on the recognition of each other's systems.[75] This was translated into an Implementing Act by the Commission[76] and a Determination by the CFTC[77] the following

[72] *Ibid.*, Art. 25(6).

[73] Thus, *ibid.*, Art. 22 requires Member States to establish a supervisory authority for CCPs 'established' on its territory but not for CCPs established in third countries and providing services into that state. For this reason a requirement for the recognition of a foreign CCP is the establishment by ESMA of a memorandum of understanding with the foreign supervisor. However, this is required also in the case of substituted compliance. The CFTC has supervisory and enforcement authority, but it cannot exercise it effectively without the cooperation of the home state regulator.

[74] 'Volumes of cleared Euro-denominated interest rate swaps between US and EU counterparties dropped 77 per cent between 2013 and 2014, underscoring a breakdown in cross-border trading relationships' (Artamonov, 'Cross-Border Application of OTC Derivatives Rules: Revisiting the Substituted Compliance Approach' 1 *Journal of Financial Regulation* (2015) 206, at 218).

[75] The United States Commodity Futures Trading Commission and the European Commission, 'Common approach for transatlantic CCPs', 10 February 2016.

[76] Commission Implementing Decision (EU) 2016/377, OJ 2016 L 70/32.

[77] CFTC, 'Comparability Determination for the European Union: Dually-Registered Derivatives Clearing Organizations and Central Counterparties', 81 Federal Register (2016) 15260.

month. But a long and stony path had to be followed to reach this point. Three years earlier the Commission and the CFTC had jointly announced that they had reached agreement on a 'Path Forward' in relation to the regulation of OTC derivatives, after discussions which Commissioner Barnier described as having been already 'long and sometimes difficult'.[78] In relation to the regulation of CPPs, that document identified only one 'key material difference'. Yet, it took a further three years of sometimes acrimonious debate to reach a final agreement on CPPs. In a comment on the CFTC Determination, Commissioner Giancarlo, who had advocated quicker progress throughout, expressed the view that the process had been 'made needlessly complex because both the EC and the CFTC insisted on a line-by-line rule analysis contrary to the flexible, outcomes-based approach advocated by the OTC Derivatives Regulators Group'.[79] Such an approach was bound to highlight differences rather than focus on common outputs.[80]

The difficulty and delay were particularly surprising because both the EU and the US had implemented the broad outlines for regulation which had been agreed at Pittsburgh and because the significant differences in substantive regulation in the two jurisdictions were limited. As Yadov and Turing commented, '[a]s regards risk management in clearinghouses, however, it is difficult to conclude that one system is evidently weaker or stronger than the other'.[81]

The principal difference between the two systems concerned the basis on which CCPs should collect margin (collateral) from members. The EU permitted the netting of margin, whilst the CFTC required it to be collected on a gross basis. Thus, under the US system a CCP would end up with more collateral than would be the case under the EU rules (though the US is somewhat more flexible than the EU on the definition of collateral). On the other hand, the EU required margin to be calculated on a two-day liquidation period (i.e. on an assumption that the CCP would take two days to sell the defaulted contract into the market), whereas the CFTC assumed only one day, so that the period the CCP was considered to be at risk was shorter under the CFTC rules and so less collateral was needed to cover the risk. As to the default fund, the EU's rules on the size of the default fund were arguably somewhat more demanding than those of the CFTC, the EU requiring a default fund which could cope with the default of its two largest members, whilst the CFTC had a general requirement based on the default of only the largest member, though it required use of the two largest for systemically important CCPs. Overall, the CFTC's margin requirements were possibly somewhat more rigorous than the EU's, whilst the opposite was the case with the default fund.

[78] CFTC, 'The European Commission and the CFTC reach a Common Path Forward on Derivatives', Press Release 6640–13, 11 July 2013.

[79] See note 77, Appendix 3. The OTC Regulators group consists of representatives of the authorities from the leading jurisdictions with regulatory responsibility for derivatives and it reports periodically to the G20.

[80] For the EU's initial approach, see ESMA, 'Technical advice on third country regulatory equivalence under EMIR—US: Final Report', 1 September 2013 (ESMA/2013/BS/1157)—a document of some 286 pages.

[81] See Yadov and Turing, note 60, at 46.

Finally, the EU requires CCPs to adopt a policy to counteract procyclicality,[82] whilst the CFTC has no such requirement. Such a policy requires the CCP to demand higher collateral from members in good economic times than would otherwise be the case, but to relax that requirement in bad times.

The ultimate deal involved the CFTC accepting net margining. 'Despite the importance of gross margining of customer accounts and the collection of this additional initial margin, in an effort to promote comity'[83] the CFTC decided not to apply the gross margin requirement to foreign CCPs and their foreign members. By contrast, the EU agreed to recognize US CCPs as eligible to provide services in the EU on condition that they added to their internal rules (articles of association) provisions which required them to maintain a default fund large enough to cope with the default of the two largest members and to adopt a procyclicality policy.[84]

4. Evaluation

From the above account, it might be said that the EU made good use of the mutual recognition procedure to export its views on the appropriate regulation of CCPs. US CCPs wishing to offer their services in Europe must calibrate the size of their default fund on the basis of the 'two largest' defaults rather than the 'single largest' and must adopt a policy of adjusting their margin collection to the state of the economic cycle. On the other hand, these are not large gains. The CFTC itself applies the rule of the 'two largest' to its most systematically important CCPs, so this was not a policy option which the CFTC had ruled out in principle. The procyclicality policy was arguably more important, at least in bad times, since it implies a time-varying collateral policy which the CFTC seems not to have adopted, but it is unclear what its overall impact upon the collateral decisions of a US CCP will turn out to be.[85]

Equally, it might be said that the EU made good 'defensive' use of the mutual recognition procedure, by resisting pressure to move to the US model of gross margining and by inducing the CFTC to accept the freedom of EU CCPs to offer services in the US on the basis of a net margining model. From the point of view of the US, this concession offers some potential for regulatory arbitrage, since membership of a CCP is more attractive under a net margining system. However, for reasons which need not be set out in full, the situation was not as clear-cut as it might appear. Net margining benefits members of the CCP, who, as against the CCP, hold on to a proportion of the collateral provided to them by their clients (derivative participants), but does not benefit the clients to the same extent because, as against the

[82] To reduce the impact of defensive measures that CCPs might take in an economic downturn which could prolong the downturn.

[83] CFTC statement, note 77, at 15267.

[84] Decision (EU) 2016/377, note 76, Art. 1. Once an agreement on EMIR had been reached, it was relatively easy to do the linked job on trading venues for derivatives: 'European Commission and CFTC Joint Statement on Mutual Recognition of Derivatives Trading Venues', available at https://ec.europa.eu/info/sites/info/files/business_economy_euro/banking_and_finance/documents/171205-joint-statement-ec-cftc_en.pdf.

[85] In good times the gross margining approach of the US CPP is likely to overtake any anti-procyclicality policy.

member, they have fewer netting possibilities. On the other hand, a two-day liquidation assumption demands more collateral than a one-day period. So, the EU net system means that clients pay more margin than clients of members of US CCPs, because of the 'two-day' requirement, but less of the collateral provided to the members gets through to the CCP itself, because the members can engage in net margining. In short, the EU's defensive victory was a Pyrrhic one: it permitted the EU to preserve a rule under which EU CCPs were less well collateralized than US ones and so less well positioned to resist economic shocks, but their clients paid more margin (because of the two-day rule), thus exposing EU CCPs to a competitive disadvantage as against US CCPs. In the course of the dialogue with the US, the EU seemed to have come to realize these shortcomings of its margin rules. The up-shot was that in 2016 ESMA moved to offer EU CCPs the option of gross margining coupled with a one-day liquidation period.[86] One might say that the impact of mutual recognition dialogue was in fact to undermine, not to preserve, the EU net margining rule.

Standing back from the details of the ultimate resolution of this clash of jurisdictions, the puzzle still remains why it took so long for the deal to be reached. Why did the EU Commission and the CFTC embark on the line-by-line approach, criticized by Commissioner Giancarlo, to a comparison of the two regulatory systems, which was bound to highlight differences, whilst at the same time claiming they were pursuing an 'outcomes based' approach? This was especially puzzling since the joint Commission/CFTC statement of 2013 had identified only one 'material difference' between the two systems of CCP regulation, namely, the initial margin rules discussed earlier. In the meantime the Commission reached agreement with regulators elsewhere in the world, easily and quickly.[87]

It is certainly true that the stakes were much higher in relation to the EU/US deal since derivatives trading globally is concentrated in these two jurisdictions. However, it is not clear how the parties viewed the nature of those stakes. It might have been an issue of competitive advantage. As we have seen, the EU net margining system coupled with a two-day liquidation period meant that US CCPs were likely to be more competitive for clients than EU ones. On the other hand, since the EU system led to less well collateralized CCPs, it was very unclear what financial stability benefit emerged from the EU arrangements. From a financial stability perspective, it was entirely rational for the EU to move towards the US system of gross margining and a one-day liquidation period, as eventually happened.

It may have been that regulators on both sides of the Atlantic were nervous and uncertain about how best to regulate CCPs. As we have seen, the CCP approach to the reform of OTC derivatives trading involves an enormous concentration of risk in a small number of CCPs. Some have argued, not implausibly, that this step

[86] ESMA, *Final Report: Review of Article 26 of RTS No 153/2013 with respect to MPOR for client accounts*, 4 April 2016 (ESMA/2016/429). Para 5 stated: 'Therefore under the current EU system, if not changed, clients of EU CCPs will always be required to post more initial margins than what they would be required to post in a US CCP.'

[87] As early as October 2014 the Commission adopted Implementing Acts in respect of CCP regulation in Australia, Hong Kong, Japan and Singapore: Artamonov, note 74, at 218.

increases rather than mitigates the threat to financial stability which OTC derivatives pose.[88] In this context, the capacity of CCPs to withstand economic shocks through appropriate collateral, default fund, and capital provisions becomes central. However, the appropriate level of this provision cannot be identified in advance with complete confidence, and regulators could conceivably be nervous about accepting any departure, even of a minor character, from their own adopted system, in case this should later turn out to be the route to the failure of a CCP they regulate. In this case, it is concerns not about competitive advantage but about regulatory responsibility which make agreement difficult.[89]

Financial stability concerns might also relate to matters not capable of being dealt with in the mutual recognition agreement relating to ongoing regulation. In particular, if a CCP's financial resources were inadequate to enable it to survive an economic shock, it would need to be put into resolution. In the case of failure of a large CCP, it is unlikely that bail-in or sale to a third party would be available to avoid a disorderly collapse. A substantial injection of state funds (bail-out) would be necessary to minimize the threat to financial stability. The US is probably the only state which could easily meet the costs of a large bail-out, but state bail-outs in the US are surrounded by political uncertainty. The pre-crisis capacity of the executive and its agencies to act without Congressional approval has been constrained in the Dodd-Frank Act.[90] In the EU the recovery and resolution instruments,[91] whilst favouring sales and bail-ins, are not set firmly against bail-outs. However, even the largest EU states would find the financial challenge of a bailing out a large CCP daunting and so there is uncertainty about how far they would undertake it, whilst the EU's own resolution fund is still small. Concerns about whether there would be effective state action in resolution might thus easily feed back into unwillingness to relax control over ongoing prudential rules.

A final contentious issue in mutual recognition is supervision and enforcement. As we have seen, the CFTC's substituted compliance is a truncated form of mutual recognition because it covers only the applicable rules. This limitation is normally justified on the basis of the difficulties of assessing the quality of another jurisdiction's supervision and enforcement.[92] By contrast, whereas the EU can probably rely

[88] Griffith, note 55.

[89] Lehmann, 'Legal Fragmentation, Extraterritoriality and Uncertainty in Global Financial Regulation', 37(1) *Oxford Journal of Legal Studies* (2017) 406. He, like Artamonov, note 74, proposes shifting to the international level the resolution of disputes between states about equivalence and substituted compliance. Although potentially a good step, the reasons which make it attractive are also the reasons states are unlikely to agree to it.

[90] Federal Reserve Act, §13(3), as amended.

[91] Directive 2014/59 of 15 May 2014, OJ 2014 L 173/190 and the proposed Regulation on CCP Recovery and Resolution, COM(2016) 856 final. Various forms of bail-out are explicitly recognized in Arts 56–58 of the Directive, though their use is subject to constraints, e.g., under Art. 37(10), and under Arts 45–47 of the proposed Regulation.

[92] Jackson, note 70. In relation to the EU, part of the problem for the CFTC is that ESMA is the rule-maker, but supervision and enforcement remain mainly with national supervisors. Whilst the CFTC might have confidence in the quality of the supervision and enforcement of some of the EU states, full-blown recognition would involve, in principle, acceptance of the quality of these activities in all Member States.

on the quality of US supervision and enforcement, the absence of reciprocity on these matters may inject some discord into the negotiations.[93]

In addition to these 'rational' explanations for the length of time it took the EU and the US to reach agreement on the recognition of each other's CCPs, there may have been an element of political tension present. The US, as the leading financial economy in the world, may have started from the assumption that the EU should simply accept US regulation as the best, while the EU, especially the Commission, is always struggling to assert the importance of the Union on the world stage and so may not have been inclined to accept the US starting point.

This combination of financial stability concerns and political rivalries is likely to reveal itself even more strongly in the area of CCP regulation after the UK exit from the Union ('Brexit'). Derivative clearing is dominated at the moment by institutions based in the UK, so that, for example, three-quarters of euro-denominated interest rate derivatives are cleared in the UK. Thus taking the EU's primary financial centre outside the Union will give rise to obvious financial stability concerns for the Union and, to some degree, monetary policy concerns as well. On the other hand, the Commission and some EU Member States have a political concern that the UK should not be seen to do well out of exit and so that may give them an incentive, *pour encourager les autres*, not to adopt an accommodating position towards the UK as a third country provider of financial services. In addition, some EU Member States see an opportunity to entice financial services away from London and into their own jurisdictions.

This potentially negative combination of incentives can already be seen to be playing out in the area of recognition of third country CCPs. In the middle of 2017 the Commission put forward a series of three documents[94] proposing to enhance the powers of ESMA in this area and to make recognition for third country CCPs a more onerous matter. From the core document[95] it appears that the crucial regulatory step is the introduction of a distinction between systemically important (for the Union) and non-systemically important CCPs. For the former (dubbed 'Tier 2' CCPs), the criteria for which are fairly general,[96] recognition and the consequences of recognition become much more challenging. Although the principle of equivalence, now termed a 'comparability' assessment, is maintained, it is not necessarily enough to achieve recognition nor does recognition carry the same benefits as previously. This is the crucial step, since UK-based CCPs are currently subject to EU law and therefore would easily pass the former equivalence test, whilst UK supervision and enforcement is not obviously more lax than that in any other Member State. Under the new proposals, ESMA can deny recognition to a CCP which passes the comparability test, on the grounds that 'a CCP is of such substantial systemic importance

[93] This issue is likely to become contentious post-Brexit. See Speech by Vice-President Dombrovskis on EMIR REFIT, 4 May 2017 (Speech/17/1225).

[94] COM(2017) 225 final, COM(2017) 331 final and COM(2017) 539 final.

[95] Proposal for a Regulation amending Regulation (EU) 1095/2010 establishing a European Supervisory Authority (European Securities and Markets Authority) and amending Regulation (EU) 648/2012 as regards the procedures and authorities involved for the authorisation of CCPs and requirements for the recognition of third-country CCPs, COM(2017) 331 final.

[96] See Proposal for a Regulation, note 95, new Art. 2a.

that compliance with the [comparability test and other requirements] does not sufficiently ensure the financial stability of the Union or of one or more of its Member States and should not therefore be recognised'.[97] In this situation, the CCP can continue to offer services in the Union only if it establishes itself there.[98]

Even if recognition is granted, for Tier 2 CCPs it will take a form more akin to US substituted compliance than to the form of recognition previously available, i.e. there is much less reliance on the supervisory and enforcement system of the third country and much more in the way of a role for ESMA in these areas. As a condition of recognition, the applicant must enter into a legally binding agreement, enforceable in the third state, 'to provide within 72 hours after service of a request by ESMA any documents, records, information and data held by such CCP at any time, and that ESMA may access any of the CCP's business premises'.[99] Once recognition is granted, the CCP must not only respond to requests for information, but also submit to general investigations and on-site inspections.[100] Non-compliance can result in substantial fines or periodic penalty payments for the CCP, imposed by ESMA,[101] or ultimately in loss of recognition.[102] Compliance is to be kept under review, often on an annual basis. Whilst the imposition of fines and penalties is subject to review by the CJEU,[103] no mention is made of the possibility of judicial review of a refusal or withdrawal of recognition.

Although these provisions are clearly aimed at UK-based CCPs, as a formal matter they apply to all Tier 2 CCPs. In relation to the main subject matter of this piece, it is interesting to speculate whether the EU revisions will spark increased transatlantic conflict. The Commission seems keen to avoid this. The core document states that '[n]o additional requirements have been introduced in the proposal for recognised third-country CCPs'.[104] For the moment, therefore, sleeping dogs, in the shape of recognized US CCPs, are left to lie. Whether this will remain sustainable in the long run remains to be seen.[105] In any event, the decision to apply the new regime only to future applicants suggests that political motives have come to the fore.

[97] *Ibid.*, new Art. 2c.

[98] It is likely that the ECB will use its proposed new powers to require clearing of EUR-denominated interest rate swaps within the Union, whatever happens with recognition of UK CCPs. See C(2017) 6810 final: Commission Opinion on the Recommendation of the European Central Bank for a Decision of the European Parliament and of the Council amending Article 22 of the Statute of the European System of Central Banks and of the European Central Bank.

[99] Proposal for a Regulation, note 95, new Art. 2b.

[100] *Ibid.*, new Art. 25d and e.

[101] *Ibid.*, new Art. 25g and h.

[102] *Ibid.*, new Art. 25m.

[103] *Ibid.*, new Art. 25k.

[104] See *ibid.*, at 24.

[105] The document itself states that the Chicago Mercantile Exchange has a notional amount outstanding of €1.8tn of euro-denominated interest rate derivatives: *ibid.*, at 5.

5

The Global Reach of EU Competition Law

Giorgio Monti

1. Introduction

This chapter considers the major planks of EU competition law: mergers, conduct with welfare-ambiguous effects (e.g. cases of abuse of dominance) and cartels. For each we test how far they apply to the conduct of private undertakings which takes place outside the EU but for which EU competition law applies. This structure allows us to explore how far the global reach of these rules (and the kinds of conflicts and possible solutions that may be required) may differ in the three fields. This discussion is contained in sections 2 to 4. More specifically, in each section three questions will be discussed: (i) What is the legal basis upon which the EU is able to assert jurisdiction over conduct carried out across its borders? (ii) How far does the enforcement of EU competition law over conduct occurring outside its borders give it 'global power'? (iii) What solutions have been devised to temper the EU's power and to redress the dysfunctionality of local enforcement for global issues?

Section 5 draws together the threads of the discussion above, noting that the shared concern in all three fields of antitrust is not so much the risk of a 'Brussels Effect' or of EU competition law hegemony, but that of over- and under-enforcement. Section 6 considers the extent to which two forms of collaboration by the EU might ameliorate these risks: agreements between the European Commission ('the Commission') and other competition agencies; and competition law provisions in agreements between the EU and other states.

2. Mergers

Merger control is, for most jurisdictions, an ex ante procedure: parties to a merger must notify a proposed transaction and wait for regulatory clearance before it may be completed. Many large mergers require multiple filings across a number of jurisdictions because the firms are active globally.

A. Global Reach

Two firms situated in South Africa merge: why should this be of concern to the European Commission? This was the question that was confronted in *Gencor/Lonrho*. These two firms obtained joint control of Impala Platinum Holdings, creating competition concerns in the market for platinum group metals, which are mined in South Africa but exported globally. Of all the antitrust provisions, the Commission's power to review this matter is most clearly set out in a legislative provision: the EU Merger Regulation. Provided that the parties to the merger have an aggregate worldwide turnover above €500m and an EU-wide turnover greater than €250m for at least two of the parties, the transaction has a 'Community dimension' and must be notified to the Commission.[1] Sales operations within the EU suffice to show a link between the transaction and the EU; there is no need for the firms to have production activities in the EU.[2] In addition, in this case, the Commission checked whether the commodity sales made on EU markets then remained there. It found that a significant amount of the platinum group metals under consideration would be utilized by firms in the Union, thereby concluding that the merger would affect EU markets.[3]

The General Court held that this interpretation of the Regulation is compatible with public international law provided that it was *foreseeable* that the merger would have an *immediate* and *substantial* effect in the EU.[4] On the facts these three features were demonstrated: (i) Russian stocks were depleting fast, which meant that soon after the merger the market would have been dominated by a duopoly (the merged entity and Amplats, also based in South Africa); (ii) the merger would create a long-lasting duopoly position which would result in price increases; and (iii) there was no expectation that sales in the EU would cease after the merger.[5] The Court then also considered the principle of non-interference, which was raised by the applicants. It did not concede that this was a principle of international law, but even if it was it held that there was no conflict between the Commission's decision to block the merger and the conclusion of the South African competition authority that the merger was not expected to have anticompetitive effects: the merger was not required under South African law.[6] The Court left open the question of whether, had the evidence shown that the merger would 'affect the vital economic and/or commercial interests of the Republic of South Africa' this would have made a difference to the Commission's assertion of jurisdiction.[7] In a subsequent merger case, where the US sent a message to the Commission emphasizing the significance of a merger for its military planning, the Commission did not analyse those aspects of the

[1] Council Regulation 139/2004 of 20 January 2004 on the control of concentrations between undertakings, OJ 2004 L 24/1, Art. 1. 'Exclusive competence' means that the Member States lose competence, but other jurisdictions of course retain their power to apply merger law.

[2] Case T-102/96, *Gencor Ltd v. Commission* [1999] ECR II-753 (ECLI:EU:T:1999:65), paras 79 and 85.

[3] Commission Decision 97/26/EC of 24 April 1996 (Case No IV/M.619—*Gencor/Lonrho*), OJ 1997 L 11/30, paras 14–18.

[4] *Ibid.*, para. 90. [5] *Ibid.*, paras 93–100. [6] *Ibid.*, paras 102–104.

[7] *Ibid.*, para. 105.

merger, noting briefly that it saw no competition risks in those markets, and allowing the merger.[8] Hence, quite how wide the EU's interpretation of comity is remains to be seen.

B. Global Power

Many other jurisdictions are able to review a merger of foreign firms which has an impact in their market. It follows that economically significant jurisdictions enjoy a de facto global veto over a proposed merger: parties cannot afford to merge and cease operations in the US or the EU for example. Sometimes the power of veto is the result of a negative decision; at other times one competition agency may require certain divestitures before authorizing the deal, or may raise certain preliminary concerns once the merger is notified, and these responses may lead the parties to withdraw the notification. This veto power is the one that elicits the most concern when one speaks of the global reach of competition law. Obviously competition agencies of smaller jurisdictions have no effective veto as the firms can normally pull out of that country if the merger is not cleared in that territory, but the EU is too big to ignore.

Concerns regarding the EU's approach became significant on two occasions where the mergers it considered were between two US-based firms. In the first round the Commission found a way to clear the merger between Boeing and McDonnell Douglas (MDD) because the parties to the merger agreed to make some concessions so that the transaction was cleared. In the second round, however, the merger between General Electric and Honeywell was blocked by the Commission. It is worth looking at these episodes from two perspectives: technocratic and political.

From a legal and economic perspective, the US did not object to the EU's competence to review the mergers; the clash was on the substantive analysis of the anticompetitive risks. In *Boeing/MDD* the Federal Trade Commission considered that the merger would have no adverse effects because the target firm was a spent force, unable to exert competitive pressure on the market, so whether it was acquired or not, there would be no change to the competitive dynamic.[9] The Commission agreed that MDD was no longer a viable competitor but it took the view that by acquiring it, Boeing would secure certain anticompetitive advantages. The main ones were the following: if Boeing were to invest in strengthening MDD this would create incentives for clients to buy its aircraft because now its future would no longer be put into question. Conversely if Boeing were to decide to phase out MDD aircraft, it would be in an advantageous position to convince clients to substitute them with a Boeing aircraft. Another source of concern that the Commission had was that the merger

[8] Commission Decision 97/816/EC of 30 July 1997 (Case No IV/M.877—*Boeing/McDonnell Douglas*), OJ 1997 L 336/16, paras 11–12.

[9] Statement of Chairman Robert Pitofsky and Commissioners Janet D. Steiger, Roscoe B. Starek III and Christine A. Varney in the Matter of The Boeing Company/McDonnell Douglas Corporation (1 July 1997) available at: https://www.ftc.gov/ (All website references in this chapter were last visited on 7 February 2019.)

would facilitate Boeing's strategy to enter into exclusive supply agreements with airlines, by being able to combine sales of Boeing and MDD aircraft. It noted that in the three exclusive supply agreements with America, Continental and Delta (all announced in proximity to the merger), the three airlines were among the major purchasers of MDD aircraft.[10] These concerns were resolved by commitments offered by the merging parties: for a period of 10 years Douglas Aircraft Company would be held separately from the merged entity so as not to risk Boeing using it strategically to enhance its market power; likewise for a period of 10 years the merged entity cancelled the exclusivity agreements with the three airlines and agreed not to seek other exclusive supply agreements.[11] These resolved the Commission's competition concerns. Judged merely by reading the texts published by the Commission and the Federal Trade Commission (FTC) the divergence is purely a difference as to the competitive strength and significance of the target firm. It is worth noting that one FTC Commissioner disagreed and considered that the merger did raise competition concerns along lines similar to those averred by the Commission.[12] A similar conclusion would be reached by comparing the approach of the Department of Justice and the Commission in *GE/Honeywell*.[13] This was a merger between two firms which both manufactured jet engines and other aviation products. The Commission had four concerns: first, that the parties were competitors in markets for certain types of jet engines and that the merger would create a dominant player; second, that the two firms sold complementary products and by joining up they could sell these in bundles, foreclosing rivals who did not have a full set of products to sell; third, Honeywell was a major supplier of engine controls and it could sell these on favourable terms to GE, thus strengthening the latter's position on the market for jet engines; fourth, GE also owned GECAS (GE Capital Aviation Services) which had a 'GE only' buying policy for the aircraft that it bought and leased. The Commission feared that the merger would mean this policy would extend to Honeywell products as well.[14] None of these concerns troubled the Department of Justice, which did not consider GE to be a dominant player; it felt that the likely bundling of products would serve consumers well rather than harm them, and that GECAS's purchasing practices would not be likely to foreclose market access to rivals.[15]

[10] *Boeing/McDonnell Douglas*, note 8, paras 61–71. The Commission had another set of concerns related to the acquisition of government funded patents, participation in US-supported R&D programmes and relationships between Boeing and suppliers that are beyond the scope of this chapter.

[11] *Ibid.*, paras 115 and 116.

[12] Statement of Commissioner Mary L. Azcuenaga in The Boeing Company (1 September 1997), available at https://www.ftc.gov.

[13] Commission Decision of 3 July 2001 (Case No COMP/M.2220—*General Electric/Honeywell*). Upheld in part Case T-210/01, *General Electric Company v. Commission* [2005] ECR II-5575 (ECLI:EU:T:2005:456).

[14] An excellent, lively account is provided by E. M. Fox, see Fox, 'GE/Honeywell: The US Merger that Europe Stopped', in E. M. Fox and D. A. Crane (eds), *Antitrust Stories* (2007).

[15] D. P. Marjoras, 'GE-Honeywell: The U.S. Decision', 29 November 2001, available at https://www.justice.gov/atr/speech/ge-honeywell-us-decision.

However, political actors played a significant role in both cases: in *Boeing/MDD*, press reports indicate that the US exercised considerable pressure on the Commission to authorize the transaction, threatening a trade war.[16] Likewise, in *GE/Honeywell* many US politicians were critical of the Commission's approach, although it seems the US government did not raise the stakes to the same level as in *Boeing/MDD*.[17] This pressure suggests that the unilateral veto power can be softened through political means, at least some of the time. It is also worth stating the obvious point that although the US has such countervailing power, a jurisdiction with less economic weight will be unable to act in a similar manner. At the same time, there have only been these two major instances of disagreement out of a much larger number of mergers that have been considered by both jurisdictions without similar friction. We turn to the modalities that facilitate cooperation in section 1.C.

C. Solution: Inter-Agency Agreements

From the previous discussion, it emerges that the EU's global power is largely a concern for parties to a merger who have to ensure that their transaction is notified to the Commission, and that, given the global reach of certain mergers, some transactions will be scrutinized by multiple agencies at the same time. The risk of the EU dictating the result globally is present, but appears to be a secondary concern given that divergence with other jurisdictions is episodic.

Competition agencies place much emphasis on bilateral agreements in order to address mergers that are filed in multiple jurisdictions. A particularly strong link exists, for example, between the European Commission and the US Department of Justice, which have agreed a code of best practice that they follow when reviewing mergers together.[18] Parties to a merger normally waive confidentiality to allow the two agencies to share information and discuss how to assess the competitive effects and what remedies to request in order to authorize a deal (normally parties are asked to divest certain assets in markets where the merger would lead them to hold a dominant position). This level of coordination allows for sharing expertise and developing mutual understanding of the competition issues, and may thus avoid the frictions identified earlier. Such cooperation is the norm. More recently, cooperation has been multilateral, with a number of agencies assessing a merger jointly and issuing simultaneous press releases to clear the deal. In half of complex merger cases, the Commission cooperates with other agencies.[19]

The takeaway is that the veto power exists more in form than in substance. The so-called 'Brussels Effect' is overstated as an explanation for the global reach of EU competition law. It will be recalled that Anu Bradford argued that the EU has the

[16] A. C. Witt, *The More Economic Approach to EU Antitrust Law* (2016), at 11–14.

[17] The press reports are summarized in Fox and Witt, notes 14 and 16.

[18] US-EU Merger Working Group Best Practices on Cooperation in Merger Investigations (2011). For discussion, see EC Commission, 'International enforcement cooperation in mergers: main principles and recent experiences', Competition Policy Brief 2016–02 (May 2016).

[19] OECD, *Roundtable on the Extraterritorial Reach of Competition Remedies—Note by the European Union* (4–5 December 2017), DAF/COMP/WP3/WD(2017)35, para. 19. Mergers are complex when they are resolved with commitments in phase 1 or require a phase 2 assessment.

capacity for unilateral regulatory globalization by virtue of its market power, regulatory capacity, preference for strict rules, focus on inelastic targets, and non-divisibility of standards. At first blush many of the conditions may be said to apply: as we saw earlier, parties cannot afford not to have the merger cleared by the EU, and one of the criticisms of the EU's antitrust law is that it is more aggressive than its US counterpart. However, while cases like *GE/Honeywell* and *Boeing/MDD* serve as examples showing the EU's capacity to exercise unilateral regulatory power, one must look more closely at the performance of the Commission as a whole before concluding that it is 'the world's de facto antitrust enforcer'.[20] In this context, as previously observed, in many merger cases there is intense collaboration between the agencies and coordination of remedies. For each example of alleged unilateral conduct, we can find counter-examples of cooperative solutions. In *Panasonic/Sanyo* the merger was investigated in parallel by the Federal Trade Commission, the European Commission and the Japan Fair Trade Commission. The US and EU agencies agreed on one of the divestitures, while the Japanese and EU requested other remedies to address concerns in their jurisdictions.[21] Another noteworthy example is *UTC/Goodrich* where it is reported that cooperation was among five agencies (US, EU, Brazil, Mexico and Canada) and the result was an agreed set of remedies (divestitures in the US, Canada and the UK). Perhaps somewhat hyperbolically, a representative of the Department of Justice, praising the joint work, suggested that the remedy 'will preserve competition in the United States and internationally'.[22] Examples such as these may be multiplied.[23] It follows that cooperative solutions are the norm, and unilateral actions the exception. Moreover, it should also be noted that the Commission (and other competition agencies) exercise some self-control at the remedies stage: by applying the principle of proportionality the least aggressive remedy will be opted for, which means that if a remedy that only applies within the EU suffices to remove the antitrust concern, then a global remedy will not be pursued.[24] In this context, a different account of the EU's global reach is necessary.

[20] Bradford, 'The Brussels Effect', 107(1) *Northwestern University Law Review* (2012) 1, at 22.

[21] Federal Trade Commission, 'FTC Order Sets Conditions for Panasonic's Acquisition of Sanyo', 24 November 2009, available at https://www.ftc.gov/news-events/press-releases/2009/11/ftc-order-sets-conditions-panasonics-acquisition-sanyo; Commission Decision of 29 September 2009 (Case No COMP/M.5421—*Panasonic/Sanyo*). Accordingly Bradford's assessment of this decision (note 20, at 21, footnote 87) is incomplete as she does not observe the degree of agreement between two agencies. Likewise Bradford cites *Intel/McAfee* (Commission Decision of 26 January 2011 (Case No COMP/M.5984—*Intel/McAfee*)) as another example of unilateralism, but this obscures the point that in spite of a difference of opinion as to the need for remedies, the EU and US authorities cooperated throughout. OECD Working Party No. 3 on Co-operation and Enforcement, *Discussion on International Co-operation: United States* DAF/COMP/WP3/WD(2012)24, 8 June 2012, at 6.

[22] Department of Justice, 'Justice Department Requires Divestitures in Order for United Technologies Corporation to Proceed with its Acquisition of Goodrich Corporation', Press Release 12–925.

[23] E.g. Commission Decision 99/287/EC of 8 July 1998 (Case IV/M.1069—*WorldCom/MCI*), OJ 1999 L 116/1. See Report of the International Competition Policy Advisory Committee to the Attorney General and Assistant Attorney General for Antitrust (2000), at 66 noting joint meetings with the parties and coordination on remedies.

[24] OECD, *Roundtable*, note 19, para. 12.

A possible option is that in merger policy a set of agencies, through joint work, are able to identify a shared vision of how to approach competition problems. The legal texts are open-textured enough for agencies to have a wide degree of interpretative latitude which facilitates the identification of shared views. Moreover, cooperation is increasingly institutionalized, which suggests that there is a belief among the agencies that coordinated approaches are valuable as a means of optimizing competition enforcement. One is left to wonder whether what is applied in merger law is in effect a universal merger regime, informed by the shared understanding, which at times is displaced when one agency takes a different position on the anticompetitive risks.

This rosy picture might be challenged by the view that this indicates the 'hegemonic' control of global mergers by a subset of agencies, in particular those of the EU and US.[25] However, for this hypothesis to be convincing we have to find ways of proving that a hegemonic view of competition is ascendant. Here, the more general demands that have been placed on developing countries to embrace market-based reforms (where the label hegemony probably fits well) should be separated from the specific issue under discussion in this chapter, which focuses only on the implementation of competition law once a developing country has embarked on some market reforms. At this juncture, then, we would expect that developing countries would have a commitment to an enforcement regime not wholly dissimilar from that of the EU and US, but which might have some divergences. For present purposes two possibilities can be considered.

The first is the degree to which industrial policy considerations form part of the competition assessment. In this context there may be instances where a merger's harmful effects on consumers might be outweighed by the expected development of an industry sector. A number of developing countries have this kind of provision in place.[26] In this context there is a risk that, if the merger has global effects, a jurisdiction like the US or the EU might block a merger which would be approved of locally in a developing country for industrial policy purposes. However, it is not clear how far this risk materializes, in particular because large jurisdictions like the EU and the US block very few mergers and it is unlikely that a domestic merger in a developing country would require notification in one of the jurisdictions that might oppose merger clearance for industrial policy reasons.

A second possibility, of which the South African competition regime is a good illustration, is the consideration of a range of public interest elements in mergers leading to stricter enforcement in less powerful states. The South African statute provides that regard should be had to: the effects of the merger on (a) a particular industry or region; (b) employment; (c) the ability of small businesses or firms controlled or owned by historically disadvantaged persons to become competitive and

[25] Krisch, 'The Decay of Consent: International law in an Age of Global Public Goods', 108(1) *American Journal of International Law* (2014) 1 (with general reference to all aspects of antitrust enforcement).

[26] See, e.g., Oxenham, 'Balancing Public Interest Merger Considerations before Sub-Saharan African Competition Jurisdictions with the Quest for Multijurisdictional Merger Control Certainty', 9 *US-China Law Review* (2012) 211.

(d) the ability of national industries to compete for international markets.[27] This provision gained global attention during the *Walmart/Massmart* merger.[28] Since Walmart had no meaningful presence in South Africa there were no conventional competition problems, but two public interest harms were signalled by reference to Walmart's commercial strategy: a risk of job losses (some dismissals having taken place before the merger) and a risk to local suppliers, as Walmart was well known for sourcing groceries from the cheapest global supplier. The merger was allowed subject to two conditions: one to protect employment rights and another requiring Walmart to invest resources into developing viable local suppliers.[29] For the purposes of this chapter, this merger, and other decisions where remedies have been imposed having regard to the public interest,[30] is not about the global reach of South African law. The merger only affected South Africa—it was not a global merger subject to multi-jurisdictional review. Moreover, it challenges the hegemony narrative as it shows the possibility for a jurisdiction to carve out a different regulatory approach than that espoused by the larger jurisdictions. Obviously, a jurisdiction like South Africa may need to balance the aggressiveness of the remedy with the importance of stimulating foreign investment, which may temper its policy somewhat. This example, however, reveals the opposite of hegemony as states in different stages of economic development appear able to craft an antitrust approach which suits them.

3. Conduct with Welfare-Ambiguous Effects

This section discusses practices by dominant firms, or agreements between non-competitors, where adverse competitive effects are contested. There are two differences from merger cases: first, this conduct is not notified ex ante so agencies will identify cases based on their own priorities; second, while for most types of mergers there is agreement on how to assess them, in the cases in this section there are deep divisions on the best analytical stance. The example that follows deals with discounts offered by a dominant firm: these practices may be beneficial (lower prices will result) but may in the long term serve to exclude rivals that are unable to match such discounts.

Intel, a dominant player in the market for microchips entered into contracts with a number of computer manufacturers to secure commitments from them that would allow it to sell high volumes of microchips. Its competitors complained that this foreclosed market access for them in a manner that was anticompetitive. In the

[27] Republic of South Africa, Competition Act (n. 89 of 1998), Section 12A(3).

[28] *Minister of Economic Development and Others v. Competition Tribunal and Others, South African Commercial, Catering and Allied Workers Union (SACCAWU) v Wal-Mart Stores Inc. and Another* (110/CAC/Jul11, 111/CAC/Jun11) [2012] ZACAC 2 (9 March 2012).

[29] For a helpful account of the background and an ex post explanation of how the remedies have played out, see Mandiriza, Sithebe and Viljoen, 'An Ex-Post Review of the Wal-Mart/Massmart Merger', Competition Commission South Africa Working Paper CC2016/03.

[30] For a survey, see R. Legh and T. Dini, *Merger Control—South Africa* (September 2017) available at https://gettingthedealthrough.com/area/20/jurisdiction/2/merger-control-south-africa.

period 2005–2010, its conduct was penalized in Korea, Japan and the EU.[31] However, its conduct was found not to infringe US antitrust law. At the time of writing, the Court of Justice had quashed a judgment of the General Court which supported the view that Intel's conduct could be judged by considering the form of the agreements; the General Court has been asked to review the Commission's assessment of the effects of Intel's conduct, paying heed to the possible efficiency justifications proffered by Intel.[32] Some of the contracts analysed by the Commission were signed in China—so why should the EU care? This is a paradigmatic example of the issues discussed in this section. For the purposes of EU law, these kinds of case may be assessed under either Articles 101 or 102 of the Treaty on the Functioning of the European Union, but the key question is the same: how can we distinguish between conduct that restricts competition and conduct that brings about efficient outcomes?

A. Global Reach

The legal basis for intervention in this context (as for cartels which are discussed later) has been controversial. Given the silence of the legislative texts and the reluctance to interfere too much in the activities of other jurisdictions, the Court of Justice has developed its case law incrementally. Two well-established grounds on which subject-matter jurisdiction can be established are the economic entity doctrine and the implementation doctrine. The economic entity doctrine allows the Commission to take action against subsidiaries situated in the EU for the infringements carried out by a parent company situated outside the EU. For this doctrine to apply, the parent must exercise decisive influence over the activity of the subsidiary.[33] The implementation doctrine instead provides that a firm outside the EU is subject to EU law when the infringement is (at least in part) implemented in the EU. In cartel cases, discussed further in section 4, this happens when goods are sold in the EU market, irrespective of where the agreement was reached.[34] One criticism of these two approaches is that while the Court of Justice tried to suggest that the basis for the jurisdiction is the principle of territoriality, the practical result of these two tests is that EU law applies when conduct takes place abroad and has an effect on the EU market.[35]

[31] Korean Fair Trade Commission, *Annual Report 2009*, at 45–47 (imposing a fine of US$26.6m); Japan Fair Trade Commission, *Annual Report on Competition Policy in Japan* (2005), at 5 (issuing an order to cease certain exclusionary practices); Commission Decision of 13 May 2009 (Case COMP/C-3/37.990—*Intel*), OJ 2009 C 227/13, by which the Commission imposed a fine of €1.060bn.

[32] Case C-413/14 P, *Intel Corporation Inc. v. Commission* (ECLI:EU:C:2017:632), judgment of 6 September 2017.

[33] This was established in Case 48/69, *Imperial Chemical Industries v. Commission* [1972] ECR 619 (ECLI:EU:C:1972:70).

[34] Joined Cases 89, 104, 114, 116, 117 and 125 to 129/85, *Ahlström Oy v. Commission* [1988] ECR 5193 (ECLI:EU:C:1988:447).

[35] A possible exception is an agreement between two non-EU firms to boycott the EU market, but for all conduct resulting in sales to the EU the agreement would fall within the implementation test.

Today, however, a more clear approach has been delineated in the *Intel* judgment, which forms the focus of discussion here. In briefest outline, Intel engaged in a commercial strategy whereby it sold its microchips to Original Equipment Manufacturers (OEMs) under contracts that provided for a rebate if the OEM bought certain quantities of chips from Intel. One of the agreements was with Lenovo, a Chinese OEM which questioned why EU law should apply to a contract in China.

The Court of Justice noted that the mere fact that an agreement is made outside the EU should not prevent the application of EU law because otherwise it would be too easy for parties to circumvent the rules. Instead, it indicated that EU competition law applies on two grounds: (1) if the agreement is implemented in the EU; or (2) if the agreement has anticompetitive effects liable to have an impact on the EU market. In the judgment this second standard is referred to as a 'qualified effects test' and the criteria are identical to those found in merger law: whether 'it is foreseeable that the conduct in question will have an immediate and substantial effect in the European Union'.[36]

On the facts of the case the Court of Justice approved the approach of the General Court, which took into consideration the overall strategy that Intel had devised, i.e. to ensure that there was no Lenovo computer with competing chips available. As some of these computers were destined for sale in the EU market, the agreement was capable of producing immediate and substantial effects in the EU.

In setting out the law the way it did, the Court of Justice gave in to the requests of its Advocates General that an effects test should be recognized. In *Intel*, Advocate General Wahl considered that it was high time for the Court of Justice to agree that this test applied to EU competition law for the following reasons: it is generally acceptable under public international law; it has been embraced by many jurisdictions; academic writing supports this test; and other provisions of EU law apply to conduct overseas.[37]

The discussion so far has addressed subject-matter jurisdiction. For completeness, it should be mentioned that this is insufficient without enforcement jurisdiction, where three key steps are relevant: (1) the capacity to serve a notification of infringement abroad;[38] (2) the capacity to secure information that is not held in the EU (although this might be available through domestic subsidiaries); and (3) the power to enforce a final decision. Often the power to enforce is exercised by exploring diplomatic channels, but a number of jurisdictions have issued so-called 'blocking' statutes, especially against US antitrust law. These blocking statutes may have little impact against the EU, however, if the firm does business within the Union, for then a notice can be served to subsidiaries established there.[39] Accordingly, while absence of enforcement jurisdiction can create problems in some instances, these can often be circumvented.

[36] *Intel*, note 32, para. 49. [37] *Ibid.*, Opinion of AG Whal, paras 297–298.

[38] In Case 52/69, *Geigy v. Commission* [1972] ECR 787 (ECLI:EU:C:1972:73) a statement of objections was posted to the Swiss offices.

[39] E.g. *Imperial Chemical Industries*, note 33.

B. Global Power

In this setting, the 'veto' power of an antitrust agency that we observed for mergers is much less prominent: in many instances the firm can simply amend its business practices to comply with the legal requirements in the various jurisdictions. An example is the Commission's concern that Microsoft was bundling the Windows and Internet Explorer software. As a result a special version of Windows 7 was sold in the EU, which did not incorporate the Internet Explorer browser.[40] Of course, in the age of supply chains, there may be instances where this adjustment is more tricky—for example, in the Intel-Lenovo agreement discussed earlier, it will be necessary for Intel to revise its conduct across all its contracts with Lenovo as it is likely that some batches of computers will be sold to the EU markets. It would be impractical and commercially meaningless for Intel to provide for a different contract for different batches of computers depending on where they are headed: not only is this costly but it also removes the commercial result which Intel seeks, which is to exclude rival chip makers.[41] However, the Brussels Effect in these instances is much weaker, as it will only apply when the dominant firm is unable to diversify its commercial strategies. In the context of distribution agreements (where the EU's rules are noted for being tougher than those of the US) most firms will be able to comply within the EU without having to rethink their strategy elsewhere. For example, in the recent Google decision, the firm can probably comply by changing its practices just in the EU.[42]

Nor is the EU the sole antitrust agency active in this context: we can also speak of the 'Seoul Effect' by reference to the decision of the Korean Fair Trade Commission to issue an order with respect to Qualcomm's global business strategy. In brief, the Korean antitrust agency took exception to Qualcomm's licensing practices for its standard essential patents, requiring it to negotiate patent licences with any willing licensee globally so as to stimulate competition in the markets for chipsets and handsets. It considered that only a global remedy would solve the antitrust harm felt on the Korean market.[43] In analogous instances, the US and EU agencies have limited the reach of similar remedies to their jurisdictions.[44]

[40] Meisner 'Working to Fulfill our Legal Obligations in Europe for Windows 7' (11 June 2009) at https://blogs.microsoft.com/on-the-issues/2009/06/11/working-to-fulfill-our-legal-obligations-in-europe-for-windows-7. For discussion, see Economides and Lianos, 'A Critical Appraisal of the Remedies in the EU Microsoft Cases', *Columbia Business Law Review* (2010) 346.

[41] On the tricky issue of how to handle liability in supply chains, see *Motorola Mobility v. AU Optronics* 775 F. 3d 816 (7th Cir. 2015).

[42] Commission Decision of 27 June 2017 (Case AT.39740, *Google Search (Shopping)*), OJ 2018 C 9/11.

[43] OECD, *Roundtable on the Extraterritorial Reach of Competition Remedies—Note by Korea* (4–5 December 2017) DAF/COMP/WP3/WD(2017)37, at 5–8. The decision was reached on 21 December 2016. An unofficial translation of the press release is available at http://www.ftc.go.kr.

[44] For instance, the settlement by the Federal Trade Commission in Motorola and Google (23 July 2013) requires that competitors should have access to standard essential patents provided that they are within the jurisdiction of the US District Courts (see http://www.ftc.gov for relevant documents), while the Commission's decision in *Samsung* is limited to the EEA because the Commission found that Samsung's conduct outside the EU had no effects in the EU market (Commission Decision of 29 April 2014 (Case AT.39939, *Samsung—Enforcement of UMTS standard essential patents*), OJ 2014 C 350/8).

C. Solution: Convergence

Divergence among competition laws is much more pronounced than for mergers or cartels. The debate here among scholars and competition authorities is fierce. Simplifying, it is between those who take a very hands-off approach and suggest (for example) that a dominant player is only infringing competition law where its conduct is likely to exclude a competitor as efficient as itself, while other jurisdictions take a more aggressive line against large firms, whereby the exclusion of new entrants is condemned without a detailed assessment of the impact on consumer welfare, but taking into account only the adverse impact on the competitive process. In particular the divergence is between the US (lax) and the EU (strict) models.[45]

The tensions that arise in this scenario are difficult to resolve: unlike in merger cases, the timing of the agencies' intervention cannot be coordinated because each agency will commence an investigation when it deems it appropriate in light of internal considerations (e.g. resources, number of complaints received, perceived gains from taking action), so it is rare that the same conduct is subjected to review by multiple agencies. Accordingly, the kind of cooperation seen in merger cases cannot occur frequently: in mergers agencies must react when the notification arrives, and this will be received nearly simultaneously by most agencies. The International Competition Network (ICN) has endeavoured to establish basic standards for intervention for the most common forms of abuse of dominance (in the ICN's jargon this is referred to as unilateral conduct) but progress is hampered by the fact that a number of agencies will wish to pursue a more (or less) aggressive policy than that prescribed by the ICN working group. Still, efforts to make the interpretation of the laws converge are ongoing.[46]

For completeness it should be noted that, when possible, agencies tend to cooperate even in these scenarios: in reviewing agreements between Apple and publishers in the e-book market the firms under scrutiny waived confidentiality and cooperated with the Commission and the US Department of Justice to reach an agreed remedy, and the *Oneworld* joint venture was scrutinized by the Commission together with the US Department of Transport.[47] However, as already noted, this kind of cooperation depends on agencies having similar enforcement priorities at the same time.

4. Cartels

Many cartels operate globally, and many have been discovered. The lysine cartel discovered by the US Department of Justice in the late 1990s was the first major global cartel of the contemporary era.[48] Since then, cartel enforcement has been a

[45] For an overview, see D. J. Gifford and R. T. Kudrle, *The Atlantic Divide in Antitrust* (2015).

[46] E.g. ICN Unilateral Conduct Working Group Predatory Pricing Analysis Pursuant to Unilateral Conduct Laws: Recommended Practices (undated, available at https://www.internationalcompetitionnetwork.org).

[47] OECD, *Roundtable on the Extraterritorial Reach of Competition Remedies*, note 19, at 9–10.

[48] Connor, 'Global Cartels Redux: The Amino Acid Lysine Antitrust Litigation', in J. E. Kwoka, Jr and L. J. White (eds), *The Antitrust Revolution* (1996).

priority for many competition agencies, with a resulting increase in the number of investigations.

A. Global Reach

The scope of the EU's global reach is largely as discussed earlier, in section 3: cartels penalized by the Commission have been implemented in the EU through direct sales, even if the parties to the cartel may have all been foreign firms.[49] In *Gas Insulated Switchgear* the Commission interpreted the scope of EU competition law rather widely: the Japanese members of the cartel agreed not to bid for contracts in the EU in exchange for EU members not bidding in Japan, and the Commission considered it was entitled to fine the Japanese firms whose absence from the European bidding market made a direct contribution to the anticompetitive effects in the EU market. This was achieved by treating this part of the cartel as a single and continuous infringement with other aspects of the same collusive conduct whereby Japanese firms made some sales into the EU.[50] After the ruling in *Intel* it is likely that these contortions will become less necessary as an agreement not to enter another market would fall under the qualified effects test.

B. Global Power

While all countries tend to agree that cartels should be prohibited, the global reach of EU competition law has been criticized for imposing penalties that are too high because it ignores possible penalties that might be imposed by other competition agencies for the same conduct. This has little to do with the proper scope of the concept of qualified effects to establish jurisdiction, and much to do with the technique used by the Commission to impose fines. Two scenarios can be distinguished: global cartels and cartels that are part of a global value chain, where the cartel harm is transmitted through the value chain.

An example of the former is the graphite electrodes cartel, where one of the members appealed against the fine. The applicant argued that the Commission, when setting fines, should take into account the fines already imposed by the US agencies. However, the Court of Justice had none of this. It noted that every state is entitled to penalize cartels for the harm that they do in their jurisdiction, and that there is no principle of international law requiring the Commission to lower its fines—the Commission may take other decisions into consideration, but there is no need to do so.[51] To a degree, the risk that the total fines may add up to quite a high value may make up for the lack of global enforcement: it is not likely that all jurisdictions will penalize every global cartel. To the extent that fines serve as a deterrent, the penalty may also benefit those jurisdictions that have not pursued the cartel.

[49] *Ahlström Osakeyhtiö*, note 34.

[50] Commission Decision of 24 January 2007 (Case COMP/F/38.899—*Gas Insulated Switchgear*), paras 314–319.

[51] Case C-289/04, *Showa Denko KK v. Commission* [2006] ECR I-5859 (ECLI:EU:C:2006:431), paras 50–63.

An example of the latter is the liquid crystal display (LCD) cartel case, where the cartel members sold LCD panels down a manufacturing chain. The Commission had no qualms in indicating that if the cartel sold directly into the European Economic Area (EEA) market then these sales could be taken into consideration; however, many sales were made either to subsidiaries of the cartel or to third parties outside the EEA before the final products arrived in the EU. The question arose whether these sales could be taken into account when imposing the fine. On the facts of the case, the Commission took into consideration only the sales of LCDs to subsidiaries of the cartel members, on the grounds that by taking into account this revenue, the fine would have a sufficient deterrent effect. The parties appealed on the basis that these sales were not made directly into the EU and should thus not be considered. However, the Court of Justice rejected this claim, largely for policy reasons: it considered that if the Commission were unable to take into account sales to subsidiaries made outside the EEA, firms would redesign their supply chains so as to avoid a large fine.[52]

The intrusive nature of Commission fines is a result of efforts that agencies have made to cooperate at the investigation stage, with coordinated inspections of premises being a prominent example: this prevents offices from destroying evidence upon hearing that other branches have been subjected to inspection.[53] Many global cartels are therefore penalized by more than one agency: after the investigation stage, where coordination is vital to secure evidence, cooperation is hampered by confidentiality, but this does not prevent multiple agencies pursuing the same infringement for the harm caused to domestic markets.[54] In this framework, the EU's global reach may be said to contribute to global deterrence.

C. Uncertain Solutions

The major concern in this field of antitrust is that national competition agencies are unable to attack cartels that operate cross-border or that are part of a global supply chain in an efficient manner. From the perspective of competition authorities in developing countries, there is a lack of cooperation between well-established agencies and newer authorities.[55] Even if channels of cooperation are open, this is hampered by confidentiality: few inter-state agreements allow for the transfer of information seized during an investigation from one jurisdiction to the next. A notable exception is found in EU law, whereby national competition agencies may carry out investigations on behalf of other agencies and transmit the information seized to other agencies. Significant procedural safeguards are necessary to protect

[52] Case C-231/14 P, *InnoLux Corporation v Commission* (ECLI:EU:C:2015:451), para. 55.

[53] In the airline fuel surcharge cartel, for instance, there was cooperation among the EU, US and Korean agencies: Korea Fair Trade Commission, *Annual Report 2011*, at 94.

[54] In the marine hose cartel, for example, at least five agencies imposed fines: Korean Fair Trade Commission, *Annual Report 2010*, at 68.

[55] P. M. Horna, 'David & Goliath: How Young Competition Agencies can Succeed in Fighting Cross-Border Cartels', Oxford Centre for Competition Law and Policy Working Paper CCLP (L) 45 (2017).

the firms' rights of defence.[56] Some agencies have entered into mutual assistance agreements that allow some information to flow (e.g. the US-Australia agreement on mutual enforcement assistance, 1999). The lack of such an arrangement is often the weakest link: a joint ICN/OECD report concluded that the primary impediment to international cooperation is the absence of a legal framework to enable the exchange of confidential information.[57]

However, under-enforcement in cartel cases is also the result of policy considerations: a number of states authorize export cartels, which are designed not to have harmful effects within the jurisdictions where they originate, but to boost exports.[58] It is odd that these provisions remain in force, given the almost religious fervour with which competition law is preached to newer competition jurisdictions. The EU has no statute that authorizes export cartels but if an agreement has no impact on the EU market then EU competition law is inapplicable.[59] It has been noted that export cartels, when sponsored by developed states, are particularly harmful to developing countries because they are unlikely to be prosecuted in those countries since the evidence for the existence of these cartels is in another jurisdiction. It has also been noted that some developing countries may be unwilling to go after a cartel which is part of a global value chain because of the higher revenues this generates for the country at the top of the chain, with losses resulting in other jurisdictions.[60] Strategically, a state that supports export cartels might find it unwise to take action against the export cartels of other nations, lest the latter retaliate with antitrust action against those export cartels.[61]

5. Global Externalities

In the previous sections it has been seen that the EU's global power in antitrust is less significant than some claim: accounts of a Brussels Effect or EU hegemony prove limited in their explanatory power. Similar remarks may be made regarding the US: in spite of concerns that the US is able to use its antitrust weight to secure market access in foreign states, there is little evidence of US agencies using antitrust in this manner.[62] Each of the three restrictive practices considered reveals different themes

[56] Council Regulation 1/2003 of 16 December 2002 on the implementation of the rules on competition laid down in Articles 81 and 82 of the Treaty, OJ 2003 L 1/1, Art. 12.

[57] Report on the OECD/ICN *Survey on International Enforcement Co-operation*, DAF/COMP/WP3(2013).

[58] E.g. the US. For discussion, see Antitrust Modernization Commission: Report and Recommendations (April 2007) chapter 4, available at https://govinfo.library.unt.edu/amc/report_recommendation/toc.htm.

[59] Case C-306/96, *Javico International and Javico AG v. Yves Saint Laurent Parfums SA (YSLP)* [1998] ECR I-1983 (ECLI:EU:C:1998:173). On other occasions the EU might support cartels. An example is a 1994 aluminium cartel, discussed by J. Stiglitz, *Globalisation and Its Discontents* (2002), at 173–176.

[60] Gerber, 'Competitive Harm in Global Supply Chains: Assessing Current Responses and Identifying Potential Future Responses', 6 *Journal of Antitrust Enforcement* (2018) 5.

[61] Jenny, 'Export Cartels in Primary Products: The Potash Case in Perspective', in S. J. Eventt and F. Jenny (eds), *Trade, Competition and the Pricing of Commodities* (2012).

[62] C. Ryngaert, *Jurisdiction over Antitrust Violations in International Law* (2008), chapter 11.

pertaining to the global reach of EU competition law: cooperation among agencies is the norm in merger cases, much less so in the other fields; conflict is much more prominent in unilateral conduct cases than it is when mergers or cartels are under consideration. In cartel cases, the picture is of fragmented enforcement which hampers an efficient approach to global cartels, compounded by the tolerance of export cartels.

An economic approach to the EU's global reach would ask a different question: how far is the application of EU competition law affecting global welfare? A clear answer which emerges in all three kinds of enforcement action discussed earlier is that each jurisdiction normally tests the welfare effects of conduct in their jurisdiction only. This is sub-optimal: a merger which yields efficiencies in one market but inefficiencies in another may be prohibited globally by a significant competition agency. Or if one agency has a narrower welfare standard than another, this might serve to block global transactions. This argument may also apply to conduct with welfare-ambiguous effects: it has been suggested that if a competition policy is overly aggressive, this might dent incentives to invest.[63] In sum, the first economic risk of local enforcement of global actors is over-enforcement which reduces economic welfare.

Under-enforcement is, however, also an issue of concern: export cartels are a clear category of instances where a state exports anticompetitive harm with the risk of no enforcement by the country that receives the exported goods for lack of capacity to take the case or the inability to secure evidence of the agreement. Another source of under-enforcement may occur when an under-resourced agency chooses to 'free ride' on the decisions of others. It may be rational to rely on other agencies in assessing the welfare effects of mergers: if the merger creates a dominant player, then the more well-resourced agencies will block this and it is likely that this will benefit the non-enforcing jurisdictions as well. However, there are risks that some adverse effects are not observed in the jurisdictions of the agencies that take the case. Free-riding is then a risky option. Finally, weaker jurisdictions might feel compelled to tolerate anticompetitive conduct to secure foreign investment.

Eleanor Fox has suggested that under-enforcement may be addressed by allowing one jurisdiction to 'stretch its law, conceptually, to embrace the whole affected market, thus approximating world welfare'.[64] The potential of this approach is revealed in the merger case law, where as we have seen, agencies can coordinate on remedies to take into consideration each other's competition concerns. It would be more complicated to expect an agency to be able to impose a fine on a corporation for the global effects of its anticompetitive conduct: procedural rules limit the scope of this approach, and it is unlikely that there will be any political interest in widening one jurisdiction's domestic antitrust rules to benefit others.[65] Another suggestion is that

[63] Gal and Padilla, 'The Follower Phenomenon: Implications for the Design of Monopolization Rules in a Global Economy', 76(3) *Antitrust Law Journal* (2010) 899.

[64] Fox, 'Antitrust without Borders: From Roots to Codes to Networks', in A. T. Guzman (ed.), *Cooperation, Comity and Competition Policy* (2011) 265, at 270.

[65] For a more optimistic position, see Michales, 'Supplanting Foreign Antitrust', 79 *Law and Contemporary Problems* (2016) 223.

a national competition authority could enforce antitrust law by recognizing the decision of a sister agency.[66] This, however, comes up against the problem that a decision of one agency is often limited to finding effects in its territory, so while such decisions can provide helpful assistance, each competition authority would still have to do some investigating to establish an infringement in its territory.

A further attempt to ensure that a single jurisdiction is able to tackle global market failures was seen in a damages claim following on from the discovery of a cartel in certain vitamin markets. Buyers based in countries like Ecuador and the Ukraine brought suit in the US for cartel losses that they had sustained when buying vitamins outside the US at inflated prices. The Supreme Court held that on these facts, foreign buyers would be unable to bring a damages claim because the adverse competitive effects that the cartel had on the US market were unrelated to harmful effects outside the US.[67] This places a high barrier for foreign plaintiffs which may wish to use the US as a global forum to secure compensation for antitrust infringements. Some have been critical of this stance, suggesting that allowing these lawsuits would afford better deterrence. Concerns about comity could have been handled on a case-by-case basis whereupon the US court would inquire about the likelihood that the foreign claimants would find their domestic courts able and willing to consider the damages claim, and whether the jurisdiction from where these claimants were situated would object to the US court considering the claim.[68] However, the restrictive approach of the Court is preferable: first, there would be significant difficulties in obtaining adequate evidence of cartel harm occurring abroad and, second, as the Supreme Court noted, it would be time-consuming for a court to carry out a comity exercise on a case-by-case basis. More generally, US law affords successful cartel plaintiffs treble damages, meaning that every claim brought by foreign plaintiffs in the US bypasses national rules that limit claims to compensatory damages.

It might be thought that there is a much simpler means of addressing the economic concerns noted above: a global competition authority. That this would work well is shown by the enforcement of competition law by the European Commission or by the US Department of Justice: supranational powers to oversee anticompetitive conduct that crosses national borders make these two agencies highly effective enforcers of competition law in their own jurisdictions. However, there is significant opposition to any global initiative that entails even just the codification of competition rules. Opposition from developing countries stems from their concern that this would benefit developed states, while the US is concerned that any codification would lead to weaker standards.[69] Although in the past the EU had pushed for a codification of competition law standards, it has now stopped doing so since there are no longer any realistic prospects of this route being followed.[70] Moreover, it has

[66] Gal, 'Free Movement of Judgments: Increasing Deterrence of International Cartels though Jurisdictional Reliance', 51(1) *Virginia Journal of International Law* (2010) 57.

[67] *F. Hoffmann La Roche et al v Empagram* 542 US 155 (2004).

[68] Ryngaert, note 62, at 133–134.

[69] See Fox, note 64, at 272.

[70] On a history of attempts to address competition at global level, see D. Gerber, *Global Competition* (2009); D. P. Wood, 'The Impossible Dream: Real International Antitrust', *University of Chicago Legal*

been argued that even if the parties were able to agree on an international treaty, the divergences are such that any resulting text would be so watered down that it would be ineffective.[71]

6. Cooperation Agreements

In the absence of a global initiative, states have engaged in bilateral cooperation. Sections 6.A and 6.B will explore how the EU has sought to engage other competition authorities and states. While in previous sections the focus was on collaboration in discrete cases, these sections will focus on bilateral agreements more generally, and they will consider how far the evidence shows a willingness to cooperate to facilitate more effective enforcement versus a desire to export norms.

A. Bilateral Competition Agreements

The EU has entered into 10 bilateral agreements of various kinds that are specifically devoted to cooperation in competition matters. Nine of these represent so-called 'first generation' agreements, while the agreement with Switzerland is the first of the second generation.[72]

The first generation agreements have a similar structure, and focus here is on the agreement with the US as the most advanced one. First, the parties undertake to notify each other of instances where one party's actions affect the important interests of the other. They establish regular channels of communication on general policy issues and specific cases.[73] These provisions have been supplemented by an Administrative Agreement on Attendance, which allows members of one agency to participate in elements of the procedure of the other. Establishing these close contacts between officials is vital in establishing trust between parties in the integrity of the other party's processes. A second aspect, which reveals an important limitation of these agreements, is a provision that allows one side to request information from the other on specific cases. However, confidential information may not be circulated unless there is a waiver by the parties. This renders the agreement less than helpful when it comes to cartel investigations.[74]

Third, the agreement provides for 'negative comity': each party endeavours to take into account the important interests of the other side. The provision sets out an

Forum 277 (1992); Aydin, 'Promoting Competition: European Union and the Global Competition Order', 34(6) *European Integration* (2012) 663, at 670–672.

[71] Bradford, 'International Antitrust Cooperation and the Preference for Non-Binding Regimes', in A. T. Guzman (ed.), *Cooperation, Comity and Competition Policy* (2011) 319.

[72] With these countries: Brazil, Canada, China, India, Japan, the Republic of Korea, Russia, South Africa, Switzerland and the US. Source: http://ec.europa.eu/competition/international/bilateral/index.html.

[73] Agreement between the Government of the United States of America and the Commission of the European Communities regarding the application of their competition laws, OJ 1995 L 95/47, Arts II and III.

[74] *Ibid.*, Arts III(4) and VIII.

indicative list of considerations that may be taken into consideration, ranging from whether the parties infringing competition law did or did not intend to harm consumers, competitors or suppliers in the enforcing party's territory to the degree of conflict between the enforcer's competition policies and the other side's economic policies.[75] It is relevant to note that the approach that has been agreed here deviates from the case law of the two countries. In the leading US case, *Hartford Fire Insurance Co. v. California*, 19 states and a number of private parties sued certain insurance companies, including some based in the UK. The defendants argued that considerations of comity militated against the US having subject-matter jurisdiction since the conduct at play was authorized in the UK. However, the US Supreme Court took the view that comity would only move the court to decline jurisdiction in a situation where there is a real conflict between the two rules: for instance if the UK required conduct that was prohibited in the US. On the facts at hand, the Supreme Court held that it was possible for the defendants to comply with both US and UK law by not colluding, so there was no true conflict.[76] The indications from the EU courts are that a similar result would obtain.[77] The more restrained approach by agencies is a recognition that a more aggressive attack on national policies would offend the other party.

The fourth element of this agreement is a positive comity clause.[78] It allows state A to request that state B take enforcement action in state B when a business entity in state B is harming the interests of state A. Within the framework of the EU-US agreement, this has only been invoked once (by the US), and the results were deemed unsatisfactory because of the slow response of the party receiving the request. This is perhaps unsurprising as competition agencies operate on tight budgets and are accountable to their masters for their results: protecting foreign markets is not their core business.

The agreement with Switzerland contains all of these plus provisions that allow for the two parties to exchange evidence that has been obtained as a result of investigations by the other agency.[79] The power to transmit such information is subject to a number of safeguards: to avoid 'fishing expeditions', evidence may only be exchanged if both sides are already investigating the same case; to avoid excessive burdens the parties are expected to engage in consultations to identify relevant information; to avoid the misuse of information, evidence may only be exchanged for the purposes of applying the other party's competition rules. Moreover, information received pursuant to a leniency application may not be transmitted, to ensure that firms may make leniency applications without fear of this being transmitted to other agencies. The depth of cooperation found here is very close to that found among the

75 *Ibid.*, Art. VI. 76 *Hartford Fire Insurance Co. v. California* 509 US 764 (1993).

77 *Gencor v. Commission*, note 2.

78 See note 73, Art. V. This was enhanced subsequently: United States and European Communities Agreement on 'Positive Comity' in Antitrust Enforcement (June 1998), available at https://www.ftc.gov/policy/cooperation-agreements/us-european-commission-enhanced-positive-comity-agreement.

79 Agreement between the European Union and the Swiss Confederation concerning cooperation on the application of their competition laws, OJ 2014 L 347/3, Arts 7–10.

national competition authorities of the Member States.[80] It is expected that the Commission will seek to replicate these provisions in other agreements.

The most significant element of these bilateral agreements is the conversations about antitrust that they facilitate, as evidenced in the intense collaboration in specific cases which is documented in sections 2 to 4. Fox's pithy assessment of comity provisions is apt: 'Comity sounds good and does very little work.'[81] It does not appear that comity serves as a break on a competition authority or national court unless the conduct in question is required by the state from which it originates; any less formal work that comity does is hard to discern. Finally, it should be noted that the scope of the EU's efforts to cooperate is limited to large economies, and there is currently no cooperation of this nature between developed and developing countries. In these cases, the EU's preference is to export its antitrust standards, as discussed next.

B. Bilateral Agreements with States

It is well known that the EU is a successful exporter of its competition laws: there is consensus that the EU's export strategy has been more successful than that of the US.[82] The competition law-related portions of the international agreements vary across time and depending on the closeness of the relationship that the EU wishes to establish.[83] Looking closely at the text of these agreements, two aspects are worth pointing out: first, there is some attempt to ensure that there is a degree of convergence between the third country's rules and those of the EU. An example where this is set out forcefully is the association agreement with Ukraine, which provides that the country 'shall approximate its competition laws and enforcement practices' to those of the EU.[84] The second aspect is that the agreements go beyond the three antitrust fields covered here and also impose obligations on the other states to make sure that competition law is applicable to public enterprises, and that subsidies are controlled.[85] These agreements are supplemented by guidance and monitoring by the EU.[86] In contrast to bilateral agreements between agencies, trade agreements appear to give more credence to the view that the EU exports its norms: the significance of the effort here is greater as the endeavour is not to influence firms to alter their conduct but to affect states.[87] A review of national legislation in countries that

[80] See Regulation 1/2003, note 56, Art. 12 and Commission Notice on cooperation within the Network of Competition Authorities, OJ 2004 C 101/43.

[81] Fox, note 64, at 269.

[82] Fox, 'Antitrust and Regulatory Federalism: Races up, down, and sideways', 75(6) *New York University Law Review* (2000) 1781.

[83] A. Papadopolous, *The International Dimension of EU Competition Law and Policy* (2010) for a comprehensive account.

[84] Association Agreement between the European Union and its Member States, of the one part, and Ukraine, of the other part, OJ 2014 L 161/3, Art. 256.

[85] E.g. Free Trade Agreement between the European Union and the Republic of Korea, OJ 2011 L 127/6, Arts 11.4–11.15.

[86] B. A. Melo Araujo, *The EU Deep Trade Agenda: Law and Policy* (2016), at 199.

[87] Young, 'The European Union as a Global Regulator? Context and Comparison', 22(9) *Journal of European Public Policy* (2015) 1233, at 1238 setting out a scale to measure the significance and ease of

have trade agreements with the EU suggests that, to some degree, national rules have been influenced by the EU.[88]

The aim of these agreements from the perspective of the EU is to ensure that European firms that export in these countries are treated fairly and that local firms are subject to rules that do not give them unfair competitive advantages.[89] However, it has been suggested that the mere existence of these rules is no guarantee that these objectives will be met: on the one hand, much depends on the way the country takes up active enforcement and how far it can successfully be embedded into the national fabric; on the other hand, while the EU can offer the incentive of future EU membership to convince certain states, for some parts of the world this carrot does not work.[90] A further limitation is that few agreements provide for any binding commitments to apply competition law in the manner prescribed therein, and the view has been expressed that these agreements are thus only 'symbolic' and rely on ex post cooperation and technical assistance.[91] This tallies with some of the theoretical literature suggesting that when there is no coercive mechanism, the EU's power wanes, and it wanes further when the EU presses for a reformist agenda, where its position is, globally, an outlier.[92] From this perspective, it is not clear how successful the EU can be in promoting the adoption of state aid policies through bilateral agreements. Moreover, it has been suggested that the strength of the EU's influence depends on the economic dependence of the other states: states that rely on exports to the EU may be more willing to follow the EU's intimations than the BRICS countries (Brazil, Russia, India, China and South Africa).[93]

In sum, while it is appealing to suggest that the EU shows some hegemonic tendencies in its export of domestic rules, this is exercised unevenly, depending on the nature of the relationship the EU wishes to have with the other party and the incentives for third states to follow the EU's requests. It is telling that with emerging global powers like the BRICS countries, the emphasis is placed more on conversation than on exporting rules. It also bears restating that for many developing countries, the presence of competition law in the books tells us little about the effectiveness of law enforcement, in particular given the challenges posed in those states by limited resources, corruption, weak legal systems and state owned enterprises.[94]

transmitting EU policy: e.g. easier (but less significant) to persuade a firm exporting to the EU to adopt EU rules, while more difficult (but more significant) to persuade a third state to alter its laws to align them to the EU's.

[88] Doleys, 'Promoting Competition Policy Abroad: European Union Efforts in the Developing World', 57(2) *Antitrust Bulletin* (2012) 337.

[89] European Commission, 'Trade, Growth and World Affairs Trade Policy as a core component of the EU's 2020 strategy', COM(2010) 612 final, at 14.

[90] Aydin, note 70, at 675 noting these arguments. [91] Melo Araujo, note 86, at 200.

[92] Young, note 87, at 1242. [93] Doleys, note 88, at 365.

[94] A. E. Rodriguez and A. Menon, *The Limits of Competition Policy: The Shortcomings of Antitrust in Developing and Reforming Economics* (2010).

7. Conclusions

The main argument in this chapter is that while the application of EU competition law by the Commission has a global reach, claims of a Brussels Effect or of hegemony appear overstated. Moreover, the scope of the global reach of EU antitrust law depends on the rule in question.

From this perspective, when we turn to merger control, the EU's global reach is rendered less salient than the cooperative manner through which these transactions are regulated, since more than one agency will have competence to review global transactions. In cartel scenarios, cooperation becomes more difficult on a practical level, but the EU's global reach might, if it is effective at all, be insufficient to counter the anticompetitive effects of cartels. In instances where the welfare effect of business practices is less clear, then some of the prerequisites for the Brussels Effect obtain, but it remains to be seen how frequently the EU will set the standards for the conduct of business globally: from recent enforcement actions it is not clear that many businesses have to adapt their conduct across the world; concomitantly the EU is not the sole actor imposing global remedies.

Hegemony is also not a helpful label by which to characterize global enforcement of antitrust law: granted there can be instances where less economically significant countries' policies might be thwarted by global antitrust, but it is equally the case that a number of weaker states are victims of export cartels against which they are incapable of reacting. Hegemony then cuts both ways: enforcement and non-enforcement of competition law. It is too sweeping an analytical tool to help explain the global reach of EU competition law and more apt to explain the negative externalities that policies of powerful states have on weaker ones at a higher level of generality.

Having focused on the actual enforcement approach by the Commission in this chapter, the themes that emerge as central to the EU's global reach are those of cooperation and convergence. The Commission seeks cooperation when possible, while convergence emerges incrementally as agencies share ideas and information. Should we be concerned about these two processes?

The presence of bilateral cooperation efforts may be read in two ways: from one perspective, it emerges from the considerations that antitrust agencies must take into account when conduct crosses borders. On the one hand, the black letter law affords states like the EU and the US a long arm to reach into the conduct of businesses abroad (as a result of the effects test to establish jurisdiction and a very restrictive reading of comity). On the other, agencies are much more cautious when tackling conduct occurring abroad and take into account the interests and policies of the other state.[95] When two agencies must consider the same conduct, cooperation has been recommended by the OECD since the late 1960s, with the US initiating some of the earliest agreements.[96] From this viewpoint, cooperation is part of a

[95] This policy is expressly set out in Department of Justice and Federal Trade Commission, Antitrust Guidelines for International Enforcement and Cooperation (January 2017), section 4.

[96] Papadopolous, note 83, at 52–58.

reasonable effort by agencies to work together in a way that is respectful of the sovereignty of other nations. From a critical political economy perspective, however, cooperation between agencies regarding mergers may be the result of pressure from industry: such cooperation facilitates a harmonious resolution of merger submissions, and larger agencies are better placed to convince smaller ones to adopt a more lax attitude to mergers.[97]

A sceptic would claim that cooperation stops when the political stakes are sufficiently high that technocratic governance yields to higher imperatives, or when disagreement among technocrats on how to diagnose market failures makes cooperation impossible.[98] However, the evidence mustered in this chapter suggests that episodes of successful cooperation far outstrip instances of disagreement. It is plausible to suggest that cooperation facilitates further cooperation, and might even weaken the state's capacity to adopt anticompetitive regulation.[99] The move by the EU to second-generation bilateral agreements in the field of competition law evidences an interest in overcoming barriers to cooperation in the field of cartel enforcement.[100]

As far as convergence is concerned, the majority of commentators welcome the identification of superior practices through institutions like the ICN.[101] Procedurally, the ICN provides for an agora, from which a voluntary choice may be made by the actors on whether to converge. A minority view questioning convergence is, however, preferable. As intimated in some of the earlier examples, there may be jurisdictions that need competition law enforcement to achieve objectives other than consumer welfare: the EU, for instance, has regularly prohibited arrangements that segment the internal market to ensure that as state-created barriers are removed, these are not re-established by agreements between private actors. In other cultures, cooperation may be valued more highly as a source of general economic welfare than the promotion of rivalry.[102] Insofar as divergences remain, it would also be advisable to temper the global reach of one's antitrust laws to facilitate accommodation of conflicting views on the role played by competition law. In the long term this may well allow a better embedding of competition law globally.

[97] H. Buch Hansen and A. Wigger, 'Too Big to Control? The Politics of Mega-mergers and Why the EU is Not Stopping Them', Corporate Europe Observatory (June 2017) available at https://corporateeurope.org/sites/default/files/attachments/toobigtocontrol.pdf.

[98] Stephan, 'The Problem with Cooperation', in A. T. Guzman (ed.), *Cooperation, Comity and Competition Policy* (2011), noting examples where states agreed to restrict competition in certain sectors.

[99] On the value of cooperation among technocrats generally, see A.-M. Slaughter, *A New World Order* (2004).

[100] This serves to respond to two of the three major factors competition agencies report as hampering cooperation (protecting confidential information and a legal basis for cooperation). The third factor is resource constraints. OECD, 'Report on the OECD/ICN Survey on International Enforcement Co-operation', DAF/COMP/WP3(2013), 2.

[101] Kovacic and Holman, 'The International Competition Network: Its Past, Current, and Future Role', 20 *Minnesota Journal of International Law* (2011) 274.

[102] For examples of the transfer of competition law in Asia, see Gerber, 'Asia and Global Competition Law Convergence', in M. W. Dowdle, J. Gillespie and I. Maher (eds), *Asian Capitalism and the Regulation of Competition: Towards a Regulatory Geography of Global Competition Law* (2013).

6

The Migration Crisis and the European Union Border Regime

Bernard Ryan

1. Introduction

The EU's recent migration crisis has been characterized by a series of policy challenges posed by irregular migration by sea in the Mediterranean.[1] This chapter is concerned with the various ways in which the migration crisis has re-shaped the EU's border control regime since the Arab Spring of 2011, in relation to migration in both the Central Mediterranean and the Eastern Mediterranean.[2] Following the Arab Spring, the scholarly consensus was to doubt its effects in the policy sphere.[3] Similarly, some commentators have concluded that fundamental policy developments have been lacking across the migration and asylum policy field since 2015.[4] In contrast, based on a detailed review of the whole period since 2011, this chapter will argue that a number of profound changes have taken place within the EU border regime.[5] Among other things, these shifts have seen a strengthening of EU powers over Schengen zone member states, and—more significantly—extensive new cooperation with third countries.

[1] The chapter was completed in May 2018. My thanks to Pablo Cortés, Alan Desmond, Marion Panizzon and the editors, for their comments on the chapter in draft (with the usual disclaimers).

[2] In support of 2011 as a turning point, see Geddes and Hadj-Abdou, 'Changing the Path? EU Migration Governance after the "Arab Spring"', 23 *Mediterranean Politics* (2017) 1 and Pastore and Henry, 'Explaining the Crisis of the European Migration and Asylum Regime', 51 *The International Spectator: Italian Journal of International Affairs* (2016) 44.

[3] Campesi, 'The Arab Spring and the Crisis of the European Border Regime: Manufacturing Emergency in the Lampedusa Crisis', Robert Schuman Centre for Advanced Studies Working Paper 2011/59 (November 2011) and Noutcheva, 'Institutional Governance of European Neighbourhood Policy in the Wake of the Arab Spring', 37 *Journal of European Integration* (2015) 19, at 24–25.

[4] Schimmelfennig, 'European Integration (Theory) in Times of Crisis. A Comparison of the Euro and Schengen Crises', 25 *Journal of European Public Policy* (2018) 969 and Scipioni, 'Failing Forward in EU Migration Policy? EU Integration after the 2015 Asylum and Migration Crisis', 25 *Journal of European Public Policy* (2018) 1357.

[5] This is in line with the conclusions concerning the EU asylum regime in Niemann and Zaun, 'EU Refugee Policies and Politics in Times of Crisis: Theoretical and Empirical Perspectives', 56 *Journal of Common Market Studies* (2018) 3, at 5–13.

For analytical purposes, the EU border regime may be divided into its internal and external dimensions. The 'internal' dimension covers the relationship between members of the Schengen open border zone, the obligations upon states concerning the control of the shared external border, and the role of Frontex, the EU's external border agency.[6] The 'external' dimension concerns the EU's engagement with states outside the Schengen zone in relation to border control and irregular migration. In Boswell's formulation, the logic of the external dimension is 'to engage sending and transit countries in strengthening border controls, combatting illegal entry, migrant smuggling and trafficking, or readmitting migrants who have crossed into the EU illegally'.[7] Drawing upon this internal/external distinction, section 2 will discuss the EU border regime as it stood prior to the Arab Spring of 2011. Section 3 will set out the ways in which the different phases of the post-2011 migration crisis triggered a transformation in EU border policy. Sections 4 and 5 will then examine the detailed shifts that resulted from the crisis, in the internal dimension, and in relation to co-operation with third states, respectively.

In thinking about recent changes to the EU border regime, a dual notion of 'reach' will be relied upon. The first aspect is substantive: how profound or intense are the implications of EU norms and policies for the states concerned? The second is territorial: which states or other political units are covered by EU law and policy? These two aspects have been addressed in political science literature on 'Europeanization', which analyses the application of EU norms and policies to EU Member States and candidate countries.[8] The more comprehensive language of 'diffusion' of EU norms and policies has also been used, to include the extension of norms and policies to third states which are neither Member States, nor likely to become so.[9] One aspect largely left unexplored in that literature, however, is the centrality of legal forms—whether secondary EU legislation, international agreements, or other arrangements—to processes of Europeanization and diffusion.[10] In contrast, the discussion in this chapter will show how the 'reach' of EU border policy finds expression in legal and semi-formal policy instruments.

The chapter as a whole will rely upon two approaches to the explanation of post-2011 developments. First, drawing upon political science literature, it will treat the extent and form of EU integration as the result of an interplay of functional and intergovernmental elements. In relation to borders, the combination of those elements has seen the establishment by the EU and Schengen states of a unique, yet unbalanced, regime: open internal borders, decentralized control of the external border, and unusual weight placed upon cooperation with third states. Second, the

[6] Triandafyllidou and Dimitriadi, 'Migration Management at the Outposts of the European Union', 22 *Griffith Law Review* (2013) 698, at 601–604.

[7] Boswell, 'The "External Dimension" of EU Immigration and Asylum Policy', 79 *International Affairs* (2003) 619, at 619.

[8] For a review, see Sedelmeier, 'Europeanization', in E. Jones, A. Menon and S. Weatherill (eds), *The Oxford Handbook of the European Union* (2012).

[9] See Börzel and Risse, 'From Europeanisation to Diffusion: Introduction', 35 *West European Politics* (2012) 1.

[10] On the centrality of law to EU international action, see Marise Cremona, Chapter 2 in this volume.

chapter will argue for a legal dimension to the explanation of recent developments aimed at cooperation with third states. Specifically, through that cooperation, the EU and its Member States have sought to avoid the domestic, EU and international legal guarantees which arise when individuals travelling by irregular routes reach the territory of a Schengen state, or otherwise come under the control of a Schengen state outside its territory. The wider point is that patterns of 'reaching' or 'diffusion' differ by policy area, and are likely to be context-dependent. At least in the case of migration policy, substantive and territorial expansion are not automatic, and neither are they a straightforward elaboration of EU norms and policies.

2. The EU Border Regime

In this chapter, the emergence and development of the EU border regime is understood as the joint product of the functional and intergovernmental forces which shape EU integration. Neo-functionalist approaches emphasize forward momentum in the EU's activities as the primary dynamic leading towards greater integration, and ascribe an agenda-setting role to the Commission in promoting such integration.[11] Within neo-functional theory, the geographical expansion of the EU and of its policies occur because successful integration between some states attracts others by changing their incentives, and their perceptions of what is possible. The theory also offers an explanation for the expansion of the EU's policy reach, as 'spill-over' across areas of competence, and also within them, leads to new tasks and action on the part of the EU. In contrast, intergovernmentalist theories treat governments and states as the central actors of the EU integration process. Within the theory of liberal intergovernmentalism, states are expected to act rationally, given the pattern of domestic preferences.[12] Others take a more critical perspective, focusing on the political and legal advantages to governments and state administrations of the transfer of decision-making to EU bodies.[13] Intergovernmentalist approaches flow in the same direction as neo-functionalist ones when government and state interests align with projects for further integration. They differ, however, in implying that there will be limits to, and constraints upon, the extent and form of integration, when states and governments anticipate economic and political disadvantages to the course of action suggested by a functional logic. These constraints are likely to be especially evident when EU integration is concerned with core state functions, including currency, defence and foreign policy, internal security, and citizenship and migration.[14]

[11] For an overview, see Niemann and Schmitter, 'Neofunctionalism', in A. Wiener and T. Diez (eds), *European Integration Theory* (2nd edn, 2004).

[12] See A. Moravcsik, *The Choice for Europe: Social Purpose and State Power from Messina to Maastricht* (1998) and Moravcsik and Nicolaïdis, 'Explaining the Treaty of Amsterdam: Interests, Influence, Institutions', 37 *Journal of Common Market Studies* (1999) 59.

[13] In the migration policy context, see Guiraudon, 'European Integration and Migration Policy: Vertical Policy-making as Venue Shopping', 38 *Journal of Common Market Studies* (2000) 251.

[14] See Genschel and Jachtenfuchs. 'More Integration, Less Federation: The European Integration of Core State Powers', 23 *Journal of European Public Policy* (2016) 42.

Sections 2.A to 2.D will outline how the interplay of functional and intergovernmental elements shaped the EU border regime prior to the migration crisis. In the internal sphere, the dynamic was for the opening of internal borders, with the expansion of the geographical reach of the Schengen zone, and measures aimed at 'deepening' the obligations upon Schengen states. In the external sphere, the participation of third states in immigration control practices was systematically favoured by EU actors, for reasons linked to difficulties with the internal operation of the Schengen zone.

A. The Schengen Framework

The evolution of the Schengen zone can appear as a textbook case of neo-functionalism in action. The abolition of internal borders had both an economic logic—promoting cross-border economic activity—and a political goal—reinforcing the tangible benefits of the EU to its citizens.[15] The origins of the Schengen regime lie in an agreement reached in 1985 among five EU states—Belgium, France, Germany, Luxembourg and the Netherlands—to abolish border controls as between them, and the Schengen zone came into existence 10 years later on 26 March 1995.[16] From the initial starting-point in 1985, further developments offer an undoubted example of 'spillover'.[17] First, there has been a marked expansion of the Schengen zone's geographical reach, so that it now covers 22 EU Member States, plus the four EFTA states.[18] Second, the initial decision to open borders led to a 'deepening' of the EU law obligations upon participating states, linked to the control of the external borders.[19] EU Member States within the Schengen zone are bound by obligations concerning surveillance and checks at the external border, now contained within the 2016 Schengen Borders Code.[20] They are obliged to impose penalties upon the carriers of improperly documented passengers, to have criminal offences for those who assist in the smuggling of irregular entrants, and to take expulsion decisions in the case of irregularly staying persons.[21] All EU and Schengen states are covered by the 'Dublin' arrangements for the readmission of third country nationals who apply

[15] Monar, 'The Dynamics of Justice and Home Affairs: Laboratories, Driving Factors and Costs', 39 *Journal of Common Market Studies* (2001) 747.

[16] The 1985 Schengen Agreement was later published at OJ 2000 L 239/13.

[17] See A. Niemann, *Explaining Decisions in the European Union* (2006), chapter 4.

[18] From the outset, Ireland and the UK stayed outside the Schengen system, and were bound only by limited parts of the Schengen *acquis*. Four EU Member States—Bulgaria, Croatia, Cyprus and Romania—are bound by the Schengen *acquis*, but not (yet) members of the open-border zone.

[19] That process began under the Schengen Implementing Convention of 1990, later published in OJ 2000 L 239/19, and continued under EU law after the Treaty of Amsterdam of 1997.

[20] Regulation 2016/399 of 9 March 2016 on a Union Code on the rules governing the movement of persons across borders (Schengen Borders Code), OJ 2016 L 77/1.

[21] Schengen Implementing Convention 1990, OJ 2000 L 239/19, Art. 26 and Council Directive 2001/51 of 28 June 2001, OJ 2001 L 187/45; Framework Decision 2002/946/JHA on the facilitation of unauthorised entry, transit and residence, OJ 2002 L 328/1 and Council Directive 2002/90 of 28 November 2002 defining the facilitation of unauthorised entry, transit and residence, OJ 2002 L 328/17; and Directive 2008/115 of 16 December 2008 on common standards and procedures in member states for returning illegally staying third-country nationals, OJ 2008 L 348/98.

for asylum, but who have a previous connection to another state's territory, and the related 'Eurodac' provision for the fingerprinting of asylum applicants and illegal entrants.[22] Third, the creation of the Schengen zone led to the establishment of two EU agencies with a role in border control. For present purposes, the more significant of these is Frontex, which was set up in 2004 to assist Member States with external border control.[23] The other is the European Asylum Support Office (EASO), which was set up in 2010, and is relevant to external border control through its powers to support asylum and reception systems in 'member states subject to particular pressure'.[24]

At the same time, however, the detail of the Schengen framework has been shaped to a considerable extent by the logic of intergovernmentalism. The principle of open internal borders implies a high degree of inter-dependence between the Schengen states, as the effects of each state's policies, actions and inactions concerning external border control will potentially be felt elsewhere. Despite that, member states have shown themselves reluctant to allow internal or external border control to be governed to any significant degree by EU law or by EU institutions and agencies. The Schengen rules have always permitted member states to reinstate internal border controls for temporary periods (see section 4).[25] The 2004 Frontex Regulation stated that 'the responsibility for the control and surveillance of external borders lies with the Member States'.[26] Moreover, the premise of the Dublin arrangements remains that of Member State responsibility for applications (and applicants) for international protection. These powers left to Member States could be understood as a matter of organizational necessity for the EU, which under current arrangements could not realistically have the resources to replace Member State external border controls. But it is also a political necessity for Schengen states and their governments, which would presumably lack domestic support for any significant transfer of authority to the EU level, or to EU bodies, in relation to a function which remains fundamental to states.[27]

[22] Regulation 604/2013 of 26 June 2013 establishing the criteria and mechanisms for determining the member state responsible for examining an application for international protection lodged in one of the member states, OJ 2013 L 180/31; Regulation 603/2013 of 26 June 2013 establishing Eurodac for the comparison of fingerprints, OJ 2013 L 180/1.

[23] Council Regulation 2007/2004 of 26 October 2004 establishing a European Agency for the Management of Operational Cooperation at the External Borders of the member states of the European Union, OJ 2004 L 349/1. On its establishment, see Mitsilegas, 'Border Security in the European Union: Towards Centralized Controls and Maximum Surveillance', in A. Baldaccini, E. Guild and H. Toner (eds), *Whose Freedom, Security and Justice: EU Immigration and Asylum Law and Policy* (2007) and Neal, 'Securitization and Risk at the EU Border: The Origins of Frontex', 47 *Journal of Common Market Studies* (2009) 333.

[24] Regulation 439/2010 of 19 May 2010 establishing a European Asylum Support Office, OJ 2010 L 132/11, Art. 8.

[25] The original provision was in Art. 2(2) of the Schengen Implementing Convention 1990. See section 4 for a discussion of provisions in the 2006 and 2016 versions of the Schengen Borders Code.

[26] Regulation 2007/2004, note 23, Art. 1(2).

[27] Genschel and Jachtenfuchs, 'From Market Integration to Core State Powers: The Eurozone Crisis, the Refugee Crisis and Integration Theory', 56 *Journal of Common Market Studies* (2018) 178.

B. The External Dimension

The creation of the Schengen zone, with its common external border, was part of the background to a growing interest at the EU level in the external aspects of migration policy from the early 1990s. The first steps came in October 1991, when the Commission proposed the 'incorporation of migration into the Community's external policy'.[28] Thereafter, the goals of external action were typically distinguished into two parts: addressing the 'root causes' of migration in countries of origin, and achieving the cooperation of third countries in the control of irregular migration.[29] The success of a 'root causes' approach was always likely to be limited, however, as it is difficult for the EU to successfully prevent conflict or to achieve economic development elsewhere in the world, while greater stability and prosperity may actually *increase* levels of emigration.[30] Instead, the focus of EU policy has typically been upon persuading third states to assist in preventing irregular migration, or to assist in the readmission of persons in an irregular situation who are present in EU Member States. (The content of readmission agreements is explored further below.) In that regard, a key policy framework was the 'Global Approach to Migration', launched in 2005, which aimed to provide multi-faceted solutions to irregular migration to the EU, in partnership with states of origin and transit, especially in Eastern Europe, Africa and the Middle East.[31] The primary outcome under the 'global approach' has been 'mobility partnerships', which are political declarations that combine third state commitments concerning readmission and irregular migration with EU and Member State promises concerning visa facilitation and liberalization and circular migration.[32]

From the 1990s, the EU agenda on irregular migration was generally taken forward at a regional level. The most developed cooperation arrangements now cover the Western Balkans. Five states in that region have entered Stabilisation and Association Agreements (SAAs) with the EU: Macedonia in 2001, Albania in 2006, Montenegro in 2007, Serbia in 2008, and Bosnia and Herzegovina in 2015.[33] These SAAs each provide for cooperation in relation to visas, border control, asylum

[28] European Commission, 'Communication on Immigration', SEC (91) 1855, 23 October 1991, paras 48–49.

[29] Boswell, note 7. Examples of early policy statements with this duality include the 'Declaration on Principles governing External Aspects of Migration Policy', in *Presidency Conclusions: European Council, Edinburgh, December 12 1992* (document SN 456/1/92 REV 1), at 41–45, para. xvi, points 2–6; and European Commission, 'Communication on Immigration and Asylum Policies', COM(94) 23, 23 February 1994, paras 47–68 and 111–117.

[30] Castles, 'Why Migration Policies Fail', 27 *Ethnic and Racial Studies* (2004) 205, at 220–222.

[31] European Commission, 'Priority actions for responding to the challenges of migration: First follow-up to Hampton Court', COM(2005) 621, 30 November 2005 and Council doc. 15744/05, 13 December 2005.

[32] Reslow, 'Deciding on EU External Migration Policy: The Member States and the Mobility Partnerships', 34(3) *European Integration* (2012) 223.

[33] These SAAs are published as follows—Albania: OJ 2009 L 107/166; Bosnia and Herzegovina: OJ 2015 L 164/2; Macedonia: OJ 2004 L 84/13; Montenegro: OJ 2010 L 108/3; and Serbia: OJ 2013 L 278/16. Prior to joining the EU in 2013, Croatia was covered by an SAA, published at OJ 2005 L 26/3.

and migration, and in the 'prevention and control of illegal immigration'.[34] The latter provision includes an obligation for these states to readmit their own nationals, and to conclude a separate readmission agreement with the EU, or to implement one if it already exists. All five states signed readmission agreements with the EU between 2005 and 2007, and these entered into force together on 18 September 2007.[35] There is a slightly different SAA with Kosovo, which again makes provision for cooperation on immigration matters and on irregular migration, but provides only that 'the parties agree to explore possibilities to start negotiations' concerning readmission.[36]

The second region which has seen extensive engagement with the EU's external migration policy covers the post-Soviet states. Partnership and Cooperation Agreements (PCAs) were concluded with Moldova, Russia and Ukraine in 1994; Kazakhstan and Kyrgyzstan in 1995; Armenia, Azerbaijan, Georgia and Uzbekistan in 1996; and Tajikistan in 2004. In different forms, all of the PCAs provided for cooperation in the prevention of irregular migration, while those of 1996 and 2004 provided for the conclusion of agreements concerning the readmission of persons present without status in the other party's territory. Since 2003, engagement with post-Soviet states has occurred under the aegis of the European Neighbourhood Policy (ENP).[37] Russia entered a readmission agreement with the EU in 2006.[38] Between 2007 and 2011, Moldova and Georgia concluded mobility partnerships and agreements on readmission with the EU, while Ukraine also concluded a readmission agreement with the EU in 2007.[39] All three of Georgia, Moldova and Ukraine then agreed to association agreements with the EU in 2014, which provided for the full implementation of the readmission agreements, and for cooperation on migration, asylum and border management.[40] Separately, Armenia and Azerbaijan entered mobility partnerships, and then readmission agreements, with the EU between 2011 and 2014.[41] Armenia subsequently signed a 'comprehensive and enhanced partnership agreement' with the EU in 2017, which included provision for cooperation in the fields of migration, asylum and border management, and a reaffirmation of the agreement on readmission, and the Council of Ministers has

[34] Arts 80 and 81 of the Albania SAA; Arts 80 and 81 of the Bosnia and Herzegovina SAA; Arts 75 and 76 of the Macedonia SAA; Arts 82 and 83 of the Montenegro SAA; and Arts 82 and 83 of the Serbia SAA.

[35] For the texts, see Albania—OJ 2005 L 124/22; Bosnia and Herzegovina—OJ 2007 L 334/66; Macedonia—OJ 2007 L 334/7; Montenegro—OJ 2007 L 334/26; Serbia—OJ 2007 L 334/46.

[36] The Kosovo SAA is at OJ 2016 L 71/3. Its Arts 85–88 concern migration cooperation.

[37] European Commission, 'European Neighbourhood Policy: Strategy Paper', COM(2004) 373, 12 May 2004, at 3.

[38] The readmission agreement with Russia is at OJ 2007 L 129/40.

[39] The text of the mobility partnership with Moldova is in Council doc. 9460/08 ADD 1 (21 May 2008), and that with Georgia in Council doc. 16396/09 ADD 1 (20 November 2009). The readmission agreement with Moldova is at OJ 2007 L 334/149, that with Georgia at OJ 2011 L 52/47, and that with Ukraine at OJ 2007 L 332/48.

[40] These association agreements were published as follows—Georgia: OJ 2014 L 261/4; Moldova: OJ 2014 L 260/4; Ukraine: OJ 2014 L 161/3.

[41] The texts of these mobility partnerships are in Council docs 14963/2011 (11 October 2011) and 16399/2013 (26 November 2013), respectively. The readmission agreements are at OJ 2013 L 289/13 for Armenia and OJ 2014 L 128/17 for Azerbaijan.

given approval for negotiations for an equivalent agreement with Azerbaijan.[42] Kazakhstan signed an 'enhanced partnership and cooperation agreement' with the EU in 2015 which contains detailed provisions on 'co-operation on migration, asylum and border management', obligations to readmit the participants' own nationals, and provision for the negotiation of a specific readmission agreement.[43] Finally, Belarus entered a mobility partnership with the EU in October 2016, though without that leading to an agreement on readmission.[44]

The EU has historically been less successful in securing agreements concerning migration and readmission in other regions. Beyond the post-Soviet states, only four states and territories in Asia have entered readmission agreements with the EU: Hong Kong (2002), Macao (2003), Sri Lanka (2004) and Pakistan (2009).[45] In the pre-2011 period, the only case of successful engagement in Africa concerned Cape Verde, which concluded a mobility partnership with the EU in 2008 and a readmission agreement in 2013.[46] For other African states, the main EU achievement in the pre-2011 period was the launch in 2006 of the 'Rabat process', involving consultation between EU and West and North African governments in relation to irregular migration.[47]

The 16 EU readmission agreements referred to earlier in the discussion are substantively very similar. For non-EU states and territories, the core obligation is to take back *their own* ('third country') nationals who are residing without authorization in an EU Member State, if specified proof or *prima facie* evidence of nationality is provided.[48] The agreements also contain an obligation to readmit the nationals of *other states*—here termed 'fourth country' nationals—upon the provision of specified types of proof or *prima facie* evidence of prior presence in the requested state or territory. These fourth country obligations typically arise where either of two conditions is met: that the person has a current visa or residence permit from the non-EU state/territory, or the person 'illegally' and 'directly' entered the territory of the EU 'after having stayed on, or transited through, the territory' of the requested state/territory. A review of EU-level readmission agreements by the Commission, published in early 2011, found that they worked far better in relation to a third state or territory's own nationals than fourth country nationals.[49] Readmission agreements

[42] Arts 14 and 15 of the 'comprehensive and enhanced partnership agreement' with Armenia, text in Council doc. 12548/17 (24 October 2017), which was signed on 24 November 2017. In relation to Azerbaijan, see Council doc. 14418/16 (14/15 November 2016).

[43] Enhanced partnership and cooperation agreement with Kazakhstan, OJ 2016 L 29/3, at Art. 238. The agreement's provisional validity does not cover the commitment concerning the readmission of the parties' own nationals: see Council Decision 2016/123, Art. 3.

[44] The text of the Belarus mobility partnership agreement is in Council doc. 9393/1/15 (10 June 2015).

[45] These readmission agreements are published as follows—Hong Kong: OJ 2014 L 17/25; Macao: OJ 2004 L 143/99; Sri Lanka: OJ 2005 L 124/41; Pakistan: OJ 2010 L 287/52.

[46] The text of the mobility partnership agreement with Cape Verde is in Council doc. 9460/08 ADD 2 (21 May 2008), and the readmission agreement is published at OJ 2013 L 282/15.

[47] See Casas, Cobarrubias and Pickles, 'Stretching Borders beyond Sovereign Territories? Mapping EU and Spain's Border Externalization Policies', 2 *Geopolítica(s)* (2010) 71, at 83–84.

[48] In the cases of Hong Kong and Macao, this obligation refers to permanent residents.

[49] European Commission, 'Evaluation of EU Readmission Agreements', COM(2011) 76, 23 February 2011.

have, moreover, proven difficult for the EU to conclude without specific incentives for the other side, such as the prospect of accession to the EU, or association, or at least visa facilitation and liberalization. The Commission's assessment was that all third states had a 'deep aversion' to readmission agreements which contained clauses concerning fourth country nationals, and that it was not worthwhile to insist upon them, save in the case of major transit countries.[50] Section 5 will show that this perspective has shaped EU thinking in response to the migration crisis, both in relation to transit countries, and through the EU's pursuit of formal and informal readmission arrangements with a wider range of third countries of origin.

Within a neo-functionalist perspective, EU policy in relation to the external dimension area could be treated as a straightforward example of spillover from the establishment of the Schengen zone. Such an interpretation does not, however, account for the priority given to the EU's external policy concerning irregular migration.[51] Indeed, no other state or group of states is as engaged as the EU in developing an external dimension to immigration control which operates in a diffuse way in various regions of the world. Genschel and Jachtenfuchs offer a more persuasive—broadly intergovernmentalist—analysis, which treats 'externalization' as inherently unobjectionable to Member States, as it does not call their core sovereignty into question.[52] On their view, it is precisely because of the Member States' objections to EU regulation and intervention in the internal domain that the EU focuses on policies aimed at cooperation with third states. While their argument refers specifically to the migration crisis, it is no less applicable to the evolution of an external policy since the early 1990s. In essence, Member States favour EU external action as a way of bypassing the difficulty of making progress in the internal sphere, by reducing irregular migration pressures upon the EU as a whole.

That essentially intergovernmental explanation of EU external policy links to legal considerations. Cooperation with third countries is thought likely to lead to a reduction in the level of arrivals if it is focused on the prevention of arrivals, or if readmission arrangements act as a deterrent to departure. The implication in either case will be a reduction in the number of persons for whom *any* Member State has legal responsibility, whether to consider an application for international protection, or to process an expulsion.[53] That is something which has no obvious counterpart in the Member States' 'internal' dealings with one another, where the issue is the allocation of responsibility as between them for a given pool of migrants. For these legal reasons as well, externalization is a policy direction which all Member States are likely to support, notwithstanding their reluctance to cede sovereignty in the internal sphere.

[50] *Ibid.*, at 9. At that time, the Council took a different position, which was that it would continue 'as a general rule' to include fourth country clauses in the negotiating directives for readmission agreements: 'Council Conclusions defining the European Union strategy on readmission', Council doc. 11260/11 (8 June 2011), para. 9.

[51] On the success of the external dimension, relative to internal migration policy development, see Lavenex, 'Shifting Up and Out: The Foreign Policy of European Immigration Control', 29 *West European Politics* (2006) 329.

[52] Genschel and Jachtenfuchs, note 27, at 190–191.

[53] Ryan, 'Extraterritorial Immigration Control: What Role for Legal Guarantees?', in B. Ryan and V. Mitsilegas (eds), *Extraterritorial Immigration Control: Legal Challenges* (2010).

3. From the Migration Crisis to EU Border Reform

Arrivals in the EU after irregular sea journeys in the Central and Eastern Mediterranean have been a frequent occurrence at least since the 1990s, and the policy questions to which they give rise are not therefore new ones.[54] The period since 2011 has, however, been different in several significant respects: there has been a large increase in the number of migrants involved; the Schengen open border regime has been questioned; EU institutions have taken responsibility for a policy response; and, ultimately, cooperation with third states has had greater territorial and substantive reach. This section will show how migration developments in the Central Mediterranean and Eastern Mediterranean have acted as a catalyst for these changes.[55] The actual changes to policy are then considered in sections 4 and 5.

A. Central Mediterranean Routes

In the Central Mediterranean, the first substantial irregular arrivals of migrants by sea were from Albania, starting in 1991, and continuing through the 1990s.[56] A significant number of persons arriving from Tunisia were also seen from 1993 onwards. The Italian authorities succeeded in disrupting migration on each of these routes through bilateral cooperation with the authorities of those states in the 1990s.[57] From about 2002, Libya became the main departure point for substantial transit migration of persons of various nationalities to Italy—especially the island of Lampedusa—and, to a lesser degree, to Malta.[58] In this case, the Italian state responded through bilateral agreements with the Libyan Government in 2000, 2007 and 2009.[59] Under the last of those, the two states agreed for the first time to the repatriation of 'clandestine immigrants', and in May 2009 Italian vessels began to intercept migrant vessels on the high seas, and to return the persons concerned to Libyan ports.[60] The result was a fall of the order of 90 per cent in the number of

[54] On irregular migration in this region, see A. Triandafyllidou and T. Maroukis, *Migrant Smuggling: Irregular Migration from Asia and Africa to Europe* (2012), chapters 2 and 3. In relation to policy, see Lutterbeck, 'Policing Migration in the Mediterranean', 11 *Mediterranean Politics* (2006) 59.

[55] H. Crawley, F. Düvell, K. Jones, S. McMahon and N. Sigona, *Unravelling Europe's 'Migration Crisis': Journeys Over Land and Sea* (2017), at 25–27, emphasize the distinctiveness of the crisis in Italy and in Greece in 2015–2016. Irregular migration by sea in the Western Mediterranean towards Spain is not considered here, as the scale of these phenomena has not provoked a policy debate at the EU level in recent years. For earlier developments, see García Andrade, 'Extraterritorial Strategies to Tackle Irregular Immigration by Sea: A Spanish Perspective', in B. Ryan and V. Mitsilegas (eds), *Extraterritorial Immigration Control: Legal Challenges* (2010).

[56] In relation to the period to the mid-2000s, this paragraph draws on information in Monzini, 'Sea-Border Crossings: The Organization of Irregular Migration to Italy', 12 *Mediterranean Politics* (2007) 163.

[57] Cuttitta, 'I confini d'Europa a Sud del Mediterraneo: Strumenti e incentivi per l'Esternalizzazione dei Controlli', in P. Cuttitta and F. Vassallo Paleologo (eds), *Migrazioni, Frontiere, Diritti* (2006).

[58] Monzini, note 56, at 177–179.

[59] Di Pascale, 'Migration Control at Sea: The Italian Case', in B. Ryan and V. Mitsilegas (eds), *Extraterritorial Immigration Control: Legal Challenges* (2010), at 297–300.

[60] ECtHR, *Hirsi Jamaa v. Italy*, Appl. no. 27765/09, Judgment of 23 February 2012, paras 13, 14 and 19. All ECtHR decisions are available online at http://hudoc.echr.coe.int/. (All website references in this chapter were last visited on 31 May 2018.)

Table 6.1 Irregular arrivals to Italy, 1997–2017

Year	Total arrivals	Places of embarkation (where available)					
	TOTAL	Algeria	Egypt	Greece	Libya	Tunisia	Turkey
1997	22,343	—	—	—	—	—	—
1998	38,134	—	—	—	—	—	—
1999	49,999	—	—	—	—	—	—
2000	26,817	—	—	—	—	—	—
2001	20,143	—	—	—	—	—	—
2002	23,719	—	—	—	—	—	—
2003	14,331	—	—	—	—	—	—
2004	13,635	—	—	—	—	—	—
2005	22,939	—	—	—	—	—	—
2006	22,016	—	—	—	—	—	—
2007	20,455	—	—	—	—	—	—
2008	36,951	—	—	—	—	—	—
2009	9,573	—	—	—	—	—	—
2010	4,406	—	—	—	—	—	—
2011	62,692	163	1,620	2,928	28,431	28,123	1,427
2012	13,267	4	1,401	2,782	5,087	2,294	1,699
2013	42,925	24	9,215	1,892	27,314	908	2,077
2014	170,100	155	15,283	1,480	141,484	1,297	10,340
2015	153,842	—	11,114	—	138,422	—	—
2016	181,436	—	10,689	—	165,448	833	—
2017	119,369	—	—	—	108,409	5,200	—

Sources: For 1997–2014, UNHCR data available at http://www.ismu.org/wp-content/uploads/2015/02/Sbarchi-e-richieste-asilo-1997-2014.xls; for 2015–2017, UNHCR publications entitled 'Italy Sea Arrivals Dashboard', available at https://data2.unhcr.org/en/situations/mediterranean/location/5205.

persons arriving on the Italian coasts between 2008 and 2009.[61] (See Table 6.1 for a summary of available data on irregular arrivals by sea to Italy from 1997 to 2017).

The first significant effects of the Arab Spring upon irregular migration to the EU arose out of developments in Tunisia. After a popular rebellion there led to the removal of the Ben Ali regime in January–February 2011, the previous controls on irregular emigration by sea became ineffective. As a result, there was a sharp increase in irregular arrivals to Italy in February (5,603 persons detected) and March 2011 (14,390 persons detected).[62] In response, a revised bilateral agreement was reached with the new Tunisian Government on 5 April 2011.[63] That provided for a simplified procedure for the readmission of persons arriving after that date, for the resumption

[61] 'Immigrazione irregolare dalla Libia: Diminuiti del 90% gli sbarchi', Ministero dell'Interno, 9 September 2009. The figure was based on a comparison of 1 May–31 August 2008 with the same period in 2009.

[62] Nascimbene and di Pascale, 'The "Arab Spring" and the Extraordinary Influx of People who Arrived in Italy from North Africa', 13 *European Journal of Migration and Law* (2011) 341, at 343, quoting official data.

[63] *Ibid.*, at 352–353 and 'Immigrazione, siglato l'accordo tra Italia e Tunisia', Ministero dell'Interno, 6 April 2011.

of action against departures by the Tunisian authorities, and for Italy to supply boats and vehicles to those authorities. The agreement would lead to a sharp fall in irregular arrivals from Tunisia in the subsequent period.[64] For those who arrived before 5 April 2011, however, Italy's solution was to confer a temporary residence permit, which had the effect of enabling travel to other EU states. That resulted in a diplomatic row with France—which temporarily re-introduced border controls—and then to a process of reform of the Schengen zone rules (see section 4).[65]

After this solution for the Tunisian route, transit migration through Libya became the centre of the migration crisis in the Central Mediterranean. This migration has typically been of a 'mixed' character, in that it has included nationalities likely to have plausible claims to international protection (especially Eritrean, Sudanese and Syrian), but also many other nationalities where the primary motive of migration is likely to be economic (including nationals of states in West Africa and South Asia).[66] The disorder in Libya during and after the February–October 2011 civil war prevented the application of the 2009 agreement with Italy, and the effect was that the number of irregular arrivals in Italy increased sharply in 2011, to over 28,000 that year.[67] On 3 April 2012, the Italian Government and the new Government in Tripoli re-confirmed their joint strategy against irregular migration.[68] By then, however, the legal context had been transformed by the European Court of Human Rights (ECtHR) ruling in *Hirsi Jamaa* in February 2012, which concerned the first of the 2009 interception operations referred to above.[69] The ECtHR held, *inter alia*, that Italy had jurisdiction over migrants intercepted by its vessels on the high seas, that the return of *any* migrants to Libya was contrary to the prohibition on exposing persons to the risk of inhuman and degrading treatment, and that such returns amounted to collective expulsion.[70] In May 2012, the Italian Government announced that, in the light of the ruling, it would no longer seek to return migrants to Libya.[71] Instead, Italy's policy became one of allowing irregular arrivals, and the number of such arrivals was more than 27,000 in 2013. That year saw the first of the large-scale tragedies which would mark the EU's migration crisis, when a shipwreck off the island of Lampedusa on 3 October 2013 claimed the lives of an estimated 366

[64] The official figures quoted in Nascimbene and di Pascale, note 62, show 597 arrivals in May 2011, 164 in June 2011 and 258 in July 2011.

[65] *Ibid.*, at 352–355; S. Carrera, E. Guild, M. Merlino and J. Parkin, *A Race against Solidarity: The Schengen Regime and the Franco-Italian Affair* (CEPS briefing, April 2011).

[66] There does not appear to be a comprehensive public data source covering nationalities of arrivals since 2011 for the Central Mediterranean. The conclusion in the text is based on information for the most significant nationalities each year published in the Frontex *Annual Risk Analysis* series.

[67] Table 6.1 shows an increase from 4,406 arrivals in total in 2010 to 28,431 from Libya alone in 2011.

[68] Statewatch, 'Italy/Libya: Documents unveil post-Gaddafi cooperation agreement on immigration', 5 September 2012, available at http://www.statewatch.org/news/2012/sep/01italy-libya-immigration-cooperation.html.

[69] *Hirsi Jamaa v. Italy*, note 60.

[70] Den Heijer, 'Reflections on Refoulement and Collective Expulsion in the Hirsi Case', 25 *International Journal of Refugee Law* (2013) 265.

[71] Remarks of Interior Minister, Anna Maria Cancellieri to a committee of the Italian Senate (Commissione Straordinaria per la Tutela e la Promozione dei Diritti Umani), 16 May 2012, available at http://www.senato.it/service/PDF/PDFServer/DF/283163.pdf, at 7.

persons.[72] The Italian Government responded by launching the *Mare Nostrum* operation on 18 October 2013, under which migrants at risk in international waters off Libya were rescued by naval assets, and taken to Italy. That operation contributed to a further increase in the number of migrants reaching Italy by sea, with the total rising to 170,100 in 2014, of whom more than 140,000 had departed from Libya.

The events of 2013–2014 would prove a turning-point in the EU's assumption of policy responsibility for control of irregular migration by sea in the Central Mediterranean. The scale of the October 2013 tragedy led to unprecedented media and civil society attention being paid across Europe to migrant deaths in the Mediterranean.[73] It was followed by a European Council declaration that 'determined action should be taken in order to prevent the loss of lives at sea and to avoid that such human tragedies happen again'.[74] The Council of Ministers then established the 'Task Force Mediterranean' to identify measures to be taken at the EU level, which reported in December 2013.[75] After an Italian Government request for EU support, the Council of Ministers agreed to the replacement of the *Mare Nostrum* operation by Frontex's Operation Triton, with effect from 1 November 2014.[76] Operation Triton was, however, limited in two respects: it was essentially a border surveillance mission, rather than a humanitarian one, and its reach extended only 30 nautical miles from the Italian coast.[77] Those limits to Operation Triton were then implicated in two major tragedies off Lampedusa on 13 and 19 April 2015, which led to an estimated 400 and 800 deaths, respectively.[78]

After the 2015 tragedies, the EU took a yet more central role in relation to the border regime in the Central Mediterranean. On 20 April 2015, the EU's High Representative for Foreign Affairs and its Commissioner for Home Affairs presented a plan of 'immediate actions' to be taken.[79] At a special meeting on 23 April, the European Council declared that 'the European Union will mobilise all efforts at its disposal to prevent further loss of life at sea'.[80] These steps would be followed by the Commission's 'European Agenda on Migration', published in May 2015, the premise of which was that the 'need to restore confidence in our ability to bring together European and national efforts to address migration, to meet our international and ethical obligations and to work together in an effective way, in accordance with the

[72] Figure in Amnesty International, *Lives Adrift: Refugees and Migrants in Peril in the Central Mediterranean* (September 2014), at 15.

[73] This was exemplified by an intervention by Pope Francis, who described the deaths as 'shameful': 'Lo sfogo di Francesco: "Una vergogna" ', *La Stampa*, 4 October 2013.

[74] 'European Council 24/25 October 2013: Conclusions', EUCO 169/13, 25 October 2013, para. 46.

[75] European Commission, 'Communication on the Work of the Task Force Mediterranean', COM(2013) 869, 4 December 2013.

[76] 'Council conclusions on "Taking action to better manage migratory flows" ', 10 October 2014.

[77] Carrera and den Hertog, 'Whose Mare? Rule of Law Challenges in the Field of European Border Surveillance in the Mediterranean', CEPS, January 2015, at 7–10.

[78] Heller and Pezzani, *Death by Rescue: The Lethal Effects of the EU's Policies of Non-Assistance* (2016), available at https://deathbyrescue.org/

[79] 'Joint Foreign and Home Affairs Council: Ten point action plan on migration', European Commission press release IP/15/4813, 20 April 2015.

[80] 'Special meeting of the European Council: Statement', EUCO 18/15, 23 April 2015.

principles of solidarity and shared responsibility'.[81] It also set out an ambitious list of initiatives, which would provide the blueprint for many of the developments that have followed concerning the external border. The 'European Agenda' was supplemented by later announcements, made at the height of the migration crisis in the Eastern Mediterranean, aimed at strengthening cooperation with third states in Africa.[82] Sections 4 and 5 will show how these declarations transformed the external dimension to the EU external border policy.

B. The Eastern Mediterranean Route

In the second half of 2015 and early 2016, the crisis in the Central Mediterranean would be overshadowed by dramatic increases in irregular migration by sea in the Eastern Mediterranean. These developments were largely a product of the Syrian civil war, which had its origins in popular protests against the Assad regime during 2011. The scale of this migration can be seen from Table 6.2, which summarizes Frontex data concerning irregular arrivals by land and sea to Eastern Mediterranean EU Member States (Greece, Bulgaria and Cyprus) from 2011 onwards. It shows that there was a rapid increase in 2015 in the number of Syrian nationals arriving irregularly by sea, from 31,000 in 2014 to almost half a million that year. It also shows a sharp increase in the number of persons of other nationalities—principally, from Afghanistan and Iraq—from 19,000 arrivals in 2014 to 389,000 in 2015.[83] These irregular sea journeys led to increased fatalities: the International Organization for Migration (IOM) estimated that there were 806 deaths of migrants at sea in the Eastern Mediterranean in 2015, compared to 59 the year before.[84]

Table 6.2 Irregular arrivals in the Eastern Mediterranean, 2011–2017

Year	Land			Sea			All arrivals			
	Syrian	Other	Total	Syrian	Other	Total	Syrian	Other	Total	Sea %
2011	1216	54342	**55558**	76	1391	**1467**	1292	55733	**57025**	3
2012	6216	26638	**32854**	906	3464	**4370**	7122	30102	**37224**	12
2013	7366	5602	**12968**	5361	6470	**11831**	12727	12072	**24799**	48
2014	4648	2129	**6777**	27025	17032	**44057**	31673	19161	**50834**	87
2015	7329	4878	**12207**	489011	384168	**873179**	496340	389046	**885386**	99
2016	3015	4657	**7672**	81570	93035	**174605**	84585	97692	**182277**	96
2017	2438	5135	**7573**	13957	20775	**34732**	16395	25910	**42305**	82

Source: Frontex, *Annual Risk Analysis*, various years. These data cover arrivals in Bulgaria, Cyprus and Greece.

[81] European Commission, 'A European Agenda on Migration', COM(2015) 240, 13 May 2015.

[82] European Commission and High Representative, 'Addressing the Refugee Crisis in Europe: The Role of EU External Action', JOIN(2015) 40, 9 September 2015.

[83] Frontex data show 214,000 Afghan nationals and 93,000 Iraqi nationals arrived in Greece in 2015, accounting for 79% of the 389,046 who were not Syrian: Frontex, *Risk Analysis for 2017*, Table 1.

[84] Information available at https://missingmigrants.iom.int/region/mediterranean. It records 59 deaths in 2014, as compared with 806 in 2015 and 434 in 2016.

In the summer of 2015 and in early 2016, the aim of most of those arriving in the Greek islands appears to have been to proceed onwards towards Northern Europe via Macedonia, Serbia and Hungary.[85] Initially, sympathy for Syrian refugees led to tolerance of irregular movements by governments and public opinion in many Member States. On 25 August 2015, the German Interior Ministry announced that it would no longer seek to use the Dublin Regulation to return Syrian nationals to other Member States.[86] The German prime minister, Angela Merkel then declared on 31 August 2015 that Germany would cope with any arrivals ('wir schaffen das').[87] This benign moment came to an end after the discovery on 2 September 2015 of the drowned body of Alan Kurdi, a three-year-old Syrian child, on a beach in Bodrum, Turkey.[88] Thereafter, growing political opposition to the large numbers of persons arriving on the Greek islands, and/or travelling via the Western Balkans, led to a more restrictive policy approach.[89]

At the EU level, prior to the events of August and September 2015, there had already been agreement to include Greece in a burden-sharing mechanism adopted under the 'European Agenda'. In late May 2015, the Commission proposed a relocation scheme for 40,000 applicants for international protection in both Italy and Greece, and that proposal was agreed in principle by the Council of Ministers on 20 July 2015.[90] In a related development, on 15 July, the Commission began securing Member State support for 'hotspots' in those two states, where international protection applicants would be processed.[91] As the sense of crisis grew, the Commission responded with a series of initiatives on 9 September.[92] These included a second proposal for relocation, covering a further 120,000 persons.[93] That would be adopted for the benefit of Greece and Italy on 22 September, despite the opposition of the Czech Republic, Hungary, Romania and the Slovak Republic.[94]

The first stage of the more restrictive approach taken from September 2015 was a series of new border controls, starting with restrictions placed by Germany and Austria at internal Schengen borders.[95] Internal border controls would be imposed by other EU Member States in the following months, including Denmark, Norway,

[85] See P. Kingsley, *The New Odyssey: The Story of Europe's Refugee Crisis* (2016), at 259–266.

[86] 'Germany suspends "Dublin rules" for Syrians', 25 August 2015, available at https://www.dw.com/en/germany-suspends-dublin-rules-for-syrians/a-18671698.

[87] 'How much longer can Germany keep its doors open to refugees?', *Guardian*, 16 September 2015.

[88] Crawley *et al.*, note 55, at 116, note that Alan Kurdi's death came to be used as a justification for measures limiting irregular movement by sea.

[89] In relation to public opinion, see Harteveld *et al.*, 'Blaming Brussels? The Impact of (News about) the Refugee Crisis on Attitudes toward the EU and National Politics', 56 *Journal of Common Market Studies* (2018) 157.

[90] COM(2015) 286, 27 May 2015; and 'Outcome of the Council meeting on Justice and Home Affairs Brussels, 20 July 2015' (Council doc. 11097/15). This measure would be formally adopted as Council Decision 2015/1523 of 14 September 2015, published at OJ 2015 L 239/146.

[91] European Commission, 'Explanatory note on the "Hotspot" approach', 15 July 2015, available at http://www.statewatch.org/news/2015/jul/eu-com-hotsposts.pdf.

[92] 'Refugee Crisis: European Commission takes decisive action', European Commission press release IP/15/5596, 9 September 2015.

[93] The Commission proposal had initially covered applicants in Hungary too: see COM(2015) 451, 9 September 2015. Hungary did not accept this assistance, however.

[94] Council Decision 2015/1601, OJ 2015 L 248/80.

[95] 'The Day Borders Came Back to Europe', *EUObserver*, 14 September 2015.

Slovenia and Sweden.[96] When this situation persisted into 2016, the European Council identified a need to 'safeguard the integrity of the Schengen area', and the Commission declared that one of the major achievements of European integration had been 'shaken to its core'.[97] Section 4 will show that this perspective would lead to significant changes to the EU's internal border regime, including new powers and practices of intervention in respect of border states. The EU also encouraged action by third states in the Western Balkans. On 25 October 2015, the Commission held a meeting in Brussels of representatives of leaders of eight Member States—Austria, Bulgaria, Croatia, Germany, Greece, Hungary, Romania and Slovenia—with Albania, Macedonia and Serbia, to discuss responses to the migration crisis, including the discouragement of secondary movements.[98] That meeting would be followed by the gradual closure by Croatia, Macedonia, Serbia and Slovenia of their borders to irregular migrants between November 2015 and March 2016, a process which would culminate in a humanitarian crisis at Idomeni, on the Greece-Macedonia border.[99] That restrictive turn at the EU level would also lead to an unprecedented degree of cooperation concerning the control of irregular migration with Turkey (see section 5).

4. The Internal Dimension: Effects upon the Schengen Zone

This section will consider the changes to the role of Frontex, and to the rules relating to the governance of the Schengen zone in the period of the migration crisis. Changes in each of these areas were initially adopted after the Arab Spring, and would be revisited in the more intense period of the migration crisis in 2015 and 2016. These various reforms since 2011 have extended the substantive reach of the Schengen border regime, by strengthening powers and sanctions against Member States. Nevertheless, the primacy of Member States over border control has been preserved.

A. Strengthening Frontex

When Frontex was set up in 2004, its role was limited to the 'coordination' of Member State action relating to the external border.[100] Under the 2004 Regulation, where Member States faced particular pressures at external borders, they could request Frontex to initiate a joint operation, which would involve the making available of personnel and assets from other Member States.[101] Other Frontex tasks included the development of 'risk analyses' concerning the external border, and supporting

[96] European Commission, 'Back to Schengen—A Roadmap', COM(2016) 120, 4 March 2016, at 9–10.

[97] 'European Council meeting (18 and 19 February 2016)—Conclusions', EUCO 1/16, para. 5; European Commission, 'Back to Schengen', note 96, at 2.

[98] 'Meeting on the Western Balkans Migration Route: Leaders Agree on 17-Point Plan of Action', European Commission press release IP/15/5904, 15 October 2015.

[99] 'Migrants Stranded as Balkans Close Borders', *The Times*, 20 November 2015; 'Europe's New Jungle Grows on Greek Border', *The Times*, 11 March 2016.

[100] Regulation 2007/2004, note 23, Art. 1.

[101] *Ibid.*, Art. 3.

Member States who organized joint return flights for persons without permission to remain.[102]

In February 2010, the Commission had proposed an amending Regulation aimed at strengthening the powers of Frontex, but progress on that proposal had been limited.[103] The events of the Arab Spring led the European Council to call, in March 2011, for 'rapid agreement' on the amending Regulation, and the final text was approved in October that year.[104] These amendments included several incremental changes to Frontex's role, which began to shift the balance away from the sole responsibility of the Member States for the external border. Frontex risk analysis was now expressly stated to concern Member States' 'capacity to face upcoming challenges'.[105] It also acquired its own powers to coordinate and organize joint returns, where requested to do so by Member States.[106]

More profound changes to Frontex's role followed the intensification of the migration crisis in 2015–2016. In the aftermath of the April 2015 tragedies, the Commission proposed that Frontex should have a greater role concerning returns.[107] It also called more generally for 'reflections' on the implications of 'shared responsibility' concerning the external border.[108] The events of the summer of 2015, linked to irregular migration in the Eastern Mediterranean, prompted a more ambitious proposal, announced by the Commission on 9 September, to 'develop [Frontex] into a fully operational European border and coast guard system'.[109] After that idea received the support of the European Council, the Commission published a legislative proposal in December 2015, which would lead to the adoption of the European Border and Coast Guard Regulation in September 2016.[110]

Under the 2016 Regulation, the relative position of the Member States and Frontex has been re-drawn. The Agency's official title is now the 'European Border and Coast Guard Agency', which goes beyond the previous references to the (mere) coordination of Member State action.[111] Frontex and the national authorities now jointly make up the 'European Border and Coast Guard', with responsibility for the external border 'shared' by them.[112] Similarly, reference is now made to the 'European integrated border management', which carries with it the implication of a common EU policy.[113] Significant changes have also been made to Frontex's powers. First, the previous idea of risk analysis has been replaced by a 'vulnerability assessment',

[102] *Ibid.*, Arts 4 and 9.

[103] COM(2010) 61, 24 February 2010.

[104] 'Extraordinary European Council, 11 March 2011: Declaration', EUCO 7/11, 11 March 2011, para. 10 and Regulation 1168/2011 of 25 October 2011, OJ 2011 L 304/1.

[105] Regulation 2007/2004, note 23, as amended by Regulation 1168/2011, Art. 4.

[106] *Ibid.*, as amended by Regulation 1168/2011 of 25 October 2011, Art. 9(1).

[107] European Commission, 'A European Agenda on Migration', COM(2015) 240, 13 May 2015, at 10.

[108] *Ibid.*, at 17.

[109] Announced in the 'State of the Union' speech to the European Parliament by the President of the European Commission, Jean-Claude Juncker, 9 September 2015, available at http://europa.eu/rapid/press-release_SPEECH-15-5614_en.htm.

[110] 'European Council meeting (15 October 2015)—Conclusions', EUCO 26/15, 16 October 2015, para. 2(h); COM(2015) 671, 15 December 2015; and Regulation 2016/1624 of 14 September 2016 on the European Border and Coast Guard, OJ 2016 L 251/1.

[111] Regulation 2016/1624, note 110, recital 11 and Art. 6.

[112] *Ibid.*, Arts 3 and 5.

[113] *Ibid.*, Art. 4.

focused on 'the capacity and readiness of Member States to face upcoming challenges, including present and future threats and challenges at the external borders', and covering Member States' 'capacity to deal with the potential arrival of large numbers of persons on their territory'.[114] These assessments are backed up by recommendations by the Frontex executive director to a Member State, which may be made binding by the Frontex management board.[115] Second, where external border control is 'ineffective to such an extent that it risks jeopardising the functioning of the Schengen area', the Council—acting on a Commission proposal—may require Frontex to prepare an operational plan, while the Member State concerned is under an obligation to cooperate in its implementation. Third, whereas Frontex's previous mandate over returns had only concerned joint operations by several Member States, it has now acquired a central role in relation to *all* aspects of return by Member States within what is termed an 'integrated system of return management'.[116] While preserving the primacy of Member States over border control, the logic of these various developments is a shift in relation to the substantive reach of EU law: the EU institutions have new powers of intervention where Member States are unwilling or unable to maintain fully effective external border controls.

In parallel, the 2011 and 2016 Regulations strengthened the provisions concerning Frontex's engagement with third states. The 2004 Frontex Regulation had provided for Frontex to facilitate Member State operational cooperation with third countries, including by entering its own 'working arrangements' with their authorities.[117] The 2011 amendments added that Frontex could cooperate with third countries' authorities to identify 'best practices' concerning the returns of persons without status, and provided for Frontex liaison officers to be deployed to third countries, with a view to preventing irregular migration and achieving returns.[118] One significant new possibility allowed by the 2016 Regulation is Frontex coordination of operational cooperation between Member States and neighbouring third states, including through the deployment of Frontex teams to the third state's territory.[119] Second, in order to implement the enhanced return possibility referred to earlier, specific provision is made for Frontex to cooperate with third countries.[120] These developments are to be seen as an enhancement of the territorial reach of Frontex, by enabling far closer cooperation with third states.

B. Schengen Governance

As discussed in section 3, the Arab Spring led to a dispute between Italy and France over the former's granting of temporary residence permits to Tunisian nationals. In response, in order to defend the Schengen zone against unilateral border restrictions by Member States, the Commission and European Council included Schengen

114 *Ibid.*, Art. 13. 115 *Ibid.*

116 *Ibid.*, Arts 27 and 28.

117 Regulation 2007/2004, note 23, Art. 14, and now Regulation 2016/1624, note 110, Art. 54.

118 Regulation 2007/2004, note 23, as amended by Regulation 1168/2011 of 25 October 2011, Art. 9(2) and Art. 14. (The latter provision is now in Regulation 2016/1624, note 110, Art. 55.)

119 Regulation 2016/1624, note 110, Art. 54. 120 *Ibid.*

reforms among the migration policy items to be addressed after the Arab Spring. In September 2011, the Commission therefore set out what it termed the 'Schengen governance package'.[121]

'Schengen governance' firstly concerns the evaluation of Member State border control practices. The pre-2011 approach was evaluation solely on an intergovernmental basis, under a Schengen decision taken in 1998.[122] The Commission had long considered that EU institutions should have the lead role in those evaluations, and had made proposals to that effect in March 2009 and November 2010.[123] After the Arab Spring, the Commission included an amended proposal in similar terms within its Schengen governance package. The legislation eventually adopted in 2013 provides for a system of evaluations led by the Commission, involving Member State experts and observers from Frontex and Europol.[124] These evaluations may propose remedial action by a Member State, which the Council has the power to recommend, on a proposal from the Commission.

The second element of Schengen governance is provision for re-introduction of internal border controls by Member States. The pre-2011 position was that, in the event of a 'serious threat to public policy or internal security', Member States could unilaterally re-introduce controls, for renewable periods of 30 days, or for the foreseeable duration of a threat.[125] Under amendments adopted in 2013, this unilateral power of Member States was limited to a maximum of six months, with a separate possibility to introduce border controls for up to two months in urgent cases.[126] At the same time, a new possibility of authorization of internal border controls at the EU level was introduced, whereby the Council, acting on a Commission proposal, may recommend that one or more Member States re-introduce internal border controls for up to six months at a time, for a maximum of two years.[127] The preconditions to recourse to this new power are a finding in a Schengen evaluation report that a Member State is 'seriously neglecting its obligations', and the institutions' conclusion that 'the overall functioning of the area without internal border control is put at risk' by 'persistent serious deficiencies relating to external border control'.

[121] The calls for legislation are in European Commission, 'Communication on Migration', COM(2011) 248, 4 May 2011, at 8; and European Council, 'Conclusions—23/24 June 2011', EUCO 23/11, 24 June 2011, para. 21. The proposals are in 'Schengen Governance: Strengthening the Area without Internal Border Controls', COM(2011) 561; and the amended proposal for a Schengen evaluation and monitoring mechanism, COM(2011) 559, both published on 16 September 2011.

[122] Decision of the Schengen Executive Committee of 16 September 1998, OJ 2000 L 239/138.

[123] For the earlier proposals, see COM(2009) 102 and COM(2009) 105, both 4 March 2009, and COM(2010) 624, 16 November 2010.

[124] Council Regulation 1053/2013 of 7 October 2013 establishing an evaluation and monitoring mechanism to verify the application of the Schengen *acquis*, OJ 2013 L 295/27.

[125] Regulation 562/2006 of 15 March 2006 establishing a Community Code on the rules governing the movement of persons across borders (Schengen Borders Code), OJ 2006 L 105/1, Art. 23.

[126] See now Arts 25 and 28 of the Schengen Borders Code of 2016. These changes were introduced to Arts 23 and 25 of the Schengen Borders Code of 2006 by Regulation 1051/2013 of 22 October 2013, OJ 2013 L 295/1. Modifications in 2013 to the procedure for notifying the Commission and other Member States are not discussed here: see now Arts 27 and 28 of the Schengen Borders Code of 2016.

[127] See now Arts 29 and 30 of the Schengen Borders Code of 2016. These provisions were introduced as Art. 26 and 26a of the Schengen Borders Code of 2006 by Regulation 1051/2013 of 22 October 2013, OJ 2013 L 295/1.

The 2015–2016 phase of the migration crisis would lead to further consideration of the rules relating to the re-introduction of border controls. First, the 2016 Regulation on the European Border and Coast Guard Agency provides that, where a Member State fails to comply with a Council decision concerning a Frontex operational plan (see above), the EU institutions may authorize the re-introduction of internal border controls.[128] Second, in September 2017, the Commission proposed an option for a Member State to unilaterally re-introduce controls in 'foreseeable' cases, for up to one year, with an additional possibility to retain internal border controls for a further two years in 'exceptional' circumstances.[129] If adopted, these Member State powers would provide a further basis for them to respond, without an EU level authorization, to problems of external border control elsewhere in the Schengen zone.

These actual and potential Schengen governance reforms show an incremental enhancement of the substantive 'reach' of the EU border regime. There are new options for the supervision and sanctioning of Schengen states facing pressures at their external borders by Frontex, by the Commission and Council, and (paradoxically) through the introduction of border restrictions by other Member States. In recent years, that process has, moreover, been evident in relation to Greece. Evaluation reports in 2015 and 2016 identified many deficiencies in the details of its external border management, on the basis of which the Council made a series of recommendations to its Government.[130] Continuing difficulties in Greece then led to a series of Council decisions permitting five Schengen states (Austria, Denmark, Germany, Norway and Sweden) to re-introduce controls at defined internal borders.[131]

5. The External Dimension: New Cooperation with Third States

A key feature of the EU response to the migration crisis since 2011 has been the EU institutions' repeated emphasis upon cooperation with third states as the preferred solution, either to prevent irregular migration to the EU, or to ensure the return of persons to those states. In the aftermath of the Arab Spring, in November 2011, the Commission relaunched what it now termed the 'Global Approach to Migration and Mobility'.[132] The new version of the strategy introduced the idea of a 'Common Agenda on Migration and Mobility', which prioritized dialogue with third states, and did not imply specific commitments as mobility partnerships had. After the Lampedusa tragedy of October 2013, the European Council emphasized the importance of 'enhancing cooperation with countries of origin and transit', and the

[128] Regulation 2016/1624, note 110, Art. 19(10).

[129] Proposal for a Regulation amending Regulation 2016/399 as regards the rules applicable to the temporary reintroduction of border control at internal borders, COM(2017) 571, 27 September 2017.

[130] See Council docs 5985/16, 12 February 2016, and 6353/17, 17 February 2017.

[131] The original measure was Council Implementing Decision 2016/894, OJ 2016 L 151/8. That was renewed by Council Implementing Decisions 2016/1989, 2017/246 and 2017/818. The motivations of individual Member States may of course be linked to arrivals from other places, Italy in particular.

[132] COM(2011) 743, 18 November 2011.

Task Force Mediterranean Report of December 2013 set out the objective of strengthening third states' capacities 'to manage mixed migration flows'.[133] The tragedies of April 2015 led the European Council to propose extensive cooperation with third states in Africa and Asia with the aim of preventing illegal migration flows, while the Commission's 'European Agenda on Migration' called for 'partnership with third countries to tackle migration upstream'.[134] As the migration crisis deepened in the Eastern Mediterranean, on 9 September 2015, the Commission and the High Representative for Foreign Affairs published a paper entitled 'Addressing the Refugee Crisis in Europe: The Role of EU External Action', which set out the detailed steps that the EU was taking with third states.[135] That was followed in June 2016 by a policy statement by the Commission outlining a new 'Partnership Framework' on migration with third countries.[136] Starting from the premise that 'External migratory pressure is the "new normal"', it proposed 'comprehensive cooperation' with individual third countries on migration, to be reflected in formal 'compacts' with them.[137]

Sections 5.A and 5.B will show how, in the period of the migration crisis, this strategy has had many concrete effects, by broadening the range of third counties with which the EU is engaged, while altering the forms of cooperation with them. Developments linked to migration in the Central Mediterranean have led to cooperation with African states and Bangladesh, while developments linked to migration in the Eastern Mediterranean have led to new forms of cooperation with Turkey and Afghanistan. It is in this area that transformations in the EU border regime as a result of the migration crisis have been most apparent.

A. Cooperation with African States

In 2011, in the immediate aftermath of the Arab Spring, the EU priority in relation to the Central Mediterranean was to establish formal dialogues over migration, mobility and security with selected North African countries.[138] In December 2013, the Task Force Mediterranean report added the strategic goal of dialogues with other states in Africa, aimed at combating migrant smuggling.[139] This orientation towards cooperation with African states would become even more apparent in the more intense phase of the migration crisis from April 2015. The European Council's

[133] 'European Council 24/25 October 2013: Conclusions', EUCO 169/13, para. 47; and 'Communication on the Work of the Task Force Mediterranean', COM(2013) 869, at 5.

[134] 'Special meeting of the European Council: Statement', EUCO 18/15, 23 April 2015, at 3–4; and 'A European Agenda on Migration', COM(2015) 240, 13 May 2015, at 5.

[135] JOIN(2015) 40.

[136] European Commission, 'Communication on establishing a new Partnership Framework with third countries under the European Agenda on Migration', COM(2016) 385, 7 June 2016.

[137] *Ibid.*, at 5. For a review, see E. Collett and A. Ahad, *EU Migration Partnerships: A Work in Progress* (2017).

[138] 'A partnership for democracy and shared prosperity with the Southern Mediterranean', COM(2011) 200, 8 March 2011, at 6–7; and European Commission, 'A dialogue for migration, mobility and security with the southern Mediterranean countries', COM(2011) 292, 24 May 2011.

[139] Communication on the Work of the Task Force Mediterranean, COM(2013) 869, at 7.

statement of 23 April 2015 included dialogue and cooperation with the African Union and key African countries concerning irregular migration and migrant smuggling among the EU's priorities.[140] That aim would be taken forward through the Valletta summit of November 2015, which was attended by representatives of 31 EU and Schengen states, and 35 African states.[141] The summit participants declared that they were 'deeply concerned by the sharp increase in flows of refugees, asylum seekers and irregular migrants', and that they were 'determined to strengthen the fight against irregular migration'.[142]

Since 2015, the EU Trust Fund for Africa has provided a key mechanism for engagement with African states. It was launched by the Commission as part of its package of 9 September 2015, and was formally established in October 2015, before being endorsed by the Valletta Summit in November 2015.[143] Its overall aim has been the reduction of irregular migration flows from Africa through improved opportunities and better migration management.[144] Its work has been arranged into three regions: North Africa; the Horn of Africa; and Sahel/Lake Chad, covering a total of 26 states.[145] By December 2017, a total of 120 programmes had been approved, with a total commitment of nearly €2bn.[146] The Fund has been used to improve local employment opportunities and the provision of social services in regions of origin, and to fund initiatives aimed at migration control and assistance to migrants.[147]

Looking to individual countries, dialogue with North African states has had more limited success. Mobility partnerships were concluded, under the Global Approach to Migration and Mobility, with Morocco in June 2013, and with Tunisia in March 2014.[148] Negotiations on readmission agreements with these states have proven

[140] 'Special meeting of the European Council: Statement', EUCO 18/15, 23 April 2015, para. 3, point (g).

[141] Information taken from 'Valletta Summit: list of participants', available at http://www.consilium.europa.eu/media/23727/v-summit-2015-trombinoscope.pdf.

[142] 'Valletta Summit, 11–12 November 2015: Political Declaration', available at http://www.consilium.europa.eu/media/21841/political_decl_en.pdf.

[143] 'Refugee Crisis: European Commission takes decisive action', 9 September 2015; Commission decision C (2015) 7293, 20 October 2015; and 'Valletta Summit, 11–12 November 2015 Action Plan', available at http://www.consilium.europa.eu/media/21839/action_plan_en.pdf.

[144] European Commission, 'The European Union Emergency Trust Fund for Stability and Addressing Root Causes of Irregular Migration and Displaced Persons in Africa: Strategic Orientation Document', 15 February 2016, available at https://ec.europa.eu/europeaid/eu-emergency-trust-fund-strategic-orientation-document_en.

[145] Information available at https://ec.europa.eu/trustfundforafrica/region_en. For these purposes, the North Africa region covers Algeria, Egypt, Libya, Morocco and Tunisia; the Horn of Africa region covers Djibouti, Eritrea, Ethiopia, Kenya, Somalia, South Sudan, Sudan, Tanzania and Uganda; and the Sahel/Lake Chad region covers Burkina Faso, Cameroon, Chad, Gambia, Ghana, Guinea, Ivory Coast, Mali, Mauritania, Niger, Nigeria, Senegal.

[146] Information in 'Commission contribution to the EU Leaders' thematic debate on a way forward on the external and the internal dimension of migration policy', COM(2017) 820, 13 December 2017, Appendix 2.

[147] See European Commission, 'Progress Report on the Implementation of the European Agenda on Migration', COM(2018) 520, 14 March 2018, at 11–15.

[148] The text of the mobility partnership with Morocco is in Council doc. 6139/13 ADD 1, 3 June 2013. The text of the mobility partnership with Tunisia is in Council doc. 16371/13, 25 November 2013.

unsuccessful, however.[149] In the case of Egypt, EU attempts to commence a dialogue over migration were declined in 2012, and thereafter were compromised by political instability.[150] Similarly, the Algerian Government indicated its lack of interest in a dialogue over migration in 2014.[151]

In contrast, the EU institutions have developed many new forms of engagement over migration with the Libyan authorities, notwithstanding the difficult political and security conditions there. The first significant step was the establishment in 2013, with the Libyan Government's agreement, of the 'EUBAM Libya' mission under the EU's Common Security and Defence Policy, to support the Libyan authorities' control of land, sea and air borders.[152] A second initiative was the naval mission EUNAVFOR Med—also known as Operation Sophia—which was established in May 2015 with the aim of disrupting migrant smuggling activities in international waters off Libya.[153] After the Libyan Government of National Accord agreed to cooperate with the mission, the Council widened its mandate in May 2016, to include capacity-building, training and information-sharing with the Libyan Coastguard and Navy.[154] Cooperation with the Libyan authorities developed more rapidly from 2017, in response to continued high levels of irregular departures. A key initiative was a memorandum of understanding between the Italian Government and the Libyan authorities of 2 February 2017, in which the former agreed, *inter alia*, to provide support and funding for Libya's border and coast guards, for its southern land border control system, and for reception centres for irregular migrants.[155] During 2017, the EU Trust Fund for Africa would then provide financial support for an Italian project with the Libyan coastguard, for UNHCR and IOM assistance to migrants in detention centres and disembarkation points in Libya, and for IOM assistance for the voluntary return of migrants to countries of origin in

[149] See 'Joint Commission-EEAS Non-Paper on Enhancing Cooperation on migration, mobility and readmission with Morocco', Council doc. 5949/16, 9 February 2016; 'Joint Commission-EEAS Non-Paper on Enhancing Cooperation on migration, mobility and readmission with Tunisia', Council doc. 7408/16, 31 March 2016; and European Commission, 'Fifth Progress Report on the Partnership Framework with third countries under the European Agenda on Migration', COM(2017) 471, 6 September 2017, at 9 and 10.

[150] 'Implementation of the European Neighbourhood Policy in Egypt Progress in 2012 and Recommendations for Action', SWD(2013) 89, 20 March 2013, at 12; European Commission scorecard on the implementation of the Task Force Mediterranean report, Council doc. 16222/14, 4 December 2014, at 3.

[151] Council doc. 16222/14, 4 December 2014, note 150, at 3.

[152] 'EUBAM Libya' is the European Union Integrated Border Management Assistance Mission in Libya. See Council Decision 2013/233/CFSP, OJ 2013 L 138/15, 22 May 2013.

[153] Council Decision 2015/778 on a European Union military operation in the Southern Central Mediterranean (EUNAVFOR MED), OJ 2015 L 122/31. For a discussion, see T. Tardy, 'Operation Sophia: Tackling the Refugee Crisis with Military Means', European Union Institute for Security Studies, September 2015.

[154] 'Council conclusions on EUNAVFOR MED Operation Sophia', Council doc. 9064/16, 23 May 2016.

[155] Memorandum d'intesa sulla cooperazione nel campo dello sviluppo, del contrasto all'immigrazione illegale, al traffico di esseri umani, al contrabbando e sul rafforzamento della sicurezza delle frontiere tra lo Stato della Libia e la Repubblica Italiana', 2 February 2017, available at http://itra.esteri.it/vwPdf/wfrmRenderPdf.aspx?ID=50975. For a discussion, see Palm, 'The Italy-Libya Memorandum of Understanding: The baseline of a policy approach aimed at closing all doors to Europe?', EUmigrationlaw blog, 13 September 2017.

West Africa.[156] Taken as a whole, these various initiatives show a level of involvement by EU bodies in the migration control of a third state which is unprecedented in the history of EU external migration policy.

In a related series of developments, the EU has increasingly engaged in cooperation with African states further south which are countries of origin or transit for irregular migrants. One set of initiatives has concerned migration towards Europe from the Horn of Africa—especially Eritrea and Ethiopia—via Egypt and Sudan. This is the so-called 'Khartoum Process', which was launched in Rome on 28 November 2014, and involves the EU institutions, the African Union, all 28 EU Member States, and Djibouti, Egypt, Eritrea, Ethiopia, Kenya, Somalia, South Sudan, Sudan and Tunisia.[157] That initiative led to more concrete agreements with Ethiopia, which is a state both of origin and of transit for irregular migration to Europe.[158] A 'Common Agenda on Migration and Mobility' was agreed with Ethiopia in 2015, and was followed by agreement with the EU on a document covering readmission procedures.[159]

The EU has also engaged to a far greater extent with states in West Africa. There has been a particular orientation towards cooperation with Niger, as the point of departure for many migrants looking to travel to Libya and then to Europe.[160] The EU Trust Fund for Africa has provided support for activities aimed at strengthening the capacity of the Niger state authorities to combat migrant smuggling, the rescue of migrants in the desert travelling in the direction of Libya, and the repatriation of migrants to other states. There has also been a new focus on the part of the EU on cooperation with the Government of Nigeria, because its nationals make up a large proportion of those reaching Europe by irregular routes.[161] A Common Agenda on Migration and Mobility was signed with Nigeria in 2015.[162] Following that, a negotiating mandate for a readmission agreement was approved by the Council in September 2016, and a first round of negotiations took place in

[156] 'EU Trust Fund for Africa adopts €90 million programme on protection of migrants and improved migration management in Libya' (European Commission press release IP/17/951, 12 April 2017) and 'EU Trust Fund for Africa adopts €46 million programme to support integrated migration and border management in Libya' (European Commission press release IP/17/2187, 28 July 2017).

[157] European Commission, 'Progress Report on the European Agenda on Migration', COM(2017) 669, 15 November 2017. See Oette and Babiker, 'Migration Control à la Khartoum: EU External Engagement and Human Rights Protection in the Horn of Africa', 36(4) *Refugee Survey Quarterly* (2017) 64.

[158] 'Communication on Establishing a New Partnership Framework', COM(2016) 385, at 15.

[159] For the text of the CAMM, see Council doc. 13430/15 ADD 1, 4 November 2015. The CAMM was signed on 11 November 2015. The text of the agreement on admission procedures is in Council doc. 15762/17, 18 December 2017.

[160] European Commission, 'Fifth Progress Report', note 149, at 3–4.

[161] *Ibid.*, at 4–5. In 2015, 22,237 Nigerian nationals arrived in Italy (14% of the total), which made it the second nationality behind Eritrea. In 2016, 37,551 Nigerian nationals arrived (21% of the total), and in 2017, 18,158 (15% of the total), which was the highest number for any nationality during those years. See UNHCR, 'Italy update #10 December 2016', available at https://data2.unhcr.org/ar/documents/download/53355 and UNHCR, 'Italy: Sea Arrivals Dashboard January-December 2017', available at https://data2.unhcr.org/en/documents/details/61547.

[162] The CAMM with Nigeria was signed on 16 March 2015. The text is in Council doc. 11745/1/14, 3 September 2014.

October 2016.[163] (This is in line with the conclusions of the Commission's 2011 review of readmission agreements, discussed in section 3, that the EU should prioritize agreements with countries of origin.) Finally, a less formal solution was adopted with Mali, in response to significant numbers of its nationals seeking to reach Italy by irregular sea routes.[164] In 2016, an agreement was reached between Mali and the EU on 'standard operating procedures' for the return and identification of persons irregularly staying in the EU, which focuses on time-limits for specified steps to be taken by the Malian authorities.[165]

The cumulative effect of these various EU initiatives, together with Italy's cooperation with the Libyan authorities, has been a reduction in the level of irregular migration in the Central Mediterranean. As can be seen from Table 6.1, the numbers remained at historically high levels after the EU's change of perspective in 2015. Over 150,000 persons reached Italy by irregular sea journeys that year, over 180,000 in 2016 and nearly 120,000 in 2017, and roughly 90 per cent of these arrivals were thought to have come from Libya. Deaths at sea also remained frequent, with the IOM recording 13,457 deaths in the Central Mediterranean between 2014 and 2017.[166] In 2018, however, numbers fell significantly, with arrivals from Libya to Italy down by 82 per cent in the first four months of 2018 by comparison with the year before.[167]

In the terminology of this chapter, these recent developments show an expansion of both the territorial and the substantive reach of EU policy. In 'territorial' terms, there has been new cooperation with several states, principally Libya, Ethiopia, Niger, Nigeria and Mali. In 'substantive' terms, the cooperation with Libya and Niger is especially significant because of the detailed arrangements that are envisaged. A further new element is the recourse to operational arrangements with Ethiopia and Mali, which is to be seen as a new technique for achieving an effective policy.

From a legal perspective, it is significant that the EU has succeeded in pursuing a novel strategy of working with countries of transit (Libya, Niger) in order to prevent migrants from departing on irregular journeys towards its Member States. This strategy of prevention of departures from Libya, Niger and elsewhere appears calculated not to export EU norms, but rather to reduce the level of protection for migrants, while avoiding imposing legal responsibility for them on the EU and its Member States. Where the individuals concerned are from 'fourth' states, they may have international protection needs which cannot be met in the third state

[163] European Commission, 'First Progress Report on the Partnership Framework with third countries under the European Agenda on Migration', COM(2016) 700, 18 October 2016, at 7.

[164] European Commission, 'Fifth Progress Report', note 149, at 5–6. In each of 2016 and 2017, Malian nationals made up 6% of irregular arrivals by sea to Italy: UNHCR, 'Italy: Sea Arrivals Dashboard January–December 2017'.

[165] 'Draft Standard Operating Procedures between the EU and the Republic of Mali for the identification and return of persons without an authorisation to stay', Council doc. 15050/16, 6 December 2016, available at http://www.statewatch.org/news/2016/dec/eu-council-standard-operating-procedures-mali-return-15050-16.pdf.

[166] Information available at https://missingmigrants.iom.int/region/mediterranean. This records 3,165 deaths in the Central Mediterranean in 2014, 2,877 in 2015, 4,581 in 2016 and 2,834 in 2017.

[167] UNHCR data shows a fall from 36,099 arrivals from Libya to Italy in January–April 2017 to 6,782 in January–April 2018: 'Italy: Sea arrivals dashboard: May 2018'.

concerned. This is a particular issue in relation to Libya, which is not a party to the Refugee Convention, and where the conditions of detention for migrants are known to be very poor.[168] While these negative elements are partly offset by the resettlement by UNHCR of migrants in need of international protection, from Libya and Niger to EU Member States, those arrangements are not based on any legal obligation.[169] These developments can be read as a response to the ruling in the *Hirsi* case that those who are intercepted or rescued by a state's vessel on the high seas are the legal responsibility of that state. The next legal question is likely to be whether support by the EU and Member States for the preventive actions of third states is sufficient to trigger Member State responsibility, under the European Convention on Human Rights (ECHR) or other international law instruments. Presumably the EU and its Member States expect a simple, negative answer to that question, with the argument that the threshold requirement of control over a person or place would not be met in such a scenario.[170] It is possible, however, that a different basis of responsibility will emerge—either that the EU or a Member State has knowledge of international wrongdoing by the third state, or that the EU or a Member State has control over the third state's actions.[171]

B. Cooperation with Turkey and other States in Asia

The migration crisis has had no less profound effects upon the EU's cooperation over migration with states closer to the Eastern Mediterranean routes, which can again be traced back to the period after the Arab Spring in 2011. After the EU proposed dialogues on migration, mobility and security with North African states in 2011, the Government of Jordan requested an equivalent process with the EU. That led in turn to a mobility partnership with Jordan in 2014, and to a Council mandate for a readmission agreement in 2016.[172] These were followed by a recommendation of the Task Force Mediterranean in December 2013 for a similar dialogue with Lebanon, which commenced in 2014.[173]

[168] In relation to conditions of detention in Libya, see Amnesty International, *Libya's Dark Web of Collusion: Abuses against Europe-bound Refugees and Migrants* (2017).

[169] The UNHCR scheme is based on resettlement commitments from Canada, Finland, France, Germany, Italy, Malta, Netherlands, Norway, Sweden, Switzerland and the United Kingdom. Between September 2017 and May 2018, some 247 persons had been resettled from Libya or Niger. See UNHCR, 'Resettlement update #9: Libya-Niger situation' (May 2018).

[170] On the concept of 'control' in a migration context, see Klug and Howe, 'The Concept of State Jurisdiction and the Applicability of the Non-*refoulement* Principle to Extraterritorial Interception Measures', in B. Ryan and V. Mitsilegas (eds), *Extraterritorial Immigration Control: Legal Challenges* (2010).

[171] Moreno-Lax and Giuffré, 'The Rise of Consensual Containment: From "Contactless Control" to "Contactless Responsibility" for Forced Migration Flows', in S. Juss (ed.), *Research Handbook on International Refugee Law* (forthcoming). These questions may be tested in a complaint to the ECtHR concerning Italy's support for the Libyan authorities, taken by the Global Legal Action Network: 'Italy's Deal with Libya to "Pull Back" Migrants Faces Legal Challenge', *Guardian*, 8 May 2018.

[172] A mobility partnership was entered into with Jordan on 9 October 2014: for the text, see Council doc. 10055/14 REV, 12 September 2014. The decision authorizing negotiations on readmission is in Council doc. 6171/16, 5 April 2016.

[173] European Commission scorecard on the implementation of the Task Force Mediterranean report, Council doc. 16222/14, 4 December 2014, at 3.

More significantly, the EU's response to the Arab Spring gave new impetus to its engagement with Turkey concerning migration. The Council had approved a mandate for a readmission agreement with Turkey as far back as 2002, and progress in the negotiations from 2009 led to the signature of an agreement in January 2011.[174] However, the eventual conclusion of the agreement came to depend upon a Council of Ministers decision to open a dialogue on visa liberalization with Turkey, which it took in June 2012, because of concern at 'illegal immigration flows reaching the EU external borders from Turkey'.[175] The readmission agreement was then formally concluded by the EU and Turkey in December 2013, and made provision for the readmission of each party's own nationals from 1 October 2014, and of 'fourth country' nationals three years after that, on similar terms to the EU agreements discussed in section 3.[176] In addition, in December 2013, the Task Force Mediterranean report recommended 'dialogue and cooperation' with the Turkish authorities with the aim of disrupting migrant smuggling networks, and that agenda was subsequently taken forward through the visa liberalization process.[177]

The pace of developments quickened as Turkey's cooperation came to seem indispensable to EU attempts to reduce the number of arrivals to the Greek islands in 2015–2016. On 15 October 2015, the Commission and the European Council announced agreement in principle with Turkey on a 'joint action plan', which was then confirmed at a meeting with Turkey's Prime Minister on 29 November 2015.[178] The action plan committed the EU to substantial financial support for state authorities and humanitarian organizations assisting Syrian refugees in Turkey, and this was taken forward through a 'Refugee Facility for Turkey', a €3bn fund made up of EU and Member State contributions.[179] This 'Facility' provided financial support for Turkish authorities—and in particular Turkey's coastguard—in combating migrant smuggling towards the EU. Faced with continued flows to the Greek islands, a further 'statement' was then agreed by the two sides on 18 March 2016.[180] For the EU, its core purpose was to ensure readmission to Turkey of Syrians and other fourth country nationals, irrespective of the coming into force of the EU-Turkey readmission

[174] European Commission, 'Cecilia Malmström welcomes the finalisation of the EU-Turkey Readmission Agreement negotiations', MEMO/11/50, 27 January 2011.

[175] Bürgin, 'European Commission's Agency Meets Ankara's Agenda: Why Turkey is Ready for a Readmission Agreement', 19 *Journal of European Public Policy* (2012) 883. The Council authorized the visa dialogue in 'Council conclusions on developing cooperation with Turkey in the areas of Justice and Home Affairs', Council doc. 11748/12, 21 June 2012.

[176] Text published at OJ 2014 L 134/3.

[177] Communication on the Work of the Task Force Mediterranean, COM(2013) 869, at 8; European Commission scorecard on the implementation of the Task Force Mediterranean report, Council doc. 16222/14, 4 December 2014, at 4.

[178] European Commission, 'EU-Turkey joint action plan', MEMO/15/5860, 15 October 2015; 'European Council meeting (15 October 2015)—Conclusions', EUCO 26/15; European Council, 'Meeting of heads of state or government with Turkey—EU-Turkey statement', 29 November 2015.

[179] Commission Decision of 24 November 2015 on the Refugee Facility for Turkey, OJ 2015 C 407/8.

[180] 'EU-Turkey statement, 18 March 2016', available at http://www.consilium.europa.eu/en/press/press-releases/2016/03/18/eu-turkey-statement. Despite the title and online location of this statement, in Case T-192/16, *NF v. European Council* (ECLI:EU:T:2017:128), the General Court held that it was not an act of the European Council, so that it could not be the subject of an act for annulment. At the time of writing, that ruling is under appeal to the Court of Justice as Case C-208/17.

agreement. In exchange, the EU made a series of new commitments to Turkey. These included a promise to resettle Syrian nationals from Turkey to the EU, initially on a one-for-one basis for each Syrian national returned from Greece, and then through a Voluntary Humanitarian Admission Scheme. The EU also promised the acceleration of the visa liberalization process, and that was followed in May 2016 by a positive Commission recommendation, conditional upon a number of outstanding matters being addressed.[181] (As those included changes to Turkey's laws on public order, security and fundamental rights, further progress was precluded by the Turkish Government's suppression of dissent and opposition after the failed *coup* of 15 July 2016.) Other EU promises concerned the speeding up of disbursement of funds under the Facility for Refugees in Turkey, and a 're-energizing' of the accession process.[182]

From a legal perspective, the EU-Turkey arrangements must be taken to weaken guarantees of international protection. First, these arrangements imply acceptance at the EU level of the possibility of return of *current* applicants for international protection to third states. That is fundamentally different to the expulsion of persons without status who have never applied for international protection, or whose applications for protection have been definitively refused. Second, the arrangements imply acceptance by the EU that applicants for international protection may be transferred to a state that does not apply the Refugee Convention to them. In this regard, the legal issue is that Turkey has never removed the original geographic restriction on the scope of the application of the Refugee Convention, the effect of which is that it has never extended the Convention to non-Europeans. It is true that Turkey is bound by the ECHR principles concerning international protection, and has its own laws on the subject.[183] That legal framework may be sufficient to satisfy the EU law definition of a 'safe third country', which permits an application to be declared 'inadmissible' if a person may request refugee status in another state, and receive protection 'in accordance with' the Refugee Convention there.[184] Tolerance by the EU of transfers to a state that does not fully respect the Refugee Convention is unprecedented, however, and appears inconsistent with the principles

[181] European Commission, 'Third Report on Progress by Turkey in Fulfilling the Requirements of its Visa Liberalisation Roadmap', COM(2016) 278; and Proposal to amend Regulation 539/2011, COM(2016) 290, both 4 May 2016.

[182] For a review of the EU's carrying-out of its commitments, see European Commission, 'Seventh Report on the Progress made in the implementation of the EU-Turkey Statement', COM(2017) 470, 6 September 2017.

[183] For an outline of Turkish law, see Ineli-Ciger, 'Protecting Syrians in Turkey: A Legal Analysis', 29 *International Journal of Refugee Law* (2017) 555, at 557–566.

[184] The test of a 'safe third country' is in Art. 38 of the Asylum Procedures Directive (Directive 2013/32 of 26 June 2013 on common procedures for granting and withdrawing international protection, OJ 2013 L 180/60). In a ruling on 22 September 2017 the Greek Council of State accepted that Turkey was a safe third country, see 'Greece: The ruling of the Council of State on the asylum procedure post EU-Turkey deal', 4 October 2017, available at http://www.asylumineurope.org/news/04-10-2017/greece-ruling-council-state-asylum-procedure-post-eu-turkey-deal. For an academic argument to the same effect, see Hailbronner, 'Legal Requirements for the EU-Turkey Refugee Agreement: A Reply to J. Hathaway', *VerfassungsBlog*, 11 March 2017, available at https://verfassungsblog.de/legal-requirements-for-the-eu-turkey-refugee-agreement-a-reply-to-j-hathaway/.

underlying that Convention.[185] Nor are these points an academic matter: from the coming into effect of the statement on 20 March 2016 to April 2018, some 1,601 persons were returned from Greece to Turkey under the statement, the majority of whom appear to have had an ongoing application for protection in Greece.[186]

In the Eastern Mediterranean, the effect of EU cooperation with Turkey and the border restrictions in the Western Balkans (see section 3) was a dramatic fall in the number of arrivals to the Greek islands in 2016 and 2017. That can be seen from Table 6.2 (above), which shows that the number of irregular arrivals by sea in the Eastern Mediterranean fell to roughly 175,000 in 2016 and to roughly 35,000 in 2017. In parallel, the number of migrant deaths at sea fell, from 434 in this area in 2016 to 62 in 2017.[187] Unsurprisingly, these developments led EU bodies to conclude that EU-Turkey cooperation had substantially reduced irregular migration in that region.[188] That in turn probably explains why the EU-Turkey arrangements have not been affected, on either side, by the Turkish Government's suppression of dissent and opposition after the failed *coup* of July 2016.

Beyond cooperation with Turkey, the crisis in the Eastern Mediterranean would lead the EU to develop new forms of cooperation with Afghanistan. This reflected the fact that—after Syria—in 2015 it was the second-largest country of nationality of persons reaching the EU by irregular sea routes. In March 2016, the Commission and the High Representative jointly proposed that the EU should develop a dialogue on migration questions with its Government.[189] That would lead to the conclusion, on 2 October 2016, of a 'joint way forward on migration issues' between the two sides.[190] While not a binding international agreement, that document set out commitments concerning the return of Afghan nationals who were in the EU without status, and who had failed in any international protection claim. The 'joint way forward' would be followed by the signature in February 2017 of a Cooperation Agreement on Partnership and Development between the EU and Afghanistan.[191] In the field of migration, Article 28 of the agreement—which is among those provisionally in

[185] On the latter point, see Hathaway, 'Taking Refugee Rights Seriously: A reply to Professor Hailbronner' *VerfassungsBlog*, 12 March 2016, available at https://verfassungsblog.de/taking-refugee-rights-seriously-a-reply-to-professor-hailbronner/.

[186] UNHCR, 'Returns from Greece to Turkey (under EU-Turkey statement) as of 30 April 2018', available at https://data2.unhcr.org/en/documents/details/63523. This document states that, of those returned '47 per cent did not express a will to apply for asylum or withdrew their will to apply for asylum or withdrew their asylum claims in Greece'. The implication is that 53% still had a current application when returned.

[187] Based on International Organization for Migration information, available at https://missingmigrants.iom.int/region/mediterranean.

[188] See European Commission, 'Contribution to the EU Leaders' thematic debate', COM(2017) 820, 13 December 2017, at 3; and Frontex, *Risk Analysis for 2018* (March 2018), at 19.

[189] 'Joint Commission-EEAS non-paper on enhancing cooperation on migration, mobility and readmission with Afghanistan', Council doc. 6738/16, 3 March 2016, available at http://statewatch.org/news/2016/mar/eu-council-afghanistan-6738-16.pdf.

[190] 'Joint Way Forward on migration issues between Afghanistan and the EU', 2 October 2016, available at https://eeas.europa.eu/sites/eeas/files/eu_afghanistan_joint_way_forward_on_migration_issues.pdf.

[191] The text is available at OJ 2017 L 67/3.

force since December 2017—commits the parties to the conclusion of a readmission agreement, and to cooperation in the prevention of irregular migration.

Lastly, the migration crisis has led to the development of cooperation concerning returns with Bangladesh. In September 2017, the Commission approved 'Standard Operating Procedures', which had been agreed with the Bangladesh authorities, concerning the identification and return of persons without an authorization to stay.[192] The focus of these procedures is on time-limits for specified steps by the state requested to take back a given person (in practice, likely to be Bangladesh). This semi-formal arrangement was linked to irregular migration patterns in the Central Mediterranean, after a sharp increase in persons of Bangladeshi origin arriving irregularly by that route in 2016 and 2017.[193]

In the case of Turkey and the other Asian states, again a mixture of 'territorial' and 'substantive' developments have taken place. While the idea of cooperation over migration with Turkey pre-dates 2011, it was only confirmed after the Arab Spring, and was then taken in novel directions after the increased arrivals in the Eastern Mediterranean in 2015–2016. Equally, the engagement with Afghanistan and Bangladesh is both new in itself, and novel in its form. From a legal perspective, any prevention of departures and returns under the EU-Turkey statement do not involve the export of EU norms, but rather their dilution in practice.

6. Conclusion

This chapter has shown how, in the period of 'crisis' over migration which began in 2011, the reach of the EU border regime has changed in fundamental respects. In the internal sphere, Frontex has more clearly become an EU agency with power over Member States, especially those considered to be failing to fully control the Schengen external borders. Meanwhile, all Schengen states have acquired greater powers to re-introduce internal border controls. In the external sphere, the EU has come to engage with a far broader range of third states, and also to explore new forms of cooperation with them. In this regard, the most significant developments are the EU's support for migration control by Libya's authorities, its detailed arrangements with Turkey, cooperation with new states in Africa (Niger, Nigeria, Ethiopia, Mali) and Asia (Afghanistan, Bangladesh), and new forms of cooperation (such as those under the EU Trust Fund for Africa, the EU-Turkey statement and operational agreements).

Any notion of a relatively seamless expansion of the substantive or territorial reach of EU policies and norms is, however, inadequate for the interpretation of these recent developments in the EU border regime. Rather, it is preferable to look

[192] Commission Decision C(2017) 6137 of 8 September 2017 on the signature of the EU-Bangladesh Standard Operating Procedures for the Identification and Return of Persons without an Authorisation to Stay (Council doc. 12031/17, 21 September 2017), with Annex.

[193] See recital 2 to Commission Decision C(2017) 6137. The number of Bangladesh national arrivals increased from close to zero in previous years to 4% of the total in 2016, and 8% of the total in 2017. UNHCR, 'Italy: Sea Arrivals Dashboard January–December 2017', available at https://data2.unhcr.org/en/documents/details/61547.

to the main theories of European integration for explanations. The pattern of EU action in this area has long been shaped by the co-existence of functional pressures to greater integration and intergovernmental constraints upon the power of EU law and of EU agencies. While the migration crisis has led to new outcomes, it has not altered these basic dynamics. That explains why, in the internal sphere, even though there is a functional imperative to protect open Schengen borders, nevertheless there has been only a limited increase in the powers of Frontex, while paradoxically the 'sanction' of allowing Member States to re-introduce internal border controls has been strengthened. The EU's basic integration dynamic—the mixture of functional and intergovernmental logics—also explains why the crisis has led to hyperactivity in the external sphere. Here, the 'functional' need to defend the Schengen zone co-incides with intergovernmental reasons to expand EU activity, with Member States willing to agree to EU external action which reduces migration pressures upon those states, without creating EU obligations for them.

There are also important legal factors in play in the recent transformation of the EU border regime. The legal significance of the EU-Turkey arrangements includes the fact that they permit the return of current asylum applicants to a third state, and to a state which is effectively not a party to the Refugee Convention. In both the Turkish and the Central Mediterranean/African contexts, the logic of the strategy of seeking to prevent departures to EU Member States is avoidance by the Member States of legal responsibility for international protection applicants and other migrants. In this respect, the new 'reach' of the external dimension to EU border policy involves, not the 'diffusion' of EU norms, but rather a weakening in their significance.

Looking to the future, there is no obvious reason for the trends concerning the EU border regime covered in this chapter to come to an end. The perception of a migration 'crisis' is unlikely to disappear, with the continuing potential for the EU's arrangements to be unstable (e.g. with Turkey or Libya), or for other migration routes to pose policy challenges (e.g. in the Western Mediterranean). At the same time, the dynamics of European integration in relation to migration and border control are such that the internal border regime is likely to develop gradually, while a more expansive approach may be anticipated in the external sphere.[194] While the territorial and substantive reach of the EU border regime remain to be determined, its direction of travel appears relatively certain.

[194] Soon after this chapter was completed the EU Member States debated the possibility of persuading third states to host the processing of applications for international protection on their territory: 'EU to Consider Building "Migrant Centres" Outside Bloc', *Financial Times*, 19 June 2018; and E. Collett and S. Fratzke, 'Europe Pushes to Outsource Asylum, Again' (June 2018).

Index

The manufacturer's authorised representative in the EU for product safety is Oxford University Press España S.A. of El Parque Empresarial San Fernando de Henares, Avenida de Castilla, 2 - 28830 Madrid (www.oup.es/en or product.safety@oup.com). OUP España S.A. also acts as importer into Spain of products made by the manufacturer.
Printed and bound by CPI Group (UK) Ltd, Croydon, CR0 4YY
14/09/2026
02216305-0003